THE SEPOY REVOLT

ITS CAUSES AND ITS CONSEQUENCES

THE SEPOY REVOLT

ITS CAUSES AND ITS CONSEQUENCES

BY
HENRY MEAD

Gian Publishing House
29/6 SHAKTI NAGAR · DELHI-110007 · INDIA

THE SEPOY REVOLT

ITS CAUSES AND ITS CONSEQUENCES

BY
HENRY MEAD

GYAN

GYAN PUBLISHING HOUSE
New Delhi - 110002

ISBN : 978-81-212-0024-0

Published, 2018

Published by

Gyan Publishing House
5, Ansari Road
Daryaganj, New Delhi-110002
Phone: 011-47034999, 9811692060
www.gyanbooks.com
E-mail: books@gyanbooks.com

Printed at: G. Print Process, Delhi.

PREFACE.

In the following pages I have condensed, to the best of my ability, the results of ten years' labour in the busy fields of Indian journalism. My opportunities of acquiring a knowledge of political and social affairs have been great; it is for the public to decide if I have made good use of them.

Were my book to be written over again, I should like to deepen the colours in which some pictures of Indian life have been painted; but the experience which enables a man to write on the subject of Eastern government, tends to blunt his sympathies, and in some degree to injure his moral sense. Torture and lawlessness, and the perpetual suffering of millions, are so familiar to me, that I am conscious of not feeling as I ought to do when wrong is done to individuals and nations. The man who lives in the vicinity of the undertaker and boiler maker, is not likely to join in the agitation against barrel organs and street cries.

There is a malady common to savages in certain parts of the world, which is termed "earth-hunger." It provokes an incessant craving for clay, a species of food which fails to satisfy the appetite, and which impairs the power of digestion. The East India Company have laboured under its influence for a century past; and as yet the disease shows no signs of abatement. The last mail informed us that 25,000 acres, in the districts recently assigned by the Nizam, had this season been thrown out of cultivation; and current advices express the satisfaction of the Indian Government at the prospect of new confiscations. In Madras, Bombay, and the Punjab, for every acre that is cultivated, at least three remain untilled; and still we continue to make nobles landless, and to increase the sum total of Asiatic misery.

If Heaven had not a great work for us to do in the East, the cruelty, the oppression, and the measureless folly of our rule would before this have produced its natural fruits, and we should have been cast out from India, a scorn and example to the nations. We have been heavily punished, and there is yet a fearful blow to be endured; but after a while we shall comprehend the nature of our responsibilities, and try to fulfil them. England's difficulty is England's opportunity. If we are wise henceforth in dealing with India, the well of Cawnpore will so fertilise the land, that every corner of it will yield a crop of blessings.

H. M.

CONTENTS.

THE SEPOY REVOLT.

CHAPTER I.

THE ILLUSION.—THE REALITY.—MILITARY DEFENCES.—COOKING ACCOUNTS.—PRETENSIONS OF CASTE.—LORD DALHOUSIE AND HIS POLICY.

In the course of an article on the disturbed state of feeling in the native army, the "Times" of the 19th of May last had the following:—

"Now that the whole of India has been thoroughly subdued, and that from Affghanistan to the borders of Siam there is no power which even aspires to oppose us, we may be humane while we are politic, and be content to punish disobedience by loss of pay and pension, without a resort to artillery or a charge of the bayonet. It is reassuring, moreover, that the Mussulman, the Sikh, the Ghoorka, has no share in the prejudices of the Hindoo. The Government may always count on the votaries of Islam for support in any tumult arising from the teaching of an idolatrous creed. Still we could wish to see a larger number of European troops at hand on such an occasion. Our Indian empire is not what it was, and yet the number of white regiments remains pretty nearly stationary. Within the last fifteen years we have annexed Scinde, and the Punjaub, and Pegu, not to speak of Oude and half a dozen protected or tributary districts. The cares and duties of the army are therefore largely increased. Although the European force is costly and sickly — although every man sent out is said to cost 100*l.*, and many are only sent out to be laid, before long, in the barrack cemetery,—yet we must not shrink from the duties which our situation necessitates. We have conquered India by British hands, and by them it must be retained. Nothing will render the improvement of the country so difficult, nothing will so unsettle the minds of a people easy to be impressed, and likely to find evil advisers to impress them, as the suspicion that there is any weakness in us. The belief that on any point, whether ten miles or one thousand miles away, the authority of England can be overthrown for a day by Asiatics of any race or creed, will go far to nullify all our character of superiority, and all the authority of civilisation."

When this extract was first read in India, rebellion was triumphant in the Sepoy army over the length and breadth of Bengal, from the farthest corner of Peshawur to the hills of Cuttack. The flame of insurrection had been leaping from post to post throughout the vast extent of country still nominally under British rule, until it had become a point of honour to rebel with men who had no previous thought of disloyalty; who urged, in reply to kind words and remonstrances, that they were bound to do what all the rest of the Sepoys were doing. Away up to the hills of Nepaul, along the wide plains of the North West, on through the Punjaub, and over the wastes of Central India, the flag of revolt was flying, the mutineers gaining strength and boldness with every hour. More than 60,000 men, who had been trained to fight by the side of English soldiers, were eagerly availing themselves of every chance to murder the wives and little ones of their defenceless officers and comrades in arms. They had plundered more than a million sterling from the public treasuries; captured hundreds of guns; they were in possession of numerous places of strength; they had won intrenchments vainly defended for weeks by one of the most gallant veterans in the service, and after admitting the garrison to terms, had murdered man, woman, and child. A wall as of fire impassable cut off communication between upper and lower Bengal; trade was at a standstill, and the hopes of the best and bravest soldiers dared not soar beyond the possibility of holding the ground covered by their encampment. Relief was certain, but it seemed far distant. Vengeance was the cry that rose from every lip, but no sound of thunder was heard on the horizon. The labours of the giants had disappeared. Six weeks had sufficed to undo the work of a century.

Men in Calcutta ask of each other, What will they say of this in England? And the answer is, that our countrymen will take comfort in the thought, so consoling to a certain class of prodigals, that India has been royally spent, and that all have had a share in dissipating the rich inheritance. The people's House of Commons have scarcely ever bestowed a thought on Hindostan. Cabinets, whether Whig or Tory, have sent out men to rule over us just as faction or family interest ordained. The favourite of the Army has seldom had a chance against the favourite of the Court; and hence it is that, at the close of a century, we have to begin a new career in the East, without money and without friends, backed only by our strong right hand and indomitable hearts. Be it so; the work will be done, though the task is heavy: the labourer asking only for a competent overseer.

Had the apprehension to which the "Times" gave currency been entertained a few months back in the proper quarter, either the mutinies would have never commenced, or have never been successful. The following statement of the means of defence in the shape of European regiments provided for India, and our new possessions to the eastward of the Bay of Bengal, will show how little danger has been apprehended from internal foes or outward aggression during the last three years.

	1854.	1855.	1856.
Agra	8th Foot.	Do.	3rd Eur.
Allahabad	None.	None.	6th Drag.
Burmah	29th, 10th, 2nd Eur.	Do.	35th.
Calcutta Chinsurah	35th, 98th.	35th, 3rd Eur.	53rd.
Cawnpore	None.	None.	1st Eur.
Dugshan	53rd.	Do.	1st Eur.
Dinapore	3rd Eur.	None.	10th.
Ferozepore	70th.	Do.	61st.
Jullundur	60th.	Do.	8th.
Kussowlie	32nd.	Do.	75th.
Lahore	10th.	10th, 81st.	81st.
Lucknow	None.	None.	32nd.
Meerut	14th Drag. 81st.	52nd.	60th.
Nowshera	None.	None.	27th.
Peshawur	75th.	87th.	87th, 70th.
Rawul Pindee	87th.	75th.	24th.
Sealkote	24th, 27th.	27th.	None.
Subathoo	52nd.	None.	2nd Eur.
Umballah	9th Lan.	Do.	Do.
Wuzeerabad	61st.	Do.	None.
Ordered home	22nd, 96th.	None.	None.
Total	2 Cavalry. 21 Infantry.	1 Cavalry. 18 Infantry.	2 Cavalry. 18 Infantry.

From the above, it will be seen that in December 1854, before the annexation of Oude took place, we had three more European regiments than we had when the rebellion occurred. Of the English troops serving in the country, it is considered that seven regiments should be always stationed in the Punjaub, two in Burmah, one at Calcutta, one at Dinapore, one at Agra, and one at Meerut. This leaves us a balance of five regiments; but some of these are in absolute need of their customary rest in the hills, so that our whole movable force is actually reduced to, say, three regiments. Of course, as in the instance of the advance upon Delhi, a strong division can be improvised at a few days' notice; but the case is very much like that of the citizen who abandons his house and property to combat rebels in a different quarter of the city. He cannot fight the enemy and protect his own valuables as well. If Sepoys mutiny, or the rabble rises at our great stations, there is not much to prevent them from working their will for a season. Luck may serve us as on many previous occasions. Those who have old scores to settle with us may lack means or courage to improve the tempting opportunity; but there is no counting upon what is really before us in the way of work, and for our means we have to thank both the Home and Indian Governments that they were scarcely adequate to the ordinary requirements of a state of profound peace. We had eighteen European infantry regiments, giving perhaps a total of fifteen thousand effectives, to occupy and defend the whole country from Peshawur to Rangoon, a line of sixteen hundred miles in length, with a population of not less than eighty millions, including three countries recently conquered—the Punjaub, Pegu, and Oude. An outbreak surprised us with no European regiments at Benares, Allahabad, Cawnpore, Furruckabad, Bareilly, Fyzabad, or Delhi; none at Dacca, Berhampore, or Patna. Calcutta was protected by a single wing of the 53rd, whilst five native regiments lay fourteen miles off in a state of disaffection, and the Commander-in-Chief was shooting in the Hills. We met the emergency by withdrawing three regiments from Burmah—one of them belonging to Madras—and so perilling Pegu; by claiming two more Madras regiments, and so leaving that Government with only four European Corps for the protection of its widely extended line of defence; by begging help from Ceylon, which not many years ago was itself in a state of rebellion; and by stopping the expedition to China. At this moment we have but one regiment in Pegu, with no John Lawrence to serve in lieu of horse and foot, and only a couple of thousand British bayonets in the country of the Sikhs. It is said that Lord Dalhousie, just before his departure, applied for more European troops. If so, he failed to obtain them, but nevertheless carried out his intention of annexing Oude, the Cabinet at home approving of his policy, but neglecting to give him the means of sustaining it. To the Board of Control and the Court of Directors we owe the insufficiency of the army, but the blame must not be laid wholly at the door of the Ministry. To the best of their ability our military chiefs have made the worst of the means at their disposal. Of the old and worn out men they make generals of division and brigadiers; of the able and adventurous, administrators of civil affairs. Of course there are men in the highest departments of the army who are still able and vigorous; but of the five major-generals of the Company's service in command of divisions, the youngest has been fifty years a commissioned officer. Of four brigadiers commanding field forces, the junior has been thirty-seven years in the service, and the oldest forty-nine. Of our most distinguished soldiers, such men as Chamberlain, Coke, Hodgson, and Lumsden, are allowed to grow old in minor posts on the frontier, whilst others no less capable of doing the state service are shelved in political employ. Why should we be hard then upon General Hewitt for allowing the mutineers to escape at Meerut? Another Elphinstone, it is happy for us that he was not in command at another Cabul. We owe him and his incapacity to the system. Had he been only ten years younger, he might have been as active as General Gomm, and we dare say quite as useful to the country.

Lord Dalhousie quitted the shores of India in October 1856. Before he reached home, he composed a state paper, in which the whole of his policy during eight years' occupation of the Government was reviewed and justified, and in the main the public were disposed at that time to adopt his own estimate of the results of his administration. He had done some harsh things, and had stooped to petty reprisals upon personal enemies, or upon men who had dared to exhibit an unpalatable independence. He was not above the suspicion of having connived at jobs in favour of his relatives and dependants; but when his faults were all summed up and charged with the heavy interest which the world adds in all cases where it has to deal with truly able men, it was asserted that his merits far outweighed his defects. He had dominated over all classes — as much over the civilian as the soldier. He had borne down all enmity from without, and claimed to have exacted respect from within. It was said that he had given up the whole of his talents and time to the public service; that he thought like a statesman, and worked like a secretary; that he had added two fair provinces to the dominions of Britain, and extinguished a crying evil in the annexation of Oude; that he had spent the best years of his life amongst the people of India, and was now going home only to die.

But the truth must be told with regard to his conquests. Perhaps they were made, in the first place, for the honour of his country; but it was the nature of Lord Dalhousie to make a policy that he was proud of personal to himself, and after a while he became interested more from egotism than right feeling, more as an individual than as a Governor-General, in the prosperity of his new acquisitions. Prudence would have dictated that, with the increase of territories, the increase of physical strength should have gone hand in hand; for if the addition of 100,000 square miles of country required no extra troops to guard it, it followed as a matter of course that the previous military expenditure had been needlessly lavish. The mode adopted by the late Governor-General to make the Punjaub and Pegu appear self supporting, was the not very dignified process of "cooking accounts," by debiting the whole military charge of the troops occupying these provinces to the Bengal and Madras Presidencies. He had pandered skilfully to the weakness of our countrymen, for wherever it is possible to combine the merchant's love of gain with the soldier's desire of distinction, the rule of force is sure to dominate. The English are a Christian nation, but they trust to the civilising influences of commerce, rather than of creeds, and acknowledge a "mission" to teach the Bible wherever the sword can find a ready and profitable entrance. No one doubted the ability of the British Government to retain a permanent hold of Affghanistan, had they chosen to put forth the strength of the empire, but it was abandoned because it would not pay to be constantly fighting with the inhabitants. Had the latter been Bengalees or Cashmerians, it is quite certain that, whatever opinions might be entertained at home with regard to our right of interference on behalf of Shah Soojah, the majority of statesmen would have decided that, having once advanced, we could not retreat with safety to the rest of the Queen's dominions in the East.

Scinde was acquired by means not more nefarious than those which have given us possession of half our Indian Empire, but the gain was dubious at best, and the conqueror was unpopular at the India House. So it was resolved to set down the province in the annual accounts at its true commercial value, and there is no saying what point a constant deficiency of revenue as compared with expenditure in this instance may not have given to the harangues of parliamentary orators, who think that the career of conquest ought to be put an end to. The Court of Directors have always deplored the achievement in question, as a merchant would annually sigh over a branch of business which he was obliged to maintain at a certain loss.

If the wars which gave us Pegu and the Punjaub were shown to be as unproductive as those which planted the British flag at Cabul and Hydrabad, it is quite certain that the Court of Directors would no more honour Lord Dalhousie than they honoured Sir Charles Napier, and that in like manner the legislature would denounce his evident passion for extending the boundaries of our rule as strongly as they assailed Lord Auckland on the score of a similar policy. The sole advantage which the marquis has over the earl is in the superior commercial results; but that is sufficient to convert aggression into beneficence, censure into glory. In the one case, blood has been transmuted into gold; in the other, it was poured out on a barren soil, and bore no harvest save that of unavailing tears.

And it is not merely that the insane passion for territorial extension is nourished by the deception resorted to; but it inflicts gross injustice on the inhabitants of the old

Presidencies. It is felt to be but right that the available Indian surplus should be laid out in works of improvement; but when the distribution comes to be considered, the districts that contribute the most to the fund will, of course, put forward claims to the largest portion of outlay. There is no part of our Eastern empire where profitable employment cannot be found for all the sums that Government and private capitalists combined are ever likely to furnish: so that on no decent pretence could the surplus taxation of the Punjaub be appropriated to public works in Madras. Each part of India, then, is vitally interested in guarding against attempts to saddle it with the payment of charges that ought to be defrayed by another portion of territory. What would Middlesex say if it were compelled to pay, in addition to its own share of war taxes, the quota that ought to be contributed by Scotland? How would our notions of equity be outraged, if a law were passed which compelled poor labourers in Dorsetshire to defray the costs of a rural police in Somersetshire? Yet in neither case would more injustice be done than was perpetrated by Lord Dalhousie, for the benefit of his pet provinces.

It is not requisite that we should enter into arguments to show the necessity of debiting each part of the British dominions in the East with the cost of the troops employed in it, so long as the revenue and expenditure of each province is kept distinct. The English public acknowledges the justice of the arrangement in the case of Scinde. Taking, then, the annual cost of the 40,000 troops stationed in the Punjaub at 53*l.* for each European, and 28*l.* for each native soldier, an estimate which does not include the expense incurred on account of the Commanders-in-Chief and the army-staff, we find the whole amounts to upwards of a million sterling! Not an item of this charge was allowed to appear in the accounts furnished to Parliament, the whole of the burden being thrown on the other Presidencies; and though the Madras Government earnestly protested from time to time against being saddled with the military charges of Pegu, the districts assigned by the

Nizam, the Saugor and Nerbudda territories, and the Straits Settlements, their remonstrances were of no avail. Wherever a surplus revenue could be obtained, it was paid, of course, into the Bengal treasury; where a deficit occurred, as in the case of Burmah and the country of the five rivers, Bengal or Madras made things appear pleasant. Meanwhile the Sepoys of the former Presidency complained that they were harassed by long marches, sent far away over the sea in one direction, and in another, beyond the confines of Hindostan, where they must expect to live in perpetual conflict with tribes of men who surpassed them in physical power and daring. A feeling compounded of the weariness that possessed the Greeks of Alexander when they arrived from the path of the setting sun on the banks of the Jhelum, and of the insolence of the Roman Prætorians, filled their minds, and the far-sighted Napier warned the Government that the fidelity of the Indian host was not to be relied on. They had come to despise authority, and felt themselves to be objects of dread to their nominal masters, who anxiously availed themselves of every chance pretext for enlarging their immunities, and increasing their store of comforts. The system under which they held together had grown utterly unsuited to the maintenance of discipline; age, and not merit, constituted the only claim to promotion; strength of will and vigour of brain were of no use to the man who could not show gray hairs and an increasing stomach. The guards were relieved weekly, and when the Brahmin was not on sentry, he took off his uniform, tied a native cloth round his loins, and took his ease like any Sybarite. Before he could cook his food, he must undergo ablutions and say his prayers, and if the shadow of a Sudra or of a commanding officer was projected upon his brass lotah or his heap of rice, the food and the utensil became accursed.

The Mussulman Khitmutgar, who performs his daily devotions before the shrine of the prophet, will bring the flesh of the unclean beast from the kitchen, where it has been boiled by the Mahomedan cook, and place it on the table before the infidel, his master; the punka-wallah will fan the flies away from the joint of beef; the bearer will throw away dirty water, though each of them in doing so commits an offence against the prejudices of caste. A prospect of good pay on the one hand, and a life of hardship on the other, has sufficient weight with them to overcome religious scruples, and if successive Governments had been as firm with the Bengal Sepoy as necessity has obliged us to be with our domestics, we should have heard nothing of greased cartridges at the present moment, or of the thousand insolent requirements of caste in times past.

Those who are acquainted with the inner life of the Brahmins know that the bonds which they would fain persuade Europeans are harder than adamant, and dearer to them than life itself, are in reality but feeble strands, which they break and reunite at will. We have tried to ignore the differences of nature's creating; we have made a law of kindness which is only observed by ourselves, and petted the dark-skinned mercenary to the top of his bent, whilst soldiers of our own kith and kin have been left to find a refuge for their heads, or food for their families, as they best might. As usual, we have forgotten that charity properly begins at home, and, as usual, have had our reward.

And Lord Dalhousie is to be blamed for something more than wilful blindness to the state of the native army. He would ill deserve the credit which the world gives him for sagacity if he had not foreseen the necessity for a large addition to the European force; and it is no good defence of his reputation to allege, as may perhaps be done, that he urged the Court of Directors and the Board of Control to send out reinforcements. Placed as he was with the public opinion of England and India at his back, and for a long while standing out amongst the politicians of his time as the only man who could govern India, he might have carried out his policy in spite of all opposition; but his heart was in the balance sheet of his administration. He cared more for results which were favourable to his personal reputation, than for strengthening the defences of the empire. He passed away from the scene of his labours, and, following his footsteps, we discern the shadows of the Company's Raj, the mastership of the Brahmin, and the phantoms of want and misery which, for a century past, have kept in the wake of the conquerors of British India. We have a terrible loss to repair, a mighty vengeance to inflict; but when the twofold work is done, the brightest days of the East will follow. Let us have fair play for the energies of England, and the desert places of Hindostan shall flourish and blossom like the rose.

CHAP. II.

THE GOVERNMENT OF INDIA.—SKETCHES OF LEADING STATESMEN.—STRANGE UNANIMITY OF UNFITNESS.

In an evil hour for the country, Lord Canning was appointed to succeed the Marquis of Dalhousie. Such a choice could only have been made under the supposition that government in India was so purely a matter of routine, that it was not of the least moment who occupied the vice-regal palace in Calcutta, and took the wages of chief ruler. He had been more than twenty years in the House of Peers, and had never exhibited a sign of the capacity for empire. The impression which he left on the minds of men who transacted business with him was that of plaintive imbecility. He could never acquire experience, and he had no insight into character. One man's opinion was as good to him as that of another. He took counsel from all, and received help from none. The last man that encountered him on his way to the council-chamber had him as a prey. He was haunted with the idea that the secretaries were supposed really to govern India; and in order to disabuse the public mind of that belief he would occasionally reverse a conclusion which they had adopted for the best of reasons, or substitute in the wording of a despatch the term *expedient* in lieu of "necessary." An honest, courageous English gentleman, he only wanted breadth of understanding and the power of reliance. He would have ruled with credit to himself, but the secret of how to manage wisely was never disclosed to him.

The Supreme Government of India is carried on by two

councils, the first of which, with the assistance of the Secretaries, forms the Indian Ministry. The Executive Council consists of the Commander-in-Chief for the time being, who takes his seat, when in Calcutta, as an extraordinary member, and four ordinary members; at present Messrs. Dorin, Peacock, Grant, and General Low. Mr. Dorin is Vice-President, and what is familiarly termed the Indian Chancellor of the Exchequer.

The Legislative Council is composed of seven members, each Presidency having its representative. Mr. Dorin is Vice-President, Mr. D. Elliot sits for Madras, Mr. Le Geyt for Bombay, Mr. Currie for Bengal, Mr. Harrington for the North-West Provinces. The Chief Justice and Sir Arthur Buller are assumed to represent the law and the general public.

The Honourable Mr. Dorin had been thirty-six years in India. He had achieved reputation as the presumed author of the financial measures which reflected so much discredit on the closing years of Lord Dalhousie's administration. Versed in statistics and skilful in the use of figures, he would always acquit himself successfully in times when there was a surplus revenue, a contented population, and a reign of peace. So long as the qualities which made up the model official were sufficient to uphold his *prestige*, Mr. Dorin took high rank; but, like his honourable masters, he has fallen on evil days. The clay has come in contact with the brass, to the infinite damage of the former.

Of General Low it is almost sufficient to say, that he had been fifty-three years in the service. He was known throughout India as a kind-hearted honourable man, ripe in knowledge of the native character, and friendly to the support of Asiatic dynasties. He was opposed to the annexation of Nagpore, and looked with no friendly eye on the absorption of Oude. His heart was with the memories of the past, and his mind too feeble to sustain the anxieties of state policy. Had his faculties answered to his will, a vast amount of evil would have been averted.

The Honourable Mr. J. P. Grant was a civilian of thirty

years' standing. He belonged to a family distinguished for obstructive ability, and like some other men enjoyed a reputation which always outran his actual performances. People valued him more for what he was thought capable of doing, than for what he had done. His stock of political capital, if small at first, had never been diminished, though it would seem that the interest could never be sufficient to maintain him. Thoroughly schooled in forms and precedents, he walked by rules which he seemed to despise, and obtained credit for having the most liberal ideas, whilst no one could point to acts which justified such a belief. Under Lord Dalhousie, he would have been an accession to the strength of Government; but acting with Lord Canning, he was attracted by the vast bulk of mediocrity, and gravitated to the dull level of his colleagues. He might really have possessed great capacity, which he was too indolent to exhibit to the world.

The guiding spirit in the Legislative Council, and who exercised, we believe, no small influence as well in the Executive, was the Honourable Mr. Barnes Peacock. This gentleman, a barrister-at-law, became famous at the period of Mr. O'Connell's trial, when, to the bewilderment of statesmen and judges, he found out a flaw in the proceedings, which being duly commented upon through hundreds of hours and thousands of pages, led to the liberation of the arch agitator. From that hour the fortune of Mr. Peacock was achieved: he was at once acknowledged as the first of special pleaders, the great master of quibbles. His mind was a perfect microscope, incapable of taking large views of the simplest and nearest objects, but making all small things appear large. His precise knowledge of the framework of legislation, and undeniable skill in the more recondite mysteries of jurisprudence, gave him, as a matter of course, commanding influence over his colleagues, who looked up to him with the same feelings of respect that a martial volunteer feels for the accomplished veteran who has seen unlimited service, and knows how to make disposition of an army. Mr. Peacock was transferred in the decline of life from the Courts of Westminster to make law for the vast population of British India, composed of a hundred nations, all differing from each other. We owe it to him that the Black Acts have almost been promulgated, a calamity from which we have been at least temporarily relieved by the scarcely greater evil of rebellion. Had the plans of the Court of Directors been carried out, the Hindoos and Mussulmans might have inaugurated the revolt by the previous imprisonment, according to law, of every Englishman of wealth or influence in the country. Meanwhile Mr. Peacock earned his salary by the quantity, if not by the quality, of his labours, and scarcely a Saturday passed over, on which he did not come down with a draft, which was made law in about forty minutes. Of the rest of his colleagues in the Legislative Council, it is needless to say anything. The Queen's judges seldom or never cared to interfere against the will of the Government, and no one thought of holding Messrs. Currie and Le Geyt responsible for what was enacted.

Next, perhaps, to the Governor-General, the Secretaries take the most important part in the work of administration. It is their duty to rough hew the business about to be brought before the supreme authority; to abstract cases and reports, hunt up whatever has been done previously on the subject, and suggest what ought to be done on the current occasion. Such an office, of necessity, gives its holder great power, and where the head of the Government and Secretary understand the true requirements of their position, and have no desire to go beyond it, the aid of the latter is almost invaluable. The task of all others the most irksome and wearying, is that of searching for acts and precedents; whence it follows, that if the secretary can instil a feeling of reliance upon his industry, impartiality, and judgment, he is enabled to influence most of the acts of Government. Under an idle viceroy he is all powerful; under a foolish one, who has not the capacity to understand the affairs submitted for his decision, he may be unreasonably snubbed, and unwisely meddled with, but in the main he will have his own way. It is of much importance then to the interests of British India, that the persons who fill those respectable posts should be men of good capacity and enlarged experience.

The secretaries of the Indian Government are Mr. Cecil Beadon, Home Department, Mr. G. F. Edmonstone, Foreign, and Col. R. J. H. Birch, C. B., secretary in the Military Department. The two first named were intellectual and painstaking, supposed to be always capable of giving good advice, and we should hope equally disposed to offer it. They had an intimate acquaintance with the machinery of administration, and as workers up of the raw material of government could hardly be superseded with advantage to the state. How far they are responsible for the present state of affairs is a matter that we need not inquire into, seeing that the onus, if any, is cheerfully taken by their superiors. No such thing as resignation is ever contemplated by an Indian placeman when balked in the attempt to carry out his views. He has no public to appeal to who will do justice between him and his opponents. He is a part of the machinery, which, if worn out or broken, can at once be replaced, and when thrown aside is forgotten by all men. The fact of no responsibility serves the civilian in lieu of a conscience. He advances no interest, public or private, by refusing to execute an order of which he disapproves, or renouncing the service when the policy of his masters offends his moral sense. In our days Sir Charles Napier afforded the only instance of a voluntary surrender of rank and dignity in obedience to the promptings of insulted feeling, and he was a Queen's officer, said to be avaricious, and known to have an inordinate fondness for power. It has been thought a matter of wonderment that Indian politicians who have acquired the widest reputation in that country, fail without a single exception on the theatre of home politics; but does not the fact of their moral subjugation furnish a key to the mystery?

There is but little to remark on the subject of Col. Birch. The public which extols the ability of Messrs. Beadon and Edmonstone have no unjust predilections, and their verdict must be taken as impartial in both instances.

In a lottery there are sometimes two chances, one for

the highest and one for the lowest throw; and in the struggle for high office and consideration, the Military Secretary had made a cast below which it was impossible to score. But he held on to his salary of more than 4000*l.* per annum, with a tenacity of purpose that indicated considerable strength of character. Of the Bengal army as it existed, he knew nothing: he was barely conscious of the fact of the rebellion, and utterly ignorant of the causes that led to it; but his task is ended, and he has had his wages. The Indian army has abolished itself, and Col. Birch will soon have to follow its example.

The Honourable Mr. Halliday was Lieut.-Governor of Bengal. Mr. Halliday was a man who had a right to consider himself aggrieved if any class of politicians spoke ill of him. He was in the habit of denouncing with great force abuses which, by some fatality, never grew less under his immediate rule. The Indian reformer quoted his evidence, and the old civilian cited his practice. His theories suggested freedom, and his policy upheld tyranny. He had written against "boy magistrates," and against the fearful iniquities perpetrated by the police; but no youthful member of the civil service lacks employment in Bengal; no darogah, or chief constable, cares more, in consequence, for the liberty of the subject. In July last, Mr. Halliday announced to the deputy magistrate of Serampore, an Armenian gentleman who was content to do at half-price the work of a covenanted officer, that he should remove him from that station in consequence of proved unfitness. There had been a holy fair at Serampore, at which 80,000 pilgrims were present. It commenced on the anniversary of Plassey, and lasted for a week. The disarmed regiments at Barrackpore, on the opposite bank of the river, were in a highly excited state, and two or three men had been put to death for urging them to mutiny. A general rising was expected, and at the earnest request of the inhabitants, the deputy-magistrate wrote to the brigadier at Barrackpore for the aid of a few Europeans whilst the fair lasted, whereas he should have applied in the first instance to the magistrate, who lived at Hooghly. The magistrate would have written to the commissioner of the division, the commissioner of the division would have forwarded the request to the brigadier, the brigadier in due course would address the general commanding at Barrackpore, who would write to the military secretary, who, if he took the responsibility upon himself, would tell the general to order the brigadier to instruct the commanding officer of a certain regiment to send a detachment across the river, at the same time taking care that the commissioner, the magistrate, and the deputy, all had the opportunity of corresponding again with each other on the subject. When the humbled official meekly remarked that before all the above formalities were gone through every European might be murdered, Mr. Halliday replied, "Well! and what is that to you?" to which the deputy was obliged of course to say, "Oh, nothing, sir," at the same time backing out of the Presence.

Mr. Halliday had a strong dislike to the press, his antipathy being as reasonable as that of a child who hates the fire because it has had the misfortune to burn its fingers. He was foolish enough to enter into a public controversy with the private secretary of Lord Dalhousie, who was unaccountably permitted by that nobleman to impugn the veracity of the Lieut.-Governor. Mr. Halliday was one of the chief promoters of the act which gagged the Indian journals, and took care to make use of the power with which the law invested him. At the date of the revolt he was not popular with any class of the Anglo-Indian community, the members of his own service not excluded.

The Governor of Madras was the son of the man who took Seringapatam. Lord Harris was polished, benevolent, and replete with a melancholy grace of person and demeanour; the kind of nobleman that a respectable solicitor likes to have always on hand, for taking the chair at public meetings, and reflecting credit on joint-stock enterprises. He rather loved all mankind than otherwise; but if he had a dislike, it was to Roman Catholics, and people who made a noise about things. Nature had given him a liberal disposition, Christianity had made him a socialist, circumstances had converted him into a warm supporter of bureaucracy. He loved sincerity, and was always to be influenced by the counsels of conscientious persons. No trouble was too great which promised to afford relief to oppressed multitudes; no odium was too formidable to be encountered in the discharge of duty. He originated the famous Torture commission, and wrote a long minute against the liberty of the press. He was opposed to the private ownership of land in Madras, and set on foot a survey of the soil, which will be completed in about thirty-six years, if nothing occurs to interrupt the work. His politics in August last were anti-Mahomedan, but liable, of course, to modification.

Lord Elphinstone, who, about twenty years since, was Governor of Madras, was the Governor of Bombay at the time of the revolt. Whilst at the former Presidency his hospitality and love of gaiety were remarkable; but if he had any chance of distinguishing himself at Bombay, it was suffered to pass unimproved.

The North West Provinces were under the rule of Lieut.-Governor the Hon. J. R. Colvin, a distinguished member of the civil service. Mr. Colvin commenced his public life as the private secretary of Lord Auckland, was afterwards commissioner of the Tenasserim provinces, and Sudder Judge, being promoted from the latter post to his present appointment. He was not fortunate in his mode of dealing with the mutiny, and died on the 9th day of September last.

It was with such tools, good and bad, that the Government of India had to be carried on from January 1857, until such time as the good genius of England should decree otherwise.

CHAP. III.

COMPOSITION OF THE INDIAN ARMIES.—CASTE PREJUDICES OF THE BRAHMIN.—CAUSES OF THE REVOLT.—CONDITION OF OUDE.

THE military force in India comprises four distinct armies, made up of the Queen's Regiments and the separate armies of Bengal, Madras, and Bombay. The services of the Bengal Troops are rarely required beyond the limits of their own Presidency; but it has occasionally happened that special emergency has demanded their aid, which has never been accorded without much dissatisfaction, and in some instances the outbreak of mutiny. The sea,—Kalapawnee, or blackwater,—is an object of special dread to them, involving damage to their caste and impairing their efficiency as soldiers, since their religion will not allow them to cook food on board ship, but compels them to live on dry pulse, sugar, and stagnant water. According to the strict rule of their faith, no Brahmin can be a soldier, since the law forbids them to take life; but they overlook this vital principle for the sake of pay and profit. The cow is a sacred animal in their estimation, but they consent to wear shoes made of leather rather than march barefoot, and have no objection to relax the observance of any article of devout profession, whenever it stands in the way of repose or rupees. Tall and handsomely made, with a love of idleness and display which makes up in no slight degree the character of a model soldier, they are to outward appearance the beau ideal of a warrior race. The rules of the service provide that only a limited number of Brahmins, out of the thousand men composing the regiment, shall be entertained; but it seldom happens that less than two thirds are really borne on the muster roll, their custom being to enrol themselves as Rajpoots or Chettryas, which they may do with impunity, the Brahmin being permitted to take up and lay down his caste at pleasure. Where they are really religious, their conscientious scruples interfere with the performance of half the duties which a soldier should perform; and where otherwise, their idleness and insolence make them even worse servants of the state. They must live and mess by themselves, no man of any inferior caste being allowed to come within a certain distance of their cooking places lest the wind should sweep the taint of his pollution across the food intended to nourish the stomachs of the twice born. The strength of discipline is materially impaired by the reverence which the chief native commissioned officer entertains for the rawest recruit who may happen to be a member of the priestly class. The feeling in this respect is exactly analogous to that which most London tradesmen would entertain with regard to the son of a nobleman, whom poverty or eccentricity might compel to serve behind the counter. Whilst regiments belonging to the other Presidencies will cheerfully take spade and pickaxe, and work when occasion calls for their services, the Bengal Brahmin would rather submit to any inconvenience than contaminate his hands with the marks of labour. He is never more, but often less, than a fighting man, who has been pampered till, as was natural to an Asiatic under such circumstances, he lapsed into rebellion. Happily, he has now abolished himself, and his family traditions of pay and pension, enjoyed from father to son for generations, are brought to a close.

The nominal proportion of the various castes as borne on the books of the 34th Regiment, N. I., may be taken as a fair index to the composition of the whole Bengal army, it being always understood of men entered as Rajpoots and Chettryas, that numbers belong in reality to the superior class. The roll on the occasion of the disbandment stood as follows: —

Brahmins	335
Chettryas	237
Lower Caste Hindoos	231
Christians	12
Mussulmans	200
Sikhs	74
Total	1089

The orders of Government provide for the enlistment of 200 Sikhs in every regiment, and had the instruction always been complied with, it might have fared better with the army at large. The Sikh is a born soldier, caring nothing whatever for caste, save in the instance of a veneration for the cow, and anxious above all things to uphold his reputation as a genuine fighter. In the field he is a match for any two or more Hindoos, and prides himself upon his near resemblance to the European; whose prowess he regards with dread and admiration. He messes with the rest of his comrades, cooks with them at a common fireplace, eats pork and drinks rum like an Anglo-Saxon, and will handle with equal relish the musket and the pioneer's axe: but then he is independent, and lacks the cringing spirit which too many of our countrymen are fond of. He refuses to cut his beard, and does not look seemly in the ranks amongst the neat, smooth-shaved Brahmins, and so he has got to be disliked by adjutants and commanding officers, snubbed when offering himself for service, and looked down upon if entertained, instead of being cared for and led to identify himself with the feelings and interests of the dominant race. Then his sect is dying out in the Punjaub, and the spirit of the Khalsa no longer lives in the sons of the men who shook our power at Ferozeshah and Moodkee, and needed but the aid of honest men as leaders to come to death grips with us in the rice-fields of Bengal. With but one partial exception, they have stood true to us throughout the present troubles when embodied in separate corps, but have been too weak to withstand the united influence of Brahmin and Mussulman. They despise the Hindoo and hate the Mussulman, and we believe may be safely trusted under wise restrictions for the future.

The Mahomedan element in the ranks of the native army has hitherto been looked upon as a counterpoise to the power of the Hindoos, but recent events have shown how thoroughly they can fraternise with the latter, when the object is to destroy a common foe. There is nothing of the ennobling qualities which dignify the creed of the prophet in the persons of Turks and Arabs to be found in the Mussulmans of India. Brutally ignorant and superstitious, they have engrafted the idolatry of Asia upon the tenets of the Koran, and look upon all Europeans as being infidels and unclean, whom it is a duty to slay whenever occasion serves. The bitter hatred with which Orangemen and Roman Catholics used to regard each other in Ireland has its intensified type in the feeling entertained towards us by the whole Mussulman race. Fierce antipathy to our creed, intense loathing of our persons, and never-ceasing dread of English valour and ability, make up the impression which is stamped on the minds of their children in early infancy, and deepens with every year of growth. We are a perpetual barrier in their path in whatever direction their footsteps tend. We will not let them win heaven by slaughtering Kafirs, enjoy liberty by oppressing Hindoos, or achieve wealth by plundering whoever is too weak to offer resistance. Prophet, king, and noble, we are the enemies of all, and the time is come when the faithful perceive a chance of avenging themselves. Here and there a man may be heard of, who from interest, or through taking a more enlarged view of public affairs, supports the English Government; but the vast majority of all classes detest us with a fervour which blood hardly suffices to allay.

The Madras and Bombay Sepoy armies, though composed of men far inferior in appearance to the Bengal regiments, are yet infinitely more efficient as soldiers, because caste has little or no weight with them. They will go anywhere and perform every part of a soldier's duty, as cheerfully as Europeans. A large proportion of the Madras regiments are composed of low caste Hindoos, with whom no scruples on the score of religion weigh against the performance of duty. In the Southern Presidency the families of the men always accompany them, a custom which, however inconvenient in general, and at times productive of dissatisfaction, affords an almost certain guarantee for the fidelity of the men. Their sons, as they grow up, hang about the lines and the officers' quarters, pick up a modicum of English, eagerly avail themselves of every opening to play at servants or soldiers, and by the time they arrive at manhood, or the age at which they are permitted to be taken on the strength of the corps, have been thoroughly identified with it. A certain number of them are enlisted under the denomination of "recruit boys," and the sons of Sepoys who have died in battle or on foreign service receive a monthly allowance. Throughout the native Indian army, the nearest relative of the soldier killed in action or who dies abroad is pensioned.

It is hardly to be expected that men, however honest and highminded, should be found willing to denounce the evils of a system from which they derive the means of existence; but never have Bengal and Madras troops been brigaded together, that dislike and dissension have not sprung up on the part both of officers and men. The Bengal officer, proud of the magnificent appearance of his troops, experienced, as his eye glanced along the line on parade, the feeling with which a man of wealth contemplates the aristocratic air of his butler, and the glorious calves of his footman. By the side of the small, meagre Madrassee, mean in look, and low in moral estimation, the Brahmin or Rajpoot from Oude suggested a comparison between the high-blooded racer and the drudging hack; and if war was not another name for work, such as tasks the highest capacity both of body and will, the superiority would be real as well as apparent. But the comparison which holds good on the review ground halts in the trenches, on the nightly bivouac, or the guarded post. The Madrassee will handle a spade as readily as a musket. He eats and sleeps in his uniform when on guard, crosses the sea without a murmur, and cooks his food wherever he can obtain fire and water. The handsome high-caste Brahmin lords it over him as naturally as a member of the peerage dominates over a Sheffield radical, and he avenges himself much after the Yorkshire fashion, by vaunting his more useful gifts. He can walk further, shoot straighter, and fight better, according to Madras traditions, and we are not sure that the boast is ill-founded. "Who will follow a damned black fellow?" was the exclamation of a little Madras sepoy, as he dashed into the open in the face of a withering fire. The implied sense of degradation and consciousness of bravery were shared in, perhaps, by the great majority of his comrades.

Nearly a third of the Bombay army is made up of Poorbeah Brahmins: from one to two hundred men in each regiment are Mussulmans, and the remainder is composed of low caste Hindoos with a sprinkling of Jews. The high caste Sepoys are of course as factiously disposed as their brethren in Bengal, and it is more than probable that, but for the occurrence of the war with Persia, which drew away so large a portion of the western army, and their subsequent employment in small detachments scattered over the whole of the Presidency, they would have followed in a great measure the example of Bengal. He would be a bold man who would venture to risk much that he cared to lose on the fidelity at this moment of any portion of the Sepoy army.

For Sepoys, as well as for English soldiers, discipline must always have a certain force; and before habits of obedience however slight could be broken, and advantages dearly prized be put to hazard, a powerful influence must have long been at work. The sense of individual wrong, the hope of individual gain, or a feeling of sympathy for the victims of oppression, may in any part of Europe turn the soldier into a rebel; but we may put the latter motive wholly aside where the Bengal Sepoys are concerned. These men ever have been, and will continue to be, the willing tools of power, no matter how it was acquired, or in what way it was exercised. They have no regard for deposed Rajahs, no pity for tortured ryots. The word patriotism has no place in their vocabulary. The leopard may refuse for a time to hunt for its former master, but not from any kindly feeling towards the helpless deer. It might be hard for us to make out a claim to be considered the friends of the Indian peasant, but the Sepoy is his hereditary enemy, in whose eyes the gains of industry are always a lawful prey.

The origin of the mutiny must be ascribed to various causes: the want of discipline in the Bengal army, and the general contempt entertained by the Sepoys for authority; the absence of all power on the part of commanding officers to reward or punish; the greased cartridges, and the annexation of Oude. The spread of disaffection was owing to the marvellous imbecility of Government in Calcutta, and the supineness of the Board of Control. The fire raged unchecked amongst the dry wood, and at last attacked the green.

The notoriously relaxed state of military discipline forbids the idea that ill usage has anything to do with the revolt. The general regulations for the government of the army have been so constantly modified of late years in favour of the Sepoy, that scarcely a trace of subordination remained in practice, and but little of it in theory. Commanding officers had gradually been deprived of the power of interfering except in cases of extremity; and from head quarters came the constant admonition to treat him tenderly and with exceeding care. There may of course be isolated instances of regimental hardship, but we are now dealing with an army of mutineers, and it is beyond possibility that military grievances should be heavy or general. And were it otherwise in a few isolated instances, the cause is not sufficient to explain the recklessness of consequences and fiendish barbarities of the mutineers. So far from having given these men cause of deadly hatred, we had gone into the opposite extreme. We have never read a more touching passage than the following, in which an officer writing from Neemuch details his latest experience of Sepoy gratitude:—

"I have been many years with my regiment; I have lived among the men, marched over the length and breadth of the land with them; I have fought with them, trusted them, respected them, cared for them, treated them with kindness and consideration always, attended to all their wants, redressed as far as lay in my power their grievances; and yet these men have been hatching treason against the State for months--perhaps years. While coming to me and in daily intercourse with me, they have been treacherously plotting against my life, and with the foulest and blackest ingratitude I ever heard or read of, they sent me away with such a shower of bullets over my head as I never had before except at Chillianwalla; and not content with this, they burnt my house to the ground, and leave me and my family beggars."

We have not space to dwell upon the interior economy of the Sepoy ranks in Bengal, but crowds of instances might be cited in proof of the laxity of military rule which prevailed amongst them; and, to show the little account that was made latterly of commanding officers, we need only cite the minute of Lord Canning on the subject of the Divisional Order issued by Major General Hearsey, on the 5th of April last, announcing the promotion to the rank of havildar of Sepoy Shaik Phuttoo, of the 34th N. I., who, to use the words of Government, "gallantly defended his officer against the murderous attack of the mutineer Mungul Pandy." His lordship goes on to remark, "It is not in the power of the Major-General commanding the division to make this promotion, which can proceed only from the Government of India, and therefore should not have appeared in a Divisional Order without the sanction of the Government." The officer thus reprimanded has attained all but the highest rank in the service, which he entered before Lord Canning was born; and his offence was that he had elevated to the rank of sergeant a man whose merit consisted in this, that he had hindered individual murder, and perhaps stayed for a season the mutiny of a regiment. We are also cognisant of a case, wherein the commandant of an irregular corps tried for a whole twelvemonth to get a man, who had saved his life in action, promoted to the rank of naick or corporal, and was obliged to give up the attempt in the end. The officer in command of a corps cannot advance a Sepoy to the lowest grade of promotion, or sentence a non-commissioned officer to an hour's drill. He is only like the private, a portion of the military machine, and not its motive power. He cannot mark his dislikes or show his sense of merit. One man is made the same to him as another, and it is scarcely to be wondered at that in the day of trial he was found to have inspired but little respect, and to have no influence. The Asiatic never rates a man as above the rank accorded to him by their common superiors.

Of the officers of the Indian army in all the Presidencies a full moiety are absent from their regiments. There is one Bengal corps without a single captain, and six that have but one each. The battalion of artillery commanded by the late Sir Henry Lawrence only musters three officers for duty, two of whom are lieutenants. Two hundred and forty-one officers at the head of the Bengal list average forty years' service each; two hundred and forty-two at the bottom count but nineteen months and have been with their regiments less than a year each. Of the absentees, two hundred and twelve are in civil or political employ.

It is a defective system which leaves an average of only twelve officers present with their regiments out of a nominal complement of twenty-six, and which makes the corps a penal settlement; but it is not without its advantages, and has certainly had no share in causing the mutinies. There are very few men who display at an early age the ability that is found to be so valuable in the East, and hence it is of much importance to have a wide field from which to select the men that are required for the various posts unsuited to the habits or the expectations of the civil service. A military or medical man is only too happy if, at the end of ten years' service, he can draw 800 rupees monthly, when the civilian will decline an appointment below 1500 or 2000. Every office in Pegu is administered by military men, and their law is not much worse than that of the ordinary judicial department. If sitting on the bench were like sitting in the saddle, and the administration of justice were a kind of fighting, we should perhaps hear of the distinction between regular and irregular judges, the real difference being a matter of uniform. So far as the junior officers are concerned, we can recognise no benefit to discipline from their performance of regimental duties. They can alter nothing and influence nothing. They dare not enter a Sepoy's hut or even walk down the lines at his feeding time. What little authority was permitted by army head quarters the commanding officer naturally engrossed, and the subaltern found himself in all respects a veritable cipher. And beyond the range of regimental duty, what sympathy could there possibly be between himself and the native soldier, whether Sepoy or subadar? The latter had risen from the ranks, and, if a Brahmin, was in five cases out of six unable to read his own sacred books. A quarter of a century back a state of things somewhat different prevailed. There might have been seen at that time, in the officers' quarters, a native female occupying the position of mistress of the household; the future Clive sitting on the floor in the loosest of garments, eating pillau with his fingers; Sepoys coming to and fro with gifts of sweetmeats to their little nephews and nieces, or bearing nuzzurs and petitions to the "Bebee sahib" for pardon or promotion. Under such circumstances there could have been no conspiracy hatched of which the European would be ignorant. He had identified himself with native interests, albeit of the baser sort, and was a brother in feeling, if not in features. But should we sigh for a return of the days, which a few old Indians still mourn? Should we exchange the task of raising the Hindoo to the European, for the easier one of lowering ourselves to the Asiatic level? Happily, the growth of Christian feeling has left no alternative in the matter. The officer must continue to comport himself as a gentleman, even at the cost of allowing the Sepoy to forget that he is a soldier.

We have a change to propose with regard to the present mode of officering the army and making staff appointments, but must for the present pass on to the consideration of the greased cartridge question. In spite of all that has happened of late years to make a state of disaffection chronic on the part of the Bengal Sepoys, in spite of the general enlistment order and the annexation of Oude, we are firmly of opinion that the rebellion would never have occurred, but for the introduction of a grievance which united all classes in a bond of deadly and needful enmity towards us. There was but one subject which concerned all ranks and embraced all interests, and the men to whom the destinies of India were intrusted made the worst of it. It is scarcely credible that the Directors of the East India Company should have deliberately sanctioned a measure which was as certain to cause rebellion as the issue of a decree of extermination. A child playing with gunpowder is a sight of terror only; but here were the rulers of a mighty empire carefully carrying the torch to the magazine with no purpose of causing explosion.

The Enfield rifle was not introduced into the Indian army until a recent period; but in November 1853, we are told by Colonel Birch, the present Military Secretary to the Indian Government, that the Court of Directors sent out to India, at the request of the Board of Ordnance, a supply of greased cartridges, which they desired to submit to the test of climate. "The cartridges were greased in England in four ways, with common grease, laboratory grease, Belgian grease, and Hoffman's grease, and in each there was a mixture of creosote and tobacco." The cartridges, placed in waggons, in magazines, and the soldiers' pouches, were under trial in Cawnpore, Rangoon, and Calcutta, until June 1854, when, it is stated, they were sent back to England, and reported upon. The Adjutant-General, Colonel Tucker, addressed the Military Secretary on the subject, pointing out the mischief that would ensue if the Sepoys took it into their heads that they would have to handle substances the touch of which was defilement; but no heed was given to his representations. It was nobody's official business to take notice of such matters. When the wind was low and the sky cloudless, why speak of precautions against danger?

So much pains have been taken by the Indian Government to disavow all connection with missionary efforts, that the most bigoted and ignorant of Hindoos could hardly suspect them of even a leaning towards Christianity. Piety has never been popular with the Court of Directors, who are not in all respects an inconsistent body of rulers; but it has strangely enough happened that the Sepoys have been enabled, as they fancy, to discern a political motive of vast weight and influence for the destruction of caste, both in the case of Hindoos and Mussulmans. It will be recollected that during the Russian war the Government were frequently counselled in the public prints to make the Indian army available in the struggle. Sometimes it was suggested that regiments should be sent to the colonies to relieve the Queen's troops, and on other occasions that cavalry and artillery should be landed in the Crimea, the one arm to take outpost duties, and the guns to be brigaded with the royal artillery. By degrees the notion took root that the Russians would be victorious unless the Sepoys could be made use of in Europe, the latter result involving of course the previous annihilation of caste. The Persian war and the outbreak at Canton deepened the prevailing impression that Sepoy aid was indispensable in localities where they must starve or eat forbidden food; and Government being furnished with this powerful reason, it was not long before the subtle Asiatic intellect discovered the supposed method by which they sought to accomplish their object. The employment of force was out of the question, and neither bribes nor persuasion would induce the devout masses to pollute themselves. It was necessary to keep the design strictly secret, and to carry it out in every station and camp as simultaneously as possible. The production of a new rifle, involving the use of a new style of cartridge, afforded the very means requisite for the success of the plot. It was dipped in cow's grease for the Hindoos, and pork fat for Mussulmans. Every man must bite it before loading; and once his lips had touched the paper, his honour was gone for ever, and he was the bond slave of Government, degraded in this life and ruined in the next. The ignorant masses were frantic with rage and fear, and there were not wanting men willing and able to turn their madness to the account of worthless princes. These latter took counsel together, and summing up the chances of mutiny, found the Bengal Sepoy master of the situation.

It is more than probable that under a commander-in-chief who knew his duty and took care to perform it, the signs of discontent would have been confined to a small area. The Sepoys would have allowed the explanations of Government their due weight, and in time have owned the folly of their suspicions; but matters of late had come to such a pass, that it was the fact of mutiny, and not the pretext for it, that they cared about. They had become so insubordinate that outbreak was inevitable; only what would have been a slight *émeute* under Sir Charles Napier's *régime*, to be repressed on the spot with merciless vigour, became under Sir George Anson a military rebellion of such dimensions as to threaten the safety of our Eastern empire.

Naturalists have a story of a horse who once overcame a lion in single combat, and ever afterwards was untameable. Luckily for equestrians the fact is unknown to horses in general, but otherwise we might hear of a great many successful mutinies on the part of those useful quadrupeds. When the 38th Regiment refused to embark for Burmah, and escaped without punishment, the horse overcame the lion, and the lesson has not been forgotten. Government in that case committed the fatal error of omitting to enforce obedience to its mandates, on the ground that the order ought not to have been issued. The Sepoy, allowed to choose for himself as to what portion of the commands of his superior shall be obeyed, is naturally led one day to take a step in advance and refuse to own any mastership whatever. A Government can commit no breach of faith to its soldiers so mischievous as that which it commits to the public when it allows a command to be disregarded. Had the order to the

38th to go to Burmah never been issued, or never disobeyed, it is not likely that at this moment their lives would be forfeited to justice.

A narrative of the introduction of the greased cartridges would occupy too much space in these pages. They were greased with a composition made of five parts tallow and five parts wax and stearine, and were sent out last year with the Enfield rifles by the Court of Directors. It is believed that none of them got into the hands of the Sepoys at the various schools of instruction; but it happened that the cartridges prepared in India for the new rifle were made of paper greased also at the ends, and having a shiny appearance, which was supposed to be produced by the use of grease in its composition; and, to quote the words of the Inspector-General of Ordnance, "no extraordinary care appears to have been taken to ensure the absence of any objectionable fat." Whether the rumour was invented for political objects, or was merely one of the thousand bazaar reports that owe their origin to the mere love of lying, it is impossible to say; but it got abroad that it was by the aid of the new cartridge that the Government designed to make Christians of the native army. The news spread like wildfire over the face of the land. On the 23rd of January the first report on the subject was made to Government, and in little more than a month afterwards the 19th Regiment had mutinied, and the Bengal army was converted into a rabble.

Detach credibility from a lie in England, and, however huge its proportions, it is as harmless as a snake deprived of its fangs. But in India, if you draw the teeth, the virus often remains, and is active and venomous as ever. The Asiatic considers words as mere breath. If a thing is worth having, it is worth lying for. If deceit is the only coinage in which your biddings will be taken, or if it is the cheaper currency, why make your payments in it by all means, and swear if need be to the genuine ring of the metal. Given a desire on the part of the English government to destroy caste, and it was certain that they would set about the way to gratify it. It was the habit of the Feringhee to compass his ends by force, that method being most facile to him; but if the "Zubberdustee" mode was either impossible or impolitic, surely he would not hesitate to employ fraud rather than let the design fail? The Government would of course repudiate any such intention, else how could they carry out the scheme? The more they were distrusted, the more anxious they would naturally be to do away with unfavourable impressions. They would make speeches, get books written, despatch circulars and proclamations, and try by every artifice to lull the nation into a sense of security. It was only by such a line of proceeding that the great object could be gained, and the English were not accustomed to fail. All the protestations and assurances, then, of the Governor-General and his chief officers concerning the cartridges went for nothing. The question presented for Asiatic consideration was simply as follows: Was there a plot to make all the Sepoys break caste unconsciously? and the query being answered in the affirmative, the disclaimers were not worth a moment's notice.

The thousand men sent adrift at Barrackpore, had at least on an average five persons dependent upon each of them for the means of existence. What did they think of themselves, and what was thought of them by their relatives? Were they fools or martyrs? had they flung away their birth right, receiving no mess of pottage? or were they the champions of the gods on whose side the deities might be expected to fight in the day of battle? The answer is easily divined. They called themselves the victims of principle, and spread everywhere the story of their sufferings for conscience' sake. Their wives and fathers in the villages of Oude were content to forego their share of pay and pension, when the Sepoy had been obliged to choose between rebellion and apostacy. The disbanded men told how otta, in which bone dust was mixed, had been served out by Government as rations, and how magistrates, under threats of the lash and gibbet, had compelled prisoners in many of the jails to eat pork and cow's flesh. In several stations otta was refused by the troops, and they encouraged each other to stand firm if Government, as was intended, should persist in the attack upon their religion. Everywhere the fuel was gathered into heaps, and the torch was at hand to light up the conflagration.

And if the mutiny of the 19th was defended as a religious act, it was equally clear that, as a military offence, the Government held it in such light estimation that honest Hindoos need not care for the consequences of revolt. They might hold what erroneous opinions they pleased with regard to the designs of superior authority; but they knew as well as the more enlightened Englishman that the crime of refusing to bite a cartridge was as great as that of a disobedience of orders to storm a fortress. The course of the Government was as clear as their own. The issue to be decided was one of life or death, and it had gone against the Sepoy. Government had won the game and demanded the stakes. A slight incident will show what the losers must have thought of the wisdom of their antagonists.

Tidings of the Berhampore outbreak and its consequences had travelled all over India in the month of April, and reached amongst other places a remote corner of Oude, where two outlying companies of irregular infantry were stationed, under the command of a young and popular officer. It was his duty to read out the general order of disbandment to the men of his detachment, but when he came to the passage where the sentence was promulgated, they burst out into a universal shout of "Wah, wah, is that all? Why if we had mutinied in the Nawab's service, we should have been blown from guns, or had our heads cut off and stuck up over the city." In the evening the subadar came to the quarters of the commanding officer and said, "Is it really true, sahib, that the 19th have been paid up and sent away without punishment?" The reply was of course in the affirmative, on which he rose and took leave, but not before assuring the lieutenant that the result would be disastrous to the British rule. The young officer had some further talk with his subordinate, and before going to bed he sat down and wrote a letter to his father in Calcutta, in which he predicted that within two months from that date there would be mutiny from Calcutta to Peshawur. All that he had to guide him in coming to such a conclusion was an appreciation of native character, a knowledge of general disaffection throughout the army, and the example of an act of deplorable weakness on the part of the executive in dealing with the first experiment of revolt. Pity that the subaltern in Oude and the councillors in Government house had not previously changed places.

Neglect and incapacity have produced their unwholesome fruit in every portion of our Indian empire; but in no quarter was the example of supineness more glaring than in that of the newly acquired province of Oude. The quarrel between the deposed monarch and the East India Company, partakes of the nature of all other strife, neither side is wholly right or wholly wrong; but it requires more study of the subject than politicians generally care to give to such cases to enable a member of the Queen's Government or of Parliament to find out how the scale of justice inclines. If a man cares for the strict interpretation of treaties, for the separation of motives pecuniary and patriotic; if he looks upon a solemn agreement to uphold a throne as an undertaking to be carried out at any time, without reference to the happiness of subject masses, he is bound to pronounce against the dethronement of the king of Oude. And if the rigid moralist would have paused before deposing him on the sole ground that he governed his people unwisely, the statesman would have hesitated for politic reasons. It is well known that the profession of arms is subject to the same unchanging rules that govern all other kinds of employment in India, wherever circumstances do not interfere with its operation. In addition to the 40,000 men with which the province furnished our army, the king's forces, at the time the country was annexed, amounted to 60,000, and the troops employed by the nobility and zemindars were quite as numerous. To these men the musket and bayonet were heir looms, the service was their natural inheritance. They counted themselves the aristocracy of the land, the actual lords of the soil. The country was in a chronic state of warfare; the taxgatherer was always a Sepoy, the landlord a feudal chieftain, who paid taxes only when forced to do so by the employment of superior physical force, and the peasant was always a partisan and slave. The country had been for generations the paradise of adventurers, the Alsatia of India, the nursing-place and sanctuary of scoundrelism, such as is without a parallel on earth. When the fiat of Lord Dalhousie went forth, there were left standing in the country 246 forts, mounting 436 guns, and having 8000 gunners to work them. We took into our service about 12,000 of the regular forces and 500 artillery men; and the rest, with arms in their hands, were sent adrift to seek their fortune. Surveyors were sent throughout the length and breadth of the land; new laws were introduced; and a new scale of taxation laid down, and then, having sold off the horses and elephants, dismissed the dancing girls, and put all the king's foppery up to public auction, we left part of a solitary European regiment and two companies of artillery to keep a country so tenanted in good order. It was supposed that British rule would yield an instantaneous crop of blessings, which all men could behold, and which they were sure to be thankful for.

And if the happiness of the masses was the object alone to be secured, such a belief would not have been without foundation. Men who have traversed Oude from one end to the other since the Company's Raj has been established, and whose testimony may be relied on, agree in stating that everywhere the peasants were delighted with the change; and they had a right to express such opinions, for under the native dynasty their lot was one of unmitigated wretchedness. The exact measure of profit sufficient to enable them to carry on cultivation had long been ascertained by the Zemindars. The sum total of their worldly wealth was known to the value of a pice, and beyond what was needful to enable them to till the soil and keep body and soul together, they were not permitted to indulge the appetites of the flesh or the desires of the soul. Their lot was that of stereotyped wretchedness; they had never heard of luxury, and stood daily face to face with starvation. The man who possessed the smallest superfluity looked upon his neighbours as being in consequence his natural enemies.

When the Company's Sepoy came home on furlough, he shut up his house at night; unwound from the folds of his cloth the ornaments of silver or gold which he had managed to purchase during his absence, and placing them on his wife contemplated his treasures with stealthy rapture; but he took care that the sight should never be witnessed by others, and on the morning of his departure, the valuables were hidden in the ground, to be brought forth again only on the occasion of his next visit. An example of the style in which revenue was wont to be collected in Oude is to be found in the following narrative furnished to the present writer by a native correspondent of the Delhi Gazette in 1850. The comments that follow appeared at the same time, and are worth reprinting as a sample of opinions entertained by an English editor on the subject of Oude, long before Lord Dalhousie contemplated annexation: —

"'The collection of the revenue of the districts of Daowrayrah and of Eesanugger, situated in the northern portion of Oude, was, from the commencement of the present Fusli year, made over by the Nazim of the Khyrabad Elaka (in which are to be found both the districts abovementioned) to the care of Lieutenant P. Orr. The Rajah of Eesanugger had, for some time past, shown himself most reluctant to pay the portion of revenue due by him to the Oude government. After many unsuccessful expostulations on the subject, Lieutenant P. Orr determined on having a final interview with the Rajah before requesting the Nazim to have recourse to more stringent measures; and with this intention he met the Rajah in a kutcherry hut, situated in a mango tope, close under the bastions of the fort of Eesanugger. The Rajah was accompanied by his brother-in-law, his dewan, his vakeel, &c., and escorted by about two hundred armed followers. Lieutenant Orr had with him but a few men of his own corps, H.M.'s 1st Light Infantry Battalion. In the discussion which ensued, the Rajah's vakeel made use of most insolent language, and was requested by Lieutenant Orr to leave the kutcherry; he did so, and shortly afterwards the Rajah himself wished to withdraw without coming to any final settlement as regarding the payment of money due. Lieutenant Orr again urged on him the necessity of fulfilling his engagement, but the Rajah seemed bent on leaving the kutcherry, and had, in fact, risen from his chair, when Lieutenant Orr seized him by the arm with the intention of detaining him, until he should come to terms. The Rajah's brother-in-law and dewan now drew their swords, and the latter struck Lieutenant Orr, inflicting a severe wound on the right shoulder. Seeing the hostile aspect affairs had taken, Lieutenant Orr felt his only chance of life was to cling to the Rajah, whose followers, apprehensive of wounding their master, feared to strike home. A fearful struggle now ensued; the Rajah's brother-in-law inflicting a second wound of about seven inches on the right thigh. Lieutenant Orr's jemadar, Rajonath Singh, and a havildar, Ram Singh, took part in the affray and behaved extremely well; the former with one blow of his sword struck off the head of the Rajah's brother-in-law, and the havildar, seizing a formidable tulwar, made right good use of it, cutting down the dewan and two others, Lieutenant Orr, though covered with wounds, still retained his hold on the Rajah, until, receiving a violent sword cut on the head, he fell stunned. The Rajah immediately rose, and, himself wounded (by whom it is not known), was carried off by his followers to his fort. Lieutenant Orr shortly afterwards regaining his senses, and thinking the scoundrels would return after seeing the Rajah safe in his fort, rose and reeled a few yards out of the kutcherry, ordering his servant to place him on a bed and carry him off as speedily as possible. Most fortunately did he thus act; for no sooner had he abandoned the place than the guns from the fort bastions opened out, and grape was fired at the kutcherry: by this two of Lieutenant Orr's men fell. To the grape succeeded round shot. Scarcely had his few men placed their officer on the bed and commenced their retreat, when a strong gang of fellows armed with matchlocks, issued from the fort, and commenced following up Lieutenant Orr's small party. Still that officer preserved his presence of mind, though faint and sick from the great loss of blood, and suffering fearfully from the jolting of the bed and the great heat of the sun (it was now about 10 o'clock A.M.). When hard pressed by the villains, he ordered his small party to stand and return the fire. He thus gained a little time, which his servants took advantage of by hurrying on with their burden as speedily as possible. Several times was this manœuvre had recourse to, and for three mortal hours did this retreat last, the enemy following up, and all the villagers on the road presenting too hostile an appearance to allow of any hope of refuge. Once, indeed, so close was the poor fellow pursued, that, fearing he had no chance of life otherwise than by mounting his horse, he, with supernatural strength, left the charpoy and actually rode a short distance; but again staggering in his seat, he was obliged to abandon his horse, and submit again to be placed on the charpoy. Fortunately, one of the villains had during this momentary halt fallen, struck dead by a ball from one of the muskets of Orr's escort, and this event caused them to pause and thus allow our harassed party to gain ground. At last Orr, with wonderful presence of mind, steering his course through the fields, avoiding all villages, gained the village of Kuttowlee, belonging to the Rajah of Mullahpore; and here a community of Gooshaën fuqueers received him, and to the number of about 300 (others from the adjacent villages having joined) turned out, and gallantly opposed the Eesanugger men, who, not daring to attack them on the territory of a rival rajah, at last retraced their steps. The Gooshaëns now turned their attention to the wounded officer, whose state then may be more easily imagined than described—seven very severe, and three slight wounds! They immediately relieved the burning thirst under which he was suffering, and sewed up his wounds, applying their own remedies—none the worse for being so simple! Two whole days and nights did they attend on him with the greatest care and solicitude; and on the third day the native regimental doctor reached from the head-quarters of the corps and co-operated with them. Lieutenant Orr is still at Kuttowlee, being in too weak a state for removal to better quarters. His health and wounds, I am happy to say, are improving, and soon, I trust, he will be able, if not to resume his duties, at least to be entered on the convalescent list.

"'Such, sir, is a succinct account of this most sad affair. Lieutenant Orr's escape has been a miraculous one, — one in which we cannot but recognise the hand of a kind and overruling Providence! I may add, the brave jemadar was severely wounded on the left shoulder, and also a small fragment of his skull shattered; but I am glad to say he is recovering fast. The Rajah has abandoned his fort and district; the former is occupied by men of Captain Barlow's corps, to which belongs Lieutenant Orr.

"'It is useless making any comments on the vile and treacherous conduct of the Rajah's people. It is one of the many sad episodes in the daily history of this most unfortunate country!'

"Thus far our correspondent; but much as we sympathise with Lieutenant Orr and his gallant Sepoys, whose valour is so graphically detailed in the above narrative, we cannot hope for better results from the degrading part which English officers are found willing to perform in the territories of this king of fiddlers and females of the household. They are compelled to assist in his quarrels, no matter whether the service expected be the enforcement of an unjust claim or the destruction of a band of thieves. They are bound to work with the worst of tools, often for the accomplishment of the worst of ends. The ancient process of levying tithe in Ireland was safe and pleasant as compared with the mode of collecting rent in Oude. If European officers are to execute the work of the king's government, allow them to do the business after their own fashion, and ensure a state of peace, by making resistance an act of insanity. Some thirty-five years since a Company's officer was sent to gather in the rent of his majesty of Oude, and he demanded a certain sum from a zemindar, who was always accustomed to stand a siege before he paid his tax. The agent selected, however, on this occasion, was a man in the habit of achieving his objects by the speediest methods, and he assured the debtor, that if he injured one of his men, he would carry his fort by escalade, and put every living soul to the sword. The zemindar laughed at his communication, and forthwith knocked over two or three sepoys by a well directed fire. But he had not so well calculated his means of defence as his range of practice. In a very short time, the place was surrounded, and the threat fulfilled to the letter. The vengeance was worthy of Cromwell, but it was perhaps an act of mercy, for the district in which it was inflicted was converted into the quietest and most productive portion of the royal territory. We do not advocate such terrible measures of repression now-a-days, for we grudge every rupee that is gathered for the support of a government which is a curse to millions, and an advantage to none but the basest of mankind. What we contend for is, that our countrymen should either govern Oude or abandon its rulers to their fate. As it is, we are powerless for good, and unwilling accomplices in evil. We do infinite and perpetual wrong, because some of our nation in times past made treaties which it is immoral to observe. When the doctrine which prevails in Europe, that the good of the people is the first, and, indeed, the only end of government, shall be applied to the worn-out dynasties of Hindostan, we may expect to see Oude and its king receive the justice to which they are entitled at the hands of the British authorities."

When Oude is re-conquered, which will be accomplished with much more difficulty than is counted upon, we may rely upon it that no trouble will be found in reducing the ryots to order. We may hear occasionally in the interim of plundering on their part, since a state of warfare is the normal condition of the country, and the men who have hitherto had nothing to do with rupees but hand them over to a landlord and to fight in his quarrel from January to December, are scarcely likely to forego the tempting opportunity of doing a little business for themselves. But when soldier and cultivator have been alike disarmed, and security is once more established, the ryot will not hesitate to prefer the safety of life, the chance of acquiring property, and the certainty of obtaining more justice than he could hope for at the hands of the rulers of his own race. We know that, in some districts at least, the assessment has been lowered to one-fourth the amount exacted under the king's rule, and it is most likely that the reduction has been universal. The progress of events has made it impossible that the dynasty of Wajid Ally should ever be restored; and, were it otherwise, we should earnestly deprecate such a result, for the sake of the toiling millions.

CHAP. IV.

THE STORY OF THE GREASED CARTRIDGES.—GOVERNMENT WARNED, BUT USELESSLY, OF THE GROWTH OF DISAFFECTION.—THE BERHAMPORE OUTBREAK.

It is not possible that hurricanes should occur in the social or physical world without giving timely warning of their growth. To sagacious minds, the tokens of great impending changes always exhibit themselves. Unluckily for the people of Calcutta, they had no hand-book of storms to guide the politician; no barometer to note the changes in public feeling; but still the uneasy feeling prevailed, which denotes that important disturbance is about to take place. There was a vague inquietude in the bazaar—a belief that all was not sound, in the minds of Englishmen unconnected with the services; every class, except the members of the governing body, was impressed with a foreboding of evil. No one, however, without the pale of authority dreamt of the magnitude of the dangers by which we were about to be assailed; and inside that potent circle not a soul had gained an inkling of the coming horrors. The ship of the state was struck by a white squall, with every sail set and not a man at his post to warn the crew of their peril.

On the 22nd of January last, Captain Wright of the 70th N. I., brought to the notice of Major Bontein, commanding the depôt of musketry at Dum-Dum, the fact that there was "a very unpleasant feeling among the native soldiers who were at the depôt for instruction, regarding the grease used in preparing the cartridges, some evil disposed person having spread a report that it consisted of a mixture of the fat of pigs and cows." Captain Wright added, "The belief, in this respect, has been strengthened by the behaviour of a classie attached to the magazine, who, I am told, asked a Sepoy of the 2nd Grenadiers to supply him with water from his lotah; the Sepoy refused, observing he was not aware of what caste the man was; the classie immediately rejoined, 'You will soon lose your caste, as ere long you will have to bite cartridges covered with the fat of pigs and cows,' or words to that effect. Some of the depôt men, in conversing with me on the subject last night, said that the report had spread throughout India, and when they go to their homes their friends will refuse to eat with them. I assured them (believing it to be the case) that the grease used is composed of mutton fat and wax; to which they replied, 'It may be so, but our friends will not believe it: let us obtain the ingredients from the bazaar, and make it up ourselves; we shall then know what is used, and be able to assure our fellow soldiers and others that there is nothing in it prohibited by our caste.'"

Major Bontein wrote next day to the station staff adjutant, forwarding the above report. A rumour to the same effect had attracted his attention for some days previously, but he had not thought it a matter of importance. On receipt of Captain Wright's letter, he paraded all the native portion of the depôt, and called for any complaint the men might wish to prefer. At least two-thirds of the detachment immediately stepped to the front, including all the native commissioned officers. In a manner perfectly respectful, they very distinctly stated their objection to the present method of preparing cartridges for the new rifle musket: the mixture employed for greasing cartridges was opposed to their religious feeling, and as a remedy they begged to suggest the employment of wax and oil, in such proportion as in their opinion would answer the purpose required.

General Hearsey, commanding at Dum-Dum, was the next link in the usual chain of communication; and he appreciated the gravity of the matter, losing not an hour in addressing the Deputy Adjutant-General on the subject.

"It will be hard," he wrote, "most difficult, to eradicate this impression from the minds of the native soldiers, who are always suspiciously disposed when any change of this sort affecting themselves is introduced." As a remedy for the misunderstanding, General Hearsey proposed that authority should be given for obtaining from the bazaar whatever ingredients were necessary for the preparation of the bullet patch, which the Sepoys themselves should be allowed to make up.

The Deputy Adjutant-General took three days to con over the affair, and then sent the correspondence to the Military Secretary, who answered, on the 27th January, that the Governor-General in council had adopted General Hearsey's suggestion, which might be carried out as well at Umballah and Sealkote, if the men wished it. The Inspector-General of Ordnance was applied to for information as to what the composition used in the arsenal for greasing the cartridges of the rifle muskets consisted of, "whether mutton fat was or is used, and if there are any means adopted for ensuring the fat of sheep and goats only being used; also, whether it is possible that the fat of bullocks and pigs may have been employed in preparing the ammunition for the new rifled muskets which has been recently made up in the arsenal." The reply was, that the grease used was a mixture of tallow and beeswax, in accordance with the instructions of the Court of Directors; that the tallow was supplied by a contractor; but that "no extraordinary precaution appears to have been taken to ensure the absence of any objectionable fat." The first ammunition made in the arsenal was intended for the 60th Rifles, and it was probable that some of this was issued to the depôt at Dum-Dum. The Inspector-General regretted that, "ammunition was not prepared expressly for the practice depôt, without any grease at all," but the subject did not "occur to him." He recommended that the Home Government should be requested not to send out any more made ammunition for the Enfield rifles.

On the 28th January, General Hearsey again addressed the

Government on the subject of the greased cartridges. He believed that members of the orthodox Brahminical party had first spread the report that the Sepoys were to be forced to embrace the Christian faith, and that on this report was grafted, as an overt act to cause them to lose caste, the distributing amongst them ball cartridges for the new Enfield rifle, that had the paper forming them greased with the fat of cows and pigs. The general connected the rumours in question with the nightly acts of incendiarism that had begun to take place in various quarters. He thought the object of the fires was to obtain the support of a party of the ignorant classes in the ranks of the army. Parades had been held of the four regiments at Barrackpore; and their commanding officers had declared their men to be "perfectly satisfied." Colonel Wheeler, of the 34th, was told by his native officers and men that they were satisfied; but one native officer respectfully asked if any orders had been received repecting the new Enfield cartridges. Ten days afterwards General Hearsey, in forwarding the proceedings of a court of inquiry assembled to ascertain the "cause of their continued objections to the paper of which the new rifle cartridges were composed," wrote as follows: — "A perusal of the several statements and opinions recorded in these proceedings clearly establishes, in my judgment, that a most unreasonable and unfounded suspicion has unfortunately taken possession of the minds of all the native officers and Sepoys at this station, that grease or fat is used in the composition of this cartridge paper; and this foolish idea is now so rooted in them, that it would, I am of opinion, be both idle and unwise even to attempt its removal. I would accordingly beg leave to recommend, for the consideration of Government, the expediency (if practicable) of ordering this rifle ammunition to be made up of the same description of paper which has been hitherto employed in the magazines for the preparation of the common musket cartridge, by which means this groundless suspicion and objection could be at once disposed of."

On the same day that General Hearsey stated his conviction that the idea of forcible conversion was so rooted in the minds of the native soldiers, that it would be "both idle and unwise even to *attempt* its removal," the Government addressed the Court of Directors in a despatch wherein it was stated that "the men were appeased on being assured that the matter would be duly represented;" and again, that "they appear to be perfectly satisfied that there existed no intention of interfering with their caste." On the 8th April the Court of Directors were "gratified to learn that the matter has been fully explained to the men at Barrackpore and Dum-Dum, and that they appear perfectly satisfied that there existed no intention of interfering with their caste;" and on the same day the Government of India addressed the Court of Directors detailing the mutiny and disbandment of the 19th regiment, who had refused to take the cartridges "in consequence of the reports in circulation that the paper of which they were made was greased with the fat of cows and pigs."

General Hearsey wrote to Government on the 11th of February that they had been dwelling at Barrackpore "on a mine ready for explosion." His belief was based on a series of facts, which were duly set forth in his statement. The taunt of the classie already alluded to had sunk deeply into the minds of the Sepoys. Fires had taken place at Raneegunge and Barrackpore, the combustibles used being Santal arrows, which fixed suspicion on the 2nd Grenadiers, who had recently been stationed in that district. A Sepoy of good character had reported to his officer that there was to be a meeting of the men belonging to all the regiments a night or two back, in continuation of a previous one, at which the Sepoys were to discuss the measures proper to be taken to prevent Government from destroying their religion. On the 10th February a native lieutenant deposed before a European court of inquiry, that on the night of the 5th instant Sepoys had come to him and made him go with them to the parade ground, where he saw a great crowd of men assembled, with their heads tied up in cloths, so as to expose only a portion of the face. They asked him to join in a rising to take place next night, when they proposed to kill all the Europeans, plunder the station, and go where they liked. General Hearsey stated that he had the regiments paraded on the 9th February, and impressed upon them the absurdity of their conduct. He pointed out to Government that there was great danger in having a brigade of four or five native corps so close to the capital, and went on to remark, "You will perceive in all this business the native officers were of no use; in fact, they are afraid of their men, and dare not act: all they do is to hold themselves aloof, and expect by so doing they will escape censure as not actively implicated. This has always occurred on such occasions, and will continue to the end of our sovereignty in India. Well might Sir C. Metcalfe say, 'that he expected to awake some fine morning, and find that India had been lost to the English crown.'"

The day after the above was despatched, General Hearsey again wrote, to say that a native doctor had heard a Sepoy of the 2nd Grenadiers, tell another native that a messenger had been sent by his regiment to Dinapore and to the 19th N. I., asking if they would join in raising a disturbance. Search was made for the messenger, but he was not found; and after a few days things appeared to have settled down into something like calmness; the Sepoys were allowed to make up their own cartridges, and a new method of loading was adopted, by which the men broke the cartridge instead of biting it, whilst the officers were "confidentially" instructed to stop short of loading in the drill, and in this way, the ulcer, destined so soon to eat into the vitals of the body politic, was supposed to be healed up for the present.

Matters continued without change till the night of the 19th February, when the call to arms was heard in the lines of the 19th N. I. at Berhampore, and the men rapidly breaking open the kotes in which the arms were kept, seized their muskets, and with loud shouts assembled as if on parade. A great many of them loaded, and when the occurrence is studied by the light of after transactions, it seems almost marvellous that the outbreak should have been got under without bloodshed. There was not a European soldier in the place. Moorshedabad, where the descendant of Suraj-oo-Dowlah, who had lost Bengal just a century before, resides, a city containing not less than a hundred and fifty thousand inhabitants, was distant but five miles, and any amount of sympathy and perhaps of aid might have been expected from its fanatic Mahomedan population. The regiments at Barrackpore had invited the 19th to co-operate with them, and a detachment of the 34th sent on duty to Berhampore still lingered at the station, waiting—it was supposed—for the news that the work of mutiny had been commenced. On the report of the disturbance being made to him, the commanding officer, Col. Mitchell, ordered out the Irregular Cavalry, consisting of 180 men, and two guns, manned each by 12 Golundauz or native gunners. The mutinous troops were asked why they had paraded without orders, and replied that they were told Europeans were being brought to murder them, because they objected to receive the cartridge. Col. Mitchell expostulated with them on their conduct, and ordered them to lay down their arms, which after much hesitation they agreed to do, provided the guns and cavalry were withdrawn. The latter were kept on the ground until the greater portion of the regiment had replaced the muskets in the kotes, and then, on the assurance of the officers that the remainder were following their example, but feared they might be set upon when deprived of the means of defence, the artillery and troopers were ordered to return to their quarters, and after four hours of anxious suspense, quiet was restored. The next day a parade was held, and the native officers with a few Sepoys were invited to inspect and test the cartridges. Water was used as a test, and one kind of paper being more highly glazed than the rest, as shown in imbibing moisture, was decided to contain fat of some kind. The glazed cartridges were put aside in deference to their prejudices, and they were told that no attempts would be made to compel their use of them. A report was made of the whole affair to superior authority, and the regiment continued to perform its duties as usual with ordinary regularity.

When the behaviour of the 19th was made known at Calcutta, Lord Canning resolved to make a signal example of the mutineers. The steamer "Oriental" was ordered down to Rangoon, to bring up H. M.'s 84th, and it was thought that a sentence of disbandment, carried out in the case of the entire regiment, would put an effectual stop to the progress of disaffection. But the resolve was bruited abroad. There were nearly 4000 Sepoys brigaded at Barrackpore and in Fort William, and though H. M.'s 53rd with a European battery would have made short work of them in a conflict, what was there to hinder the success of a rising, judiciously planned and carried out simultaneously at both stations? There were neither Europeans nor guns at Barrackpore. If the telegraph wires were cut and the roads taken possession of, they could march down to Calcutta without a soul being aware of the movement, and at the moment that their comrades in the fort assailed the Europeans, they could attempt a surprise from without with every chance of success. By a strange laxity of rule which deserves the most severe reprobation, the pouches of the native soldiery are only examined by their officers twice a week, and of course, except upon these occasions, they may use their cartridges without any fear of detection. We believe that in almost every instance where the Sepoys have had cause to dread punishment, or were waiting for the signal to mutiny, their muskets if examined would have been found loaded. There would have been no difficulty then in every armed native shooting his fellow soldier on duty, without awakening suspicion or affording the opportunity of resistance. Now that we can look back and sum up the incentives to rebellion, we feel abundant cause to rejoice that these men, with arms in their hands and treason in their hearts, could not find a leader, or muster up courage sufficient to strike a blow which must have proved fatal.

Perhaps no actual conspiracy was formed to carry out a plan of assault such as has been suggested, but it is certain that an understanding, involving an attack upon Fort William and the murder of the European officers generally, was come to. The order to the 19th N. I. to march down to Barrackpore hastened the necessity for action, and the 34th sent the men of that corps a message, urging them to slaughter their officers on the road, in which case they would be ready to effect a junction at Barrackpore, and try conclusions with the Government. Their overtures might perhaps have been successful, but Col. Mitchell took the precaution of making an unexpected halt within fourteen miles of Barrackpore, and sending for the native officers, kept them at his quarters for some hours, the time chosen for the durbar being that supposed to be fixed upon for the mutiny. Baffled by those simple but efficacious measures, the 19th were unable to transmit the expected signal to Barrackpore, and the rest of the conspirators were afraid to begin without it. But Mungul Pandy, a Sepoy of the 34th, was not to be balked of the pleasure he had anticipated in shedding the blood of the Feringhees. Roused to frenzy by the copious use of bhang, he seized his musket, and rushed upon the parade ground on the afternoon of Sunday the 29th of March, calling upon his comrades to come forward and fight for their religion. The serjeant-major of the regiment came up at the time, and the fellow deliberately fired at him but missed. The quarter guard, consisting of nineteen men of the same regiment, turned out to witness the scene, but without exhibiting the smallest intention of affording assistance. Whilst the struggle was going on, the adjutant made his appearance, and Mungul Pandy, having carefully reloaded his musket, fired a second time, and shot the adjutant's horse. A hand-to-hand fight now ensued, the Sepoy hacking with his sword at both officers, whilst numbers of men belonging to the regiment, who had gathered round the spot, attacked them from behind with the butt ends of their muskets, repeating their blows whilst the latter lay on the ground. The strife would have soon been over, had not Major-General Hearsey galloped up, and ordered the guard to move forward to the rescue. The fellows hesitated to obey, on which the General drew a revolver, and pointing at them, repeated his commands, when they slowly advanced and rescued the bleeding and insensible men. The jemadar, a high caste Brahmin, who had ordered them not to stir from their post, was, with the rest of the guard, placed in close arrest; and on the night following, the 19th regiment, weary with their march of fourteen miles, arrived at the station. Next day they were disbanded with expressions of regret on the part of the General commanding the brigade, and apparently a little compunction on the side of the Governor-General, who thought he would strike terror by such an act to the hearts of their co-religionists. Supported by H. M.'s 84th Regiment and a wing of the 53d, two troops of artillery, and the Body-guard, General Hearsey pronounced the sentence contained in the following order:—

"The 19th Regiment N. I. has been brought to the head quarters of the Presidency Division, to receive, in the presence of the troops there assembled, the decision of the Governor-General in Council upon the offence of which it has been guilty.

"On the 26th of February, the 19th Regiment N. I. was ordered to parade on the following morning for exercise, with fifteen rounds of blank ammunition for each man.

"The only blank ammunition in store was some which had been made up by the 7th N. I., the Regiment preceding the 19th Regiment at Berhampore, and which had been left at that station on the departure of the 7th Regiment. This ammunition had been used by the recruits of the 19th Regiment up to the date above mentioned.

"When the quantity of ammunition required for the following morning was taken to the lines, it appears that the men objected to the paper of which the cartridges were made, as being of two colours; and when the pay havildars assembled the men to issue the percussion caps, they refused to receive them, saying that they had doubts about the cartridges.

"The men have since stated, in a petition addressed to

the Major-General commanding the Presidency Division, that for more than two months they had heard rumours of new cartridges having been made at Calcutta, on the paper of which the fat of bullocks and pigs had been spread, and of its being the intention of the Government to coerce the men to bite these cartridges; and that therefore they were afraid for their religion. They admit that assurance given them by the Colonel of their regiment satisfied them that this would not be the case; adding, nevertheless, that when on the 26th of February they perceived the cartridges to be of two kinds, they were convinced that one kind was greased, and therefore refused them.

"The Commanding Officer, on hearing of the refusal, went to the lines, assembled the native commissioned and non-commissioned officers, and explained that the cartridges were unobjectionable, and had been left at Berhampore by the 7th Regiment. He instructed them to inform their men, that the cartridges would be served out in the morning by the officers commanding companies, and that any man who refused to take them would be tried by a Court Martial and punished.

"This occurred at 8 o'clock in the evening.

"Between 10 and 11 o'clock a rush was made by the Sepoys to the bells of arms; the doors were forced open; the men took possession of their arms and accoutrements, and carried them to their lines.

"On learning what had occurred, Lieutenant-Colonel Mitchell ordered out the 11th Regiment of Irregular Cavalry and the post guns.

"When the Cavalry reached the parade, the men of the 19th Regiment rushed out of their lines with their arms shouting, and assembled near to the bells of arms, where many loaded their muskets.

"Upon Lieutenant-Colonel Mitchell and the European officers approaching the men, they were warned not to go on, or the men would fire.

"The native officers were assembled, and Lieutenant-Colonel Mitchell, after addressing the men, directed the officers to separate the companies, and to require them to give up their arms.

"The men hesitated at first, but eventually gave up their arms and retired to their lines.

"These are the principal features of the outbreak at Berhampore on the 26th of February.

"The men of the 19th Regiment have refused obedience to their European officers. They have seized arms with violence. They have assembled, in a body, to resist the authority of their Commander.

"The regiment has been guilty of open and defiant mutiny.

"It is no excuse for this offence to say, as had been said in the before mentioned petition of the native officers and men of the regiment, that they were afraid for their religion, and that they apprehended violence to themselves.

"It is no atonement of it to declare, as they have therein declared, that they are ready to fight for their Government in the field, when they have disobeyed and insulted that Government in the persons of its officers, and have expressed no contrition for their heavy offences.

"Neither the 19th Regiment, nor any regiment in the service of the Government of India, nor any Sepoy, Hindoo, or Mussulman, has reason to pretend that the Government has shown, directly or indirectly, a desire to interfere with the religion of its troops.

"It has been the unvarying rule of the Government of India to treat the religious feelings of all its servants, of every creed, with careful respect; and to representations or complaints put forward in a dutiful and becoming spirit, whether upon this, or upon any other subject, it has never turned a deaf ear.

"But the Government of India expects to receive, in return for this treatment, the confidence of those who serve it.

"From its soldiers of every rank and race, it will, at all times, and in all circumstances, enforce unhesitating obedience. They have sworn to give it, and the Governor-General in Council will never cease to exact it. To no men who prefer complaints with arms in their hands will he ever listen.

"Had the Sepoys of the 19th Regiment confided in their Government, and believed their commanding officer, instead of crediting the idle stories with which false and evil-minded men have deceived them, their religious scruples would still have remained inviolate, and themselves would still be, as they have hitherto been, faithful soldiers, trusted by the State, and laying up for future years all the rewards of a long and honourable service.

"But the Governor-General in Council can no longer have any confidence in this regiment, which has disgraced its name, and has lost all claim to consideration and indulgence.

"It is therefore the order of the Governor-General in Council, that the 19th Regiment N. I. be now disbanded; that the native commissioned and non-commissioned officers and privates be discharged from the Army of Bengal; that this be done at the head-quarters of the Presidency Division in the presence of every available corps within two days' march of the station; that the regiment be paraded for the purpose; and that each man, after being deprived of his arms, shall receive his arrears of pay and be required to withdraw from the cantonment.

"The European officers of the regiment will remain at Barrackpore until orders for their disposal shall be received from His Excellency the Commander-in-Chief.

"This order is to be read at the head of every regiment, troop, and company in the service."

The arms were piled, the colours deposited, and the 19th N. I. was erased from the army list.

It is difficult to say how far the disbanded soldiers really went in heart with the promoters of insurrection, but before scattering themselves over the face of the land, they asked to be allowed one of two favours, either to be re-enlisted for general service, or failing that request, to be allowed the use of their arms for half an hour, and brought face to face with the 34th, in which latter case they promised to avenge the quarrel of the Government as well as their own. Perhaps their anger was felt against the men who had brought them into temptation without having had the courage to share their offence, rather than against the evil advisers who had lured them to an act of folly. Some alarm was entertained lest they should plunder the villages on their way up-country, but they seem to have conducted themselves peaceably. Many got employment as durwans, or gate-keepers, and a few were entertained by magistrates for whom they have since done efficient service in the capture of fugitive mutineers. Hundreds died of cholera by the way side, and a large proportion went into the service of the Nawaub of Moorshedabad. It has not been ascertained if any of the 19th have been found in the ranks of the existing rebel army.

It took five weeks from the date of the occurrence last mentioned, to enable the Government at Calcutta to make up their minds as to what they should do with the 34th. The Commander-in-Chief was far away in the recesses of the Himalayas, and justice must neither seem hurried nor cruel. In the interval, Mungul Pandy and the jemadar of the guard had been tried and hung, the former glorying in his crimes to the latest moment, and asserting that he was about to suffer for the good of religion. Two Sepoys had also been transported as accomplices in a plot for capturing the fort, and a native officer of the same regiment, the 70th N. I. was dismissed the service for treasonable practices. In the Executive Council Mr. J. P. Grant appears to have been prepared to inflict capital punishment, in the case at least of the quarter guard of the 19th, but if so, the milder counsels of the Governor-General secured a majority in favour of merely sending them about their business. Lord Canning had a notion, which it took two months of terrible experience to conquer, that disbanding was a fearful punishment to the Indian Sepoy, accustomed as he is to rely absolutely on the Government for his own subsistence and that of his family in manhood and old age. It was no use pointing out to him that these men had committed the worst offence known to the military code; that they were mutineers in fact and murderers in intention, saved only by their intense cowardice from finishing a work which they undertook *con amore.* He had got it fixed in his mind, that a mutiny was a mere strife of discontented labourers, which a little coercion, a little persuasion, and much talk upon the folly of the proceeding were sure to put down. It was true he might recognise a difference between the Bengal Sepoy and the Manchester spinner, to the great advantage however of the former, seeing that he kept his tools and received his wages when on strike, whilst the latter was entirely disbanded with very little chance of re-enlistment. At one moment it appears to have been thought advisable to overlook the conduct of the regiment altogether. The "Oriental" which was supposed to be lying at Madras, was twice telegraphed for to convey the 84th back to Burmah, and but for the accident that sent her across to Rangoon, the capital would have been left as before with only the wing of a European regiment. It is hard to say what might have occurred had either the steamer been available when applied for, or the reports of growing disaffection become less frequent. Fortunately neither contingency occurred. The Government were roused to a partial sense of duty, and on the 6th of May, the whole of the disposable troops in and around Calcutta were concentrated at Barrackpore, to carry out the order for disbanding such officers and men of the 34th N. I. as were present in the lines on the 29th March, when Adjutant Baugh was wounded. At daylight two sides of a square were formed by H. M.'s 53rd and 84th, the 2nd, 43rd and 70th N. I., two squadrons of Cavalry, consisting of the Body Guard and the 11th Irregulars, and a light field battery with six guns. When the line was formed, seven companies of the 34th, about four hundred strong, were halted in front of the guns; the order for disbandment was read out by the interpreter, Lieut. Chamier, and after a few energetic remarks upon the enormity of their offence, General Hearsey commanded them to pile their arms and strip off the uniform which they had disgraced. Of course they obeyed without a moment's hesitation. The work of paying up their arrears was then commenced, and in two hours the disorderly Sepoys, now converted into an orderly mob, were marched off to Pulta Ghaut for conveyance to Chinsurah, the grenadiers of the 84th and a portion of the Body Guard attending their footsteps. When they left their lines, order had been taken for sending their families and baggage on to Chinsurah. Instructions were given to the various police authorities to hinder them from crossing the river, and it was hoped that the public had heard the last of the *second* mutiny of the 34th B. N. I.

The following order appeared next day in the *Government Gazette,*—

"Fort William, 4th May.—On the 29th of March, a Sepoy of the 34th Regiment of Native Infantry, stationed at Barrackpore, armed himself with a loaded musket and sword, advanced upon the parade ground in front of his lines, and, after conducting himself in a violent and mutinous manner, and calling upon the men of the regiment to come forth and to join him in resisting lawful authority, attacked and wounded the adjutant and sergeant-major of his regiment, who approached to restrain him.

"This man has been tried, condemned, and hanged.

"On the same occasion the native officer, a jemadar in command of the quarter guard of the 34th Regiment Native Infantry, refused to obey his superior, by whom he was ordered to seize the above mentioned Sepoy.

"After being tried by a court of native commissioned officers, this man, himself a commissioned officer, has paid the penalty of his mutiny by the same ignominious death.

"But these men were not the sole offenders upon that occasion.

"The Governor-General in Council laments to say that the conduct of the native commissioned and non-commissioned officers and men of the 34th Regiment who were then present, has been shown to be such as to destroy his confidence in them as soldiers of the state, and to call for severe and exemplary punishment.

"The mutinous Sepoy was permitted to parade himself insolently before his assembled comrades, using menaces and threatening gestures against his officers without an attempt on the part of any to control him.

"No such attempt was made even when he had deliberately fired at the serjeant-major of the regiment.

"None was made when upon the appearance of the adjutant, Lieutenant Baugh, and after having reloaded the musket unmolested, the mutineer discharged it at that officer and shot his horse.

"When the horse fell, not a sign of assistance to Lieutenant Baugh was given either by the quarter guard or by the Sepoys not on duty, although this took place within ten paces of the guard.

"During the hand-to-hand conflict which followed between the mutineer and Lieutenant Baugh, supported by Serjeant-Major Hewson, the men collected at the lines in undress, looked on passively; others in uniform and on duty joined in the struggle; but it was to take part against their officers, whom they attacked with the butts of their muskets, striking down the serjeant-major from behind, and repeating the blows as he lay on the ground.

"The Governor-General in Council deeply regrets that of the ruffians who perpetrated this cowardly act, the only one who was identified has escaped his punishment by desertion.

"There was, however, one amongst those who stood by, who set an honourable example to his comrades. Sheik Pultoo Sepoy (now havildar), of the Grenadier Company, obeyed the call of his officer for assistance unhesitatingly. He was wounded in the endeavour to protect Lieutenant Baugh from the mutineer, and did all that an unarmed man could do to seize the criminal. His conduct was that of a faithful and brave soldier.

"When the adjutant, maimed and bleeding, was retiring from the conflict, he passed the lines of his regiment and reproached the men assembled there with having allowed their officer to be cut down before their eyes without offering to assist him; they made no reply, but turned their backs and moved sullenly away.

"For the failure of the quarter guard to do its duty, the jemadar who commanded it has already paid the last penalty of death. In this guard, consisting of twenty Sepoys, there were four who desired to act against the mutineer, but their jemadar restrained them; and when eventually the order to advance upon the criminal was given by superior authority, the majority yielded obedience reluctantly.

"Upon a review of these facts and of all the circumstances connected with them, it is but too clear to the Governor-General in Council that a spirit of disloyalty prevails in those companies of the 34th Regiment Native Infantry which are stationed at the head-quarters of the Presidency Division. Silent spectators of a long continued act of insolent mutiny, they have made no endeavour to suppress it, and have thereby become liable themselves to the punishment of mutineers. The Governor-General in Council can no longer put trust in them, and he rejects their services from this time forward.

"Therefore, it is the order of the Governor-General in Council that the native commissioned and non-commissioned officers and men of the seven companies of the 34th Regiment Native Infantry, now quartered at Barrackpore, be disbanded and dismissed from the army of Bengal, with the following exceptions in favour of those who in the course of recent events have given the Governor-General in Council good reason to believe in their fidelity to their officers and to the Government:—

* * * *

"There remains one point which the Governor-General in Council desires to notice.

"The Sepoy, who was the chief actor in the disgraceful scene of the 29th of March, called upon his comrades to come to his support for the reason that their religion was in danger, and that they were about to be compelled to use cartridges, the use of which would do injury to their caste; and from the words in which he addressed the Sepoys it is to be inferred that many of them shared this opinion with him.

"The Governor-General in Council has recently had occasion to remind the army of Bengal that the Government of India has never interfered to constrain its soldiers in matters affecting their religious faith. He has declared that the Government of India never will do so, and he has a right to expect that this declaration shall give confidence to all who have been deceived and led astray.

"But whatever may be the deceptions or evil counsels to which others have been exposed, the native officers and men of the 34th Regiment Native Infantry have no excuse for misapprehension on this subject. Not many weeks previously to the 29th of March it had been explained to that regiment, — first by their own commanding officer, and subsequently by the major-general commanding the division, — that their fears for religion were groundless. It was carefully and clearly shown to them, that the cartridges which they would be called upon to use, contained nothing which could do violence to their religious scruples. If, after receiving these assurances, the Sepoys of the 34th Regiment, or of any other regiment, still refuse to place trust in their officers and in the Government, and still allow suspicions to take root in their minds, and to grow into disaffection, insubordination, and mutiny, the fault is their own, and their punishment will be upon their own heads. That it will be a sharp and certain punishment the Governor-General in Council warns them."

It is no insignificant branch of the art of governing, which teaches the right use of language with reference to compositions intended for the eye of the public. The vagueness and want of meaning charged against royal speeches and ministerial statements in general, give those utterances their chief value; to say nothing now, is to leave you the opportunity of saying anything hereafter. When the case is thoroughly stated, and the argument has been heard in support of it, the matter in question is remitted to the sole cognisance of the jury, and the ruler, who is always defendant, lies at their mercy.

The Governor-General forgot the lessons of state craft, when he penned the above General Order. It was far too explicit to be successful. It vindicated the mildness rather than the wisdom of the executive; it showed the necessity for adopting a stern policy, and how very far the fulfilment halted behind the purpose. The physician details all the symptoms of a terrible disease and gives it its right name. He knows the exact state of the patient; he declares that violent remedies must be resorted to, and winds up by prescribing fresh air, low diet, and an abstinence from labour, as a cure for the malady, and a panacea against infection. In the above narrative, nothing is omitted that could make the story of the mutiny more effective. The universal complicity, the common blood-thirstiness, the cruelty, and the cowardice are exhibited in the strongest light. But for the Governor-General the public would not have known how deep was the offence of these men against law and humanity, and it is much to be regretted, that the intellect, which could so clearly portray the crime, had not in this instance been joined with the strength of will that should have decreed its proper punishment.

The position of the Governor-General is, however, with regard to military affairs, a very anomalous one. If he exercises the independent jurisdiction which the law has vested in him, his situation is much like that of the captain of a ship who supersedes the pilot. He may have the best possible reasons for the step, but, if the vessel is lost, the insurance is vitiated, and, under any circumstances, he must expect to be blamed by the pilot interest. On the first report of disaffection in Bengal, it was the duty of the Commander-in-Chief to hasten to Calcutta, and initiate the measures to be taken. Ease and comfort are needful as well as pleasant in that climate, and no one grudges such enjoyment to the seniors of the service; but emergency sometimes calls on the old as well as the young, and the head of the Indian army is not entitled to claim exemption from the common lot of soldiers. We hope we are not doing injustice to the memory of General Anson, in imputing the delay that occurred in dealing out what was called "severe punishment" to mutineers, to his personal inactivity. We should indeed be sorry to hear that it was owing to his deliberate counsels.

Pickpockets who have left us the story of their lives, have recorded the feelings of terror with which the entry of a police officer into a den of thieves is regarded. He is a common foe, and to a certain extent they are all interested in preventing the capture of an offender, but it is rare in the extreme that resistance is offered. The thieftaker's warrant represents the whole authority of the courts of justice; his truncheon symbolises all the physical force of the country. The criminal who is "wanted," surrenders, not to the individual, whom a single blow might dispose of, but to the law, which is enduring and resistless. Had Government, instead of waiting till a force of Europeans numerically superior to the mutinous regiments could assemble, organised, at the first moment of outbreak, a movable column, consisting of a single corps of English troops, a battery of guns, and such cavalry as were available, they might have disarmed and punished treason wherever it dared to lift its head. If authority can only maintain itself by opposing man to man, it should abdicate with as little delay as possible.

Delay and comparative impunity for crime had much to do with the widespread growth of mutiny; but it is something to know that the whole military system in Bengal is at an end. So long as the Brahmin dominated in its ranks, so long might we expect to hear of plots and disaffection, by means of their results. A native officer of the 34th was complaining of his hard fate in being ruined for a revolt in which he had no share. He was reminded that he must have known what was going on in the ranks; and at once he admitted that such was the case, but asked, in turn, how it was supposed he ought to have acted? Had he reported the facts, the Brahmins would most likely have murdered him, and, at any rate, they would have brought forward hundreds of witnesses to swear that he was either perjured or insane. There was no denying the force of this plea; the poor wretch vowed that he was a martyr to our system, and we incline to believe him.

An army has often been likened to a machine, and we wish the comparison were thoroughly accepted. When your engine goes wrong, it is found needful to have at hand a man who understands every portion of it. Being able to place his hand on the defective spot, he knows exactly what is required in the way of reparation, and how to set about the work. But we never, except by chance, have a capable engineer in the person of the exalted official, who has to guide the vast and powerful mechanism that holds the soil and collects the revenues of India. It is hard to divine in most cases the cause of his appointment, harder still to justify the fact of it. It is a miserable thing to say that the State gains by the idleness of a commander-in-chief; and yet in most cases all ranks of the community would join in wishing that he would fold his hands, and only open them to clutch what ought to be the recompense of zeal, intellect, and energy.

Show that your highest office might be a sinecure, and ought never to task the body and brain of the man who fills it, and every general who is old or constitutionally indolent will naturally imitate the example of his chief. Wherever duty can be delegated, it will be done, if at all, by deputy. The general of the division will rely on the colonel, who will rely on his officers, who in turn will rely on native subordinates, who of late could not rely on their men. If the world would only stop for us, so that we could all grow old together, what a pleasant state of things might ensue: but it refuses to halt for a moment; it declines to accept age and idleness in lieu of vigour and industry, however highly recommended to do so. And as we cannot conquer the necessity, we had better submit to it quietly. Clearly enough, the Indian army requires better guidance, and it will be wise to provide at once the indispensable material.

The way to make men invincible is to place them in a situation where they must gain the victory in order to save their lives; and if we made military rank the sole reward of the Indian officer, it would soon be found that he would both love and adorn his noble profession. But so long as he finds the great prizes of his career in the ranks of the civil service, it is not likely that he will take a pride in soldiership. He cannot fail to observe that his superiors in general seem to lay it down as a maxim, that he is wisest who does the least work, and he the most to be envied who gets the highest pay. It would ill beseem him to ignore their example, and he imitates it. The day comes when the Sepoy fancies that he discerns an injury to his religion, or feels more than the usual strain upon his loyalty. He refuses to recognise the authority of one who is scarcely known to him, or to listen to a voice that has never spoken kindly in his ear; and the result is mutiny and ruin on the one hand, disappointment and shame on the other. We hold that rebellion can never break out amongst a people, unless their rulers are greatly in fault; and we are equally convinced that mutiny would never show itself in a regiment, where the officers knew their duty, and performed it.

CHAP. V.

THE OUTBREAK AT MEERUT.—THE MARCH TO DELHI.—MR. COLVIN'S DESPATCHES.—GOVERNMENT KEEPING BACK INTELLIGENCE.

On the 8th of May the new cartridges were offered to the 3rd Cavalry. They refused to accept them, and on the following day eighty-five of the mutineers were tried by court martial, and eighty of them sentenced to be imprisoned for ten years with hard labour, and the remaining five for six years. The offence had been grappled with vigorously, and the display of force for the purpose of carrying out the punishment was sufficiently imposing. The Carabineers, 60th Rifles, the 11th and 20th Regts. N. I., a light field battery, together with the Horse Artillery and the mutinous regiment, were drawn up on the parade ground, and the prisoners were brought forward, stripped of their uniform, and ironed on the spot. The majority of them uttered loud cries of rage and despair, and great agitation was evinced by the native soldiery; but no attempt at resistance was made, and the criminals were marched off the ground under a strong guard, and lodged in jail. It is reasonable to suppose that, for the next thirty-two hours, they showed no signs of an intention to revolt, for not a single precaution was taken by the authorities, though nothing would have been easier than to have rendered mutiny impossible. The custom of hutting the Sepoys would seem designed for the express purpose of isolating them from outward control. Each caste has its own quarter, and none but Brahmins can know what occurs in the Brahminical portion of the cantonment, where the low caste man is not allowed to enter except upon duty. There is no doubt that during the night of the 11th the whole plan of the rising was matured; but the bare design implied in them a too well founded reliance upon the incapacity of the general commanding, or a degree of daring which could only be the result of fanaticism wrought up to the pitch of madness. They were scarcely a match, numerically speaking, for the European troops, and had never been taught that against odds of two to one the Gora logue had failed to be victorious. There were in the station two troops of European horse artillery, together with a field battery, whilst they were wholly destitute of guns. The dragoons could have fairly ridden down a couple of native cavalry regiments, and the 60th Rifles were at least a match for 2000 Sepoys. With such a prospect of speedy annihilation before them, they rose at six o'clock on Sunday afternoon, and set the first example of rebellion and murder. The sound of the church-going bell was soon mingled with the roaring of flames, the wild shouts of revenge and unavailing shrieks for mercy. Whilst a party of the 3rd Cavalry rushed to the jail, and liberated without the slightest difficulty their comrades and the whole of the prisoners in confinement, the rest were galloping about, cutting down their officers and such other Europeans as came in their way. Torches were everywhere applied to the bungalows; the ruffians from the jail and the thieves of the bazar rushed into every house; and, whilst some slaughtered the inmates with circumstances of shocking barbarity, the others plundered whatever they could lay hold of, and wrecked such valuables as they were unable to carry away. For two hours the work of butchery and burning continued, though the authorities had it in their power to have cut up within that time every living soul of the mutineers. Whether the apathy, which it is more painful to contemplate than the scenes of bloodshed, was the result of fear or imbecility, we have not the means of judging; and part of the vengeance invoked upon General Hewett ought to fall on the heads of those who are responsible for the appointment to such an important post of an old man of seventy years and upwards. When the work of destruction had been completed, and every English man, woman, and child whom they could lay hold of were murdered, the rebels prepared to leave the station, and were allowed to do so without hindrance. They took the Delhi road, and went on their way rejoicing; when at last the dragoons and rifles made their appearance and shot down a few without in any way impeding the march of the rest. Their place of refuge was forty miles distant, the highway was level as a bowling green the whole way, and they had to cross two rivers to get into Delhi. A few guns placed on the road, a forced march of the Rifles, and smart gallop of the cavalry, would have placed the British force in a position to effect their total annihilation. The mischief at Meerut had been done; the safety of the station was past praying for; and what had 2000 of Her Majesty's choice troops to do but to plant themselves in the path of the bloodthirsty traitors and trample out the mutiny, so far at least as *they* were concerned? But the chance, which many a gallant heart must have prayed for all that night in agony of spirit, was allowed to pass away, and the cowardice or folly of a single man has entailed the slaughter of countless thousands, and put to hazard the fairest dominion that ever the sun shone upon. There is no punishment great enough for such weakness, and we had better let it rest under the shield of ignominy and universal execration.

For weeks afterwards the wrecks of what had once been beautiful women and stalwart men straggled daily into the station, adding fresh stock to the stories of horror and disaster. The mutilated remains of the murdered were collected and decently disposed of, and a sense of the propriety of retribution began to dawn on the minds of the authorities. Some of the assassins were arrested and hung, and hopes were whispered abroad that in a few days ample justice would be done on the mutineers. Tidings of the outbreak were sent off to the commander-in-chief, who, however, could not be found for some time, having gone on a shooting excursion amongst the hills, and for the next three weeks no direct intelligence of his movements was received at Calcutta.

He reached Umballa on the 18th of May, with the European regiment from Sealkote, Dughsi, and Kussowlie, and pushed on to Kurnaul, but halted for guns and carriage accommodation. Neither artillery nor beasts of burden were to be had at the head-quarters of the Queen's forces.

General Anson had sadly neglected his duty as Commander-in-Chief of the Bengal Army in the evil days that he had fallen upon, but the spirit of a brave soldier was strong within him, and he proposed to move on Delhi at once, without waiting for reinforcements. The guns might follow as he thought, but it was pointed out to him that there was no commissariat, no camels, not a day's allowance of provisions for troops in the field. Well! he would supply his men in the villages on the route, and make the military chest serve in lieu of gomastahs, and baggage waggons. Such unwonted energy might have borne down opposition; but another reason for delay was urged. There was not a single medicine chest available: that objection was insurmountable, and the general bowed to the influence of the Military Secretary. He remained at Kurnaul till the 27th of May, and then succumbed to a mightier influence, dying of cholera after a few hours' illness.

On the 11th of May Mr. Colvin telegraphed to Government that a message had been received at Agra, at 9 P.M. the preceding evening, from the niece of the post-master to the following effect:—"The cavalry have risen, setting fire to their own houses, and several officers' houses, besides having killed and wounded all European soldiers and officers they could find near their lines." On the 12th, the Lieutenant-Governor telegraphed that the 3rd Cavalry mutineers had been released, that guns were heard all the night of the 10th and morning of the 11th. A young Sepoy, with his arms and a cavalry troop horse, travelling down, it was believed, to acquaint other regiments with the mutiny, had been arrested, and the Delhi road was in possession of the mutineers; the villagers had risen between Meerut and Haupper. The next day Mr. Colvin urged that the troops from Persia should be ordered to Calcutta, and sent up-country at once. He stated that the villagers between Agra and Meerut robbed and ill-used all passengers, that men of the 11th and 20th regiments were apprehended at Allyghur, but "were obstinately silent as to what has occurred." He suggested the use of irregular cavalry in clearing the roads in the disturbed districts.

On the 13th, Government telegraphed to Meerut, to know what had taken place, and on the same day Mr. Colvin received a letter from that station, dated May 12th. A detachment of carabineers might have easily escorted a mail to Agra in twenty-four hours after the occurrence of the outbreak, the distance being only fifty-six miles; but neither the faculties of the general commanding nor those of the commissioner of the division were equal to such an effort. On the 14th, Mr. Colvin informed Lord Canning, that he had received a letter from the king; that the town and fort of Delhi and his own person were in the hands of the insurgent regiments stationed there, who had joined a hundred of the Meerut mutineers, and opened the gates. The commissioner and his assistant, as well as Miss Jennings, were reported to be killed. Mr. Colvin recommended the proclamation of martial law, and to show the state of feeling amongst the Sepoys, about English designs against their caste, he enclosed the extract of a letter received that day from the collector of Muttra, who wrote, "I have just heard what makes me doubtful of the fidelity of our Sepoy guard here. The subadar told one of the clerks to-day that he was convinced the Government intended to take their caste, and had for that purpose mixed ground bones in their flour." Scindiah had offered the services of his body guard, and a battery of guns, which the Lieutenant-Governor proposed to accept "for a short time only," remarking in his message, "though we really do not want more troops."

On the following day, the 15th of May, the Lieutenant-Governor announced that thirty Europeans had been massacred, that all the troops had fraternised and proclaimed the heir apparent king, and were apparently organising a regular Government, their supposed policy being to "annex all the adjoining districts to their newly acquired kingdom." They were not likely, therefore, to abandon Delhi, and would probably strengthen themselves. They had secured, perhaps, 500,000*l.* Bhurtpore and Gwalior were giving us hearty aid. The native regiments in Agra were weak in numbers; and, said Mr. Colvin, "whatever their feelings may be, they are not likely to rise of themselves without any other support. We do not, therefore, show distrust of them. I have every confidence that they will all be put to rights in a few days." On the same day Mr. Colvin sent another message as follows: —"I have had a very satisfactory review of the troops this morning. I had previously ascertained, from undoubted authority of natives of confidence of all classes, that a deep and genuine conviction, however absurd, has seized the minds of the Sepoys of the army generally, that the Government is steadily bent on making them lose caste by handling impure things. Men of their own creed, trusted by them, were sent by me into their lines, and the most distinct assurances given them on the subject. I spoke to the same effect at the parade, and the men said this was all they wanted to be certain of. I believe that under the present circumstances the men are now staunch. If mutineers approach in any force it is our determination to move out the brigade and fight them. We shall go with the brigade: a reinforcement of a battery of guns, and some of the Contingent cavalry will be here from Gwalior the morning after to-morrow. It is most earnestly recommended, from the result of present experience, that a proclamation to the army be at once issued by the Supreme Government, saying, if it be so thought fit, that the Lieutenant-Governor, North-West Provinces, has informed them that he has found a gross misconception to be prevalent; that, being so informed, it at once declares to its faithful troops that it would in every manner respect and protect their feelings and usages of religion and caste, as it has always scrupulously protected them; that it declares the notions which have got abroad on the point to be an utter delusion, propagated by some designing persons to mislead good soldiers; and the army may remain thoroughly satisfied that no attempt whatever will be made in any way to hinder in the least their religious rites and practices. Armed with a simple and direct assurance of this kind, it would rapidly, I think, quiet the minds of the troops. An inducement, too, is wanted for not joining the mutineers and for leaving them. I am in the thick of it and know what is wanted. I earnestly beg this to strengthen me."

Up to this date an apology may be suggested for the conduct of Lord Canning. He had been but fourteen months in the country, and there are powerful minds that are slow to receive new impressions. His colleagues in the executive, with one exception, were men of ripe Indian experience, the picked statesmen of the entire civil service. In the Legislative Council he had the advantage of the advice of Her Majesty's judges, and they had all been unanimous in support of the measures that were adopted. To risk the chance of being wrong in company with his council was a safer course than to aim at being right in opposition to their opinions.

But what shall we say of the policy which, after the receipt of Mr. Colvin's message, still trusted the native army? Blindness is no proper name for it, for there were sounds as well as sights, the trumpets of alarm in the ear, as well as the handwriting on the wall. To give point to General Hearsey's opinion, that argument and remonstrance were hopeless, two regiments had been disbanded, seven were in open rebellion, many others had been tampered with, and "a deep and genuine conviction had seized the minds of the Sepoys generally, that Government were steadily bent on making them lose caste." But Lord Canning was in no hurry to act, and saw no occasion to take a gloomy view of affairs. Lord Elphinstone telegraphed on the 17th of May, that he could at once despatch a steamer to Suez, which would be in time to catch the French steamer of the 9th of June at Alexandria, and thought that an officer sent off at once in a swift vessel, might even overtake the mail that left Bombay on the 13th. The Governor-General answered that he was not desirous of sending to England by an earlier opportunity than the mail of the 18th of May from Calcutta. Time was of course required for earnest consultation by the members of Government, and the result of their deliberations was a communication to the Court of Directors, dated the 19th of May, giving the first intimation of the revolt, and embodying the following suggestions of a remedy:—"The necessity for an increase of the substantial strength of the army on the Bengal establishment, that is to say, of the European troops upon this establishment, has been long apparent to us; but the necessity of refraining from any material increase to the charges of the military department, in the present state of our finances, has prevented us hitherto from moving your Honourable Court in this matter. The late untoward occurrences at Berhampore, Fort William, Barrackpore, and Lucknow, crowned by the shocking and alarming events of the past week at Meerut and Delhi, and taken in connection with the knowledge we have lately acquired of the dangerous state of feeling in the Bengal native army generally, strange, and, at present, unaccountable as it is, have convinced us of the urgent necessity of not merely a positive increase of our European strength, but of a material increase in the proportion which our European troops bear to the native regular troops on the establishment. We are of opinion that the latter is now the more pressing necessity of the two.

"We believe that all these objects, political, military, and financial, will be immediately attained in a very material degree by taking advantage of the present opportunity in the manner we have now the honour respectfully to propose; and we see no other way in which all the same objects can be attained in any degree, now or prospectively. We recommend that the six native regiments, which are in effect no longer in existence, should not be replaced, whereby the establishment of regular native infantry would be reduced to sixty-eight regiments; and that the European officers of these late regiments should be used to officer three regiments of Europeans to be added to your establishment at this Presidency.

"We confidently affirm that the Government will be much stronger in respect of all important internal and external purposes, with three additional European regiments of the established strength, than it would be by embodying six native regiments of the established strength; and we anticipate no inconvenience in respect of minor objects, in time of peace and tranquillity, from the consequent numerical reduction of regular troops. Indeed, the financial result of the measure, if carried out as we propose, will leave a considerable surplus available, if it should be thought fit so to employ it, for an augmentation of irregulars, who, for all such minor objects, are much better, as well as much cheaper, than regulars of any description."

We have here at least one example on the part of Lord Canning of a sense of the fitness of things. It was certainly not worth while to send a special messenger with such a very ordinary communication as the above. As the emergency for European soldiers could wait until the Court of Directors had made up their minds to empower the recruiting serjeant at home to act, the delay of a mail on this side was of no moment whatever. The reader will now be at no loss to understand the grounds on which, when the news of the outbreak reached England, the ministry and Mr. Mangles expressed their high admiration of his Lordship's firmness and capacity. When did a nobleman acquit himself more ably than this Governor-General, who could afford to take such a hopeful view of a troublesome affair? When was mutiny made so pleasant to the Court of Directors? They would positively gain money by it! No blame was imputed to them for the parsimony which had left the country so truly defenceless; no reproaches were directed against the folly which had sanctioned and sent out the greased cartridges. There are doctors who, on system, make the most nauseous medicine taste pleasant; and Lord Canning has gained their secret, though, in this case, he has practised it to the imminent danger of his patient.

With the same dislike to diminish the amount of human happiness, which dictated the tone and substance of his correspondence with the Court of Directors, Lord Canning withheld from the people of Calcutta the intelligence of the Meerut and Delhi massacres, which reached the newspapers as a mere rumour on the 14th of May. The native merchants had full particulars the day previous as a matter of course. On the 15th the "Hurkaru" said:—"We hear that some bad news was received from Meerut, by the Military Secretary to Government—the 3rd Cavalry had mutinied and murdered their officers." "There is also a report that the troops at Delhi have also risen, and, after having overcome the Europeans, had taken possession of the fort. It is to be hoped that this is a mere rumour, but we have heard it on sufficient authority to justify publication."

The "Englishman" was instructed to contradict this the next morning, which it did in the following terms:—"We can authoritatively contradict the statement in yesterday's 'Hurkaru' that a report of the murder of the officers of the 3rd Cavalry has reached the Secretary to Government in the Military Department. No such report has been received. Alarming reports were in circulation yesterday as to the state of affairs in Meerut and Delhi. We published all that was certain, believing there must be great exaggeration in the rest. We are now informed that all was tranquil at Meerut on the 12th instant. The Cantonment and Treasury all right, and the troops quite ready to meet any attack. The interruption to the communication was caused by the refractory troopers of the 3rd Cavalry, who had fled from Meerut, and their villages being on the road, they persuaded their friends to join them, and it is feared that some of their officers have been killed.

"At Delhi there had been disturbances, and a party of the marauders got possession of the fort, as it is called,—not a place of any strength. Two European gentlemen have been murdered, but we refrain from mentioning names till more positive information reaches us."

The same journal came out in its evening edition with "authentic particulars from Government."

"There has been a rising of some of the native troops at

Delhi, some Europeans have been killed, but the names and number not known. Meerut is quiet, and the troops are ready. European regiments are on the march from the hills."

The admission on the 16th of May, that "there had been disturbances at Delhi," and the statement, that the losses at Meerut were the work of those men of the 3rd Cavalry who had fled from that place, reads oddly enough, when we call to mind that Lord Canning knew, at the time he allowed this information to be furnished, that six thousand men had revolted and proclaimed a king. The concealment of intelligence grew afterwards into a habit, and gave the natives a handle for inculcating all kinds of false rumours. When these inventions were met by denial on the part of Europeans, the Bengalee would reply, "The Government know that what we say is true, only they don't choose to make the thing public." The rejoinder was always felt to be unanswerable, for the authorities had sole control of the telegraph, and daily experience showed how unwilling they were that the whole truth should be known by their countrymen. It was not long after the outbreak of insurrection, that the English population, having to choose only between the tales of the bazar and the bulletins of Government, gave the largest credence to the former.

CHAP. VI.

STATE OF THE DEFENCES OF BENGAL.—THE GOVERNMENT URGED TO OBTAIN REINFORCEMENTS.—AVAILABLE RESOURCES.—FACILITY OF RELIEVING CAWNPORE AND LUCKNOW.—JUNG BAHADOR AND THE GHOORKAS.

AMONGST the causes of the mutiny should be ranked, as well, the notorious weakness of our means of defence at the outset, and the ease with which revenge and plunder were to be obtained at the subsequent stages of the revolt. On the 10th of May, there was not a single European soldier at Delhi, Allahabad, or Cawnpore. Benares was hurriedly reinforced by a company and a half of the 10th, and General Wheeler obtained the aid of two companies of the 32nd from Lucknow, which he sent back again on the arrival at Cawnpore of a detachment of the 84th. At army head-quarters, as we have seen, there were neither commissariat nor medical stores. At Meerut, on the 18th of May, the commanding officer reported that the reinforcement for the army of Delhi must stand fast for the want of carriage. At Allahabad there were guns in abundance, but no men to work them; Benares was wholly without fortifications, and had only half a bullock battery; Barrackpore had to depend upon sailors to man the six guns sent up there from Calcutta, when the safety of the capital was threatened. Often, during the months of June and July, were the English prompted to thank their stars that the rebels had neither a leader nor a plan of action, but blundered almost as much as the Supreme Government; for, had it been otherwise, every living soul in Bengal would have perished, or been forced to abandon the country.

If we admit that Lord Canning, after a residence of fourteen months in the country, could not be expected to detect the signs of weakness, which all men now unite in deploring, and that the warnings of General Hearsey, and the occurrences in the 19th and 34th regiments were not grave enough to induce fears for the safety of the empire, the question of competency on the part of the Indian Government, is restricted to a single inquiry: —Did the Governor-General use all possible exertions to obtain more troops, and make the best use of them when they arrived?

The first portion of the query must be answered in the affirmative. No means were left untried to collect reinforcements of English soldiers from the various stations in the Indian and China seas; but the credit of suggesting such vigorous measures, must not be allowed to rest with the Calcutta authorities, to whom it has hitherto been assigned. On the 13th of May, Mr. Colvin telegraphed to Lord Canning as follows:—

"It will, no doubt, have been already thought of, but I cannot do harm in suggesting that the force returning from the Persian Gulf, or a considerable portion of it, be summoned in straight to Calcutta, and thence sent up the country. Necessarily it will give a powerful movable force free from local influences, and have an excellent effect in showing that the Government has large means, independent of the usual army here."

On the 16th, Sir Henry Lawrence telegraphed from Lucknow:—"All is quiet here, but affairs are critical; get every European you can from China, Ceylon, and elsewhere; also, all the Ghoorkas from the hills; time is everything."

Lord Elphinstone offered, on the 17th, a regiment of Beloochees, and the 1st Bombay Europeans, both of which were accepted. On the same date Sir John Lawrence proposed to embody 5000 men from the corps of Police and Guides in the Punjaub, and to raise 1000 more, if necessary, both of which suggestions were adopted. The message of Lord Canning to the Governor of Bombay was dated May 16th, and is as follows:—

"Two of the three European regiments which are returning from Persia are urgently wanted in Bengal. If they are sent from Bombay to Kurrachee, will they find conveyance up the Indus? Are they coming from Bushire, in steam or sailing transports? Let me know, immediately, whether General Ashburnham is going to Madras."

On the 17th the Governor-General asked Lord Elphinstone if he could send a steamer to Galle, to bring troops from thence to Calcutta; and the Fusiliers, at Madras, were called for on the 16th of May, after the receipt of the message from Sir Henry Lawrence. We have thus the whole of the reinforcements accounted for, and in no single instance is the merit of having called them to Bengal to be ascribed to the Supreme Government.

The question of the wise employment of means is equally capable of solution.

At the outbreak of the mutiny, there were in Calcutta, and the adjoining stations of Dum Dum and Barrackpore, two regiments of European infantry, the 53rd and 84th, mustering about 1700 effective men. These, with the 10th at Dinapore, and a company of artillery in Fort William, comprised the whole English force between the capital and Agra, 900 miles distant. The native corps consisted of the 2nd Grenadiers, 43rd and 70th N. I., the Calcutta militia, and the remnant of the 34th, in all 4000 men, stationed within the limits of the Presidency division. At Berhampore, there was the 63rd N. I.; at Dinapore, the 7th, 8th, and 40th, together with a regiment of irregular cavalry. Benares was occupied by the 37th, and the Loodianah regiment of Sikhs. The 6th were at Allahabad; the 65th at Ghazepore, the 2nd Cavalry, 1st and 53rd N.I. at Cawnpore. The total available force of Europeans throughout this great extent of country, was not more than 2500, against 14,000 native troops; vast odds as seen upon paper, but not sufficient to alarm a man of energy and decision as to the result of a struggle for the mastery.

A thousand English volunteer infantry, 400 cavalry, and 1500 sailors, were at the disposal of Government a week after the revolt became known. It only needed the utterance of a few words of ordinary sympathy and encouragement, to draw out the entire available European population; no great price to pay for such service as they were able and willing to perform; but small as was the estimated cost, Lord Canning grudged it. It was not until the 12th of June that he consented to the enrolment of a volunteer corps; and only then, after much misgiving as to the propriety of showing special favour to any particular class of the population. The use that might have been made of such auxiliaries was pointed out at the time with sufficient clearness; but, at this moment, we can see that it would have been literally invaluable.

The waters of the Ganges do not rise until the latter end of June; and it would have been scarcely advisable to push troops up by that route, so long as there was a prospect that the vessels might get aground. The railway and the road offered the greatest facilities for the transit of men, guns, and stores; and both were in the best condition. The line was opened to Raneegunge, a distance of 120 miles from Calcutta; and up to that point there was no difficulty in sending a couple of regiments by a single train. Whilst the volunteers were learning how to load and fire, and the merchant seaman were being instructed in the use of artillery, Government might have placed on the road from the terminus to Cawnpore a line of stations for horses and bullocks at intervals of five miles, guarded, if necessary, by posts of armed men; the studs at Buxar and Ghazeepore, the streets and the course of Calcutta, could have supplied any number of horses. There were 1600 siege bullocks at Allahabad and 600 at Cawnpore; carriages and commissariat stores of all kinds might have been collected for the use of a division with seven days' hard work; and had Government only consented to do just a fortnight beforehand what they were coerced to do on the 14th of June, they might have had, on the first day of that month, a force of 2000 Europeans at Raneegunge, fully equipped with guns and stores; the infantry capable of being pushed on at the rate of 120 miles a day, and the artillery, drawn by horses, elephants, and bullocks in turns, following at a speed of two miles an hour, day and night. The Madras Fusiliers had arrived, 830 strong. The disbanded native troops could have been kept easily in check by a detachment of 300 men at Barrackpore and 200 in Fort William, in addition to the volunteers and seamen; and by the 8th of June, at latest, a column of 1500 men would have reached Cawnpore; the guns, escorted by half a wing, arriving seven days afterwards. The 10th, after having disarmed the native regiments at Dinapore, could have spared 200 men for Benares, and the same number might have been detached from the column as it passed through Allahabad. The attack upon Sir Hugh Wheeler was not made until the 4th of June, and only succeeded on the 27th; and we have only to recall the narrative of Havelock's raid to infer the result of a march made six weeks earlier.

The "Englishman" has said that there were two stamps in the Calcutta post-office, one marked "insufficient," and the other "too late;" and that one or the other ought to have been impressed upon every act of the Indian Government. The arrangements suggested in the previous paragraph were partially carried out when it was too late; when the veteran Wheeler with all his force and their precious charge slept in their bloody shrouds; when the wives and children of the gallant 32nd had all been massacred, and the gentle and gifted Lawrence had perished miserably by the hand of a traitor. The volunteers were allowed to enrol themselves on the 12th of June, and the native troops in Calcutta and Barrackpore were disarmed on the 14th of that month. The Fusiliers, despatched in relays of twelve, fourteen, and on one occasion of eight men, arrived at Allahabad in the last days of June, when the 1600 bullocks offered by the commissariat on the 27th of May were all dispersed, and there was not a beast of burden or chest of medicine to be had. On the 24th of May Lord Canning telegraphed to Sir Henry Lawrence:—"It is impossible to place a wing of

Europeans at Cawnpore in less than twenty-five days. The Government dawk and the dawk companies are fully engaged in carrying a company of the 84th to Benares, at the rate of eighteen men a day. The entire regiment of the Fusiliers, about 900 strong, cannot be expected at Benares in less than nineteen or twenty days." The plea of impossibility was not to be gainsaid, and hence it occurred that General Havelock started from Allahabad the day after the death of Sir Henry Lawrence; twice essayed to relieve Lucknow; and twice returned, unable, from numerical weakness, to accomplish the object. But the success obtained satisfied the minds of the authorities. Every petty detachment reached its destination. Benares was saved by a reinforcement of forty men; Allahabad had been preserved by seventy decayed European gunners. The people at home would overlook the neglect of prevention, when they heard of the rapidity of the cure; the chance of a relapse not being taken into consideration.

Each of the large towns enumerated are situated on the banks of the Ganges or Jumna, the former stream being navigable at all seasons for vessels of light draught as far as Dinapore. There were hundreds of cargo boats at Calcutta, which, furnished with mat roofs and partially decked over, would have carried each a large gun, and the men to work it. Steamers, of which there were numbers available, would have towed them to Dinapore, where they might have waited till the rivers rose, and then, either by sailing and rowing, or tugged by steam, they could have got up to the walls of Delhi. If it were thought advisable to ascend the Jumna in the first of the rains, the armament and stores could have been transferred to boats built expressly for the navigation, which are always to be found waiting at Benares and Ghazepore for their upward cargoes at that season of the year. These vessels, long, low, and heavily built, carry forty tons on a draught of eighteen inches, and are admirably fitted to serve as gun boats. The notion of taking advantage of the facilities afforded by steamers and small armed vessels for attacking towns situated on the banks of navigable rivers, appears to have been suggested in an official way to Lord Canning early in August, when it was settled that Captain Peel should ascend the Ganges with a force of men and guns; but there were difficulties in the way which required long deliberation, and Captain Peel started when it was too late in the season, and hence had to relinquish the main object of the enterprise. There is an old maxim which recommends that you should never put forth your hand, without being sure that you can draw it back again. The Indian Government appear to value the advice, and always to have acted upon it.

The column of 1500, arriving at Cawnpore in the second week in June, could have been reinforced on the 25th of that month by at least 4000 men, even if a regiment had been left behind to strengthen Calcutta. The 64th, 78th, and a company of the Madras artillery, in all nearly 1900 men, arrived at Fort William between the 1st and 10th of June. The 37th from Ceylon, with a company of the Royal Artillery, the 29th and 35th from Pegu, reached almost at the same time. The rebels in heart at Calcutta wrote to their friends in the north-west, that "the sea was throwing up soldiers every day;" and the slightest knowledge of the oriental character would have suggested the propriety of benefiting by their natural tendency to exaggeration. Had the regiments, after a day's rest, been marched in each case to the wide plain near the fort, and there, with all the pomp and circumstance that could have been devised, been put through the evolutions of a sham fight, the story of their numbers and warlike appearance, magnified tenfold, would have spread over the whole country. But the rulers of British India had no idea of dramatic effect; and except when the occupants of carriages on the course stood up as one man to cheer a passing troop ship, and, with full hearts, felt that they ought to be uncovered in the presence of the rudest soldier that wore the livery of England, the gallant men passed on to their work of toil, perhaps to sickness and death, with no sign of recognition from the Government they came to serve. Want of food, bad lodgings, and pitiless exposure waited upon them till they got clear of Calcutta.

The 5th and 90th arrived early in July, and two Madras regiments in August; yet Lucknow was not relieved, but only strengthened on the 20th of October. The elements of a force, with which a Napier would have undertaken to traverse the length and breadth of the land, were scattered over the country, shattered in brilliant but useless actions, worn down by incessant toil, or decimated by disease and lack of sustenance and shelter. God's curse lies heavy on the nations, when it takes the form of pestilence or famine; but it is never, perhaps, so deadly and terrible as when, in time of trial, it visits the people with a Government such as that which is presided over by Viscount Canning.

But there was still another means of saving the brave and helpless of Cawnpore and Lucknow, apart from the march of Europeans to their aid. At the outbreak of the mutiny, Jung Bahador, the virtual ruler of Nepaul, offered the use of his army, and the services of 3000 were accepted. The best men of the Nepaulese forces were picked out for the expedition; and the daring little Ghoorkas, elated to the highest pitch at the prospect of fighting by the side of the English, and plundering the hoards of the hated Sepoys, came down from their hills by forced marches, and expected to be in Oude about the 15th of June. Though the prime troops of Nepaul, they were the ugliest and dirtiest of warriors, not much amenable to discipline, nor fond of temperance in eating or drinking; but the Sikh, who cares nothing for Brahmin and Mussulman, shrinks with dismay from a conflict with the Ghoorka. They were a match in this case for more than 10,000 Sepoys; and had they been permitted to join Sir Henry Lawrence at Lucknow, he would have raised the siege in twenty-four hours after their arrival, and then, clearing a road to the Ganges, have crossed over to Cawnpore and liberated Sir Hugh Wheeler. But the blight of Calcutta was upon all concerned. When the Ghoorkas had passed through the deadly jungle that surrounds the base of their hills, Jung Bahador received a despatch from Lord Canning, requesting that they might be recalled, as their services could be dispensed with. They went back to Katmandoo, heavy-hearted, and suffering greatly from sickness which broke out amongst them on their return march; but had scarce reached the capital, when another despatch came from Lord Canning, asking Jung Bahador to send them back again to Oude, where they were now wanted. They left Katmandoo for the second time on the 29th of June, two days after the massacre at Cawnpore; and only arrived in the British territory, much reduced by disease and death, when Sir Henry Lawrence had been dead for a fortnight. There are widows and orphans who have more need to complain than Jung Bahador; but that chieftain considers that he has been ill used in the matter; and writing to his friend, Mr. Hodgson, late of the Bengal Civil Service, a narrative of the affair, he wound up with the exclamation, "You see how I am treated. How do you expect to keep India with such rulers as these?"

CHAP. VII.

THE MARCH ON DELHI. — THE DEFENCE OF THE MAGAZINE. — THE GREAT MOGUL AND HIS COURT. — NARRATIVES OF THE CAPTURE AND CONDITION OF THE CITY.

WE left the Meerut mutineers on the night of the 10th of May, encamped on the road to Delhi. They made good use of their time, performing the distance, thirty-six miles, before noon the following day. They met several Europeans on the road travelling in dawk carriages, who were of course slaughtered; and then hastening into the city, the rebels set about their separate tasks of seducing the men of the regiments stationed there, calling out the thieves to plunder, and murdering every European that could be laid hold of. Riding furiously through the cantonment, the men of the 3rd cavalry sought everywhere for the officers, in whose faces they discharged their pistols with shouts of savage triumph. The city was full of munitions of war; though, with a blind reliance upon destiny, for which our race have only the excuse that they believe in the Providence which watches over fools and madmen, no Europeans have been stationed in Delhi for many years.

The arsenal contained three siege trains and vast stores of warlike material, the loss of which has been felt severely by the troops of the avenging army; but the rebels were not permitted to reap all the benefits of Government supineness. The magazine held a vast quantity of powder and warlike stores, and they hastened to it in the hope of a speedy capture; but its little garrison of nine men were of the true English mould, and the rebels obtained nothing in the end but a speedy entrance into the Indian paradise. Some days after the loss of Delhi, Lieutenant Willoughby, the officer in charge of the magazine, made his appearance at Meerut, blackened with gunpowder, and sinking rapidly from the effects of wounds and exhaustion; and it was then learned that he had blown up the place to prevent it falling into the hands of the mutineers. He died soon afterwards, and it was thought that the story of his gallant conduct would never be told; but, after an extraordinary delay, the Government published a despatch from Lieutenant Forrest, from which it appears that, on the first alarm of the outbreak, he hastened to the magazine, together with Messrs. Buckley, Shaw, Scully, and Crow, warrant officers, and Serjeants Edwards and Stewart. What followed had better be told in his own words.

"On Sir Theophilus Metcalfe alighting from his buggy, Lieutenant Willoughby and I accompanied him to the small bastion on the river face, which commanded a full view of the bridge, from which we could distinctly see the mutineers marching in open column headed by the cavalry; and the Delhi side of the bridge was already in the possession of a body of cavalry. On Sir Theophilus Metcalfe observing this, he proceeded with Lieutenant Willoughby to see if the city gate was closed against the mutineers. However, this step was needless, as the mutineers were admitted directly to the palace, through which they passed cheering. On Lieutenant Willoughby's return to the magazine, the gates of the magazine were closed and barricaded, and every possible arrangement that could be made was at once commenced on. Inside the gate leading to the park were placed two 6-pounders, double charged with grape, one under acting sub-conductor Crow and Serjeant Stewart, with the lighted matches in their hands, and with orders that if any attempt was made to force that gate, both guns were to be fired at once, and they were to fall back on that part of the magazine in which Lieutenant Willoughby and I were posted. The principal gate of the magazine was similarly defended by two guns, with the chevaux-de-frise laid down on the inside. For the further defence of this gate and the magazine in its vicinity, there were two 6-pounders so placed that either would command the gate and a small bastion in its vicinity. Within sixty yards of the gate and in front of the office, and commanding two cross roads, were three 6-pounders and one 24-pounder howitzer, which could be so managed as to act upon any part of the magazine in that neighbourhood. After all these guns and howitzers had been placed in the several positions above-named, they were loaded with double charges of grape. The next step taken was to place arms in the hands of the native establishment, which they most reluctantly received, and appeared to be in a state not only of excitement, but also of insubordination, as they refused to obey any orders issued by the Europeans, particularly the Mussulman portion of the establishment. After the above arrangements had been made, a train was laid by conductors Buckley, Scully, and Serjeant Stewart, ready to be fired by a preconcerted signal, which was that of conductor Buckley raising his hat from his head, on the order being given by Lieutenant Willoughby. The train was fired by conductor Scully, but not until such time as the last round from the howitzers had been fired. So soon as the above arrangements had been made, guards from the palace came and demanded the possession of the magazine in the name of the King of Delhi, to which no reply was given.

"Immediately after this, the subadar of the guard on duty at the magazine informed Lieutenant Willoughby and me, that the King of Delhi had sent down word to the mutineers that he would without delay send scaling ladders from the palace for the purpose of scaling the walls, and which shortly after arrived. On the ladders being erected against the wall, the whole of our native establishment deserted us by climbing up the sloped sheds on the inside of the magazine, and descending the ladders on the outside, after which the enemy appeared in great numbers on the top of the walls, and on whom we kept up an incessant fire of grape, every round of which told well, as long as a single round remained. Previous to the natives deserting us, they hid the priming pouches; and one man in particular, Kurreembuksh, a durwan, appeared to keep up a constant communication with the enemy on the outside, and keep them informed of our situation. Lieutenant Willoughby was so annoyed at this man's conduct, that he gave me an order to shoot him, should he again approach the gate.

"Lieutenant Raynor, with the other Europeans, did everything that possibly could be done for the defence of the magazine; and where all have behaved so bravely, it is almost impossible for me to point out any particular individual. However, I am in duty bound to bring to the notice of Government the gallantry of conductors Buckley and Scully on this trying occasion. The former, assisted only by myself, loaded and fired in rapid succession the several guns above detailed, firing at least four rounds from each gun, and with the same steadiness as if standing on parade, although the enemy were then some hundreds in number, and kept up a continual fire of musketry on us, within forty or fifty yards. After firing the last round, conductor Buckley received a musket-ball in his arm, above the elbow, which has since been extracted here. I, at the same time, was struck in the left hand by two musket-balls, which disabled me for the time. It was at this critical moment that Lieutenant Willoughby gave the order for firing the magazine, which was at once responded to by conductor Scully firing the several trains. Indeed, from the very commencement, he evinced his gallantry by volunteering his services for blowing up the magazine, and remained true to his trust to the last moment. As soon as the explosion took place, such as escaped from beneath the ruins—and none escaped unhurt—retreated through the sally port on the river face. Lieutenant Willoughby and I succeeded in reaching the Cashmere Gate. What became of the other parties, it is impossible for me to say. Lieutenant Raynor and conductor Buckley have escaped to this station. Severe indisposition prevented my sending in this report sooner."

It is little more than half a century since Lord Lake, whilst engaged in a campaign against the Mahrattas, encamped near the city of Delhi, and, making his way into the palace, found there the representative of the royal house of Timor, in the person of an aged man, poor, helpless, and blind, the plaything of fortune, the prize by turns of numerous adventurers. His ancestors had by the law of force at one time acquired the dominion of all India, and the rule which had raised them to the pinnacle of greatness had sunk him to the lowest depths of abasement. He had lived to see the dominions over which he had himself reigned, the prize of successive conquerors, his wealth scattered, his wives dishonoured, and had reached the climax of human misery, when a brutal soldier scooped his eyes out with a dagger, and left him without the hope of better days. The English general seated him again in the chair of royalty, and, in return for a parchment gift of the countries which he had won and intended to keep by the sword, allotted to him the first rank in the long line of mockery kings that once reigned, but now who merely live in India. In public and private, the Padshah, as he is called, received the signs of homage which were considered to belong to his pre-eminent station. He has never forgiven the English since a Governor-General insisted upon having a chair in his presence; and, until recently, the agent of the latter, when vouchsafed the honour of an audience, addressed him with folded hands, in the attitude of supplication. He never received letters, only petitions; and conferred an exalted favour on the Government of British India by accepting a monthly present of 80,000 rupees. Merely as a mark of excessive condescension, he tacitly sanctioned all our acts, withdrew his royal approbation from each and all of our native enemies, and fired salutes upon every occasion of a victory achieved by our troops. Hitherto, it would have been impossible to have found a royal ally more courteously disposed; and, we believe, it never entered the brain of the most suspicious diplomatist, that the treaties between the Great Mogul and the Honourable Company were in any danger of being violated by His Majesty. To sweep away the house of Tamerlane would not have added one jot to our power. Outside the walls of his palace, the

King of Delhi, as he was termed, had no more authority than the meanest of those whom he had been taught to consider his born vassals; but within that enclosure, his will was fate, and there were 12,000 persons who lived subject to it. The universal voice of society ascribed to this population the habitual practice of crimes of which the very existence is unknown at home, except to the few who form the core of the corrupt civilisation of great cities. Its princes lived without dignity, and its female aristocracy contrived to exist without honour. The physical type of manhood was debased, whilst the intellectual qualifications of both sexes, with one or two exceptions, did not reach even the Mahomedan standard of merit, perhaps the lowest in the scale of modern humanity.

But a "Light of the World" could not exist even in these days without experiencing earthly troubles. His Majesty had no fear of Mahratta daggers, and his pension was paid far more punctually than were the revenues of his ancestors. Domestic troubles were more burdensome, perhaps, to his effulgent shoulders than would be the cares of the universe, and there were no less than 1200 little lights which radiated upon him from all parts of Hindostan, and required a great deal of oil to keep them burning. It was no uncommon thing for one of this celestial race to be obliged to live on fifty shillings a month, but in no case did he forget the dignity of his birth. A Mussulman is obliged to settle a dowry upon his wife, and a member of the *Soolatun* never endows her with less than 50,000*l.* Their sole occupation was confined to playing on the Indian lute, and singing the King's verses. Too proud to work with their hands, too ignorant to be useful with their heads, they would have been content to continue for generations to come in their late miserable condition — forlorn mortals, empty alike in pocket and stomach, in heart and brain, and conscious only of the possession of unsatisfied appetites. The evil had not escaped the notice of Government, who felt that they must pull down the nest, if they would have the young brood fly abroad. When the title of the late heir apparent was recognised, it was arranged that, on the death of the late occupant of the musnud, the palace should be evacuated, and the family residence fixed at what is now the King's country seat, situated about twelve miles from Delhi. His Majesty consented to the terms with much reluctance, and, his son dying before him, perhaps he felt morally released from the bond. He has had his own little quarrels with his despised protectors on the usual score of accounts; but it is likely that all outstanding claims from the 11th May last will find speedy adjustment.

In spite of the utter subjection in which the Padshah lived for well nigh a hundred years, the Mussulmans still continued to regard him as being the fountain of honour, the rightful monarch of Hindostan. This belief is easily accounted for, since, with the exception of the Princes of Rajpootana and a few insignificant rajahs, there are no dynasties which can lay claim to a much greater antiquity than that of the British rule in the East, whilst again there is hardly a single monarch who has not at some time sworn fealty to the house of Tamerlane, and received investiture at its hands. The Mogul is the only person to whom the Mahomedans can look up as their natural head. The founders of the royal houses of the Deccan, Carnatic, and Oude, of Holkar and Scindiah, were the deputies and servants of his ancestors. His divine right to universal dominion still exists; only in the East, as elsewhere, Toryism, however sincere, is seldom able to bring the law and the fact into complete harmony. Nothing was more natural than the proclamation by Mussulmans of the Delhi Raj when they fancied they saw a chance of throwing off the English yoke; but a rebellion requires something more than a name to make it successful, and the adherents of the new rulers have not failed to recognise the fact. They used the King of Oude as they have used the credulous Hindoo. The deposed prince has vast hoards of money, and unbounded influence amongst the Sepoys; and hence, when it became possible to employ the pretensions of the Padshah, the wrongs of the King of Oude, and the superstition of the Hindoos, a confederacy was created, the strength of which we have scarcely yet ascertained. Meanwhile the King of the Sepoys' choice has shown himself worthy of his Tartar progenitors. At an early date of the mutinies he caused letters to be sent to various regiments, requesting them to seize the treasuries and loot all they could find, bringing, in every case, the plunder to his royal receiving house. Favour and twenty-four shillings per month would reward the obedient Sepoy; punishment sure, but not specified, was to overtake him who elected to remain honest. Some of His Majesty's ancestors were emphatically the greatest thieves in the world, and their descendant has availed himself of this the only opportunity he has had of pursuing the family vocation.

The complicity of the Sepoy King of Délhi in the rebellion was evident from the first moment of alarm. The corps that commenced the revolt were Mussulmans almost to a man; and the place of their destination, with the nature of the welcome that would be given to them, was not for an instant in doubt. They made for the palace at once on entering the city, the King having it in his power to shut the gates against them, without any danger to his own personal household. The mutineers would not have dared to shed blood within those sacred precincts without his previous authority to do so; and had he chosen to give shelter to the helpless fugitives who implored his protection, not a finger would have been lifted against them. It rested with him to give the word which would have converted the revolt to a mere strife between men of opposing races,— Sepoy against European, Mussulman and Brahmin against Christianity and civilisation; but the descendant of Tamerlane inherited the ancestral thirst for blood, and thought, perhaps, like a chief of pirates, it was necessary to make forgiveness hopeless. Ladies and others who had sought shelter in the palace were dragged before him, their captors asking what should be done with them. The royal answer, "Do what you like to them," was of course a sentence of death; and the brief reign of the heir apparent, whom his majesty gave them as a sovereign, was inaugurated with the blood of English women and children whose lives had wrought him no harm, and whose death could yield him no profit. Later still the last of the Great Moguls issued a decree of extermination against the Sikhs as well as the hated Feringhee, and in both cases committed what politicians say is worse than moral guilt,—a deplorable blunder. For every drop of the innocent blood spilt at Delhi and elsewhere a tide has poured from the veins of his adherents; and the act of H. M. 5th Fusiliers, who scratched a crucifix on their bayonets, and, kissing the weapon, swore to wash out the mark in the hearts' blood of the rebels, only embodied the feelings of every man of British extraction. To win back our losses and vindicate our ancient reputation, were felt to be but small matters. The cry was for vengeance, full and complete; and nothing short of that will satisfy our countrymen.

Narratives of what took place after the mutineers got possession of Delhi have been furnished by native writers, whose habit of chronicling minute facts gives great value to their descriptions of passing events. We subjoin translations of two Hindoo letters, which throw great light upon the state of feeling in the city at the time of the revolt, and show how little reason there is to suspect that the commercial and trading classes had anything to do with it. The extract now given is from a communication to the Rajah of Jheend by his newswriter in Delhi, dated May 17th, six days after the arrival of the mutineers:—

"On the 16th Ramzan, on Sunday, eighty-five sowars of the cavalry were sentenced to imprisonment at Meerut. The regiments proceeded to the gaol, and released the prisoners, and took them away, slaying the European sentries: they then set fire to the houses in the lines, and slew old and young. Some 300 Europeans and natives were killed in the conflict; some cavalry and a regiment of infantry have arrived at Delhi. Mr. Fraser and some other gentlemen went with some sowars to quell the disturbance: the cavalry attacked and killed all the Europeans, and then went down to cantonments, and burnt the artillery and infantry lines, and the blackguards of the city looted the shops. In the afternoon the sowars offered their services to the King, and said they would place him on the throne, and that he should take the opportunity, and give up to them his guns and magazine. What they required, he did. He promised, and gave up his son to them. They attacked the Government magazine, when they knocked down the wall of the magazine, which caused much injury to the people. There were many Europeans killed; in short, only those of the English who concealed themselves escaped, but none others. The King has appointed one Meer Nawab as kotwal. The whole place is in disturbance. The King has sent his son to inspire confidence, but the ill-disposed are plundering everywhere. The King has encamped outside the city with six regiments; he is old. The officials are those of a worn-out government. The Jahgeerdars, in deference to the English, have not girded their loins. There are no arrangements for any provision, much less for anything else. The Sepoys are ready to give their lives, and to take the lives of others. To-day, Wednesday, some fifty odd Europeans, who had secreted themselves, were killed. They are hunting for more, and if any be found they will be killed. If they have escaped, so much the better. It is like the atrocities of Nadir Shah. On Tuesday, the King rode through the city, and encouraged the people to throw open their shops; but the people would not be comforted; many shops have been deserted. The civilisation of fifty-three years has been destroyed in three hours; good men have been plundered, scoundrels enriched. A regiment has come from Allygurh; they have not spared their officers. Three regiments and one battery of artillery of Delhi, two regiments and 500 troops from Meerut, and a regiment from Allygurh, are now in Delhi. All the magazine has been placed in the fort. The King has summoned different principal men of Delhi to make arrangements; they have pleaded sickness and incompetency, and sowars have been despatched to Utwur and Jaipoor. It remains to be seen what will come of it. The Delhi people have fallen into difficulties: God's will be done. This has been composed with care, and in a spirit of loyalty. The state of the people is not to be described. They are alive, but they despair of their lives. There is no cure for such a curse. The Sepoys are without a leader."

The story of the second eye-witness is even more circumstantial, the writer having had opportunities of witnessing all that occurred in the place from the commencement of the outbreak.

"On the morning of the 11th instant we were proceeding in a bhylee from Delhi to Mussoorie, and after we had crossed the bridge of boats and had proceeded 200 yards, we were met by eighteen troopers, with drawn swords; they asked us who we were? We replied, 'Pilgrims proceeding to Hurdwar.' They desired us to turn back to Delhi, or they would murder us; we accordingly returned. On arriving at the bridge of boats, the troopers plundered the toll-chest; and a regiment of Sepoys crossed the bridge and entered the city, after having killed a European whom they met on the bridge. The regiment had crossed, but the troopers were on the other side of the river, when the boatmen broke the bridge; the troopers crossed the river on horseback, and entered the city by the Delhi gate, and cantered up to the Ungooree Baugh (under the palace), to murder the 'Burra Saheb.' The kotwal, on hearing of this, sent word to Mr. Simon Fraser, the commissioner, who immediately ordered the records of his office to be removed into the city, and, getting into a buggy, with a double-barrelled gun loaded, with two orderly horsemen, proceeded towards the mutineers. The troopers advanced upon him; Mr. Fraser fired, and shot one dead through the head, and with the second barrel killed a trooper's horse; he then got out of the buggy, and entered the palace at the 'Summun Boorj,' closing the gate, and proceeded to the Lahore gate of the palace, and there called out to the subadar on duty to close the gate (*i. e.* the palace-guard gate), which he immediately did. A trooper then rode up, and called out to the subadar to open the gate. He asked 'Who are you?' and on his replying 'We are troopers from Meerut,' the subadar observed, 'Where are the other troopers?' The man replied, 'In the Ungooree Baugh;'

when the subadar desired the troopers to bring them all, that he would open the gate, and on their arrival did so, when all the troopers entered the palace.

"Mr. Simon Fraser and Captain Douglas, the commandant of the Palace Guards, called out to the subadar 'What treachery is this? Desire your men to load' (an entire company, if not more, was on duty at the palace-guard gate). The subadar abused the commissioner, desiring him to go away; on hearing which both Mr. Fraser and Captain Douglas left the quarters, and ran towards the interior of the palace, and were pursued by the troopers, one of whom fired a pistol at Mr. Fraser, on which he staggered and leant against a wall; when another trooper went up, and with a sword severed his head from his body at a single blow, and also in a similar manner killed Captain Douglas, the commandant of the palace, and then proceeded to the king's hall of audience, where they killed two more Europeans, and then proceeded to Durreeougunge, and set fire to all the houses there. Another regiment of Sepoys arrived into the city, and desired all the budmashes to plunder the houses, since they (the mutineers) considered it 'huram,' and would not condescend to touch the booty themselves. The troopers then murdered five gentlemen and three ladies in Durreeougunge, and the remainder took shelter in the Kishungur Raja's house. They then came to the Delhi bank, set fire to it, and killed five gentlemen; they then went up to the kotwalee, desiring the budmashes to commence plundering; on hearing which the kotwal absconded, and took no steps to protect the people, and even allowed the kotwalee to be plundered. The mutineers then came to the late Col. Skinner's house, which they did not touch, but set fire to all the houses in the vicinity of the church, killing all the gentlemen, ladies, and children therein.

"After this five troopers galloped to the cantonments, and on their approach all the Sepoys set fire to their officers' houses, murdering all the gentlemen, ladies, and children they could find in cantonments; the remainder of the troopers proceeded to the magazine in the city. On their approach four officers were standing before the magazine gate, which they closed, and from inside fired two shots at the troopers, and then set fire to the magazine: all the four officers, and upwards of a thousand men of the city, were blown up with the magazine. Two regiments from the Delhi cantonments joined the mutineers at the Delhi kotwalee, and commenced plundering the city. The two Delhi regiments then went and encamped near the Ellenborough tank before the palace. A guard was sent to the Kishunghur Raja's house, on suspicion of his having given refuge to Europeans. Upwards of thirty-four Europeans (men, women, and children) were concealed in the house. The mutineers set fire to the house, and it kept burning all day and night; but the Europeans were safe in the 'tykhana.' The next morning the troopers brought two guns from the magazine, and kept firing at the house all day, but without effect. They then took to plundering the city in every direction. The late Colonel Skinner's house, which the mutineers did not touch, was regularly plundered by the scamps of Delhi. On the 13th, the mutineers again attacked the Europeans that had taken shelter in the Kishunghur Raja's house. The Europeans commenced to fire, and shot thirty of the mutineers; but on their ammunition and supplies being out, thirty Europeans came out, and four remained in the 'tykhana.' The heir apparent now rode up to the house, and begged the mutineers would deliver them into his custody, and that he would take care of them; however, paying no attention to what he said, they put all the Europeans to death. Mr. George Skinner, his wife, and children had taken refuge in the palace; spies gave information; they were seized, taken to the kotwalee, and there most cruelly put to death. Dr. Chimmun Lall, the sub-assistant surgeon, was also killed at the dispensary. For three days the dead bodies were not removed, and on the fourth day the mutineers caused them all to be thrown into the river.

"The mutineers then asked the king either to give them two months' pay or their daily rations. The king summoned all the shroffs and mahajuns, telling them if they did not meet the demands of the mutineers, they would all be murdered; on which the shroffs agreed to give them dall rotee for twenty days, adding they could not afford more. The mutineers replied, 'We have determined to die; how can we eat dall rotee for the few days we have to live in this world?' Whereupon the king ordered four annas a day. The mutineers have placed two guns on each gate in the city, and have brought a thousand maunds of gunpowder from the cantonment magazine, and have taken possession of all the shot and shell in the city magazine. Supplies have been stopped, and everything becoming exceedingly dear, viz. attah thirteen seers, wheat eighteen seers, ghee one and a half seers, &c. All the neighbouring villages are up and plundering: the king has accordingly burnt five Goojur villages. The late Col. Skinner's house at Balaspore has also been plundered. After plundering Delhi, 200 troopers proceeded to Goorgaon, and set fire to the houses, murdered the collector, and plundered the treasury, bringing away 7 lakhs 84 thousand rupees; and, with the Delhi treasury, the mutineers have in their possession 21 lakhs 84 thousand rupees, which is kept in the palace, guarded by them and the king's troops. The troopers have also advanced towards Allyghur and Agra, with the intention of persuading the troops there to join them and set fire to houses and murder all the Europeans there. At Delhi there are three regiments, one from Meerut and two of the Delhi regiments, and two hundred troopers; the rest have all proceeded towards Allyghur and Agra. The great banker, Lutchmee Chund Sett, from feeding the mutineers daily, has saved his firm from sharing the fate of the others, and is the only shroff who has not been plundered."

We think that a careful perusal of the above narratives will strengthen the theory that there was no plot to create a rebellion, but that the outbreak was the result of a sudden impulse, hardened into purpose and plan by the sense of general disaffection. The relatives and adherents of the Delhi family were spread all over the country, and had tampered, no doubt, with the major part of the Mussulman Sepoys, urging them to seize the first favourable opportunity to rise for the recovery of their ancient dominions. They would say that although the Padshah was too old to place himself at the head of such an enterprise, his son was willing to be declared their king and leader; and that the enormous military arsenals and commercial wealth of Delhi, totally undefended by European troops, would give them such a start at the outset of a rebellion, that they might reasonably expect the adhesion of all the surrounding country. Still, however, it is unlikely that the revolt would have happened but for the local grievance of the greased cartridges. The Meerut rebels knew that the heir apparent was not a soldier, and they had never heard that rebellion had prospered against the British power. The most sanguine spirit could scarcely expect to have escaped alive from the cantonment where 2000 English soldiers, guns, cavalry, and infantry, were brigaded. And when, beyond their wildest hopes, they reached Delhi, the same sense of impending doom weighed upon them. They talked of themselves as men who had fulfilled a sacred duty at the certain cost of speedy extinction. They thought, with all the English, that a very short time must witness the capture of the city, when, of course, they would be annihilated to a man; and murmured at having nothing better than "dall rotee" to feed upon for the few days that remained to them. "Let us," they said, in the emphatic language of Scripture, "eat and drink, for to-morrow we die."

The cries of a mob, hotly engaged in the work of destruction, are the heart's genuine utterances. There is no deceit in impulse — no mode of artifice by which you can employ the tiger instincts in an unnatural way. The shout of the Mussulman troopers was "Deen, deen!"—a word of fear equally to Hindoo and Christian under ordinary circumstances. It was the battle-cry of Mahomed of Ghuznee and Nadir Shah, and had been heard over the din of falling pagodas and the death-shrieks of thousands of Hindoo worshippers in many a dark cycle of Eastern history. To suppose that Mahomedan soldiers would raise it now, merely to excite the Hindoo Sepoys to join them against the Feringees, is as reasonable as to believe that the officers of an English army would, if Ireland were invaded by a foreign power, seek to animate the loyalty of the Roman Catholic population, by marching through the villages with shouts of "Down with the Pope and the priests!" The Mussulman, in this instance, roused the Hindoo to aid him in warding off an evil which threatened both equally. They had a common cause to defend, and coalesced as a matter of course, just as Archbishops Sumner and M'Hale would unite, if Christianity were in the last stage of peril. That the rebels are using cartridges against us, which they chose rather to mutiny than accept at the outset, is no argument against their foolish sincerity of belief. Once get the conviction firmly established in your mind that your servant intends to murder you in your sleep, and you are likely enough to seize him when he enters the chamber on an errand of service. The mistake may be discovered, but the distrust remains. In the identical case of the cartridges actually in use, the Sepoys might see cause to alter their first impressions; but, after all, their forcible conversion was only a matter of time and opportunity. The majority of them, at this moment, think that their religion was in imminent danger; and if they regret the past, it will be that they have not made a wise use of their chances of salvation.

CHAP. VIII.

THE SIEGE OF DELHI. — WANT OF GUNS. — DEFECTIVE INTELLIGENCE. — UNWISE CLEMENCY. — THE REBEL PROCLAMATION. — LORD CANNING'S WASTE PAPERS.

ON the death of General Anson the command of the army devolved on the senior officer present, General Sir H. Barnard, K. C. B. This officer had served in the Crimea as chief of the staff under Lord Raglan, and was fully entitled, we suppose, to whatever honours had been conferred upon him in consequence of that appointment. His march from Umballa was a rapid one, but the immediate result was not unlike that of a workman who proceeds in haste to his task, and then has to sit down and wait for his tools. The troops arrived before Delhi on the 8th June; but the siege train had not come up, and when it reached the camp, a close examination of the means of attack disclosed the fact that there were no men to work the guns. Two modes of assault were open to General Barnard. He could in half an hour have made a breach in the walls of Delhi, sufficient to admit of the passage of any number of troops, or, before proceeding to storm, he might batter the place with shot and shell, till king, mutineers, and inhabitants were buried in the ruins. The public, of course, were not aware of the obstacles that stood in the way of the latter course, and the least hopeful minds looked upon it as a matter of certainty that the place would be taken in a fortnight after our army sat down before it. This sanguine view of matters was encouraged by the conduct of Government, who promulgated from time to time stories of the capture of Delhi, sometimes gleaned from a newspaper, at other times from private messages, and once, on the 12th of June, from "a great banker at Indore."

But the day rolled by without bringing the event prayed for by so many thousands, and at last an anecdote oozed out through the columns of a Bombay journal which justified a very humble estimate of General Barnard's fitness. The general, it appears, had ordered a parade of the forces before leaving Umballa, at which the 5th and 60th N. I. showed unmistakeable signs of mutiny. The tale of their disaffection reached Calcutta, and it was said that, on their refusal to obey orders, they had been cut to pieces. Granted the fact of the revolt, and there was nothing more likely than the infliction of the subsequent punishment; for the insolence and daring could know no bounds which did not hesitate to defy a British officer at the head of four or five thousand English soldiers. It turned out, however, that the crime had been committed, and was pardoned. The general soothed the malcontents into good humour, and hushed up the matter so far as they were concerned.

The sequel may be imagined: the 5th were left behind to do garrison duty, but the 60th marched under British protection to Delhi, and reached the rebel fortress stronger in men, and richer in pocket, than if they had been simply dismissed the service, like so many thousands of their countrymen, and left to get to Delhi as they best could. We have not heard whether they ever fired a shot on our side; but if so, they took the earliest opportunity of apologising for the mistake, by going over in a body to the rebels, and heading, a day or two afterwards, one of the fiercest assaults made on our position.

People who knew nothing of the science of war, except so far as common sense teaches its rudiments, recognised in this fatal facility of pardoning, and its consequences, a melancholy likeness between the Governor-General and the Commander-in-Chief. With Lord Canning in Calcutta, and Sir Henry Barnard at Delhi, the prospect of a speedy termination to the rebellion seemed gloomy in the extreme.

It took twenty-six days to bring the main army from

Umballa, and the auxiliary force from Meerut, before the walls of Delhi. The Guides accomplished the longer march in three days; the rebels performed the shorter distance in eighteen hours. The men literally pined with impatience to get at the enemy; but there were no guns, no artillerymen, no commissariat, and no medicine chest. They were held fast, as if labouring under nightmare, with the Government of India clutching at their throats. The rebels swarmed up at leisure from all parts of the country as to a safe asylum. They kept the roads open for themselves, but entirely closed to the British authorities, and went and came at discretion. In time, the mastiffs arrived, and watched the movements of the tiger. The artillery followed after a season, and at some interval of space the gunners. The labour commenced: the tides of life began to ebb and flow in the British camp: battles were won daily, but the siege never progressed: reinforcements continually arrived, but the army grew no stronger. Death was fed sparingly, but the table was always spread. General succeeded general, and engineers followed each other in the direction of the attack, with the rapidity of the changes in a pantomime, and still the batteries remained at almost extreme range, and the enemy came out to fight us almost daily on our own ground. General Barnard had taken the place of General Anson; General Reed superseded the former by right of seniority. General Barnard was restored to the command by order of the supreme Government; General Barnard died, and General Reed again took the command of the force, to be again superseded in favour of General Wilson. Three or four chief engineers had been appointed, and at one time the direction of siege operations was vested in a lieutenant of artillery. Fighting became at last the soldiers' daily work, from the performance of which neither wages nor profit were expected. The Government grew tired of announcing the fall of Delhi, and were content to hear occasionally from remote quarters that sickness, the sun, and the sword, had not absorbed more than the total of the reinforcements sent from time to time. The natives proclaimed all over the country that we had at last met more than our match. With the aid of our Sepoys we had captured the impregnable Bhurtpore, but fighting against them we could not take the almost defenceless city of Delhi. The "so-called fort, a place of no strength," as the military secretary phrased it, had resisted all the might of the Company Bahadoor: who could doubt that the Raj had passed away from it for ever?

In the latter part of May, His Majesty of Delhi circulated the following proclamation in all directions. It was published by a Mahomedan paper in Calcutta, and, by means of religious mendicants and other agencies, dispersed over the whole country:—

"Be it known to all the Hindoos and Mahomedans, the subjects and servants on the part of the officers of the English forces stationed at Delhi and Meerut, that all the Europeans are united in this point—first, to deprive the army of their religion; and then, by the force of strong measures, to Christianise all the subjects. In fact, it is the absolute orders of the Governor-General to serve out cartridges made up with swine and beef fat. If there be 10,000 who resist this, to blow them up; if 50,000, to disband them.

"For this reason we have, merely for the sake of the faith, concerted with all the subjects, and have not left one infidel of this place alive; and have constituted the Emperor of Delhi upon this engagement, that whichever of the troops will slaughter all their European officers, and pledge allegiance to him, shall always receive double salary. Hundreds of cannon and immense treasure have come to hand; it is therefore requisite that all who find it difficult to become Christians, and all subjects, will unite cordially with the army, take courage, and not leave the seed of these devils in any place.

"All the expenditure that may be incurred by the subjects in furnishing supplies to the army, they will take receipts for the same from the officers of the army, and retain them by themselves—they will receive double price from the Emperor. Whoever will at this time give way to pusillanimity, and allow himself to be overreached by these deceivers, and depend upon their word, will experience the fruits of their submission, like the inhabitants of Lucknow. It is therefore necessary that all Hindoos and Mahomedans should be of one mind in this struggle, and make arrangements for their preservation with the advice of some creditable persons. Wherever the arrangement shall be good, and with whomsoever the subjects shall be pleased, those individuals shall be placed in high offices in those places.

"And to circulate copies of this proclamation in every place, as far as it may be possible, be not understood to be less than a stroke of the sword. That this proclamation be stuck up at a conspicuous place, in order that all Hindoos and Mahomedans may become apprised and be prepared. If the infidels now become mild, it is merely an expedient to save their lives. Whoever will be deluded by their frauds, he will repent. Our reign continues. Thirty rupees to a mounted, and ten rupees to a foot soldier, will be the salary of the new servants of Delhi."

The proclamation summed up the entire argument in favour of mutiny. It was the work of a man who thoroughly understood the Asiatic character, and appealed to all the subject masses. Our rule was about to be distinguished by the practice of an iniquity as comprehensive as if we had poisoned all the rivers and wells, or infected the universal air. Hitherto, the worst of Governments had spared the great bulk of the people, from the impossibility of reaching them; but there was no man so poor or insignificant as to escape terrible loss at the hands of the English, if we were allowed to carry out our meditated design. We "were all united on the point," and "the orders" of the "Governor-General" were "absolute." The people had the "Emperor's" word for the fact, and his wisdom had devised the best method of averting the threatened calamity. He had killed all the conspirators within reach, and recommended all who cared to preserve their faith to follow his imperial example, and "not leave the seed of those devils in any place." Double pay was to be the never-ending reward of those who murdered their officers; unavailing regret would perpetually haunt those reprobates who were foolish enough to give credence to our promises. If we were "mild," it was "merely an expedient to save our lives." We had shown, in the case of Lucknow, what we thought of pledges.

Whilst the monarch of the Sepoys *de facto* was taking the short cut to the hearts and understandings of his new subjects, the ruler *de jure* was complacently issuing proclamations, which were read only by the few, and listened to by none. A manifesto was put forth warning all classes against the deceptions that were practised on them, and asserting that the Government of India had invariably treated the religious feelings of all its subjects with careful respect. The Governor-General in council had declared that it would never cease to do so. He now repeated that declaration, and emphatically proclaimed that the Government of India entertained no desire to interfere with their religion or caste, and that nothing had been or would be done by the Government to affect the free exercise of the observances of religion or caste by every class of the people.

"The Government of India," said Lord Canning, "has never deceived its subjects:" therefore the Governor-General in council now called upon them "to refuse their belief to such seditious lies." This paternal remonstrance was expected to effect much good. No Sepoy can blame the Governor-General for being precipitate to condemn or stern to punish. Rebels with arms in their hands would hardly expect to be reasoned with, and treated as erring mortals, whose morals were to be mended by argument and admonition, and the Asiatic mind failed to imagine the real drift of the document. They saw in it a mere confession of weakness. If the Government had the power to act, they would never have condescended to discuss the question of the folly of disaffection. With them the time had gone by for talking and writing; and it would have been well for England and India both, had Lord Canning either possessed the usual sagacity of Englishmen or the never-failing cunning of the Asiatic. In either case he would have given a single emphatic denial to the rumour of intended interference with the native religions, and spoken out the rest of his mind in salvoes of great guns and volleys of musketry. Something more tangible than words was offered to the men who remained true to their salt. A list of functionaries was published, who were empowered even to bestow commissions in the Company's service for deeds of valour and fidelity; and every officer in charge of a detachment was authorised to promote deserving Sepoys to the non-commissioned grades. Great crimes might and did go unpunished; but the smallest act performed in the cause of law and order was certain to find approval and reward.

Only a month had passed away since the officer highest in rank at Barrackpore had been censured by Government for promoting a most deserving Sepoy to the rank of sergeant; and now General Hearsey could bestow commissions, and officers in command of detachments were empowered to confer the non-commissioned grades. So long as the Sepoy was orderly and obedient he was unnoticed by the State, but when he became turbulent and unruly his merits were acknowledged. Whatever the Government dreaded they were willing to conciliate; the general order made no mention of the Queen's troops, because their fidelity was unquestionable. Being in fear for our lives, we had become "mild," and were trying to "overreach" the Sepoys. The Padshah had warned the people that attempts would be made to deceive them, and advised them not to put trust in the faithless Feringhee. It was in this sense that the natives interpreted what Lord Canning considered a master stroke of policy. He spoke of clemency and gratitude, which they translated as meaning weakness and attempted corruption. About the same time he was obliged to repeal an order which had been issued, empowering all general officers, and officers commanding stations, to appoint courts-martial, composed of not less than five native officers, for the trial and instant punishment of any offence which in their judgments required to be punished without delay. It was felt to be too bad to call upon the subadars and jemadars of the army to uphold Sepoy loyalty under existing circumstances. It was patent to the Governor-General, as well as to the rest of the world, that the native officers in each regiment could not by possibility be ignorant of what was going forward amongst the men, and that if, with their commissions and lives at stake, not a man amongst them could be induced to tell what he knew, it was the wildest folly to suppose that they would have found by court-martial their accomplices guilty of treason. It has been Lord Canning's misfortune throughout his brief Indian career to be incapable of distinguishing between Europeans and natives; but the Legislative Council in this instance corrected his error, and passed an act by virtue of which the court-martial might be composed of European officers alone, if the officer commanding thought proper. Some weeks afterwards, when our prospects seemed hopeless to native eyes, his lordship thought proper to recall the powers he had unconditionally vested in the civil authorities, for reasons which have not met the approbation of the thinking portion of society.

Of course, with a thousand stories floating about of mischief and murder, the popular feeling in Calcutta took the shape of an alarm for the safety of the capital. The public journals advocated the formation of volunteer corps, and the Trades Association went up to Government on the 20th of May, offering "every assistance in their power towards the preservation of order and the protection of the Christian community of Calcutta, either by serving as special constables or otherwise in such manner as may appear most desirable to Government, and at the same time suggesting to Government that their services should be availed of in some manner, as they deemed the present crisis a most serious one, and one in which every available means should be brought into action for the suppression of possible riot and insurrection." In conveying the above offer to the authorities, the secretary of the association described it in his letter "as a copy of proceedings and resolutions held on the subject of the present disaffection evinced by the Sepoy regiments throughout India," a remark which his lordship took instant pains to repudiate. The Trade Association was thanked, and advised to register their names at the office of the Commissioner of Police, who would write to them if their services were required. "But," said Lord Canning, "the Governor-General in Council desired to assure the Calcutta Trades Association that he has no apprehension whatever of riot, insurrection, or disturbance amongst any class of the population of Calcutta; and that if, unfortunately, any should occur, the means of crushing it utterly, and at once, are at hand.

"The Governor-General in Council begs the members of the association to believe that he is not on this account less thankful to them for the ready and spontaneous tender of their aid. Nothing gives greater strength to a Government in a large community than the cordial support and co-operation of the influential classes represented by the Calcutta Trades Association.

"The Governor-General in Council is sorry to see that, in the letter of the secretary of the association, it is assumed that disaffection has been evinced by the Sepoy regiments throughout India. His Lordship in Council would greatly regret that such an impression should go abroad. Not only is it certain to lead to exaggerated fears amongst the civil population of the country at large, but, without speaking of the armies of Madras and Bombay, it is not just as regards the army of Bengal. There are in the army of this Presidency many soldiers and many regiments who have stood firm against evil example and wicked counsels, and who at this moment, are giving unquestionable proof of their attachment to the Government, and of their abhorrence of the atrocious crimes which have lately been perpetrated in the north-west provinces.

"It is the earnest desire of the Governor-General in Council that honourable and true-hearted soldiers, whose good name he is bound to protect, and of whose fidelity he is confident, should not be included in a condemnation of rebels and murderers."

When this reply was given, the mutiny, so far as Government information went, was confined to the six regiments at Delhi and Meerut and the abortive attempt of the 7th Oude Irregulars. A month afterwards, and Lord Canning had to inform the Court of Directors that half the Bengal army were in open rebellion; had to inform the Trades Association that he would gladly accept their offered aid; had to guard the Mint and Treasury with Europeans, and exhibit to all the world that he was unable to see any of the signs of the times, and had been labouring, however unconsciously, as much to discourage the loyal subjects of Her Majesty as to afford heart of grace to their enemies. Again, on the 25th of May, Mr. Cecil Beadon replied to the address of the French inhabitants of Calcutta, as follows:—"The Governor-General in Council desires me to return his sincere acknowledgments for your address of the 23rd instant, in which you evince your attachment to her Majesty the Queen by placing your services at the disposal of the Government, for the common safety, in consequence of the partial revolt of some of the native regiments in the north-west provinces.

"His Lordship in Council regards this expression of the sentiments of the French community with lively satisfaction, and feels assured that, in case of necessity, their sympathy with the British Government and their active co-operation in the cause of order may be entirely relied on; but he trusts there will be no occasion to call for their services. Everything is quiet within 600 miles of the capital. The mischief caused by a passing and groundless panic has already been arrested, and there is every reason to hope that, in the course of a few days, tranquillity and confidence will be restored throughout the Presidency."

CHAP. IX.

THE FIRST TROUBLES IN OUDE. — WEAK BEHAVIOUR OF GOVERNMENT. — REVOLT OF THE ENTIRE ARMY OF THE PROVINCE. — COMPARATIVE MILDNESS OF THE REBELS.

THE force in Oude at the commencement of the outbreak consisted of the following troops: H. M. 32nd, a troop of horse artillery, 2 companies of foot ditto, the 7th Light Cavalry, 7 regiments of native infantry, 3 field batteries of the Oude Irregular Force, 3 regiments of Oude Irregular Cavalry, 10 regiments of Oude Irregular Infantry, and 3 ditto of police; in all, about 900 Europeans and 22,000 natives. The last revolted almost in a body; but it is noticeable that the irregulars, who had but lately taken service with us, were far less bloodthirsty than the troops of the Bengal army. If, as natives of Oude, they had grievances peculiar to themselves, their conduct as mutineers certainly betrayed no special signs of it.

On the 2nd of May, the 7th Oude Regiment, stationed about seven miles from Lucknow, refused to bite the cartridge when ordered to do so by the officer commanding; and again when the order was repeated by the brigadier. The next day the corps showed signs of mutiny in an unmistakable way, and measures were at once taken to deal with it. A field battery, a wing of H. M. 32nd, and several regiments of native cavalry and infantry marched against it, and the disaffected troops were drawn up in columns facing the guns. They expressed sorrow for what had occurred and asked for forgiveness, at the same time giving up two prisoners and offering to surrender forty more; but when the port-fires were lighted, they imagined that the strong measures usually adopted against mutiny in the king's time were about to be employed, and, throwing down their arms, fled for their lives. They were pursued, and a number taken prisoners; but no blood was shed, and the runaways came back to their lines at night, and were told on the following day that Government would be asked to disband the corps, but that the innocent men might be re-enlisted. When the matter came before Government for consideration, Lord Canning proposed that the disbandment should be real to whatever length it might be carried. He disliked discharging men one day to take them back the next, and would therefore keep the good soldiers, and get rid of the bad characters. Mr. Dorin was of opinion that disbandment was not a sufficient punishment. "The sooner," he wrote, "this epidemic of mutiny is put a stop to, the better. Mild measures won't do it. A severe example is wanted. It is little or no punishment to a Local on five rupees monthly pay to be disbanded in his own country. In many instances, it might be a convenience to him than otherwise. I would rather try the whole of the men concerned for mutiny, and punish them with the utmost rigour of military law. I am convinced that timely severity will be leniency in the long run."

Mr. Dorin was of opinion that no corps mutinies that is well commanded. General Low thought it probable that the main body, in refusing to bite the cartridges, did so refuse, not from any feeling of disloyalty or disaffection towards the Government or their officers, but from an unfeigned and sincere dread, owing to their belief in the late rumours about the construction of those cartridges, that the act of biting them would involve a serious injury to their caste and to their future respectability of character. In short, that if they were to bite these cartridges they would be guilty of a heinous sin in a religious point of view.

He would try the ringleaders by court-martial, and disband the main body of the regiment; and "if it came to light that want of zeal, good judgment, or short-comings of any kind had been evinced by European officers, he would have them punished with the utmost rigour." This last sentence was in allusion to the fact that the drill instructions by which biting the cartridge was dispensed with had not been brought into operation at Lucknow.

Mr. Grant penned a very voluminous minute on the subject. He thought it very likely that the men had been influenced by an unfeigned dread of losing caste, engendered by the stories which had been running like wildfire through the country. "Sepoys," he went on to say, "are in many respects very much like children; and acts which, on the part of European soldiers, would be blackest disloyalty, may have a very different significance when done by these credulous and inconsiderate, but generally not ill-disposed, beings. These men, taken from the late Oude army, can have learned as yet little of the vigour of British discipline; and although there can be no doubt that the cartridges which they refused to bite were not the new cartridges for the Enfield musket, which, by reason of the very culpable conduct of the Ordnance Department, have caused all this excitement, yet it may be presumed that they were the first cartridges that these men were ever required to bite in their lives."

Mr. Grant's remedy for the evil shown in this case was to suspend the order for disbandment till there had been time for making a full inquiry into all the circumstances. He thought the "dismissal of the bad characters, with the trial by court-martial of a few of the worst men a month hence," was the best plan to adopt; but four weeks after the date of his minute the honourable member would be disposed to look on the mutiny, which consisted only in refusing to bite the cartridges and then running away, as a military act which deserved commendation rather than otherwise.

When the despatch box came round again, Lord Canning wrote a minute, in which he said: "I know no instance in which the punishment of any individual could, with unquestionable justice, have been made more severe; and I am not disposed to distrust the efficacy of the measures because the present ferment, in running its course over the land, after being checked in the Presidency, has shown itself in Oude and in the north-west. I would meet it everywhere with the same deliberately measured punishments,—picking out the leaders and prominent offenders, wherever this is possible for the severest penalties of military law,—visiting the common herd with disbandment, but carefully exempting those whose fidelity, innocence, or, perhaps, timely repentance, is proved. This has been the course hitherto pursued, and I earnestly recommend that it be adhered to steadily." The rest of the council concurred; but Mr. Dorin, in whose mind misgivings had sprung up, said there would "seem to be more in the present case than has yet transpired. It is to be hoped that the news from Meerut (in the telegraph message from Agra in this box) is not true." The knell of the Great Company had tolled, and his ear caught the faint sounds that were soon to reverberate throughout the universe. The straw on the surface of events, he was guiltless of having caused the tide.

After the fall of Delhi it was universally felt that if the mutiny spread it would be in the direction of Oude, where the irregular force, lately in the service of the king, might be expected to rise against us to a man. Sir Henry Lawrence, the Chief Commissioner of the Province, asked for "plenary powers," as soon as the intelligence reached Lucknow, and obtained them. He was made Brigadier-General, which enabled him to assume the direction of military affairs, and commenced to fortify himself against accidents. But his anxiety was for Allahabad, Benares, and Cawnpore, with regard to which he was constantly communicating with the Government. On the 20th of May he telegraphed "All very well at Lucknow and in the district. Our position is now very strong. In case of necessity no fears are entertained." On the 23rd he announced that he had secured his magazine stores, and had 10 days' supplies for 500 men. He had 30 guns and 100 Europeans in a fortified post called the Muchee Baun, and 291 Europeans with a European battery in cantonments, and was safe except from external influences. All his dread was for Cawnpore, and he telegraphed without ceasing to spare no expense in sending up Europeans to reinforce the place. On the 29th he intimated that there was great uneasiness, and that tranquillity could not be maintained much longer at Lucknow, except Delhi were captured. On the 30th he received back the fifty Europeans that had been lent to Sir Hugh Wheeler, and the next day the troops broke out in mutiny. During the last days of May he was constantly assured by his spies each night that the troops intended to rise that evening, and each morning of course showed that the tale was unfounded. The sentries, however, were doubled, and every precaution taken to avoid surprise, and such was the effect produced by the admirable nature of the arrangements and the well-founded reliance on the skill and bravery of the Chief Commissioner, that the people began to think there would be no mutiny after all, and the authorities at Calcutta would have backed the opinion freely. But on the night of the 30th May firing was heard in the lines of the 71st N. I., and it was evident that the tragedy had begun. From every quarter of the native encampments, the fire of musketry rained hotter and hotter; bungalows were seen blazing in all directions, and officers, galloping here and there with such irregular cavalry as they could muster, were seen engaged hand-to-hand with the mutineers, or trying to persuade their men to remain true to their salt. The Brigadier, Col. Handscombe, a brave old soldier, who had served at the capture of Ghaznee during the campaigns in Affghanistan, and been present in all the desperate battles of the first Sikh war, was shot as he rode up to the lines in the hope of being able to persuade the tigers who had already tasted blood not to thirst for more of it. Lieut. Grant, son of the Commander-in-Chief of Madras, was killed at his picket. The rebels charged his men, who turned and fled, and one of them shot the poor youth, who tottered into the guard-house, and was hidden by the subadar under his charpoy. The ruffians returned to the place, and were told that he had got away; but a scoundrelly havildar of the guard pointed out his hiding-place, and it is needless to say he was murdered with circumstances of savage cruelty. The firing continued throughout the night, the mutineers receiving occasional reinforcements from the ranks of the 71st, 13th, and 48th N. I., but being unable to make the smallest impression on the weak body opposed to them. At daybreak they had traversed the length of the encampments, the whole of which was in a blaze, and had set fire to the lines of the 7th Cavalry, nearly the entire of whom then turned and made common cause with the rebels. Retracing their steps, they made a show of giving battle to Sir H. Lawrence; but a few round shot from the artillery sent them flying in all directions, and he returned to cantonments with a hundred prisoners, having chased the rebels till the sun became too hot to continue the pursuit. During the next thirty-four days he remained cooped up in Lucknow, the circle of fire gradually closing round him, and his tone of correspondence slowly changing from a sense of complete security to that of utter hopelessness. It seemed so impossible, both to the world outside and to himself, that he could be left in Lucknow to perish. Surely Delhi would fall, and aid would come from Calcutta. With a European regiment in addition to his own force, he believed he could reconquer Oude, and, after the marvels performed by our troops, we can hardly venture to doubt that he would have forced a way through all opposition. But the vital error which pervaded all our military operations was the attempt to hold fortresses instead of merely looking to the saving of lives. Lord Canning had made it a war of posts. He would give up nothing, and yet could defend nothing. At the outset Meerut and Agra might have put down the insurrection, even after the mutineers had possession of Delhi, if the Government had only disarmed the Sepoys, trusted the defence of the women and children to volunteer guards, and made forced marches on the rebel capital. Again, had Lucknow been given up for the time, Wheeler and Lawrence combined could have held their own at Cawnpore, and we should have been spared the worst of the Indian tragedies. The junction of the two detachments, the easy advance of Neill with a flying column in June, or the aid of the Ghoorkas, each or any, would have sufficed, in all human probability, to save us bitter and unavailing regret. But it was fated to be otherwise. No succour came through all the weary June, and on the 2nd of July Sir Henry Lawrence marched out against the mutineers with nearly all his force. He reasoned that, if the native troops were staunch, he might even succeed in raising the siege, and if they joined the rebels, he should have so many less of useless mouths to feed from his slender stock of provisions. The event justified his fears. The traitors, artillery and infantry, turned upon him as soon as they got well outside the defences, and it was with difficulty that he got back to cover, seriously wounded, and with heavy loss to his little band, who, however, by springing a mine, blew up a great number of the enemy. On reaching his quarters, he sat down and wrote to Government, detailing the particulars of the action and the perilous state of affairs, but making no mention of his own hurt. Two days afterwards he died, to the infinite loss of the public service, and the sorrow of all ranks of Englishmen.

The 17th N. I., stationed at Goruckpore, and the 22nd at Fyzabad, agreed to rise at an early date, but the latter resisted the solicitations of the 17th either to kill their own officers or send them away on the road by which it was arranged that the 17th should march on Fyzabad. A company of the latter was sent to Azimgurh with 50,000*l.* in silver, and on arriving at that place they killed a couple of their officers, marched into the lines, and there being joined by the rest of the regiment, they plundered the treasury, containing, we believe, about 70,000*l.* in addition, and then broke away for Fyzabad, slaughtering, as a matter of course, every European who came in their way. Their approach to that station was duly announced, and on the night of the 8th June a couple of guns fired by the 6th Oude Irregular Infantry warned the Sepoys of the 22nd that the time had arrived for fulfilling their contract. For several nights previous Major Mills, commanding the battery with Lieutenants Currie and Perceval, had slept at the quarter guard with their guns in readiness; and Colonel Lennox, commanding the 22nd N. I., slept amongst his men. On hearing the alarm, Major Mills started off to the battery; but the company of Sepoys which had been placed to flank the guns closed round the field-pieces, and, presenting their bayonets, refused to allow any of the artillery to approach. It was then considered useless to stay any longer, and the officers assembled and sent for boats. The rebels were divided into two parties, — the Mussulmans, who wished to slaughter all the Europeans, and the Hindoos, who inclined to moderate counsels. Ultimately the advice of the latter prevailed, and the mutineers not only assisted in providing them with the means of transport, but made them a donation of Rs. 900, the money being taken from the regimental chest. When the officers tried to induce them to pause, they answered respectfully that the Company's raj was at an end. That the subadar major of the corps had been appointed to the command of the station, and that each regiment had chosen its own colonel. The subadar major, willing to do all things in order, requested the late colonel of the 22nd to produce his dress-uniform coat, and, having tried it on in his presence, observed, "it would fit very well if let out a little underneath the arms." The property of all belonging to the station was of course looted, but nothing was taken of much value, except by arrangement with the owners. An officer's wife, who was rich enough to possess a handsome service of plate, was requested by her butler to give it to him: somebody, he said, must have it, and he, as chief servant, was best entitled. Discussing the state of affairs with his mistress, he said he knew that the rebels could only hold the country while the rains lasted: with the cold weather, the Europeans would of course return as conquerors; but in the meantime they would have plenty of loot and European lives. Mutiny carried on after this fashion is perhaps less unpleasant than exciting, and there are extant notes of various conversations with the chiefs of the mutineers at Fyzabad. One of the officers states that, in a conversation with a subadar of his regiment, the latter said, "As you are going away for ever, I will tell you all about our plans. We halt at Fyzabad five days, and march viâ Durriabad upon Lucknow, where we expect to be joined by the people of the city." He added, "proclamations have been received from the King of Delhi, informing all that he is once more on the throne of his fathers, and calling upon the whole army to join his standard. Also that Rajah Maun Singh, under whose guardianship the ladies at Fyzabad placed themselves, had been appointed Commander-in-Chief in Oude." The subadar further said, "You English have been a long time in India, but you know little of us. We have nothing to do with Wajeed Ali or any of his relations; the kings of Lucknow were made by you. The only ruler in India empowered to give sunnuds is the King of Delhi; he never made a King of Oude, and it is from him only that we shall receive our orders."

When the whole of the European officers had stepped into the boats, the station resumed its usual aspect. The subadar major, as chief of the station, drove about in the late commanding officer's carriage, and each sable hero promoted after this summary fashion to be captain or lieutenant, annexed the cattle and vehicle of his predecessor; the rule of entail was pursued, the estates going with the title. The band played nightly at mess for them, the extra pay of the musicians being defrayed from the Company's treasury. Guards were planted and parades ordered as usual, and perhaps the Sepoy would have been puzzled to tell what he had gained by the change of masters. The fugitives started for Dinapore in several boats, but there appears to have been a sad want of concert between them. They were numerous enough to have made a stout resistance had they kept together; but they left at various times, and lost the advantage of company and counsel. The majority of the hapless souls were killed, some by the revolted troops, and others by the villagers, and the narratives of the escape of those who survived, teem with examples of exquisite suffering and unexpected succour. The Rajah Maun Singh, whom the English had imprisoned and the King of Delhi had promoted, showed himself a fast friend to our race, and not only made advances of money to various officers, but repeatedly supplied escorts to bring them to a place of safety, much against the will of his own adherents, who seldom omitted to taunt them with their failure in the attempt to destroy the native religion.

At Sultanpore the 15th Irregulars gave notice to their commanding officer, Colonel Fisher, that they intended to mutiny, in company with the 12th N. I. and Oude Police Corps. The Colonel was one of the most popular members of a service in which all commanding officers who succeed are favourites with their men. Above all native troops, the fidelity of the Irregulars would have been vouched for; and above all commanding officers, "Sam Fisher," as he was popularly termed, would have been voted the last man to lose his corps by mutiny. A lieutenant only in H. M. 29th, he had won his rank of brevet lieutenant-colonel three years since, by dint of desperate bravery. The record of his services shows that he was present through all the Affghanistan campaigns in 1842, the occupation of Cabul, and capture of Istaliff; in the battles of the Sutlej in 1845-6, where he was severely wounded, and in the second Punjaub war. All these dangers he had passed through, and was now to die by the hands of miserable traitors. Finding that his expostulations were of no avail with his men, he turned sorrowfully away from the groups he had been addressing, and rode in front of the 6th Oude Locals, who were breaking up, with loud shouts to seize the Treasury. A volley saluted his arrival, and he fell riddled with balls, but survived to be carried off in a palanquin, in which it is said he was finally killed by his own men, who cut up their second in command, Captain Gibbings, and fraternised with the rest of the mutineers. Messrs. Black and Strogan, civilians, took refuge in a native house, but were turned out, and also cut down. Captain Bunbury, commanding the 6th Oude Locals, had taken the precaution to have a boat in readiness, and, hastily pushing off, escaped the fate of many of his brother officers and friends.

Another popular officer who fell by the hands of the rebels was Lieutenant Joseph Clarke, second in command of the 3rd Oude Irregulars. He had distinguished himself by killing the notorious Fuzil Ali, a dacoit, who had set at defiance for years the police and the troops of the King of. Oude, and had at last displayed his indifference to consequences by the murder of a Bengal civilian. Lieutenant Clarke was stationed at an outlying post during the mutiny, and the tidings of defection throughout the province reached him before his men got to hear of it. As a matter of course, he knew they would rise as soon as they received the news, and his first care, therefore, was to send off his brother officer at the station, with the women and children, to a place of safety. That done, he waited quietly till the Sepoys came forward, and said they must follow the example of the rest of the regiment. They went on to assure him that they would not allow a hair of his head to be harmed, and that of course he could take what things he pleased away with him. The parting was arranged in the most amicable manner, and Lieutenant Clarke, with a couple of servants, who remained by him, started off to the nearest station of Europeans. On their way down, they were crossing the Gogra, when they saw, on the opposite bank, a regiment of infantry, and, looking back to the shore they had just quitted, a squadron of cavalry was observed occupying the river's edge, and effectually cutting off their retreat. There was no help for it but to go forward, and in a few minutes they were surrounded by the rebels. The native commanding officer merely inquired his name, and ordered a dozen men to take him out and shoot him. The servants threw themselves on their faces, and, with passionate tears, implored his life. They spoke of his bravery in battle and unvarying kindness of heart, and how loath the corps were to part with him. The rebel leader gave his assent to all that was said in his prisoner's favour. He, too, had heard of "Clarke Sahib," and would have been glad to save him, but the English were killing every black man who fought against them, and his orders were to retaliate in every instance. The poor young Lieutenant knew that his doom was fixed, and made no appeal himself to move their compassion. He only begged that his sword and medal might be sent to his father, and that he might die a soldier's death. His captor promised compliance with his request, and was as good as his word. He took the life which he considered forfeit, and went on his way of evil. The sword and medal were safely delivered, and perhaps, before this, the executioners have joined their victim.

CHAP. X.

THE REVOLT OF BENARES. — PANIC AMONGST THE SIKHS. — DEFENCELESS STATE OF ALLAHABAD. — MUTINY OF THE 6TH N. I. — THE SIEGE AND MASSACRE OF CAWNPORE.

ONE evening about the latter end of May, a river steamer filled with soldiers belonging to the 1st Madras Fusiliers, arrived alongside the railway wharf at Calcutta. They had been sent for in great haste from Madras, and were now on their way to Benares. The night train to Raneegunge, distance 120 miles from Calcutta, was just about to start; and one of the officials told Colonel Neill, the commanding officer, that unless he could get his men on shore in two or three minutes it would start without them. The reply of Colonel Neill was an order for a file of men to take his informant into custody. The man shouted for assistance; and the stokers, guard, and station master crowded round to see what was the matter, and were each in turn stuck up against the wall with a couple of bearded red coats standing sentry over them. The colonel next took possession of the engine, and by this series of strong measures delayed the departure of the train until the whole of his men were safely stowed away in the carriages. The occurrence furnished a great deal of amusing gossip in Calcutta; and there were men who saw in this act of Colonel Neill indications of a vigour and decision of purpose to which they had hitherto been unaccustomed. The "Friend of India" said, "We would back that servant of the Company as being equal to a case of emergency." But no one knew the real value of this example of Zubberdustee, the phrase for small tyrannies, till some weeks after, when it was found that the safety of the fort and city of Benares was entirely owing to the stoppage of the railway train. Colonel Neill arrived at Benares just as the mutinous elements in the fort had drawn to a state of fusion. The native corps consisted of the 37th N. I., the Loodianah Sikhs, and the 13th Irregular cavalry, opposed to which there were only three guns of Major Olphert's battery, 150 of H. M. 10th, and a detachment of forty Madras Fusiliers. It had transpired that the 37th N. I. intended to rise on the night of the 4th June; and the authorities took their measures accordingly. A parade was ordered at five o'clock, for the purpose of disarming them, the whole of the troops being in attendance. Brigadier Ponsonby commanded the station, his appointment a short time previous having been the subject of much heartburning in the Bengal army, and of a reference from the Supreme Council to General Anson as to the reasons for it. Luckily for himself, but hardly so for the public and the service, the brigadier fell ill when the moment for decisive action arrived; and the command then devolved upon Colonel Gordon, of the Sikh regiment, who was in turn superseded by Colonel Neill, in the course of the afternoon of the 4th. At first there seemed no cause for apprehending resistance on the part of the 37th; a portion of them appeared on the parade without arms according to order; but one or two companies were piling their muskets, when a few men of the corps opened fire on their officers. The rest followed their example; and the fight commenced in earnest. The Sikhs were counted upon as being loyal; but they were seized with an unaccountable impulse, and poured in a volley upon the Europeans. The little band sustained the English reputation. Eighteen or twenty rounds of grape were delivered from each gun in the course of a few minutes, a crashing discharge saluting the Sikhs as three times in succession they dashed up to the muzzles. The Irregulars ranged themselves on the side of the mutineers, and the boldest spirit might well have shrunk from that unequal contest; but native daring, with the advantage of ten to one in numbers, quailed before the indomitable courage of the English. Lieutenant-Colonel Spottiswoode, of the 37th, took a couple of port-fires, and set fire to the Sepoy lines; and the wind being strong at the time, the hiding-places of the mutineers were speedily in a blaze. In a few minutes the affair was over, and the men of the three regiments were swarming out of the fort in crowds, with the loss of 100 killed and 200 wounded, the casualties on our side amounting only to eight. Major Guise, of the 13th Irregulars, was murdered by one of his own men while he was hastening to the parade; and two officers, Ensigns Chapman and Hayter, were severely wounded. During the mutiny a portion of the Irregular cavalry and Sikhs stood firm; and next day 250 of the latter, and a considerable number of the cavalry, returned to the fort and begged to be forgiven. Their statement was that they had acted in supposed fear of their lives, and had not the slightest intention of disobeying orders. The excuse was accepted; and the Loodianah regiment, like the rest of the Sikhs, have since done good service and performed all that could be expected from brave and loyal soldiers. A company of them were on guard over the collectors' cutcherry, where the families of the Europeans had taken refuge, and the treasure was kept; but Soorut Singh, one of the prisoners taken by us in the last Punjaub campaign, went amongst them and persuaded them not to rise in mutiny, which they were strongly inclined to do on hearing that their bhaees had been so severely dealt with. A reward of Rs. 10,000 was distributed amongst them for their behaviour on this occasion; and by dint of unlimited hangings and other measures of a quieting character, Colonel Neill contrived in two or three days dissipate all fears for the safety of Benares. Whilst he was engaged in the work of pacification, the Government, true to its instinct of confounding time and place, sent orders to him to push on to Allahabad; but the reply conveyed by telegraph was, "Can't move—wanted here." Lord Canning needed somebody who could think for himself and the Government as well; and in Colonel Neill he found the requisite individual. We shall find him afterwards performing for Allahabad services almost as signal as he had rendered at Benares.

The mutiny at Jaunpore was the result of the misunderstanding which had so nearly proved fatal to our gallant countrymen at Benares. A couple of the Sikhs, who had seen their countrymen mowed down by the volleys of grape, reached the station and informed the guard of 150 men how the English had dealt with them. This intelligence, added to the exhortations of the fugitive sowars, who came crowding in to Jaunpore, turned the hearts of the Sikh detachment who fired upon their officer, Lieut. Mara, while he was standing in the verandah of his house, and mortally wounded him. The station was up and the Europeans crowded to the cutcherry, for a planter fresh from the rout of Benares hastily rode in and told what had occurred. The handful of Europeans barricaded themselves in the house of Lieut. Mara, and expected nothing but instant death; but the Sikhs were evidently not thirsting after blood. They contented themselves by firing a few shots through the windows, and then made off to plunder the treasury, and were seen no more. The magistrate Mr. Cuppage, was shot as he was returning from visiting the jail guard, and Mr. Thriepland and his wife were murdered the next day, by the sowars, under circumstances of great brutality. The country was all up in arms on the instant, and some of the zemindars threatened their people that if they concealed a Feringhee their own lives should pay the forfeit. The suppression of the mutiny at Benares, however, had the effect of staying the progress of revolt in that quarter, and an aspiring Hindoo, who one afternoon proclaimed himself independent, and set up his banner as Rajah of Jaunpore, came the following morning to the head of the relieving party from Benares, and made his salaam. The Sikhs in conjunction with the 37th carried away the whole of the treasure; but it has not been stated that, as a proof of their loyalty, they brought it all back again.

Some two or three days after the news had arrived in

Calcutta of the Meerut outbreak, the attention of Government was drawn to the state of Allahabad. This city, which is situated at the confluence of the Ganges and Jumna, is considered the key of the lower provinces. The inhabitants, amounting to about 75,000, are made up chiefly of Mussulmans, priestly Brahmins, and religious mendicants. The arsenal, situated in the fort, is one of the largest in India, having arms for about 40,000 men, and numerous cannon. Under a wise administration, such a place would be rightly looked upon as a post of strength and importance; but a fort can scarcely be called impregnable that has no gunners to defend it, and at the period in question there was not a single artilleryman in Allahabad.

The steps to be taken under the circumstances formed the subject of anxious debate at Government House. Benares could afford no help, having only men enough to work a single battery; and Cawnpore was distant twelve marches. The native troops in the fort numbered about 600 men, of whom 500 were Sikhs, and the remainder belonged to the 6th N. I., the rest of the latter regiment being quartered in cantonments. With the exception of the magazine staff, there was not a single European soldier in the place. The treasury offered a tempting prize; and what would the Court of Directors and the world at home say, if fortress, guns, arsenal, and money were lost under such circumstances? The Governor-General acknowledged the magnitude of the danger; the military secretary saw no means of arresting it. Nowhere could help be looked for, except at the cost of sacrifices not to be thought of. The Supreme Council had no suggestions to make, and the official conclave was broken up in despair, when it occurred to a non-military gentleman that he had seen, when going up the Ganges some years back, European artillerymen belonging to the veteran battalion at Chunar, a place less than sixty miles from Allahabad. The military secretary was informed of this feat of memory, and poured out his blessings on the wondrous head which contained such a store of knowledge. The valuable reminiscence was communicated forthwith to Lord Canning, who recognised its importance; and on the 19th of May sixty-nine old veterans, the youngest of whom was probably not less than fifty years of age, were hurried off in a steamer under Captain Haslewood, and arrived in due course at Allahabad. Their guns, on the night of the mutiny, saved the fort and all that it contained; and for three weeks the dilapidated old soldiers manned their batteries every night, thus justifying our countrymen at home, who occasionally adopt phrases which imply a belief that the English empire in India owes more to good fortune than to ability for its continuance.

On the afternoon of the 6th of June, a parade of the 6th N. I., who had volunteered to fight the Delhi mutineers, was ordered, for the purpose of reading out to the men the general order of Lord Canning, conveying his thanks for their loyalty and good feeling. When the paper was finished, the Sepoys gave three cheers; and in less than four hours afterwards they had murdered seventeen officers, and all the women and children they could find, and marched off to Delhi, the band playing "God save the Queen."

The commanding officer, Colonel Simpson, had exercised all his authority and powers of argument to persuade his subalterns and the public that the men were what they pretended to be; and hence the amount of loss sustained. Perhaps he scarcely thanks destiny for having preserved his own life and that of his family under such circumstances; but it was not the fault of his faithful Sepoys that his name has not been erased from the Army List. He was saluted, like the rest, with a perfect storm of bullets, but managed to get into the fort unhurt. Meantime the officer in command there acted with promptitude and decision. The guard at the main gate was composed of eighty men of the 6th, who of course longed to give entrance to their rebel comrades; but a detachment with two guns were sent to guard the bridge of boats until a couple of six-pounders could be brought up to the main gate and loaded with grape shot; and then, the veterans facing them with port-fires lighted, they were summoned to give up their arms. At first they hesitated; but an intimation from Captain Haslewood, that only a few moments grace would be allowed them, had the desired effect. They laid down their muskets, and marched out to join in the work of destruction. Thanks to the energy of this invalid Captain and of the unattached Lieutenant Brayser, in command of the Ferozepore Sikhs, not a soul inside the fort was injured. They had taken the precaution of closing the gates against egress for the last two days; and it was well they did so, for the rebels at Benares had sent a man to inform the Sikhs how their countrymen of the Loodianah corps had been shot down by Colonel Neill, and had he gained admittance, there is but little doubt that they would have joined the mutineers and thus insured the destruction of all of European blood. We hope that, when justice is administered to our brave defenders, the service of these gallant men will meet reward as well as appreciation.

For miles around Allahabad the country during the next two or three days presented nothing but scenes of devastation. Every house belonging to the English residents was burnt or gutted, and property to an enormous amount destroyed. What the city thieves and sepoys left was looted by the Europeans and Sikhs, who apparently could recognise no difference between friend and foe in this respect. The work of destruction was carried on with impunity under the very guns of the fort; and supplies which would have enabled General Havelock to reach Cawnpore a week earlier, were utterly destroyed or scattered. There were 1600 siege bullocks belonging to the commissariat available on the 27th of May; and on the 20th of June the Military Secretary was obliged to write to the officer commanding at Benares to do his utmost to collect carriage for Havelock's force; 150 bullocks would be required, which must be taken off the road where they were employed at that time in assisting the bullock train. The valuable godowns of the India General Steam Navigation Company were thoroughly sacked; and costly furniture, of no value to the plunderers, was smashed to pieces for the mere love of mischief. These did for private what the enemy had done for public property. Drunkenness was all but universal; and riot reigned supreme. The Sikhs having no taste for champagne or wine in general, sold all they could lay hands on, at prices varying from threepence to eighteen pence a bottle; but the brandy they seized for regimental use. Whatever was unsuited to their appetite was parted with for the merest trifle; but, except for edibles, there were no buyers, and the losses which had ruined many persons benefited none. The works of the railway were almost entirely destroyed for many miles. The rebels tore up the rails, burnt the stations, and, fearing to approach the locomotives, lest they should "go off" and blow them up, they fired into them from a safe distance till the engines were battered to pieces. The "lightning dawk," as a work of magic and mischief, was especially the object of rage and hatred. This state of things lasted till the 11th of June, when Colonel Neill arrived from Benares with half the Madras Fusileers, and all classes of men felt that a master had been placed over them. His first act was to adopt sanitary measures in the fort, where cholera was raging to that extent that fifty persons had died in a single day; and the result was so successful as to enable him to dismiss from his mind the dread of a lengthened pestilence. A couple of hours were given for the restoration of plundered property, after which, persons found with any portion of such in their possession were to be incontinently hung.

The authorities had very wisely passed Colonel Simpson over; and his successor had full opportunities for carrying out his daring and energetic plans. The next morning at daybreak he opened fire with shot and shell on a portion of the city suburbs where the worst and most turbulent Brahmins resided. At the same time a body of fifty Fusiliers, three companies of the Sikhs, a few of the 13th Irregulars, and a number of volunteers, railway men and others, marched into the open country. About two thousand of the rebels, under the command of a fanatic Moulvie, had strongly intrenched themselves and held the garrison in siege since the night of the 6th. Seeing the small band of Europeans, they hastily left cover; but at five hundred yards a volley from fifty Enfield rifles carried dismay into their ranks. They advanced a little nearer, and received a second discharge, after which they turned and fled back again, the assailants being prevented only from storming their position by the heavy fire of the guns inside. The rebel Sepoys had exhausted all their cartridges, and had cut the telegraph wires into slugs, the peculiar sound of which rather tried the nerves of some of our brave Irregulars. Finding it hopeless to assault the rebel works, the small force slowly retired, inflicting as much mischief in the retreat as in the advance. All this while the volunteers had been doing their portion of the combined work in the most satisfactory manner; and it is hard to say whether as incendiaries or soldiers their services were most useful. In an incredibly short time they had set fire to the whole of the disaffected portion of the town, and destroyed some hundreds of the enemy, fighting their way back to the fort without the loss of a single man. For the next four days advantage was taken of the cool hours in the morning and evening to harass the rebels, until the Moulvie found that the place was too hot to hold him, and made off with his forces. His nephew was taken prisoner by the Sikhs, who had been wrought up to the utmost exasperation by cruelties committed on two or three of their comrades who had strayed into the town. They brought the captive into the fort, when the fellow made a snatch at an officer's sword, with the intention of cutting him down. This was provocation enough to induce his captors to set at nought the rules of war; and they literally trampled him to death.

Up and down the line of road from Allahabad, the gallows and the musket were employed from morning to night. Reinforcements, as they hastened to join the garrison, were continually halted for the purpose of dispersing bands of marauders, the prisoners taken having merely the advantage of an hour's extra existence.

The philosophic native merchants of Calcutta, who may be supposed to know what style of policy is most likely to overawe their countrymen in this emergency, have been heard quietly to observe "that four lacs of people must be killed, after which there will be peace and security as heretofore." There is a large margin of human life as yet to be drawn upon before the slain number four hundred thousand; but we are bound to say that our countrymen are lessening it as industriously as possible.

For several days previous to the outbreak at Cawnpore, the sepoys were evidently unsettled and ripe for mischief. Bungalows were occasionally burnt; and threats of mutiny became so rife in the bazaar, that many of the Europeans left the station. The merchants and shopkeepers, however, remained, with a few exceptions, to watch over their property; and the place contained a large number of women and children belonging to the families of officers and soldiers serving in Lucknow or up-country stations. General Wheeler was warned of his danger, and took such steps to meet it as were in his power.

Within two or three miles of Cawnpore stood the fort and palace of Nana Sahib the Rajah of Bhitoor, the adopted son of the late Bajee Rao, the ex-Peishwa of the Mahrattas. This man had tried to obtain, on the death of his adoptive parent, the reversion of the enormous pension which the latter received from the British Government, and the continuance in his person of the jaghire of Bhitoor. His request has been rejected; and though the enormous wealth left by Bajee Rao, amounting to more than four millions sterling, placed him amongst the first nobles in the country, he conceived a deadly hatred, in consequence, to the British. Having received an English education, he was a frequent visitor at the tables of Europeans of rank, and was in the habit of entertaining them in turn at Bhitoor. With the usual craft of his tribe, he was most profuse in his professions of sympathy and friendship at a time when he had made up his mind to earn for himself the reputation of being the most bloodthirsty enemy of our race; and so far did he impose upon General Wheeler, that the latter, thinking the treasury somewhat unsafe under the care of Sepoys, applied to him for a guard for its protection. This desire was promptly complied with; and a detachment of the Nana's troops, consisting of two guns and two hundred nujeebs armed with matchlocks, were stationed as a guard over the treasury. The sepoys had previously refused to allow the General to remove the treasure to the intrenchments, assuring him that he need not be apprehensive of an attack upon it by the Budmashes of the surrounding country, as they would defend it with their lives. Declarations of loyalty on the part of sepoy regiments have been construed by experience to imply a settled intention to rebel at the first favourable moment; but if poor Sir Hugh Wheeler read the character of his men truly, the knowledge could be of no service to him. He had but two companies of Europeans and eight guns, was short of provisions, and hampered with the presence of a helpless multitude. He took, then, in good part the refusal of the Sepoys to give up the treasure to the collector, and, looking about for such means of defence as were at hand, sat down to await the coming of what might be in store for him. He was not kept long in suspense. On the morning of the 5th of June, the whole of the native troops broke out in open mutiny. They began by burning their lines, and then made for the cutcherry where the treasure was, one of the regiments staying behind to hold Sir Hugh Wheeler in check, and prevent him from sending assistance to the collector. After a while the treasure, amounting to 170,000*l.*, was packed on elephants and carts, the reserve came up; and about midday the whole force, together with the nujeebs and the Nana Sahib's two guns, moved off in the direction of Delhi. Up to this time they had committed no act of violence, and it would appear that the Nana had first meditated a rapid retreat with his plunder to a place of safety; but if so, he soon changed his mind, and returned next morning to Cawnpore, halting within two miles of the intrenchments. His own force was now increased to 600 men with four guns; and the whole body of the mutineers ranged themselves under his authority. Detachments of cavalry were sent into the town and cantonments, to slay all the Europeans, East Indians, and native converts, and set fire to the place. The wind was blowing furiously at the time; and when the houses were fired, a few moments sufficed to set the whole in a blaze. The noise of the wind, the roaring of the fire, the wild cries of the mutineers maddened with excitement and raging for blood, these mingled with oaths and prayers and shrieks of anguish, formed an atmosphere of devilry which few of our countrymen would wish to breathe again. A few of the residents fought with the fury of despair; but they were a handful against many thousands of enemies, and silence gradually settled over the place which a few hours previously was fair and flourishing.

The Nana proclaimed himself by beat of drum sovereign of the Mahrattas, and planted two standards, one for Mahomed, and the other for Huneyman, the monkey god of the Hindoos. Some 2000 Mussulmans repaired to the former; but only a few budmashes took service under the latter. Their next step was to proceed to the palace of the Nawab of Cawnpore, who was suspected of being well affected towards the Europeans. The gates were blown open with cannon, the palace thoroughly ransacked, and the nawab made prisoner, after which they took up a position in front of the intrenchments, and began to cannonade Sir Hugh Wheeler. But one feeble gun was able to reply to the increasing weight of artillery daily brought against the beleaguered garrison; but every time that the rebels attempted an assault, they were invariably beaten back with heavy slaughter. The heroic band daily expected relief, and fought as if the safety of the empire depended on their individual bravery.

Whilst the main body of the Nana's troops closed round the intrenchments, and cut off every avenue of escape, the Nana Sahib whetted his hopes of revenge by daily morsels of pleasant taste and flavour. He was accustomed to send out parties in the district to search for Europeans; and when these were brought in, no matter what their age or sex, the boon of speedy death was never granted.

An English lady with her children had been captured by his bloodhounds, and was led into his presence. Her husband had been murdered on the road, and she implored the Nana for life; but the ruffian ordered them all to be taken to the maidan and killed. On the way the children complained of the sun, and the lady requested they might be taken under the shade of some trees; but no attention was paid to her, and after a time she and her children were tied together and shot, with exception of the youngest, who was crawling over the bodies, and feeling them, and asking them why they had fallen down in the sun. The poor infant was at last killed by a trooper.

To cut off nose and ears, and hang them as necklaces on his poor miserable victims, was one of the mildest punishments inflicted by this gentle and highly educated Hindoo, who, if sufficient time had been allowed him, would have no doubt invented over again all the modes of ancient and modern cruelty. Amongst other strokes of his good fortune was the arrest of a band of fugitives, numbering about 126 souls, who were making their way from Futtyghur in boats on the Ganges. He compelled them to come on shore, promising, as usual, protection for life and property, and, when they were collected together, ordered his men to commence the work of slaughter. The women and children were despatched with swords and spears, the men were ranged in line, with a bamboo running along the whole extent and passing through each man's arms, which were tied behind his back. The troopers then rode round them and taunted their victims, reviling them with the grossest abuse, and gloating over the tortures they were about to inflict. When weary of vituperation, one of them would discharge a pistol in the face of a captive, whose shattered head would droop to the right or left, the body meanwhile being kept upright, and the blood and brains bespattering his living neighbours. The next person selected for slaughter would perhaps be four or five paces distant; and in this way the fiends contrived to prolong for several hours the horrible contact of the dead and the living. Not a soul escaped; and the Nana Sahib thanked the gods of the Hindoos for the sign of favour bestowed upon him.

For twenty-two weary days the little garrison held their

own, full of heart and hope. It was impossible to believe that aid would not come before the hour when the last round should have been fired, and the last ration of food consumed. Lucknow was but fifty miles off; and Lawrence might give up the almost hopeless task of preserving it, and bring a reinforcement sufficient to raise the siege. Delhi, it was thought, must have fallen within a few days after our troops appeared before it; and the first rumour of the approach of the victorious column would scatter the Mahratta and his followers to all points of the compass. Allahabad was but 120 miles distant; and the tramp of British soldiers would be heard some glorious night, hurrying forward to the rescue. Vain hopes! The days went and came and brought no help; and one morning towards the close of June, men whispered to each other in Calcutta that the struggle had terminated, and none were left to tell the tale. The news was carried to Government, who at first affected incredulity, though it afterwards turned out in this, as in other cases, that they were fully informed of the catastrophe, but shrank from revealing it to the public. For the next ten days we were taunted by expectations continually renewed, that the report would be found untrue, until, on the morning of the 7th of July, Lord Canning permitted the following notice to appear in the Calcutta papers. "Allahabad, July 5th. Colonel Neill reports that he had received a note, dated night of the 4th, from Major Renaud, of the Madras Fusiliers, commanding the advance column sent towards Cawnpore, that he had sent men into that place, who reported on their return that, in consequence of Sir Hugh Wheeler being shot through the leg, and afterwards mortally, the force had accepted the proffer of safety made by the Nana Sahib and the mutineers. The Nana allowed them to get into boats, with all they had, and three and a half lacs of rupees, that after getting them in boats, fire was opened on them from the bank, and all were destroyed. One boat got away ten miles down the river, was pursued, brought back, and all in her taken back into barracks and shot. One old lady was alive on the 3rd, at Futtehpore."

Later intelligence furnished some particulars of the last days of the ill-fated garrison. The fire of the enemy was kept up for fourteen days and nights without intermission.

Nunjour Tewarree, a sepoy belonging to the 1st N. I., was at Banda with his regiment, when the mutiny broke out, and he saved the lives of a clerk and his wife, named Duncan Subsequently, he marched with his regiment to Cawnpore, and falling under suspicion on account of his liking for the English, he was confined by Nana Sahib in the same house with the Europeans. His account of the destruction of the party brought back from the boats, should never be perused by those who have the power of influencing the fate of the rebels who may be captured by our troops. To our mind, the story of the Roman senators, sitting at the close of their long lives, each in his post of honour, waiting for the stab of the approaching barbarian, has far less of the heroism of self-sacrifice than the example of those English women at Cawnpore, who, clasping their husbands tenderly, sat ready, with white lips and still hearts, to share with them the first moments of the life beyond the grave.

Relief was sent at last, but too late. The fiery Neill, having quelled mutiny at Benares and punished it at Allahabad, chafed impatiently till a force of men, properly equipped, could be got together for the relief of Cawnpore, but he was not allowed in this instance to follow the impulse of his daring nature. Colonel Havelock had arrived in Calcutta, and the rules of the service would not allow a junior officer to be at the head of an enterprise, however fit he might be to carry it to a successful conclusion. Time was lost to enable Colonel Havelock to join at Allahabad, and on his arrival there a further delay of some days occurred consequent on the receipt of news that Cawnpore had fallen. There were reports of serious misunderstandings between the two officers, but these were got over. Both Havelock and Neill were made brigadier-generals, and the first division of the force, under the command of the former, left Allahabad on the 2nd July, the day on which General Wheeler was murdered and Sir Henry Lawrence mortally wounded.

CHAP. XI.

THE OUTBREAK IN ROHILCUND.—INGRATITUDE AND HATRED OF THE SEPOYS AND POPULACE.—STRANGE CONDUCT OF THE 10TH NATIVE INFANTRY.

The revolt of the troops stationed in Rohilcund was distinguished by instances of singular baseness and treachery. The force consisted of the 8th Irregular Cavalry, 16th and 68th N. I., 6th company 8th battalion Native Foot Artillery, and No. 15 Light Horse Field Battery, stationed at Bareilly; a detail of Native Foot Artillery, and the 29th Native Infantry, at Moradabad; the 28th Native Infantry, and a detail of Native Artillery, at Shahjehanpore; the 66th Ghoorkas, and the 3rd company 8th battalion Native Artillery, at Almuch; the whole amounting to about six thousand men, Of these all but the Ghoorkas at Almorah rebelled on the 30th and 31st of May.

The news of the outbreaks at Meerut and Delhi caused, of course, great excitement amongst the Sepoys in every station throughout India; and Bareilly, which is only 152 miles from the first-named place, felt the full force of the mutinous wave. The 8th Irregulars were nearly all Pathans, from the neighbourhood of Delhi, and caught the infection at once; but still the authorities were convinced that, should the service of the troops be required, they "would act as good and loyal soldiers." Brigadier Sibbald wrote to Calcutta on the 23rd of May, that they "were labouring under a great depression of spirits, caused by the fear of some heavy punishment they imagined Government was about to inflict upon them." He remarked that no open act of theirs had rendered them liable to punishment; and at a general parade addressed them on the subject, spoke of the good and sustained intentions of Government towards them, and begged of them to dismiss from their minds the causeless dread that pervaded them. The brigade received these assurances with the greatest apparent satisfaction. The native officers told him that they had "commenced a new life," and in the fulness of his heart he added in a postscript to his despatch: "I cannot say too much in praise of the 8th Irregular Cavalry; their conduct is beyond praise, and I should feel much gratified should Government consider them worthy of their thanks." The Government did thank them. Mr. Colvin authorised the brigadier to assure them publicly, that "nothing that had happened since the commencement of the recent agitation, had at all shaken his solid confidence in their fidelity and good conduct." He was glad that the strength of the Cavalry had been increased, and wished to know what officers and men could be recommended for promotion. The despatch was sent off in due course, and twenty-four hours afterwards, whilst the Sunday chimes were ringing, the brigadier was lying heedless in the sun, shot through the heart by the very men whose welfare he was so anxious to promote.

The European officers, with one exception, shared unanimously in the confidence felt by the brigadier, until the very moment of the outbreak. It was but of little use for military men to encourage misgivings, for they were tied to the stake, and must wait till the signal was given for their massacre. The Sepoys took every precaution that they could think of, both to avoid giving alarm and to increase the number of their victims. When they had laid all their plans, and placed men under a bridge to murder such of the English as might chance to pass that way; had blocked up the Futteghur road, and told off two companies to surround the house of the commanding officer of the 68th, they spoke to their officers about bringing back the women and children who had been sent to the hills on the first symptoms of discontent being visible. All was quiet now they said, and signs of distrust injured the good name of the regiment!

There were not, however, wanting some who were faithful to the oaths. The havildar-major of the 68th was sent by the subadar-major on the 29th of May to inform Colonel Troup, his commanding officer, that, whilst bathing in the river that morning, the men of the 18th and 68th had sworn to rise at 2 o'clock that day, and murder their officers. The Commissioner of Rohilcund, Mr. Alexander, had news to the same effect, and all the Europeans in the station were duly warned of their danger. The cavalry were assembled, they seemed apparently well affected, and the day passed over without any disturbance. The next day, Colonel Troup was informed, that the troopers had sworn not to act against the artillery and infantry, but that they would not harm nor raise their hand against any European. Still his tidings and his apprehensions were ridiculed. The commanding officer of the artillery was certain that there was no cause to doubt his men, though he was told that his pay havildar had addressed a letter to the 18th and 68th, calling upon them in the most urgent terms to rise and murder their officers. If they neglected this sacred duty, the writer said, the Hindoos were to consider that they had eaten beef, and the Mussulmans that they had tasted pork. With equal blindness, Major Pearson commanding the 18th N. I. asserted, at 8 A. M. on the 31st, that his men "were all right, and that he had every confidence in them." At 11 o'clock he had shared the fate of Brigadier Sibbald.

Neither the Government at Calcutta, nor Mr. Colvin, saw any mischief in allowing thousands of disbanded soldiers to wander about the country. It was so much money saved in the monthly pay accounts, and the appearance of the men in the stations and villages, instead of being an incentive to mutiny, would be a warning against the consequences of it. The fugitives from other corps passed through Bareilly in great numbers just before the outbreak, and influenced the minds of the men by all kinds of stories with reference to the intended destruction of caste, and the advance of European troops to destroy all who refused to obey. These rumours were confirmed by the Sepoys of the Bareilly regiments on their return from furlough about the same time, and at last a rising was determined upon. On the Sunday orning appointed for the revolt, the Sepoys abstained from going to bathe as usual, on the avowed plea that they would be wanted in their lines at 11 o'clock, and precisely at that hour, a gun was fired by the artillery, and the whole of the cantonment was at once in arms. The guns were turned on the officers' houses, and the Sepoys spread themselves in skirmishing order with the view of hindering the escape of any whom they had marked for slaughter. The sentry over the mess room of the 18th fired at the officer whom he had just saluted. Those who were fortunate enough to make their way to the cavalry lines thought they were safe, and after a time spent in deliberation, during which the work of murder and destruction was going on, it was decided that they should make their way to the hill station of Nynee Tal, distant about ninety miles. The cavalry accompanied them for some miles, and then asked to be allowed to turn and charge the mutineers. Permission was given as a matter of course, and under the command of Captain Mackenzie, they rode back till they reached the rebels, who had a gun and a green flag. They were ordered to charge, but the sight of the symbol of their faith was too much for their lingering feelings of loyalty. They halted and began to murmur, ending the parley by turning their horses' heads and ranging themselves on the side of the mutineers. The gun was now brought to bear on the little group that still closed round their officers, and they were told to ride for their lives, a suggestion which they were not slow in obeying. When the mutiny was complete, an artillery subadar was made commander-in-chief of Rohilcund, and a rajah was found in the person of a retired company's judge, Khan Bahadoor. This man, who was in receipt of a considerable pension, turned to account, like the Sepoys, the knowledge he had obtained whilst in the service of Government. He seized Messrs. Raikes and Robertson, the judges of Bareilly, and having tried them in due form, had them found guilty of heinous offences, and hung. The same fate was inflicted on

Mr. Wyatt, the deputy collector, author of "Panch Kouri Khan," the Indian Gil Blas, and upon many others.

The 19th rose at Shahjehanpore on the same day, and surrounding the church whilst divine service was being performed, they butchered the greater part of the congregation, and murdered the remainder in the course of their flight from the station. The 29th, at Mooradabad, remained quiet till the 3rd June, and then followed in the wake of rebellion. They had previously done excellent service against the mutineers throughout the district, but the cause of the Sepoys had become national, and they were bound to support it. A little while, and they would neither have pay nor plunder; the sahib logue would be driven out of the country, and rational Sepoys would enjoy their wealth. Actuated, then, by considerations of religion and rupees, they made for the treasury on the morning in question, but finding only 25,000*l.*, they were about to blow the treasurer away from a gun, when the judge and the collector interfered. Baulked of their plunder and prey at the same moment, the Sepoys were furious. They presented their muskets at the two civilians, and would have shot them, had not two native officers rushed forwards and reminded them that they had sworn on the Ganges water, not to touch a hair on the head of any European. The sanctity of the oath was sullenly admitted, and the Sepoys retired with their booty, giving the residents two hours to leave the station. A detachment of the 8th Irregulars formed part of the troops at Mooradabad, but these instead of imitating the example of the rest of the regiment, mounted, and rode off with the civilians and ladies to Nynee Tal. The officers of the 29th were afterwards escorted by a part of the regiment to the same station, not a man being injured in any way.

The Bareilly mutineers were six weeks on their way to Delhi. They made for the Ganges at Gurmuckteser, but the river was swollen, and they had to wait for the means of crossing. They had with them 700 carts laden with treasure, the plunder of all the treasuries of Rohilcund, and twelve miles off lay more than a thousand English soldiers, but under the orders of General Hewitt. It is said that an officer offered to prevent them from crossing, if the general would only give him fifty men; but that would have left only eleven hundred and fifty for the defence of the station against the bad characters of the surrounding country, and the gallant chief felt that he could not run such a risk. After staying some days at the Ghaut, one of the rebels swam across, and seized a small boat. By the aid of the party whom he ferried over, two more boats were gained, and the three sufficed to transport the whole three thousand men, with their wealth and stores. The work was done leisurely, there being no need to hurry the operation.

In no instance, perhaps, has the waywardness and inexplicable nature of the Bengal Sepoys been more fully exhibited than in the case of the 10th N. I. stationed at Futtehghur. Children in impulse and tigers at heart, swayed by a breath and deaf to the most exciting appeals, we find them at one moment standing up for their officers against all comers, and willing to incur all risks in their behalf, and at the next, without an atom of provocation, readily joining to murder them and their helpless little ones.

The following striking narrative from the pen of a correspondent of the Mofusillite, will enable our readers to gain an idea of the labour and anxiety requisite to keep a "staunch" regiment in the right path. The conclusion of the story, which we supply from other sources, is no less tragical than that of a score of other episodes of Sepoy fidelity: —

"All was right at Futtehghur up to the 3rd June. The residents were much alarmed, and many had provided boats in which to slip away after the regiment had mutinied and were looting the place, which they appeared to think an inevitable event. The slightest rumours were believed and repeated with additions, and as the news reached of mutiny at Lucknow, and massacre at Shahjehanpore, the panic was at its height, and many families slept in their boats on the evening of the 1st and 2nd. On the afternoon of the 3rd, information was received of the arrival of a party of insurgents at Goosaingunge, where they burnt the Dak bungalow and the house of the Tehseeldar. The civil residents all rushed to the boats. Colonel Smith and the officers of the 10th N. I. went into the lines to be with their men, and resolved not to leave them a moment. The roads were blocked up with hackeries, &c., and the regiment was ready to turn out, and proceed to any point at which danger might appear. The night passed over quietly. When the sun rose the station was deserted, and the fleet of boats was gone. About 12 P. M. a village was seen burning on the other side of the river, and the natives say, that then were the anchors weighed and the sails shaken out to the wind. It was necessary to make arrangements for the care of public property. The Treasury, with two and a half lacs, was taken care of and removed to the Fort. The clothing agency, containing stores of cloth, worth several lacs of rupees, was looked after, as well as the jail, containing upwards of a thousand prisoners. News came in during the day that the mutineers had advanced about six miles towards Futtehghur, but on hearing that the 'old Duffels,' who are looked upon almost as infidels for having volunteered to proceed to Burmah, were anxious 'to look them in the face,' they turned off towards Chilbranow for Delhi. The treasure was conveyed to the Fort about 9 A. M., when, from some misunderstanding, contrary orders, or something, we cannot tell what, there was a little disturbance in the lines, and down rushed a party to bring it back *vi et armis;* the officers accompanying, trying to restrain them. Colonel Smith had ridden down with the treasure; when he saw the excited state of the men, he very wisely gave way; they merely said, they would protect it and the regimental colours in the open air, but would not be cooped up in a fort. All went back, men, officers, and treasure, without any mischief having been done, but not without creating alarm, as we shall see presently. It had been arranged, between the magistrate and colonel, that the men should have an advance of pay, but Monday and Tuesday having been native holidays they had not received it.

"Captain Vibart, of the 2nd Light Cavalry, who was on his way from the hills to Cawnpore, volunteered his services to Colonel Smith, and he was put in charge of the Treasury and jail. The business of getting an advance of pay gave employment to the minds of the men, and when they were a little quiet, the colonel mounted a rostrum, and addressed them on their conduct in the morning. The old Sepoys hung their heads with shame, and laid the blame on the young lads of the regiment. All promised nothing of the kind should occur again. Towards afternoon the men were once more shaken, by discovering that during the tamasha in the morning, no less than four of their officers had disappeared, deserted their posts in the hour of danger, when the commanding officer required all the assistance which could be rendered to him. The Sepoys became suspicious of being deserted by all their officers, and watched their movements like cats watching mice. Everything was done to reassure them, the officers walked about and talked. Some of the ladies drove on to the parade, to show that they were not gone with the fleet, and the men became satisfied once more. Had this regiment behaved ill, it would have been caused by the civilians deserting their posts; and that they were kept quiet, was entirely through the admirable coolness, tact, and discretion shown by Colonel Smith, and the fact of the officers having never left their men for a moment since Wednesday evening. We have had alarms and reports without end, but through the blessing of God, all is quiet; and if He gives quietness, who then can make trouble? We expected that the budmashes, from across the river and the neighbouring villages and the city, would take advantage of the unprotected state of the station, and fire the bungalows. Nothing of the kind has occurred. A few things from Maharajah Dhuleep Sing's estate have been plundered, as the park ranger bolted, leaving everything to its fate; and we have sustained an irreparable loss in our poet, who is gone we know not where. Perhaps our fugitive may turn up in time at Cawnpore, and they may be glad to hear through your columns that their property is, up to the present moment all safe. We have had no Daks in for several days, and know nothing of what is going on in the neighbouring stations.

"June 6th.—All right. Sepoys this morning, of their own accord, on the parade, swore on Gunga Panee and Koran respectively, to be true to their salt, never to desert their four colours, and to protect the officers who have been faithful to them, with their lives.

"The names of the four officers have been removed from the rolls of the regiment, as being 'absent without leave.' A considerable quantity of the Maharajah's property has been found in the possession of his mootsuddie; he stole the property, and then reported that the place had been looted by the Sepoys. Six P.M., all quiet. The old Sepoys have come to an understanding with the young hands, informing them that if they do anything to injure the character and name of the regiment, they will themselves shoot the youngsters without ceremony.

"Sunday passed over quietly. Heard that some of the fugitives had taken refuge with Hurdeo Buxsh, a zemindar of Kussowra, and that the rest had gone on to Cawnpore.

"Monday morning, 8th.—The prisoners have refused for several nights to be locked up. Many have got rid of their irons, and some of the worst characters were exciting the rest to resist authority. They pulled down some brick work, and were pelting the Sepoys, when Captain Vibart went down. He told them to go into their sleeping cells, or he would make them. They begged him to try it on, saluted him with a shower of bricks, and called down blessings on himself and family in the native fashion. The Sepoys fired; and after compelling them to take refuge inside, they brought out the ringleaders and shot them. Two were under sentence of death—and the object was attained at the smallest possible expenditure of life: only sixteen killed; but these were the greatest budmashes in the jail. The prisoners are all quiet, submitting to be re-ironed; happy, and looking as if nothing had occurred. The Sepoys were as obedient as a well-ordered family. They fired when ordered—ceased firing when bidden, and would have shot every prisoner there at the command of their officer.

"Jail continues quiet. We are all, Sepoys, officers, ladies, and children, in good health and spirits, and are truly grateful to God for all his late mercies vouchsafed to us."

Ten days after the last entry in the above journal, the faithful 10th had joined the 40th. Many of them, after sharing the plunder of the regimental chest and the treasury, went to their homes, but a part of both regiments united in an attack upon the entrenchment in which the Europeans took refuge. For eight days the little band of Englishmen fought without an hour's intermission, and had they continued the defence, their lives would probably have been saved, as they had thoroughly cowed their assailants, whose ammunition also failed; but want of rest and the loss of their best men disheartened them, and on the night of the 4th of July, they left the fort and dropped down the river. Their flight was perceived, and the enemy followed in large boats. Numbers were killed by the fire of the rebels, or drowned in the attempt to escape, but the bulk of the party got away, and were induced by the promises of Nana Sahib to land at Bhitoor. We have already chronicled their fate in one of the darkest pages of the catalogue of Hindoo iniquity.

CHAP. XII.

A CONVINCING ORATOR.—MR. COLVIN'S PROCLAMATION AND DEATH.—MUTINIES IN RAJPOOTANA.

THE 9th N. I., stationed at Allygurh, about thirty miles south of Delhi, revolted on the 19th of May. They had been tempted to rise by a religious mendicant; but two of the men to whom he addressed himself, took him prisoner, and carried him before the commanding officer, who ordered a court-martial to sit upon him instantly. The proofs of guilt were clear, and the sentence of death was ordered to be carried out next morning. At the appointed time the regiment paraded, and the criminal was brought out and hung, no man appearing to feel aggrieved at his fate; but before they were marched off the ground, the rifle company, which had just been relieved from the outpost of Bolundshur, made their appearance, and a Brahmin Sepoy, stepping out from the ranks, began to harangue his comrades on their cowardly wickedness in having betrayed to death a holy man, who came to save them from disgrace in this world and eternal perdition in the next. Some commanding officers would, perhaps, have shot the incendiary on the spot; but in this case the fighting priest was allowed to finish his speech, and when he had made an end, the whole corps were converted to his way of thinking. They seized the treasury, broke open the gaol, and ordered all their officers to decamp instantly, on pain of death, doing, however, no bodily harm to any of them. The next that was heard of them was communicated from Delhi, where the regimental number of the 9th was found on the bodies of some of the most daring assailants of the British army.

The regiments stationed at Agrâ were the 3rd Europeans, and the 44th and 67th N. I. The Lieutenant-Governor, writing on the 22nd of May, was of opinion that things would remain quiet in the capital of the North West, though he believed that if they were left to themselves, or were to meet with the mutineers, the Sepoys would sympathise, and unite themselves with the revolt. There had been a great deal of excitement amongst them, and they had undoubtedly been inflamed by a deep distrust of our purpose. "The general scope of the notion by which they have been influenced," said Mr. Colvin, "may be expressed in the remarks of one of them, a Hindoo, Tewarree Brahmin, to the effect that "men were created of different faiths, and that the notion attributed to us, of having but one religion, because we had now but one uninterrupted dominion throughout India, was a tyrannical and impious one." Mr. Colvin, who saw even clearer than General Hearsey the character of the prevailing delusion, entertained a different opinion from that of the gallant officer, with regard to the possibility of eradicating it. He held a parade of the troops on the 13th of May, and spoke to them in a familiar-way, several times afterwards, upon the subject of the mania that had seized them, and offered to give discharges to any who were still dissatisfied on the subject. "They all at the moment," declared themselves content with the explanations given, but little impression was made upon them in reality, as was shown eight days afterwards, when a company of each regiment rose at Muttra, thirty-six miles from Agra, murdered their officers, burnt the cantonments, and plundered the treasury of 70,000*l.* This occurrence put an end of course to any doubts concerning the course that ought to be pursued; and next day the two regiments were assembled on the parade ground at Agra and disarmed, an indignity to which they submitted with great reluctance. Mr. Colvin was weak enough to grant furloughs to such as chose to ask for them, which of course included the whole body. Three days' march brought them to Delhi, where there were arms in abundance, so that the saving of two thousand muskets was all that could be claimed for the cause of law and order.

This appears to have been the last public service that Mr. Colvin performed. Under the pressure of a great emergency, which he saw no means of meeting, his energies gave way, and he ceased to influence the character of public events. He took no pains to keep open a communication with Delhi, which could have been easily arranged for, or to knit together the severed strands of authority in any portion of the extensive country under his care. He felt deeply the censure cast upon him by Lord Canning, for issuing his famous proclamation of pardon to the mutineers; but if he erred on the side of mercy, his policy had at least this advantage over that of Lord Canning, that it was suggested fourteen days and not three months, after the first outbreak of rebellion. On the 24th of May he wrote: "On the mode of dealing with the mutineers, I would strenuously oppose general severity towards all. Such a course would, as we are unanimously convinced by a knowledge of the feelings of the people, acquired amongst them from a variety of sources, estrange the remainder of the army. Hope, I am firmly convinced, should be held out to all those who were not ringleaders or actively concerned in murder and violence. Many are in the rebels' ranks because they could not get away; many certainly thought we were tricking them out of their caste; and this opinion is held, however unwisely, by the mass of the population, and even by some of the more intelligent classes. Never was delusion more wide or deep. Many of the best soldiers in the army, amongst others, of its most faithful section, the Irregular Cavalry, show a marked reluctance to engage in a war against men whom they believe to have been misled on the point of religious honour. A tone of general menace would, I am persuaded, be wrong. The Commander-in-Chief should, in my view, be authorised to act upon the above line of policy; and, where means of escape are thus open to those who can be admitted to mercy, the remnant will be considered obstinate traitors, even by their own countrymen, who will have no hesitation in aiding against them. I request the earliest answer to this message. The subject is of vital and pressing importance."

The following day Mr. Colvin, alarmed by the defection of a part of the 1st Gwalior Cavalry, his only effective horse, whose flight to Delhi "severely complicated his position," impressed by his knowledge of native feelings, and "supported by the unanimous opinion of all officers of experience" in Agra, took upon himself to issue the following proclamation, "under the belief that severity would be useless, and with the view of giving a favourable turn to the feelings of the Sepoys who had not as yet entered against us." A weighty reason was the total dissolution of order, and the loss of any means of control in every district. His latest letter from Meerut was seven days old, and he had not received a line from General Anson.

"Soldiers engaged in the late disturbances, who are desirous of going to their own homes, and who give up their arms at the nearest Government civil or military post and retire quietly, shall be permitted to do so unmolested.

"Many faithful soldiers have been driven into resistance to Government only because they were in the ranks and could not escape from them, and because they really thought their feelings of religion and honour injured by the measures of Government. This feeling was wholly a mistake, but it acted on men's minds. A proclamation of the Governor-General now issued is perfectly explicit, and will remove all doubt on these points. Every evil-minded instigator in the disturbance, and those guilty of heinous crimes against private persons, shall be punished. All those who appear in arms against the Government after this notification is known, shall be treated as open enemies."

The Governor-General telegraphed the next day to stop the issue of the proclamation and do everything to check its operation, except in the cases of those who might have already taken advantage of it. An improved proclamation was substituted, consisting of a preamble and three paragraphs, as follows:—"The Governor-General of India in Council considers that the proclamation issued at Agra on the 25th instant, and addressed to those soldiers who have been engaged in the late disturbances, might be so interpreted as to lead many who have been guilty of the most atrocious crimes to expect that they will be allowed to escape unpunished. Therefore, to avoid all risk of such misinterpretation, that proclamation is annulled by the Governor-General in Council, who declares as follows: —

"Every soldier of a regiment which, although it has deserted its post, has not committed outrages, will receive free pardon, if he immediately deliver up his arms to the civil or military authority, and if no heinous crimes be shown to have been perpetrated by himself personally.

"This offer of free and unconditional pardon cannot be extended to those regiments which have killed or wounded their officers or other persons, or which have been concerned in the commission of cruel outrages. The men of such regiments must submit themselves unconditionally to the authority and justice of the Government of India.

"All who before the promulgation of this present proclamation may have availed themselves of the offer contained in the proclamation issued at Agra on the 25th instant, will enjoy the full and unreserved benefit thereof."

In his reply to this message, Mr. Colvin begged that the preamble of the amended proclamation might be omitted, on the plea that openly to undo any public act of his, where really no substantial change was made, as in this case, would fatally shake his power for good. "His time," he said, "was torn by a thousand distractions," and he could not always frame his words as perfectly as he could wish. The request was acceded to, and a mere notification made at the end of the new proclamation, that all former offers of pardon by local authorities were cancelled; but, as it turned out, both announcements were only waste paper. Not a man ever came forward to claim the benefit of the greater or the lesser act of grace. Two months later, Lord Canning, when he had exhausted the utility of hanging and blowing away from guns, tried his sole hand at conciliation, and was not more successful than Mr. Colvin had been. It was his lot never to excite gratitude or fear.

The framework of society in the North-West fell to pieces, and men held life and land by the law of the strongest. The zemindars and the village communities who had been dispossessed of their estates or holdings by civil suits, entered again into possession. Old feuds were recollected and avenged. Old landmarks were everywhere obliterated. Settlements and title-deeds, the record of the decree and the property which it represented, were swept away. Government had no existence, and order no rallying point. The ruler of thirty millions of souls had no voice for good or evil, except within the boundaries of Agra, and those were soon to be contracted to the narrowest space. After leading for some weeks a harassed life in the city, and virtually losing a battle without the walls, Mr. Colvin saw the gaol opened and its population of three thousand let loose over the country, the cantonment burnt, and the town sacked; and then, betaking himself to the fort, was doubtless glad when death came and brought oblivion of the world's troubles. He died on the 9th of September last, loved and respected as an individual, but not missed as a statesman.

The 15th and 30th N. I. mutinied at Nusseerabad on the 28th of May. They were counted amongst the most faithful soldiers of the state, and there was not an officer with them who would not have vouched for their honesty under any circumstances. That quality had been often praised by their superiors; but it was not of a very durable kind, seeing that the two corps rose in rebellion a fortnight after the news of the Delhi outbreak had been received at the station. The 15th were the first to commence, and seized the guns, which were charged by the 1st Bombay Lancers, but without effect. Four officers of the latter were killed and wounded, but none of the men, — a fact which can only be accounted for under the idea that it was understood that the cavalry should not take the guns and that the Sepoys should not fire on the horsemen. After the 15th had been firing at their officers for a couple of hours, and had burnt the cantonment and threatened to attack the 30th, whom they adjured by every sacred tie to fight for their religion, the latter got tired of holding out, and took part in the revolt. The colonel summoned the European and native officers to the front, and the latter begged of them to fly with all haste. There was no other course to pursue; and the Europeans made off to Beawr, where some of the 30th came a few days afterwards, and laid down their arms. When the officers left, the villagers made their appearance in armed gangs, and plundered the station. The two regiments, with six guns, subsequently made their way to Delhi.

The Neemuch brigade mutinied on the 3rd of June. They consisted of the 4th troop, 1st brigade of Native Horse Artillery, the left wing of the 1st Cavalry, 72nd N. I., and the 7th Regiment of the Gwalior Contingent. For some days the force had been in a state of great agitation; and the people in the bazaar fled in crowds on the 30th, believing that the Sepoys had risen. Their fears were, however, quieted; and Colonel Abbott, commanding the 72nd, held a durbar on the 2nd of June, which was attended by all the officers of the native regiments. In answer to his remonstrances, they assured him that the effervescence had entirely subsided and that all were perfectly quiet, including the artillery, who had repacked the ammunition which they took out of the limbers that morning. They were dismissed with injunctions to take care of their men; but, at eleven o'clock the next morning, the signal guns were fired, and in a very short time the cantonment was in flames. The Sepoys closed round the officers and their families, who were advised to go into the house of a jemadar in the lines, with a view, as they afterwards thought, of keeping them together till the word was given to murder them; but one of the native officers came into the place, from which he turned them out, and told them to hasten away for their lives. They took the advice, and, accompanied by a handful of faithful men, reached a place of safety. The rebels joined the Nusseerabad troops, and carried the guns and the treasure to Delhi.

At Nagpore a plot, which had been in agitation for three

months, for the murder of every European in the station, was discovered just as it was about to be carried into execution. The conspirators had organised all the details of the rising and posted the men who were to carry out the design.

One of the Rissalah, the authors of the plot, had been sent to endeavour to induce the 1st N. I. to join them; but they, true to their salt, resisted the temptation, seized and confined the tempter, and spread the alarm. The ringleaders were instantly apprised of the discovery, and two of them hastened to the houses of the European officers to give the alarm, hoping by this stratagem to elude detection. The alarm was given on the night of the 13th of June, and the massacre was to have commenced an hour or two afterwards. Of course, immediate steps were taken to guard against the consequences of an attack. The 32nd N.I., which had marched to Kamptee, together with detachments of artillery and cavalry, was recalled. The arsenal, which contained an immense quantity of arms and warlike stores, was guarded by only fifty Madras Sepoys, who were now strengthened, and guns, double-shotted with canister, were placed in position. Thirty thousand pounds of powder were destroyed, to prevent its falling into the hands of the insurgents. The Seetabuldee hill, which the Commissioner had wished to dismantle, was hastily occupied, and its guns, commanding the city as well as the treasury and arsenal, overawed the conspirators, who had counted upon finding the Europeans an easy prey. So confident were they of success that they had allotted amongst themselves the wives of their intended victims, and settled the proportion in which the treasure, amounting to about 150,000*l.*, should be distributed. On the 17th of June, the irregulars were disarmed without resistance; and a proclamation was issued, ordering the inhabitants to give up their arms within five days. More troops arrived at the station soon afterwards, and the leaders were tried and hung, not a hand being raised in their behalf, though there could be no doubt that they had the sympathies of nearly the entire population. No further attempt at revolt was made in the capital of Nagpore.

At Saugor, the 3rd Irregular, 31st, and 42nd N. I., were stationed under the command of Brigadier Sage. He had a company of European artillery, and a number of officers, unable of course to make any effectual resistance. On the 29th of June the Brigadier moved into the fort with his guns and the whole of the European population. The native soldiery took advantage of the absence of control to loot the treasury and cantonments. The Brigadier was too weak to go out and attack them, and was afraid that if he fired from the fort the walls would fall down from the concussion. In this emergency, he called in all the officers, the Sepoys of the 31st loudly complaining of the desertion of their natural leaders. They said they were desirous of doing their duty, and gave the most signal proof to that effect by attacking the 42nd ten days afterwards. Not an officer of the corps was present; but with the aid of forty troopers who remained faithful, and four Englishmen, who joined them and brought some chuprassies to assist, the 31st utterly routed the rest of the rebels, inflicting great loss upon them, and captured a large gun and some elephants, which they gave up to the authorities. The Sepoy character is inexplicable enough at all times, but here was a new phase of it.

CHAP. XIII.

THE ADMINISTRATION OF THE PUNJAUB.—LORD CANNING AND SIR JOHN LAWRENCE.—THE ORGANISATION OF THE SIKHS.

THE difference between Lord Canning and Sir John Lawrence lies simply in this, that the one never succeeded, and the other never failed, in anything he undertook. The contrast of the two men exhibits something marvellous. But for Sir John Lawrence, Delhi would not have been taken; but for Lord Canning, Cawnpore would not have fallen. The one creates means, the other only dissipates them. The one finds everything within his own brain, the other can glean nothing from the whole outside world.

At the time of the Meerut revolt, there were eight British, and twenty-five native regiments in the Punjaub. The former were nearly all sent on to Delhi, the latter entirely broken up or disarmed, and not above a dozen European lives have been taken by mutineers except in fair fight with our countrymen.

Three days after the outbreak at Meerut, the 45th and 57th N. I. rose in mutiny at Ferozepore. They had previously avowed their determination not to use any more of the cartridges, and the news of what had occurred found them ready to be up and doing in imitation of their gallant black brethren; but happily there was no second General Hewitt to be dealt with on this occasion. The signs of insubordination had not escaped the notice of the military chiefs, who wisely prepared at once for the worst. There was only one corps of Europeans in the station, H. M. 61st; but this, with the European artillery, was quite sufficient to vindicate the claims of justice. As a preliminary step, the wives and children of Europeans were ordered into the intrenched magazine; and this being done, the two regiments were paraded and ordered to march to their respective cantonments. They refused to obey, and made for the magazine, a company of the 57th N. I., on duty inside, throwing over ladders and ropes to assist them in scaling the outer walls. Three hundred of the rebels made their way to the interior, and with loud shouts rushed to the ordnance stores; but a company of the Queen's troops stood in the way. A detachment of five files fired, and knocked over six of the assailants; and the remainder required no second reason for getting out of harm's way. They next tried to get in the rear of the little band, but with no better success, and were soon flying in all directions. Now and then clusters of the Sepoys outside would be seen crawling on the top of the walls like beetles, but only to be brushed away with the butt-ends of the European muskets. The party inside who had invited their appearance, were of course disgusted with this summary mode of extinguishing a plot that had cost some trouble in hatching, and prepared to do battle with the delighted Englishmen; but the sight of the levelled muskets, backed by Lieut. Angelo's two guns loaded with grape, quelled their ardour, and they promptly flung down their arms and were marched out. Before the night set in the contest was over; the magazines of the mutineers were blown up by the artillery. The 57th were entirely disarmed, and 200 of the 45th sent in their arms and colours. The next day the rebels avenged themselves by recommencing the task of burning the bungalows; but that was soon put a stop to. The 10th cavalry who stood firm throughout the affair, and the 61st, cut them up in all directions. The country round about Ferozepore is a level plain for many miles, and afforded no cover to impede the pursuers. For weeks after the occurrence of the mutiny, fugitives from the 45th were either killed daily, or brought in to meet the scarcely less inevitable doom. The last notice in connection with the above corps is that of a general parade being ordered at Ferozepore, when twenty-four mutineers were brought out to undergo the punishment for their crime. Twelve of them purchased life by consenting to give information against their accomplices; and of the remaining moiety, two were hanged, and the rest blown away from guns. A few of the rebels, no doubt, made their way to Delhi; but between the Queen's troops and the 45th and 57th N. I. the balance of mischief inflicted was vastly on the side of the former.

At Mean Meer, where the 16th, 26th, and 40th N.I., with the 8th Cavalry, plotted to murder the Europeans and obtain possession of the fort, the plan of operations for their defeat was carried out, whilst the wives and daughters of the good folks of Lahore were enjoying themselves at a ball. Europeans were marched down to the fort instead of the expected native relief; the guards were turned out and disarmed, and the rest of the bewildered conspirators were deprived of the means of doing mischief before they could realise the fact that their plot had got wind. At Peshawur, Colonel Edwardes disarmed the 21st, 24th, 27th, 51st N.I., and the 5th Cavalry, without a drop of blood shed. The 55th mutinied, and took possession of Murdaun, which they were soon glad to evacuate. A hundred of them, flying to the Swat hills for protection against the proselytising English, were compensated by being forcibly converted to Mussulmans at the hands of their humorous entertainers. The revolt of the 3rd N. I. at Phillour completed the catalogue of Sepoy crime in the Punjaub for the month of May, and up to that period not a single European had been murdered.

June opened in the Punjaub with the revolt of the 64th at Peshawur, who were disarmed without difficulty, the good work being followed by the disarming of the 62nd and 69th at Mooltan. The Jullunder force, consisting of the 36th and 61st N. I. and the 6th Cavalry, rose on the 8th of June. At Phillour they were joined by the 3rd N. I., and the united force made off to Delhi by forced marches. Brigadier Johnstone, commanding at Jullunder, left the station after the rebels quitted it, and took the same road; but it would be wrong to say that he pursued them. He made slow marches whilst they went at the top of their speed. He was able to miss his way once or twice, and finally ceased to go in the same direction. After a day or two the mutineers turned towards Delhi, the Europeans went back to their posts, and Brigadier Johnstone retired to the hills to take the repose that was needful for him. Mr. Ricketts, of the civil service, attacked the rebel column with a few Sikhs and newly raised levies, but could only exhibit on a small scale the effect that might have been produced by vigorous measures on the part of the Brigadier. The fugitives held on their way with unabated speed, and finally reached Delhi.

Whilst the Sepoys of the Barrackpore division were offering their red coats for sale in the streets of Calcutta opposite the very windows of Government House, and were deserting unmolested in batches, Sir John Lawrence was blowing their fellow soldiers away from guns for no heavier offence. He adopted, at the very outset, the line of policy which has made his name as famous amongst the people of England as it had hitherto been famous amongst the Indian nations. No trust in professions of loyalty, no mercy for signs of disaffection, were the axioms which he had laid down for the guidance of his subordinates. He knew that the Hindostanees were not to be relied upon, and that the British troops were far too few even to hold the Punjaub in the face of a rebel population in arms. The only course then was to call upon the Sikhs and exhibit to them an enemy whom they despised as well as hated. Fierce as was the animosity with which the soldiers of Runjeet Singh regarded the terrible race who had scattered to the winds their hopes of universal mastery in Hindostan, they regarded the Brahmin and Rajpoot Sepoys with a far deeper antipathy. The Sikh felt that these men, who for bravery and endurance were not to be compared with himself, were the natural aristocracy of his race, who looked upon himself as an unclean thing, and he hated them, as democrats hate a scornful noble, as sectarians in religion hate each other. The value of such antagonism was soon developed. When the 55th mutinied, the whole regiment were of course deprived of their arms; but the Sikh recruits, only a hundred in number, offered to fight the rest of the corps, if the officers would let them have their muskets back again. They were immediately reinstated, and from that hour to the present there has been no cause to regret the reliance placed on Sikh fidelity. The occupation of hunting down Sepoys in the Punjaub or elsewhere has, to be sure, been a profitable one. Where the mutineer had shared in the plunder of the treasuries, he paid his heirs and executors liberally enough for their trouble of killing; when he had merely broken bounds and went off to join the main body, the Government gave *5l.* for him if caught with arms, and half that sum if captured without them: and the King of Delhi was silly enough to aid our policy by inflicting cruel tortures on the Sikhs who fell into his hands. Some of these were sent into General Barnard's camp, frightfully mutilated, as a challenge and a warning to the inhabitants of the Punjaub. The Sikhs, who feel as one man, swore to have vengeance; and they have kept their oaths.

The 10th Irregulars were disarmed at Nowshera on the 26th of June. Their arms and horses, the latter their own property, were taken from them, and, under a guard of levies, they were dismissed to their homes, remorseful and ruined. At Jhelum the 14th were summoned to lay down their arms, but resisted and fought desperately, inflicting a heavy loss upon the detachment of Europeans who attacked them. They were, however, driven out of the station, and cut to pieces in a great measure by the people of the country; but very few finding their way to the rebel head-quarters. The mutiny of the 46th at Sealkote was more signally punished. The corps rose as if by an uncontrollable impulse, killed the Brigadier-Colonel Brind and some other officers, and took to flight. On the 12th July they were encountered by the moveable column under Brigadier Nicholson, routed after a short engagement, and compelled to betake themselves to an island in the Ravee, from which they escaped only to be hunted to death by the armed Sikhs or the eager population of the district. The corps was literally exterminated.

The mutiny of the 10th Cavalry at Peshawur, on the 10th of August, was the last instance of rebellion in the Punjaub. They killed a single officer, and wounded two or three European soldiers, and got away, after some loss, to Delhi, where it is said they were but coldly received; for they had killed, during the time they remained loyal, more of their own countrymen than they could expect to slaughter of the English in future, let their prowess be ever so great. A force intended to be augmented to 30,000, and composed of two-fifths Sikhs, one-fifth hill races, and two-fifths Mahomedans, Punjaubees, and Pathans, now occupies the place of the Bengal regiments, and as yet the result of the experiment has been eminently successful. Of all those public servants who in this generation have deserved well of their country, not one man ranks truly higher than the Chief Commissioner of the Punjaub.

CHAP. XIV.

THE GWALIOR RISING. — CONTRADICTORY CONDUCT OF THE MUSSULMAN CAVALRY.—HOLKAR AND HIS CONTINGENTS.—THE REVOLT AT MHOW AND INDORE.

THE Mahratta states of Gwalior and Indore are each bound by treaty to support a body of troops officered from the Company's army, and under the sole orders of the British residents at their respective courts. Scindiah's Contingent, consists of five companies of artillery with thirty guns, two regiments of cavalry, and seven of infantry, in all about seven thousand three hundred men. Holkar's Contingent is made up of two companies of artillery with twelve guns, a thousand cavalry, and fifteen hundred infantry. The material of which these troops were composed differed in no respect from that of the Bengal army. The men were recruited from the same districts, wore the same uniform, and were disciplined exactly like the regular forces. The Government perhaps relied upon them as a check to the insubordination of their own proper forces, but in the time of trial it was found that the Contingents were neither more loyal nor the reverse, neither more blood-thirsty nor kind-hearted than the ordinary Sepoy. That they have hitherto been so little heard of arises we believe from the fact, that their nominal masters have not been able to make up their minds, whether to declare for or against us. The dread of losing their dominions in case we are successful in putting down the rebellion, has of course considerable weight with them; but then, on the other hand, the Government of India has taken such pains to make that result appear unlikely, that we could hardly blame them if they made their selection finally in favour of independence. To a Mahratta the prospect of turmoil and plunder must be almost irresistible; and even when brought up as Scindiah and Holkar have been, at the feet of the Honourable Company, he must feel as the young pet tiger feels when a flock of chickens first falls in his way. Holkar, we believe, has hitherto done his best to uphold the connection of Indore with the British, but it is no secret that tempting offers had been made to him to place himself at the head of the Mahrattas, and convert them once more into the dominant race. Scindiah's own troops have already fraternised with the Contingent, and having no apparent means of enforcing even the observance of neutrality towards the British, he will perhaps either abdicate or go with the stream. It will be a fortunate thing for him if he can postpone his decision till Christmas next, as by that time he will find no difficulty in deciding where his interest lies.

The Gwalior Contingent was paraded on the 17th of May to hear the Governor-General's proclamation, which we are told by one who was present, was read to them most impressively by Brigadier Ramsay, who took the same opportunity of addressing the troops. This he did most clearly and pointedly, conveying as distinctly as words could convey it to the minds of native soldiery the utter absurdity of the rumours that the British Government wished to interfere with native caste or native religion in any shape or form. The speech was well delivered by a man well acquainted with the native language, and had a most excellent effect.

A day previous to the mutiny a number of houses were set on fire, and though the Sepoys readily lent a hand in conveying the furniture to a place of safety, their tone and bearing showed plainly what might be expected from them when the needful incentive to revolt should be supplied. There were Europeans of course on the spot, and a Sepoy talking to them said, "You have come to see to-day's sport but to-morrow you will behold a different kind of fun." The remark was significant, and had its effect on the minds of the hearers, but they could only sit with hands folded, and wait the course of events. The next day was Sunday, the favourite day for mutiny, and, as threatened, the Sepoys got up their "tamasha." Towards nightfall a bugle sounded, and the troops turned out on parade, and when the officers made their appearance they were assailed. A party made for the Brigadier's quarters, and with loud shouts called upon him to come forth, but a faithful Sepoy had anticipated them. This man rushing into the house laid hands on him, and hurried him out of the compound to a place of safety: the mutineers, baulked in this instance of their prey, avenged themselves by setting fire to the bungalows, and carrying away the whole of the property. Another officer was roused out of bed by his guard, and one of them coming up quietly said, "Sahib, fly; all is lost." As the man walked away the rest of the guard came up, and said, "The houses are on fire, shall we load?" The officer replied that it was useless to load muskets to put out a fire, on which they marched back to the guard-house; but watching them through the window he saw the whole of them deliberately loading, and felt that it was time to get away. A couple of shots were fired at him, and he turned to escape in another direction, but only succeeded in getting into a place of shelter by running under fire from the whole guard. By this time the whole station was in an uproar; men, women, and children were flying from all quarters towards the Rajah's palace, whilst the rebels were eagerly searching the houses in cantonments for victims. Upwards of twenty-seven persons were murdered, but the thirst for blood was not universal. Several instances occurred where pains were taken to preserve life; in one case three Sepoys saved a lady and her children by conveying them to the roof of a house, where they remained whilst the search was going on for them below, and then escaped when the mutineers had quitted the premises. The survivors were sent forward next day to Agra, under an escort furnished by Scindiah; but they had only gone a short distance when a sowar rode up to say that there was mutiny in the durbar, on which the escort turned back again. The poor fugitives, footsore and bleeding, trudged on over beds of kunkur and through thorny ravines till they reached the jaghire of a friendly rajah, who sent a few sowars with orders to see them safe to Agra. They reached that place at last, after being in hourly danger from the men of the escort, who ridiculed and abused them every step of the way.

The rest of the Contingent at Neemuch, Augur, Sepree, and Sultanpore mutinied soon after the revolt of head quarters. The 7th were the last to join the rebels at Neemuch. They guarded the treasure for twenty-four hours, but at the end of that time the Horse Artillery approached to attack them: they saw the station in flames, and felt themselves powerless to resist the rebels or to help their officers. The subadar ordered the gates of the fort to be thrown open, and the 7th marched out to join the Bengal Sepoys. Before the crowd of mutineers approached they induced their officers to seek safety in flight, and many of them accompanied the fugitives for a considerable distance, showing genuine grief for what had taken place. But the conduct of the 7th, though it exhibited as much good feeling as we had a right to expect, was not to be compared to that of the 1st Irregular Cavalry, upwards of 200 of whom, under Lieut. Cockburn, marched out of Gwalior on the 13th of June, at an hour's notice. They knew what had taken place at Meerut and Delhi, and that they were called upon to fight if need be on the side of Government, but without a murmur, they marched twenty-seven miles a day for seven days in succession; no slight task in the North-west of India at that season of the year. They reached Allyghur a few hours before the mutiny of the 9th N. I. took place, and not being led against the rebels, it is hard to say what their conduct would have been if brought into actual conflict with their co-religionists. They escorted, however, all the officers, women, and children to Hatrass in safety. Two days after they arrived at that place, a hundred of the party mounted their horses to desert, and called upon the rest of the detachment to join them, and fight for their religion. If they refused, they were false to the prophet, and would be beggars for the rest of their days. Neither persuasion nor menace had any effect, and friends of long standing and relatives, shook hands and parted, the one moiety to slaughter the Feringees, and the other remaining to protect them, and punish their enemies. For weeks afterwards the faithful few remained and performed the most essential service to the State, of which the following is only a single instance. A party of five hundred villagers had got together about three miles from Hatrass, where they had been robbing and murdering all passengers, and Lieut. Cockburn resolved to attack them. He put four men in a covered bullock cart, such as is used for conveying respectable females, and sent them on ahead of his party of forty troopers, who dodged amongst the trees so as to be out of sight. Of course when the marauders saw the bullock cart, they made a dash at it, and lifting up the curtains received the contents of four carbines from the supposed ladies. This was followed by a charge from the troopers in ambush, who rode at the insurgents, and cut down fifty of them, without injury to a man on their own side. The surprise was complete, and the neighbourhood was cleared at once of the entire band of rebels. On the day following, they rescued upwards of twenty Europeans from a village where they had been kept in confinement, and continued to perform the like services, until Asiatic nature could hold out no longer against the inducements to join the cause of the Bengal army, when they made their way to the main body of their countrymen. Such examples, which might be multiplied to almost any extent, shows beyond all question, that there never was any plot even amongst the Mussulmans, to rise against the English government. Each man found at last a reason to his liking for mutiny and murder, but assuredly there was neither a unity of feeling, nor a common purpose amongst them at the outset of the insurrection.

Holkar's troops remained steady through the whole of the month of June, and it was thought that reliance could be placed upon their loyalty; but on the morning of the 1st of July a couple of guns passed rapidly through the cantonments of

Mhow. The circumstance created some excitement amongst the officers, more especially as heavy firing had been heard previously in the direction of Indore; but queries as to their destination were soon set at rest, intelligence being received from the Resident, Colonel Durand, that the Contingent was in mutiny and had attacked the Residency. Colonel Platt, commanding the station, was requested to despatch a battery of guns immediately to assist in putting down the revolt, which he did, at the same time ordering Captain Brooke to take a detachment of Light Cavalry, and two companies of infantry, and bring back the fugitive artillery. Captain Brooke soon returned with the two guns, but reported that he had been obliged to shoot one of the gunners, who attempted to open fire on his party. A few minutes after his return, the battery that had been despatched to Indore came back, an express having met it on the road with counter orders. Colonel Durand had considered it expedient to abandon the Residency, and retire on Sehore. There was nothing then to be done but to provide for the safety of the cantonment. Patrols and pickets were appointed, and in the evening the officers sat down to mess as usual, but not in their own bungalows; the example of the 6th at Allahabad was before them, and the caution was not a vain one, for the mess house was on fire shortly afterwards, and most likely the intention of their men was to murder them as they were trying to escape from the building. In the lines the men had been talking about the hard fate of the King of Oude, and of the trooper who had been shot by Captain Brooke, and their officers, finding how ticklish matters stood, were going about amongst them, and trying to sooth them into good humour. Lieut. Martin was conversing with some men of the cavalry, who were loud in their expressions of fidelity to the Government, when a shot was heard, and the trooper whose professions of loyalty had been most vociferous, suddenly wheeled round, and fired at his officer's head: the fellow missed, and Martin, putting spurs to his horse, galloped for his life, the guard giving him a parting volley as he passed their post. Colonel Platt had been warned of the intended rising, but a reliance upon what he had done for the regiment, and belief in the assertions of the leading men, who told him that it was only a few turbulent spirits who were disaffected, made him blind to the plainest signs of impending mutiny. That evening a trooper had warned his officer not to appear in the lines, and a coolie reported that a Sepoy had asked him to join in the outbreak, which was to take place at ten o'clock. But neither Colonel Platt nor Major Harris, commanding the 1st Cavalry, would listen to statements against their faithful soldiers, and both paid for their incredulity with their lives. When the firing from the lines became general, the officers galloped off under a shower of bullets, went to the arsenal, and disarmed and turned out the native guard, armed themselves with muskets, and manned two bastions of the fort. Adjutant Fagan of the 23rd, had ridden up to the quarter guard of his regiment, and ordered the Sepoys to turn out, but their reply was a shower of musketry. Colonel Platt ordered out the artillery, and insisted upon the adjutant returning back with him to the lines, not being able to realise to his imagination that his men were traitors. Neither of them came back again; they were hacked to pieces, together with Major Harris, who was found next morning lying dead by the side of his horse. Lieutenant Dent and Dr. Thornton had narrow escapes; the former had been with the cavalry picket on the Indore road, and when the firing commenced his men remounted their horses, and were about marching to cantonment, when three troopers rode up, one of whom discharged a pistol at him; his guard, who might have shot him with the greatest ease at any moment during the previous hour, now shouted out "Kill him, kill him." The speed of his horse saved him from a second attack which might not have been so harmless. Dr. Thornton had been concealed in a drain all night, affording not the first example of hunted fugitives who have been saved from death during the rebellion, by taking advantage of the Hindoo superstition with regard to these places. Lieutenant Simpson owed his life to two of his men, who remained with him all night in the bazaar. The next morning they asked permission to look for some of their things in the lines, and returned to join the rebels. Had the outbreak been delayed an hour all the officers might have been easily murdered in their beds, and the fort perhaps captured: the women and children had been sent there the previous day, and it was five o'clock upon the evening of the mutiny before Captain Hungerford commanding the artillery could persuade Colonel Platt to allow him to move his guns into the fort. Upon such slight incidents rested the lives of the whole body of Europeans at Mhow.

The morning after the mutiny found the station entirely deserted; the rebels had moved off in a body in the direction of Lucknow, but some of the Maharajah's men returned, and were taken again into pay. It appears that the rascals had quarrelled about the division of spoil; the Bengal renegades asserted that the Contingent had no right to share in the loot taken in the regular way from the Company. For some days previous to the outbreak reports of disaffection had been floating about to the great scandal of the regiment and their officers. On the 4th of June a man of the 23rd came running into the cavalry lines with a story that the artillery were coming down to blow them away; the native officer on duty arrested him, and his "comrades" called for his punishment. Nothing could be more satisfactory, especially when it was borne in mind that, at the morning parade on the 6th, the different companies to a man, through their own officers, petitioned Colonel Platt to accept their offer of fighting against the mutineers at Delhi. The Colonel thanked the men, and promised to report to Government their tender of services. An officer narrating the latter fact to a newspaper, properly remarked, "This does not look like mutiny."

The Bhopal Contingent, stationed at Indore, mutinied in concert with the Mhow force: they consisted of a battery of six guns, four troops of cavalry, numbering 250 sabres, and eight companies of infantry, amounting to 700 men. In addition to this force there were the Malwa Bheels, consisting of 250 men, and two companies of infantry belonging to the Mehidpore Contingent. The outbreak scarcely seems to have been concocted by any portion of the Indore troops. Contrary to the usual state of feeling, the cavalry were well affected in the main, but they were disliked and suspected by the infantry and artillery; a portion of the latter, under Holkar's officers, being stationed at the opium godowns, in which two companies of the Maharajah's infantry were lodged. On the morning of the 1st, Holkar's guns opened the ball by firing a volley of grape into the square where the horses of the Bhopal cavalry were picketed, and the infantry assembled and began firing at the officers. There were two guns at the Residency, which replied to the mutineers; and if the Bheels, who were staunch enough, could have been persuaded to fight, the former would have most likely got the worst of it. But they were afraid to stir in advance, and could not be persuaded to remain in a post of danger. Colonel Travers, commanding the force, did all that a loyal soldier could accomplish, but the insurgents were too powerful for him. At the head of only five troopers he charged the Bhopal artillery and rode into the battery, the gunners lying down under their guns. Had half a troop been at his back he would have captured the battery; but though the charge gave time for the horsemen to come up and form in position, they appeared bewildered, and galloped wildly about the station, neither receiving nor doing harm. An officer went to the treasury, where the infantry, to support the Residency guns, were posted, but was told that if he did not go away they would shoot him. It soon became apparent that fighting was hopeless: the artillery, unsupported, could make no effectual resistance; more guns were coming up from the city, and the rabble were assembling in great numbers, so that there was nothing left but to retreat. Colonel Durand gave a reluctant order to that effect, and the small body of Europeans moved off, the ladies seated on the gun carriages, a small party of Sikh cavalry, which had remained neutral, covering the flanks, the two nine-pounders bringing up the rear, and the Bheels following in marching order. A few round shots were fired at them, but the mutineers were too glad to get them quickly out of the way, that they might more safely carry out their schemes of plunder. After the departure of the English they quitted the Residency, carried off 95,000*l.*, and joining next day the mutineers at Mhow, the whole body marched off towards Agra, after having murdered thirty-five Europeans, men, women, and children. The fugitives got safely to Hoosingabad after seven days' travelling.

Of the horrible tortures inflicted on our countrymen and their families both in Central India and elsewhere, we dare not trust ourselves to speak; but the imagination which can paint the worst of torments that revenge and malice can devise, will attain to the best idea of the realised atrocities. And in many cases it fared as bad with those who escaped the first burst of rebel ferocity. The troops marching on Delhi from Umballa could have found their way without a guide, by the mutilated fragments that met their gaze on each few miles of road. At one place they came across a band of plunderers, amongst whom was a fellow having the dress of an European lady tied round his body. He was seized with his companions, and marched on in the rear of the column, which a short distance in advance came upon the body of the murdered woman from whom he had taken the spoil. A few paces further, and the boots of a child apparently about ten years old were found, with the feet in them, the legs having been cut off just about the ankles. In the above instance it was felt to be a small measure of atonement which the hanging of the murderer afforded. The private soldier yearned for a retaliation, and his better-taught officer could scarcely refrain from sharing his feelings and affording the opportunity of gratifying them.

CHAP. XV.

THE REVOLT AT DINAPORE.—REFUSAL OF GOVERNMENT TO DISARM THE SEPOYS.—GENERAL LLOYD; HIS TASTES AND SYMPATHIES.

THE force at Dinapore consisted of six guns; H. M. 10th and two companies of the 37th; the 7th, 8th, and 40th N. I. The Sepoys were about three to one as compared with the English; but had it been thought advisable to reduce the odds before attempting to disarm the native regiments, there were numerous opportunities of doing so during the months of June and July, when reinforcements of Queen's troops were passing the city almost daily. But in Dinapore, as elsewhere, argument and entreaty were of no avail against the policy of illusion. Always blundering at leisure and always obliged to repent in haste, the Government insisted that the Sepoys were "staunch," and pooh-poohed each attempt to get things made safe. Upon the fidelity of those men depended vast interests, public and private. The opium godowns, the treasury of Patna, and the indigo works of Behar, would most likely be looted and destroyed by successful mutineers. Why should such risks be incurred when there was not a shadow of benefit to be gained thereby? Why care to keep in a condition of fighting efficiency, soldiers who had to be themselves guarded by fighters still braver and more skilful? Why? because Lord Canning had told the Home Government that the "panic" was not only "groundless," but temporary; that he could put it down without great difficulty, and had no fear for the army *en masse*. And hence the Calcutta merchants, a deputation of whom waited upon him in July, to beg that the Sepoys at Dinapore might be disarmed, were coldly told that their apprehensions were not shared in by the authorities, who were satisfied with regard to the trustworthiness of the native corps. A statesman weighing the comparative value of evidence would have taken time to consider whether the reports of two or three officials, who, if they were no better informed than the majority of their class, looked at the outer world only through the spectacles of their native subordinates, ought to outweigh the remonstrances of men whose very means of reputable existence were perhaps staked on the correctness of their information and their ability to turn it to good account. Not less than a million sterling has been advanced this season in Calcutta on the standing crops of indigo in Behar; and surely those who had embarked so much property, under the belief that their ventures were safe from the hand of violence, might consider themselves entitled to consideration. It was not as if compliance with their request entailed loss upon the Government or disgrace to the Sepoy. Twelve hundred British troops, whose presence elsewhere would have been invaluable, were detained at the station on the sole ground that the native corps could neither be left to take care of Dinapore nor sent to perform duty elsewhere. They were of no use as soldiers; and as for the sentimental part of the question, so many thousands who had been lauded as "staunch to the backbone" had become traitors and murderers,—so many hundreds who had been specially praised by the Governor-General had been compelled to give up their arms under the pressure of British bayonets, that the Dinapore Sepoys might have found sufficient consolation for their loss of the means of doing mischief. But the cause of mutiny has derived more support from Government House, in Calcutta, than from the royal palace of Delhi: of all Indian potentates, Lord Canning has been the most efficient ally of the Great Mogul.

General Lloyd, the brigadier commanding at Dinapore, is an officer of fifty-four years' standing, a twelvemonth older than General Hewitt; but, neither in that respect nor any other point of personal merit, had he the advantage of his imbecile junior. As a matter of duty, no less than as the utterance of an article of belief, General Lloyd sent constant assurances to Calcutta of the "staunchness" of his men; but towards the end of July he appears to have had misgivings on the subject, and at last, on the 24th of that month he issued orders to have the percussion caps taken out of the magazine which was under the care of the Sepoys. This was done in the early morning, but not without signs of mutiny on their part. The 8th made a kind of rush towards the tumbril in which the caps were removed, but drew back before they reached it, and retired, shouting, to their lines. It might have been supposed that, having shown distrust to such an extent, the general would have scarcely thought it worth while to consult the feelings of his Sepoys with regard to subsequent movements; but no one can map out the course that is likely to be pursued in cases of emergency by Bengal brigadiers of seventy and upwards. General Lloyd told the native officers to collect the fifteen rounds of ammunition in the pouches of the men, and, leaving a quantity of ball ammunition in the magazine, he sent word to the Sepoys that he would allow them till 4 P.M. to consider whether they would give up the building quietly, ordered an afternoon parade, and then went to enjoy himself on board the steamer. General and Sepoys profited by the opportunity to accomplish their hearts' desires. The former took his daily siesta and slumbered quietly; and the latter, assembling in regiments, hastily filled their pouches with ammunition, removed their families, and deliberately prepared for the march to Delhi. The European pickets noticed the movement in their lines, and the 10th and 37th, together with the artillery, were immediately under arms, but the general was nowhere to be found, and the second in command was absent looking for him. A number of the officers of the Sepoy regiments went down to their lines, in the vain hope of quieting their men: however, they were there but a short time when the Sepoys began firing at them; even the loyal 40th blazed away at every European they saw. The sick men that were in the 10th hospital, and the guard, mounted on the roof, and immediately opened fire on the mutineers, who now began to fly in every direction. Fortunately none of the native infantry officers were touched, though several of them had very narrow escapes. The 10th then advanced with the battery of artillery, the whole covered by about a hundred men of the 37th foot, who were *en route* to Benares and armed with new Enfield rifles. By the time they got to the native parade-ground, the mutineers had got almost beyond range; but the guns opened on them with round shot, and the Enfield rifles were also plied; but few, if any, were touched. They fled at the first discharge, and never attempted to rally. The only person hurt was a man of the 37th, who was wounded accidentally by a comrade. The lines were then fired by the Europeans, and the camp followers and others gutted the huts in a very short time. The mutineers left nearly everything they had behind them; and had there been but a hundred dragoons in the station they might have cut the fugitives to pieces.

The rebels had to cross a deep nullah, and did it leisurely enough; but orders came to act before the day was over, and they had scarcely got out of range before the guns opened upon them with round shot, and materially quickened their movements, if no further results were obtained. Once across the nullah, the Sepoys sat down in some mango topes and rested themselves, firing at intervals upon the Europeans. Groups of the fugitives amused themselves in this manner till 2 P.M. next day, and decamped ultimately without injury. We cannot help admiring the reliance on destiny which enabled three regiments of Sepoys, with only a scanty supply of ammunition, to beard 1000 English soldiers in this style, men who longed to be at them, and who would scarcely, if allowed to fight, have left a soul of them alive. Had the affair been the consequence of previous arrangement, it could not have been managed more harmlessly. The Sepoys fired on their officers, but hit nobody. On an officer of the 40th addressing an old acquaintance, who aimed at him in the most deliberate style, the latter exclaimed "Yes Sahib, what else would you have?" What else, indeed, under the guidance of the Lloyds and others whom it is needless to mention?

When the Sepoys left Dinapore they made their way to Arrah, a place about fourteen miles off. The three corps were in hail of the station till three o'clock on Sunday morning the 26th, but no effort was made to pursue them. There were plenty of elephants which could have carried a detachment out in pursuit and driven the miscreants beyond Arrah or dispersed them; but no move was made. Sunday passed, and the rebels reached Muneer (about twelve miles on the Arrah road), stayed to plunder and burn the railway engineer's houses, &c., still without any hindrance from Dinapore. Monday passed, and though it was known where the mutineers were, still the idea of pursuit or of saving Arrah was never entertained by the general. Having neither guns nor cavalry, they might have been pursued and overtaken without difficulty; but it took General Lloyd two whole days to recover his senses, and not a man was moved till the evening of the 27th, when a hundred and ninety of the 37th started in the Hoorungotta steamer to the relief of the handful of Europeans besieged at Arrah. After proceeding some distance, the vessel grounded, and they remained fast till midday of the 29th, when the Bombay steamer came up with 150 men of the 10th and 70 Sikhs, and took the 37th on board. The whole force, now amounting to 400 men, disembarked about twelve miles from Arrah about four P.M., and commenced their march on that place. On their way they were informed that the enemy had evacuated Arrah,—a falsehood which unhappily prompted Captain Dunbar, who commanded the force, to push on, though the night was growing very dark and they were ignorant of the road. Eager to wipe out the discredit attaching to the Europeans for allowing the mutineers to escape, and holding his enemy in contempt, he thought of nothing but getting over the ground, and marched without picket or advanced guard to the edge of a mango tope, where the rebels were planted in ambush. A crashing fire from both sides of the road was the first intimation of the presence of an enemy, and before any measures could be taken to extricate the force, volley after volley was poured into them, throwing the men into inextricable confusion. Unable to advance or retreat, afraid of firing lest they should hit their own comrades, and totally bewildered as to the whereabouts of the foe, our brave fellows remained the whole night mere helpless targets. When the morning dawned, order was restored, and about half the number that had left Dinapore closed up, shoulder to shoulder, and began their retreat. In this movement no lack of military skill was exhibited. Skirmishers covered the retiring column, and made a stand whenever it was possible; but the Sepoys followed them up, taking advantage of every spot of cover; and all the wounded unable to march were left behind to be ruthlessly slaughtered. The survivors succeeded in reaching Dinapore at noon, their appearance adding to the dismay of the station, and to the bewilderment of the wretched general, who lost no further time in going on the sick list. Amongst the list of killed were: Captain Dunbar, H. M. 10th; Ensign Erskine, ditto; Lieut. Sale, H. M. 39th; Lieutenants Ingilby and Anderson, 7th and 22nd B. N. I. Volunteers; mate of steamer, ditto; railway engineer, ditto; and about 150 men; hardly one of the rest escaping untouched. The rebels, about two thousand strong, with some small guns which had been supplied by a neighbouring rajah, pursued them to the very edge of the cantonments, though their own ammunition was so scant that they were obliged to fire buttons and stones. It was something for them to boast of, that they had routed a British force, and killed or wounded nearly the whole of them, with a loss to themselves of only half a dozen men.

Of course it was everywhere expected that the little band at Arrah would now be overwhelmed before aid could reach them from other quarters; but, however unlucky the chances that have superinduced a Johnstone upon a Hewitt, and a Lloyd on a Johnstone, the present crisis has shown that the officers of the Sepoy army have amongst them men who are equal to any emergency. Tidings of the perilous condition of Arrah reached Major Vincent Eyre at Buxar; and, knowing from experience in Affghanistan what mischief might be wrought by the delay and incompetence of a worn-out general, he started at once for the place with 150 of H. M. 5th Fusileers and three guns. He found the party whom he came to relieve still holding out against the whole force of the enemy. There were but fifteen Europeans in all, civilians, railway staff, and indigo planters, with fifty of Rattray's Sikhs. They had knocked over no less than fifty of the rebels without the loss of a man to themselves. When the besiegers attempted to mine, they ran a countermine: their water fell short, and they sank a well: provisions failed, and they made a sortie, coming back laden with provender. The advance of Major Eyre was made just in the nick of time. He attacked the rebels as soon as he could get within range, and utterly dispersed them. The siege was of course raised at once, and the garrison liberated. They had nothing but the preservation of life to be thankful for, since the mutineers had burnt or plundered all the houses and property, public and private, on their route from Dinapore. The whole of the railway works and bungalows on both sides of the Soane had been destroyed, and what the Sepoy spared the liberated convicts wrecked. The cost in blood and treasure of the outbreak at Dinapore, cannot be summed up for many months to come; but it will be enormous, and has been incurred solely that an elderly brigadier might have time to eat his luncheon in quiet.

The mutiny at Dinapore paralysed for awhile the energies of all classes of our countrymen in the fertile province of Behar. The ruin of the vast interests scattered over the country appeared imminent, and the authorities thought only of securing safety by abandoning their stations. The Commissioner of Patna, Mr. Tayler, who had, up to this time, displayed great activity and courage, ordered all the civilians to come in at once to Dinapore. He was obeyed in every case but that of the collector of Gya, Mr. Alonzo Money, who refused to abandon the treasury under his charge, containing a large sum, and ultimately brought it in to Dinapore under charge of a company of H. M. 37th. There was valid cause for alarm: the troops from Dinapore — three regiments of infantry, with the greater portion of the 12th Irregulars—and many thousands of liberated convicts were spread over the face of the country; and there was not for a season, except in Dinapore, a single European between Benares and Raneegunge, the latter place distant but 120 miles from Calcutta. Patna with its opium godowns, containing perhaps poison to the value of 2,000,000*l.* sterling, was distant but two hours' march; the Mahomedans of Bankipore, one of the city suburbs, would have been only too happy to join in the work of plunder; and if it were sacked, the commissariat supplies for the force at Allahabad would be cut off. Patna was defended solely by Rattray's Sikhs without guns; and, if that was captured, Dinapore must surrender, leaving Calcutta without any channel of communication between Bengal and the north-west. Had the rebels in their exodus shown as much skill as daring, they would have been masters of Patna and had the whole of Behar at their mercy before General Lloyd had got back his recollections.

We have no heart to chronicle the massacre of Jhansi, and no space to devote to the outbreaks in Madras and Bombay. It must suffice to say, that at Nagode and Jubbulpore the 50th and 52nd imitated at a late period the example of mutiny, and completed the defection of the Bengal army.

Marvellous are the ways by which Providence works out its ends. The leopard that we have trained to hunt for us has turned upon his master, whilst the poor dumb beasts of burden, who are cruelly oppressed, bear their heavy loads in silence. Had the Sepoys not rebelled, the wrongs of India might have gone on accumulating until God grew utterly weary of us; and had the ryots risen at this time there would have been no future for us in the East. As it is we can atone as a nation for the past. We have no apology to offer to the Brahmin, no injustice to own in the case of the Sepoy, but to ruined noble and miserable peasant, we acknowledge a debt of repentance, and trust that the first instalment of it may be paid without an hour's delay.

For twenty-one weeks, counting from the first receipt of intelligence of the Meerut revolt, the Government of India was on its trial. It was subjected to a strain which tested every joint and searched every flaw, and the result was most disastrous. Not a bolt remained in its place, not a rivet but was started, not an inch of surface but was found to be decayed and rotten. It disclosed neither the wisdom that could foresee danger nor the strength that could overcome it.

If the order of things could have been reversed, and the last acts of the Government made their first, matters would have now worn a very different aspect. They have done all that could be desired, but not at the right times. Volunteers were enrolled, troops massed, enterprises undertaken, and foreign aid enlisted, but all at the wrong seasons. Calcutta was wisely left to the chief care of the civic force and the navy, but not until the rebel fires had blazed out in a dozen stations, and it was seen that the Sepoy army had transferred its allegiance. "Too late!" was inscribed on the banner of the Ghoorkas, when for the second time they turned their faces towards Lucknow; "too late!" was graven on the lids of the empty chests in the treasury, when a loan was called for, and a second bid was made for the hoards of the capitalist; "too late!" was shouted by the public when the order was given to disarm the regiments at Dinapore; "too late!" was shrieked from the well at Cawnpore; "too late!" was echoed by the breeze that swept over the battlements of Lucknow. We saw in those days, the story of Sisyphus enacted. The ceaseless striving, and the sure defeat; the hand constantly striking, but the foe still remaining in front; the feet always marching, but the goal as far off as ever; the Sibyl's price paid, but the book of fate not forthcoming. It seemed as if a single faculty had swallowed up every other quality of national greatness. Never did English courage shine out so gloriously, never was English want of capacity so thoroughly displayed. We were giants in the field and dwarfs in the council. Our soldiers surpassed in heroism all who had gone before them; their rulers transcended all previous notions of weakness and imbecility.

The least glimmer of good sense is sufficient to light a government to a knowledge of the fact that it must have money, but the Calcutta authorities were wanting even in the instinct of pecuniary self defence. It was not until the 20th of July, when the cause of order seemed almost hopeless, that they thought of taking means to supply themselves with funds. Lord Dalhousie and the present administration of India, had inflicted a fatal blow to public credit in 1855, by reducing the interest of a large portion of the Indian debt to four per cent., opening a loan at three and a half per cent., on the plea that the rate of interest in future would not rule above that figure; and crowning a series of financial measures, by announcing a Public Works Loan at five per cent., all within ths space of a few months. It was said to be a clever stroke of policy; it turned out to be a sorry trick. The four per cents went down to a heavy discount, and great numbers of natives, who had invested in the stock at par, found themselves stripped of a large portion of their capital. The press took up the subject and showed beyond all question that the term "Public Works Loan," was a mere pretence. The Government wanted money to carry on the current business of the State, and so far from having a surplus on hand when they announced the first reduction, sufficient to pay off the whole of the bondholders, they would have been obliged to suspend the operation had a large number disbelieved their professions and demanded cash. Hence the attempt to raise large sums during a period of general alarm, with such memories fresh in men's minds, was a perilous experiment, but with the exercise of ordinary sagacity it would have succeeded. With the fact patent to all men, that money was daily growing dearer, and that doubts as to the continuance of our rule would soon more than neutralise the tendency to invest in Government securities natural to a period of general stagnation in trade, they should have advertised a six per cent. loan, and taken the four per cents at par value, to the extent of half the sum subscribed. The money received into the treasury would then have cost seven per cent, but the announcement would have caused a rush of contributors, and, by adding to the number and interest of the public creditors, have served to strengthen our hold of the country. But the idea of giving a bonus of two per cent. to the fundholders, on condition of their doubling their stake in the permanence of English rule, was not to be thought of, and the Government proposed a five per cent. loan, the subscribers having the option of paying one half in four per cents at par. Two months earlier, the scheme would have answered, and it had been pressed on the Government, of course without success, but now it failed, and the worst of the matter was that every person had the means of finding out the result. If the loan were popular, capitalists, who were not holders of four per cents, or who wished to speculate, would come into the market, and the price of that stock would go up. In this instance the quotations sank lower, and the sagacious men who could have helped the State in its sore need saw that their time had come, and that the Government must increase their biddings. A week after the first announcement, a second notice appeared, to the effect, that forty per cent. of the new subscriptions would be taken in the three and a half per cents; but the tide ran out whilst the financiers were sitting on the banks of the stream counting the cost of getting their loan afloat. Every step taken was too late; the money power followed the military power; when Government ceased to command the obedience of the soldier it ceased to possess the confidence of the citizen. The physical force melted away, and moral influence could never at any time be said to exist. It was only in dealing with English rights that the Government felt it was still a power in the land. It sought compensation for defeat and measureless indignity, and found it in trampling on the press, and imprisoning the King of Oude. The victims were equally lofty, but not equally helpless. Lord Dalhousie is safe from the ex-monarch, but his successor, in destroying the liberty of printing in India, has wrought the overthrow of the more powerful dominion of the East India Company.

CHAP. XVI.

THE INDIAN PRESS. — ITS ISOLATION, AND NATURAL ANTAGONISM TO THE INDIAN GOVERNMENT. — HYPOCRISY OF ITS ASSAILANTS. — LORD CANNING AND MR. MANGLES. — THE GAGGING ACT. — APATHY OF THE PUBLIC AT HOME.

THERE is no sadder proof of the hopeless ignorance of our countrymen upon all matters of Eastern politics than that afforded by the restraints imposed on the Indian press. They have consented to look upon it as a mere engine of mischief, a force inimical to the proper influence of Government, and the true welfare of the people. They would have resented as a national insult, an attempt to gag the "Times" during the war in the Crimea, and yet how much more needful was it to have had a free press in the great dependency where bad government has well nigh lost us an empire, and incompetency sits supreme? What would have been the bare money's worth to the nation, of a dozen leading articles disclosing at the outset of the insurrection the real state of affairs? Our home journals furnish many a country gentleman, and many a leading politician, with arguments as well as facts; but the "Times" cannot help Mr. Vernon Smith, nor tell the public that which it wants to know about India. Yet the nation which would not trust ministerial capacity, nor believe ministerial statements during the campaign before Sebastopol, is content to trust Lord Canning, and to believe in the bulletins of Colonel Birch. In the one case it demanded more light than the press, the parliament, and the London Gazette could throw upon the state of affairs; in the other, it is satisfied to see the few tapers extinguished, which enabled it at least to discern the surrounding darkness.

"But, surely," it will be said, "the press of India is licentious in its strictures, and low in point of morals, or else it is strangely belied." Perhaps it is, but at any rate it must be assumed to suit the wants of its public. If it contemns authority, the members of the service maintain the libellers; if it is depraved in taste, they take no care to screen the examples from the notice of their wives and daughters. Being gentlemen, all, they must care for decency, yet they voluntarily pay for its opposite; they cannot like what is low, and yet no one will cater for the gratification of their better impulses. And the vicious journalism has not even the attraction of low prices. If the editor is to be bought cheaply, his paper is a dear commodity. Brain and soul are perhaps reasonable enough, but types and paper inflict a heavy tax upon moderate incomes.

There are three daily papers in Calcutta: the "Englishman," "Hurkaru," and "Phœnix." The "Friend of India" and the "Dacca News" are published weekly, making a total of five separate publications for Bengal. In the North-west provinces, there are the "Delhi Gazette," and the "Mofussilite;" in the Punjaub, the "Lahore Chronicle," in Scinde, the "Kossid." Bombay has three daily papers, the "Times," "Gazette," and "Telegraph," together with the "Guardian" and the "Poona Observer." Madras has but one daily journal, the "Spectator;" and three, the "Athenæum," "Examiner," and "Crescent," published every other day. The "Bangalore Herald" completes the list of Indian newspapers, and amongst all these journals, there is not one that gives even general support to the Government, and is spoken well of by the Indian authorities. The fact tells for something more than the hostility of the press: it shows that advocacy of the ruling policy will not find a paying audience. At least six out of seven of the whole body of subscribers are in the Company's service, and in India, as elsewhere, the readers determine the policy of the paper. The wares, we take it, are made for the market.

A selection might be made in England of journals which advocate principles that are considered in some quarters subversive of the well-being of society. Every interest that pays, can get itself recognised, and whatever is worth supporting is worth attacking, so that in time, each has its enrolled corps of assailants and defenders; but in India, there is no scope for antagonism of intellect, and journalism languishes under the influence of enforced unanimity, so far as public affairs are concerned. The press is always railing at Government, because it is the sole representative of the rights of humanity, and stands in lieu of a people, and a parliament. Civilians and soldiers dare not meddle in politics, and merchants are too busy making money to interfere; but God has given each of these men a conscience, and they contend by proxy against the wrongs of the country. An old writer avers, that if an infant child were left to itself, it would be found after the lapse of a few years speaking Hebrew. We are not sure that the language of the Jews is the natural speech of mankind, but are quite certain, that to the unfettered journalist in India, abuse of the Company and its rule is a necessity of his existence.

It is somewhat superfluous to dwell upon the advantages of a free press in England, but if the right of free utterance is needful in a country where every man knows his rights, and most persons are able to maintain them, how much more are we bound to uphold it in India, where Government, from the very necessity of things, must be despotic; where the law is administered by men who have had no judicial training; where millions of public money are expended in works over which the state can exercise no real control; where there is no public opinion, no force of any kind to interpose between authority and the people? If our countrymen would make up their minds to cut India adrift, if they felt no interest in its growth, no remorse for its misery, and no responsibility for its general welfare, their indifference to the liberty of the press would be rational enough; but whilst they hold to the East, as they would to Kent or Cornwall, their conduct is inexcusable. They insist upon making laws for India, and cut off from the legislature the sources of information. They would gladly extend the operations of trade and commerce, and yet lock up the knowledge of Indian resources. They would like to improve the spirit and the details of legislation, and yet destroy the only antagonism to the existing order of things, that is at the same time useful and harmless.

For proof of the respectable character and eminent ability of the Indian journals, we refer to their columns; for argument, as to their utility, we need only appeal to the English common sense. The great plea, however, in favour of the Gagging Act passed by the Indian Government, rests upon the fact of the revolt. It is said that the liberty of the press is incompatible with a state of insurrection. Freedom of publication was dangerous to the well-being of the state, and had to be suppressed in consequence for a season.

If the above plea is made out, it is evident that complaint on the part of the Indian press is idle, and redress for their declared grievance quite out of the question. If the newspapers have been damaged for the public good, they must put up with their losses, and hush their outcries. We are content to rest their case upon the completeness with which this assertion, on the part of the Government, can be met and refuted.

A journal contains only news and opinions. Indiscretion, or the desire to steal a march upon rival prints, might occasionally induce an editor to publish information which ought to be withheld; and we know of one instance where the garrulity of the members of Government allowed a secret to escape, which was published to the possible detriment of the public service. But there is no other example on record, and the pretence that rebellion would suffer in the intelligence department, by the gagging of the press, was either foolish or dishonest. Every department of the public service, every branch of business, is throughout India virtually in the hands of natives, who are cognisant of all that transpires in the Government offices, or the counting-houses of the merchants. They knew to an ounce the weight of powder in every magazine, the number and calibre of our guns, what means of defence we had, and how we proposed to increase them. The treasuries, the arsenals, the whole public correspondence were in their hands: pains and patience, with the occasional expenditure of a few rupees, would put an inquirer in possession of every fact that he wished to know, or gain him an inkling of whatever was going forward. The natives are always taking stock of us: the writer knows your resources and those of your correspondents, the servants watch your conversation, and treasure up what they suppose to be your secrets. Such knowledge may be found useful some day, and it costs nothing to preserve. The Government *employé* knows the butler or the valet of the official under whom he serves; the one copies despatches, and the other hears remarks made in familiar intercourse, and both of them are acquainted with persons who can turn information to account. And then as to their machinery for transmitting intelligence! it was perfect before our forefathers understood the art of writing. It is only in the use of the "lightning dawk" that we surpass them, and all our working signallers are native. Every man of rank has his newswriter in the capital, and his reporter in the nearest English station. The native merchants employ their own messengers: there are 2000 runners always travelling between Calcutta and the Upper Provinces. The last resolution of the Executive Council, the names of the guests at a dinner party, the particulars of a shipment, the number of troops in a garrison—all are at your service if you are concerned to learn such matters. To an Englishman who knows the East, the assertion that it was needful to restrict the freedom of the press, in order to prevent the circulation of certain items of news amongst the people, appears not merely in the light of an untruth; — he knows that it is hypocritical as well as false, and that the men who made it, knew in their hearts that they were inflicting needless oppression upon the public in India, and wilfully deceiving the public at home.

And then with regard to the publication of opinions! What shall we say of the legislature which gags the score of editors who write in India, and are amenable to its laws and its social influences, and leaves free, as a matter of necessity, the hundreds of busy pens that are at work on the subject of India and its government at home?—that bullies the "Friend of India," and is obliged to tolerate the Sepoy articles of the Dublin "Nation," and the glad homilies of the Paris "Univers?" Surely its experience in opium smuggling might have taught a lesson in this respect, if one were needed. It was of little use that the Emperor of China blocked up two or three ports, if the rest of the seaboard were left open. The drug was in request, the Company were there to sell, and the poison was circulated through every vein of the body politic, without the slightest difficulty.

At the same time that the Indian Government were threatening the press with suppression, for expressing hopes that Christianity might reign supreme in Bengal a hundred years hence, Mr. Mangles, the chairman of the Court of Directors, was telling the House of Commons that the East India Company held the country under Providence for the propagation of the gospel. Whilst Indian newspapers were forbidden to speak in disparaging or doubting terms of native princes, to impugn the motives and designs of Government, or to bring into contempt any of its officers, the columns of the home journals were converted into a kind of French Flanders, where every man, whether friend or foe of the existing order of things, was allowed to fight his own battles. Every phase of the religious question, every plausible theory of the causes of revolt, was ventilated in the "Times." Clemency and coercion for the rebels; absorption or restitution for the native dynasties and nobles; contempt or admiration for the actual as well as the nominal rulers in India, were all suggested at once. On "mail nights" a score of dusky faces might be seen in the hall of the General Post Office, in St. Martin's le Grand, one perhaps sending out to his principal or chief a file of papers, in which Mr. Spurgeon preached against the toleration of Hindooism, and the editor of the "Morning Post" wrote against the continuance of native dominion: whilst an Irish journal howled with delight over our difficulties, and a French writer recognised in the rebellion God's judgment upon us as a wicked nation. Another would be posting a speech in the House of Commons against the inhuman practice of blowing away rebels from guns; a score of articles against Lord Canning and the existence of the Company, and paragraphs of unmeasured contempt for every member of the Indian administration. Whatever men might be disposed to say in ignorance or anger, under the influence of fear or the promptings of self-interest, was allowed to be said without hesitation in speeches, sermons, letters, and leading articles. India was the universal topic; its affairs came home to the business of many, to the bosoms of all.

And the Gagging Act was an injury to the feelings, as well as an insult to the patriotism of the English in India. When the revolt broke out, the sense of a common calamity seemed to inspire journalists with a common purpose, so far as the Government was in question. One and all they supported Lord Canning to the full extent of their ability, and far beyond the limits suggested by their consciences. The Council was known to be impracticable, the Commander-in-Chief was feared to be deficient in the required ability for the crisis; but the Governor-General had the power of uncontrolled action, and the public tried to believe that he would exert it. Credit was given to him for every sign of vigour, silence was observed with reference to obvious defects of policy; but the sham broke down at last, the empty bag could not be made to stand upright. When weeks rolled on, and it was seen that Government were without a policy or a plan, that they were content to depend for information from the seat of war to the chances of the day, and the agency of remote newspapers and stock jobbers; when danger was ridiculed, loyal offers put coldly aside, and natives of influence, who could not possibly be ignorant of the rebel designs, were soothed and caressed, the general patience gave way, and the newspapers echoed faintly the universal discontent. But as no one could foresee how much of suffering and disgrace there were in store for us, so no one dreamed of setting on foot a systematic opposition to the measures of Government. Never was a community more willing to submit to absolute control. They felt the full need of guidance, and would only have been too happy to obey a dictator, who could give the help of which all classes were in want. They were soon to feel that Government had a heel, if it had no head, that it was content to be feared, well knowing that it could not possibly be respected.

On the 13th June, Lord Canning went into the Council Chamber, and in a speech of half an hour's duration proposed a Gagging Act, to be applied to all Indian newspapers, European and native. He was obliged to own that the English journals had exhibited no signs of disloyalty to Her Majesty's dominion; but the reason he was instructed to assign for classing them with her enemies, was, that he had read articles, which might, if perverted by translation, have a very mischievous effect. The legislative council saw, with the Governor-General, that there was no difference between European and Asiatic pens, and by a parity of reasoning it might be said, no distinction between European and Sepoy bayonets. But the lawgivers made the proper allowance in fact, if not in theory. It was right to disarm the English journalist, who was certain, if tolerated, to pull down the Company's Government, and right to strengthen the British soldier, who would fight just now to preserve it. The Bill passed through the second and third stages in ten minutes, and Lord Canning assented to it with unwashed hands. Not a man of those present had a word of objection to offer to the measure. They went home, and rejoiced that, by a vigorous effort, they had got rid of responsibility; and each feeling like the person who, being worried by his tailor, gave an acceptance for the amount of his bill, and exclaimed, as he threw down the pen, "There, thank God, the fellow 's paid at last!"

At midnight on the 17th June, four days after the press law was enacted, the Commissioner of police in Calcutta, with a strong force, well armed, sallied out to make a seizure of three native presses. No resistance was offered, and next day the culprits, two Mussulmans and one Hindoo, were brought before the chief magistrate, and on the information of the Secretary of the Home Department, Mr. Beadon, and other witnesses, committed for trial, on charges of having published seditious libels. In due course, bills of indictment were offered to the grand jury, and the puisne judge of the Queen's Court, Sir Arthur Buller, spoke a column and a half of newspaper type, against the Doorbin and the Sooltan el Akbar, charged with having reprinted the proclamation of the King of Delhi, that document which every English journal republished in the next issue after it came to hand. Judges eminent for their learning, ability, and high moral worth, had in other times seconded the acts of arbitrary power; and his lordship saw no reason why judicial functionaries of that class alone should be reckoned, in trying times, as the friends of Government. He charged then heavily for true bills, and the grand jury found them, and hence brought the matter fairly to issue. But when the trial came off, Lord Canning shrank from the contest which he had invited. The Advocate-General had gone to Madras to defend the Government in an action brought against them for withholding the property of the Ranees of Tanjore; and the junior counsel came into court, and entered into a compromise in the cases of the two Mussulmans. But the case of the Bengalee was proceeded with. Three libels were charged against the defendant; and it was proved that he had taken the first of these to the Home Secretary in person, as evidence of the respectability of his paper, and on the strength of it, asked to be allowed to have the Government orders to publish. The secretary gave directions that the paper should be taken in at the office, and successive numbers were regularly received and filed. Three leading articles were picked out by the under-secretary, on which Lord Canning, it was shown, ordered a prosecution to be founded. The most virulent of these was a statement that the Governor-General had his venetian blinds regularly drawn down at 9 P.M. for fear of the Sepoys, to whom he now gave sweet words, which they refused to care for. The upshot of the case may be imagined. The jury, composed chiefly of East Indians, men as unlikely, under ordinary circumstances, to give a verdict against Government, as twelve "Castle tradesmen," acquitted the defendant without hesitation; and no more was heard of prosecutions under the common law for libel and sedition. It was known to every man in Calcutta, that the violent tone of the native press had been brought especially to the notice of the Home Secretary, months before the breaking out of the revolt, and that he had then wisely let it pass unnoticed. No man knew better than Mr. Beadon, that treason amongst natives was not hatched by leading articles, the rebels being as much influenced by Calcutta newspapers as Welsh miners are by the "Quarterly Review." He knew that in their private intercourse with each other, the natural wealth of the Eastern languages was all too poor to express the contempt or hatred with which men of influence regard us; and that as to the mass, they were not able to read or meditate. Our true policy was, to take no heed of that which we could scarcely punish, to be deaf to scurrility, and scornful of threatening. When the Marquis Wellesley rode through Benares, a Brahmin reviled him in the name of all the gods of India, and received, by way of punishment, the lowliest of reverences from the proudest of viceroys.

What kind of writing it is that the Indian Government punishes, we have shown in the appendix to this book; but the working out of the act is another matter again. At Akyab, where 150,000 tons of shipping annually take their departure, the mercantile houses find it convenient to prepare lithographed circulars containing shipping lists, the price of the great staple of Arracan, and speculations with regard to crops, present and future. No one knows what amount of contempt might be expressed for Government in those enigmatical phrases, with which the commercial class puzzle, and perhaps sometimes delude, the community at large; and hence, to guard against such a contingency, Major Verner, who represents law, justice, and revenue in those parts, refused to license the stones, and the whole rice literature of Arracan was extinguished at a blow. The order will be a source of great annoyance to merchants in the busy season, when they require every available hand in the godowns, rather than in the counting-houses, but our countrymen are very quiet on the subject. There are Dutch and French houses at Akyab, and the Englishman would rather not allude to the topic.

The military authority who presides over the destinies of Pegu, has improved upon the law. Pending the orders of the Governor-General, he has permitted the proprietor of the "Rangoon Chronicle" to receive an "ad interim order of protection," for the publication of his newspaper, but requires that every article of news or comment on the mutinies, shall be submitted to the acting magistrate, a lieutenant of the Madras artillery, previous to publication. The editor chafes at the condition, and chooses, rather than comply with it, that his subscribers should be without any intelligence on the subject which fills all minds and engrosses all attention.

Englishmen who have cast their lot in the East, feel perhaps more acutely at this moment the indifference of their countrymen to the continuance of the Gagging Act, than the wrong inflicted upon them by the East India Company in imposing it. They could not believe that tyranny so senseless would be tolerated for an hour at home. They thought that even for the sake of their own enlightenment, legislators and editors would uphold the freedom of the Indian press. Had the "Times," which leads captive the mind of the English nation, been worthy of its influence, or true to its high vocation, the fetters would have been removed before the iron had eaten into the flesh. But perhaps it has taken the proper course; the leading journal of the world writes for freemen, and the Anglo-Indian population never deserved that proud title. Let us change the subject, the prisoners may escape when the jail is battered down, and the crowbars and sledge-hammers are being got ready.

CHAP. XVII.

THE END OF THE GREAT COMPANY.—THE FINANCIAL DIFFICULTY.—IMPORTANCE OF AN IMMEDIATE ASSUMPTION OF GOVERNMENT BY THE CROWN.—NATIVE PRINCES AND THEIR RIGHTS.

THE goodly ship that in the mid-watch of the night goes down suddenly, when the crew are either asleep or lying listlessly on the deck gazing at the stars, is a type of the government of the East India Company. Leadenhall Street has foundered in deep water, and left only a spar or two floating on the surface. The catastrophe is complete, but we can hardly realise the fact of it. Power and prestige, the headship of great armies, and the control of illimitable resources, all gone in three short months!—helplessness and insolvency taking the places of the strength that seemed invincible, and the wealth supposed to be exhaustless! The events seem to belong to the world of dreams. To be a crowned king one day and a fugitive the next, is no uncommon destiny in this generation; but in the case of the East India Company, we have not only a dynasty deposed, but a dominion shattered to pieces. The Raj and the Rajahs are equally at an end. With the blessing of heaven we shall reconquer India, but it will be only by the aid of the Queen's troops, brought over in the Queen's ships, and paid out of the revenues of England. Even if it were possible, or thought desirable to revive the late order of things, with as few modifications as need be, there is no quarter in India to which we can look for the means of carrying on the government. The latest parliamentary returns show an average annual excess of expenditure, as compared with income, for the last three years, of 1,574,758*l.*; and the estimate for 1856-7 provides for an expected deficiency of nearly two millions. Out of the total land revenues, 4,753,125*l.* is contributed by the North-West Provinces, of which we hold at this moment as much ground only as is covered by the guns of our European troops. Vegetation after the rains is scarcely more rapid than the growth of prosperity under favourable circumstances in the East; but it will take some years to fill up the gaps in the population, to rebuild the factories, replace the capital destroyed, and efface the marks of the present war and the coming famine. When we take into account the wide area of ravage and the ruthless character of the contest, the universal unsettling of men's minds and the blocking up of so many channels of trade, it will be conceded that we take a very moderate estimate of the damage to the pecuniary interests of Government when we set down the loss of revenue from present sources, for some years to come, at four millions sterling. Here, then, is a deficit of six millions sterling, in relation to the ordinary scale of expenditure,—it being taken for granted that opium will continue to furnish sixteen per cent. of the gross income.

But it is not only on one side of the account that the Indian balance-sheet will show a different result in future. The cost of reconquest will make an enormous addition to the burthens of the country. The fifty thousand additional troops just sent out may not be all required three years hence; but no prudent statesman would recommend that less than half that number should form the permanent increase to the strength of the European army in Bengal and the Upper Provinces. Under the head of irregular soldiers or armed police, a force equal in number to that of the late army must be kept up; and looking at the great advance all over the country in the cost of living, it is not likely that less than the Sepoy's rate of pay and allowances will attract good men to the service. The cost of maintaining twenty-five thousand Europeans will be upwards of a million and a quarter per annum, making, with the interest of the new loan, a total annual deficit of eight millions sterling.

The loan required by the Indian Government will not be less than fifteen millions. The winter harvest in the north-west will be totally lost; and the spring crops will not produce enough for the subsistence of the people, even if our arms are so successful as to leave the cultivator at peace by the end of January next. The zemindars of Bengal will of course be called upon for their rent as usual, though, if the lower provinces were harried to any great extent, we could hardly put up their estates to auction for non-payment. Two thirds of the ordinary customs' receipts at Calcutta may be looked upon as lost for the present year: the damage done to the East Indian Railway is estimated at a million, and the loss by the plunder of treasures at a million and a half. There are the stores and public buildings destroyed by the Sepoys to be replaced, and new barracks to be built for the Queen's troops. Five millions will be required for transport charges, every soldier costing, all charges being taken into account, a hundred pounds from Chatham to Calcutta. The deduction that must be made from the revenues of Madras, Bombay, and the Punjaub, the increased cost of the army, and the expense of carrying on the war, we have not attempted to estimate; but in the above enumeration we have accounted for twelve and a half millions.

The overthrow of the Company's rule has long been felt to be only a question of time. It could not possibly have survived many years longer; but the Sepoys have simplified the labours of orators and journalists. The immediate proclamation of the Queen's Government throughout India would be worth fifty thousand men, on the side of law and order. Of the princes and nobles who have taken up arms against us, there is not a man but is fully conscious of the overwhelming might of England, and who is not impressed, in the main, with a belief in the desire of the imperial authority to do justice to the people of Hindostan. Only by such a change can we safely temper justice with mercy. An amnesty on the part of the East India Company, however narrow in its provisions or distant in date, would be attributed to fear. The fighting class would have no respect for the government which they had once overturned; the native capitalists would never forget that, even in Calcutta, the bonds of the public debt had been almost unsaleable at 25 per cent. discount. The trading millions would shrink from embarking their means in ventures beyond the reach of their own supervision and control; the servants of the state would have no reliance on the permanence of their means of livelihood. Ever in the minds of all men would survive the memory of past events, and the thought that what had been might be again.

But if we look upon government by the East India Company as an impossibility in the future, are we prepared to show that the Queen's servants can rule Hindostan in a way that will give content to the natives, and entail no loss on the imperial exchequer? The chance of another rebellion, or the steady recurrence of a deficit, would not be tolerated in England. The time has arrived when we must either assume the direct responsibility of the Government, or abandon the country altogether. If we refuse to let go our hold of the glorious East, we shall be answerable in the sight of the world for its welfare. Its poverty will accuse, its sufferings will shame us. We must pay its debts and insure its safety. The screens, both moral and physical, have been rudely torn away; substitution is at an end, and we stand face to face with the Hindoo and Mussulman, accountable henceforth for every act and deed of our countrymen.

In gauging the feelings with which we are regarded by the people of India, we may divide the latter into two classes, — those who, under any regime, must yield up the greater portion of their earnings to the ruling power, and those who, by the force of position or prestige, might hope in a great measure to escape taxation. The ryots would generally vote for us; because, although our system of land revenue is oppressive in the extreme, it displays a blind rapacity which frequently misses its aim. The native zemindar knows how to work the screw to a terrible nicety, and takes care that every portion of extractable surface is exposed to its action. Under his eye there is no such thing as "concealed cultivation," no possibility of bribing the revenue officer to furnish false measurements of fields or make untrue estimates of the harvest. He has no sympathy with the sons of toil: the ryot is one of his beasts of burden, no more, — having thews and sinews that are the property for the time being of his employers, and a soul that it rests with himself to get saved if he pleases. When we hear of the peasants helping the insurgents to rob and murder, it may be taken for granted that they are avenging some local quarrel or fighting for the livelihood of which the insurrection has deprived them. Our rule has been cruel and unjust, but in setting up native domination the working masses know that their condition would not be made more tolerable. They care much for religion, but nothing for rajahs, except in isolated instances. If we conferred upon them again the blessings of peace, and would be content to take only a fair share of the produce of their land, they might not be disposed to pray for our welfare, but they would certainly never aid in expelling us from the country.

The rajahs and nobles hate us as men hate evil destiny. They are the food for which we have always an appetite; each counts upon his destruction as a thing certain to follow sooner or later; and it is not to be wondered at if the fiery spirits amongst them should long for a chance of winning honour and safety by joining the ranks of our open enemies. As applicable to jaghiredars and princes, we have laid down a code of rules which embraces every case of ownership or succession. If a Mussulman pleads that his rent-free estate was given to him a century and a half ago in perpetuity, he is told that it was notoriously the custom of the Mogul monarchs to resume such grants at will, no matter though his title-deeds show that the land was alienated from the state for ever. Our government, then, being inheritors of the sovereign rights exercised by former emperors, are entitled to treat him as his predecessors would have done. In dealing with such claims we prefer to rank as Mussulman rulers the practice of civilised states and the precepts of Christianity not being applicable to the circumstances. Where the slice of country in question was possessed by a Hindoo who has left no heirs of his body, we disallow the adoption of a son, because, being an English government, we can recognise no such law of inheritance. The fact, adduced by friends, relatives, and neighbours, that the defunct was obliged to adopt a son for the sake of his soul's happiness in the next world, which said heir by immemorial custom had forfeited all natural rights and could now only claim under his adoptive parent, is of course acknowledged; but the claimants are told that the supposed necessity does not exist. We know as Christians that the welfare of spirits is nowise dependent upon the mode in which their property when in the flesh is distributed. The late owner can show no equitable right that can be affected by the scheme of succession; and his pretended descendant has no legal claim. If the deceased had been a Christian noble, living in England, he might have made a will and left his estates to the sweeper of a crossing; but, as a Hindoo subject of Her Majesty, he has no such privilege. The one may bequeath his lands to a stranger who has corrupted his disposition through life, and who may dishonour his memory after death. The other is not permitted to purchase with his wealth, after the customs of his faith, the inheritance of heaven.

The sovereigns of what are called Independent States live in a state of abject dependence upon the will of the British agency at their various courts. The whole functions of government are in most cases exercised by the resident, in fact, if not in appearance; and the titular monarch sighs in vain for the personal freedom enjoyed by his subjects. To know the character of his rule, and the seeming tendencies of his disposition, it is sufficient to have a knowledge of the capacity and likings of the British representative. Thus General Cullen is a savant, and the Rajah of Travancore builds an observatory and maintains men of science; the resident of Indore is a person of elegant tastes, and the Maharajah surrounds himself with articles of *vertu*. The durbar surgeon at the Mysore court, who fulfils the duties of government agent, is passionately fond of the sports of the turf, and the rajah keeps a large stud of horses, gives gold cups and heavy purses at races, wears top-boots, and has pictures of the "great events" of past and present days. These are all Hindoo princes, but the Mussulmans are not so various and flexible in their tastes. The latter shut themselves up in their zenanas, the home of their infancy, manhood, and old age, and pass their time in occupations such as Englishmen scarcely care to inquire about. As pious Mahomedans, they detest us for the sake of the Prophet; as monarchs, whether good or bad, they hate us for reasons of their own.

Whether the next generation of Englishmen interfere or otherwise with the existence of native dynasties is a matter which scarcely concerns us at this moment. It will be the fault of Eastern princes alone if their dominion does not last our time; but what concerns every man of us at this moment is the necessity of giving freedom to native sovereigns, and the means of existence to native nobles. At every court our influence is paramount, and we use it neither for the rajah's power nor for the people's benefit. The example of the King of Oude is just in point. We had made treaties with his ancestors without the slightest stipulation as to the character of their rule. We had profited more by their vices than by their virtues. We knew that the hoards of treasure which more than once afforded us assistance, of which we stood in great need, were wrung from the tears and blood of miserable peasants, and yet we spoke not of his misgovernment, except to contrast it with our own beneficent system of rule. We waited in the case of the "sick man" of the East till his complaint was past remedy. We entered his palace as undertakers, and not as physicians. As guardians to an improvident heir, we winked at excesses which could not but lead to ruin; and when the estates were hopelessly involved, we took possession with the view of administering the property for the benefit of the tenants at large.

It will be admitted that such policy is not over-creditable to the English reputation amongst Asiatic princes, while it is cruel in the extreme to their subjects. We ought to make tyranny as rare as treason, and do our best to secure the perpetuity of native dynasties by making bad government on their part impossible. The change would hardly interrupt for a day the natural process of absorption, and we need hardly say how much it would conduce to the happiness of millions who have no protectors save Heaven and the Honourable Company.

The worth of the last-named influence is not much in the case of the state of Travancore, one of the naturally richest tracts of India, and under the nominal rule of an independent Hindoo rajah. The resident at the Court of Trevandrum has occupied the post for many years; and his wondrous power of floatation has kept him on the surface, though a dozen hurricanes of public wrath have spent all their force upon him. Nine years since, the "Madras Athenæum." bent itself steadily to the task of procuring redress for the wrongs of Travancore, and employed to that end every weapon within reach. The facts of the administration of public affairs were almost too horrible for recital; the causes of the misgovernment could only be darkly hinted at; but they were laid bare so far as a sense of loathing and a regard for decency permitted explanation. There was no shrinking from responsibility; the law of libel was transgressed a score of times, under the belief that if the aid of the courts of justice were invoked, the journalist would establish a claim to the gratitude of his countrymen. The public, after a while, got over the usual dislike to the occurrence of constant attacks on the conduct of a single official, and joined heartily in the hope that the Government would compel the resident either to prosecute the newspaper by indictment or resign his appointment. But striving and sympathy were equally useless. They were only potent enough to procure an order for the abolition of slavery, which existed in its most frightful form throughout Travancore. But the attempt to purify the courts of justice, to soften down the social scandals which disgraced the British name, to reform the police, to abolish torture, and to call out the resources of the country were wholly fruitless. The rajah of a subordinate principality on the coast tried his best to strengthen the hands of the seekers after justice. He told the Madras Government how he had been refused permission by the resident to dismiss his minister, though the latter had supplanted him in the affections of one of his wives; but the authorities at Madras treated the complaint as a question of internal administration, with which they ought not to interfere. In the end, the resident effectually wore out the perseverance, if he could not shake the purpose of his assailant, and the harvest of misrule grew without ripening.

In the abstract, it appears singular that so much toil should be requisite to redress the wrongs of society, in any quarter of the globe. The spider feels at once an injury done to the remotest filament of its web, and starts on the instant to repair it. A man suffers inconvenience from the smallest pain, and is anxious to get rid of it as soon as possible. But in the case of a community oppressed by a bad government, it is ever a task of the utmost difficulty to get reparation for the mischief inflicted. A year would probably elapse before the supreme authority would take notice of the state of things in Travancore. A period of equal duration would then be wasted in debating the matter; and under the most favourable circumstances, it must be many years before a mere popular outcry in India can force itself upon the attention of the Court of Directors. It is this long and inevitable delay between the vindication of a right, and the hour of its acknowledgment, which paralyses the efforts of Indian reformers. The opportunity is lost, or the inclination to strive for it suffers diminution. The hand grows stiff, or the heart grows cold; and as no institutions are founded for the progressive emancipation of the people, the last philanthropist finds that he must not only tread in the footsteps, but also do over again the work of his predecessor. So far as the government of the country is concerned, it would appear that the last century has done little or nothing for the improvement of its character. It is still a matter of chance, as to whether the most responsible posts are filled by a man of talent or an imbecile, a Christian or a tyrant; and when the ruling authority is vested in the hands of one who is unfit to exercise it, no checks exist to mitigate the hardships of its most oppressive exercise. A British resident at Travancore is at this moment more independent of control, more absolutely the disposer of life and fortune, than the Prime Minister of Great Britain; and it is a knowledge of this debasing fact which might prompt him to defy alike the efforts of public writers, and the indignant remonstrances of an outraged people.

The following list of the tortures current in Travancore, was prepared, in 1848, by an English gentleman of the highest respectability, at that time, and for many years previous, residing in the country. It will be seen that the operator had an extensive choice in his modes of treatment, and could deal with any kind of subject, in any locality. Some of the kinds of torture were constantly practised, others with less frequency; but there were a few of the government servants who had learnt the whole system, and could apply any example of persuasive treatment that might be required. Beating hardly comes under the head of torture, though the Burmese method of laying the patient down on his face, and kneading his back with the elbows of a strong man, approaches very near to it. Our catalogue should commence, with, racking the arms backwards, with cords tightened with increasing severity. While the arms are thus tied, bearing down the neck by a heavy weight pressing on the nape. In several ways wrenching various parts of the body, even to the dislocation of bones. Using an instrument called the "kitti," formed by two sticks connected by a loose joint at one end, which serves as a fulcrum, the two sticks being levers between which the fingers, &c. are squeezed; the degree of tightness is not limited, but increasing according to the nature of the case, and the will of the torturer. Whipping with a species of stinging-nettle. Tying two women together by their long hair, and suspending a weight on that hair between them. Using a long iron rod, with rings which slide on it, each one fitted to contain a leg; when these are filled, pulling the rod with violence, through a hole in the wall or wooden frame, by one end, so that all the legs are jammed up together at the other end. Suspending by the hands on a pole, for a lengthened time. It is not needful to tie the hands together; they can be constituted self-suspenders in this manner:—while holding the hands in front with the palms inwards, towards the chest, and the fingers extended, turn them inward, and then lock them one in the other, so that the ends of the fingers on one hand, rest in the palm of the other; then a pole passed across them inside will suspend the body, its pressure preventing the fingers from slipping out. While suspended in this manner, lighting a fire beneath the victim. Adding to his sufferings, by throwing the strongest red pepper on the fire, so that its severely pungent fumes assail his eyes, nose, and throat. Shutting up in a close room, and then smoking the sufferer. Applying hot pincers, and that to parts of the body which cannot be mentioned. Enclosing a number of pinching beetles, in half a cocoa-nut shell, and tying it over the navel, so that the horrid sensation of digging into the bowels is inflicted. Rubbing the arm from the wrist to the elbow, with salt and sand, then applying longitudinally a number of eekil, or ribs of the cocoa-nut leaf, and tying them on firmly; then forcibly drawing them out, one by one, the finer end first, so that each one, by its own increasing thickness, and aided by the salt underneath, cuts burningly into the flesh, and leaves its smarting sting.

The first impression on the reader's mind, will perhaps be, that the members who were in office at Madras, ten years since, were culpably remiss in not causing inquiry to be made into such dreadful practices as the above; but let him be reasonable. Two years since, the report of the Madras Torture Commission was put into the hands of the whole English public; and what has come of it? What party do the ten members of parliament belong to, who have taken the pains to read it? Men who live in India have lost the power of being moved by the recital of such atrocities; and those who sit at home at ease, need the occurrence of a rebellion, to induce them to give even a passing thought to the subject.

If the princes of India have not made common cause against us, the fact is in no degree owing to the kindness of the treatment which they receive from the hands of the Government. A species of surveillance is exercised over them, compounded of the watchfulness exercised with regard to a lunatic and to a dangerous state prisoner. No European can visit them without permission of the Company's agent. We have known a medical man denied access to the Nabob of the Carnatic, who, it was said, expressed a wish to see him upon unimportant matters. None of them dare correspond openly with England, and they take especial care to do nothing that can possibly offend their keepers. The pupils of Dotheboys Hall would willingly tell the story of their wrongs when away from school, but the poor souls whom we dignify with the titles of "Maharajah," and "Highness," scarcely dare utter their complaints, even in the recesses of their zenanas. The Rajah of Mysore sent an agent to the editor of a Madras newspaper, about four years since, with an earnest request that some articles should be inserted, with a view to procure the removal of an English officer attached to the presidency. The agent was reminded that the rajah had the power of refusing to receive the gentleman in question. "Oh, he dare not do that," was the reply. "Well, but," rejoined the editor, "will the rajah, if he is referred to on the subject of the charges, support and justify them?" "Why, no," said the ambassador. "You see, the rajah will be obliged to say that they are all lies, if the resident asks him; and that is the reason why he wants the paper to take up his case." In theory, the Rajah of Mysore is at least master of his court, in practice, he is scarcely on a level with his humblest retainer. The rights of sovereignty and the rights of manhood have both departed from him.

And it is not alone the "mockery kings" that expiate in bondage the crime of their weakness. It is no secret that Holkar, who might if he had chosen been at this moment at the head of a hundred thousand Mahrattas, has been addressed, since the late outbreak at Indore, both by the officiating resident and the officer in command at Mhow, in a style which would have driven any proud or passionate man into open insurrection. The servants of the Government, which is powerless to prevent the deeds of Cawnpore and Delhi, tell the Mahratta chieftain that he is responsible for the conduct of his troops, and they require explanations for the use of the Governor-General, which they warn Holkar are very likely to be thought unsatisfactory. If the maharajah is very sensible or very timid, no harm may come of this mode of treating the master of armed multitudes, at such a critical season as the present. But we usually rely on our right hand to cancel the mistakes of the brain. Holkar would thrive none the better for having a good cause of battle, and we trust that he will continue to sit and wait, like the rest of us, for better times.

Five years since, Lord Dalhousie threatened the King of Ava that he would dismember his dominions if he refused to pay the sum of 90*l.*, at which sum his lordship assessed the damage that had been sustained by certain merchants at the hands of the Burmese; but a hundred and sixty years ago, one of his predecessors, Nathaniel Higginson, Esq., addressed the lord of the white elephant as follows:—"To his Imperiall Majesty, who blesseth the noble city of Ava with his prescence, Emperour of emperours, and excelling the kings of the East and of the West in glory and honour, the clear firmament of virtue, the fountain of justice, the perfection of wisdom, the lord of charity, and protector of the distressed: The first mover in the sphere of greatness, president in council, victorious in warr; who feareth none and is feared by all: centre of the treasures of the earth, and of the sea, lord proprietor of gold and silver, ruby's, amber and all precious jewells, favoured by Heaven, and honoured by men, whose brightness shines through the world as the light of the sun, and whose great name will be preserved in perpetual memory." The paragon of princes has as many titles now as formerly, and his notions of greatness are no doubt equally justified by facts, but the balance of power has been strangely altered and the nobleman who now sits in Nathaniel's chair expresses his admiration in less glowing language. Talk about the smooth adulation of shopkeepers, what draper's "assistant" ever condescended, in order to sell his wares, to such abasement as the Governor of Fort St. George, who goes on to say: "The fame of so glorious an emperour, the lord of power and riches, being spread through the whole earth, all nations resort to view the splendour of your greatness, and with your Majesty's subjects, to partake of the blessings, which God Almighty hath bestowed upon your kingdoms above all others; your Majesty has been pleased to grant your especiall favours to the honourable English Company, whose servant I am; and now send to present before the footstool of your throne, a few toys, as an acknowledgment of your Majesty's goodness; which I beg your Majesty to accept; and to vouchsafe an audience to my servants, and a gracious answer to my petition.

"I humbly pray your Majesty's fountain of goodness to continue your wonted favours to the Right Honourable English Company, and to permit our factors to buy and sell, in such commoditys, and under such priviledges, as your royall bounty shall please to grant; and allow us such conveniencys, as are necessary for the repair of shipps, whereby I shall be encouraged to send my shipps yearly to your Majesty's port, having orders from the Honourable Company, to send shipps and factors into all parts of India, when their service requires it, and pray your Majesty to give me leave to send a factor, next monsoon, to reside at Syrian."

When the renowned Turpin wished the bishop's coachman to come to a halt, it is said that

> "Dick put a couple of balls in his nob,
> And perwailed on him to stop."

We invite attention to the passage in the following paragraph, where a kindred act on the part of the King of Ava is told in language equally soft and graceful. The guileless Nathaniel treats piracy as a pleasant hospitality, and thanks his majesty for robbery and murder.

"About three years agoe I ordered Bartholomew Rodrigues, master of a small sloop, called St. Anthony and St. Nicholas, to go from Acheen to Bengall, laden with divers commodity's; while I was expecting to hear from my factors in Bengall of her arrival there, the ship that came hither the last year from Syrian, brought me advice that the said sloop was fortunately arrived within your Majesty's kingdoms, and calling there for wood and water, your officers not knowing who she belonged to, had taken care, by your Majesty's order for the safe keeping the sloop and cargoe, which great favour I thought myself obliged to acknowledge, and therefore by the first opportunity, sent your Majesty a letter of thanks, with a small present, by a shipp that went last year from hence for Syrian: but unfortunately lost by the ignorance of the pilott. I have now sent this by my factors Edward Fleetwood and James Lesly, and humbly pray your Majesty to cause Bartholomew Rodrigues and his people, and that sloop and cargo, to be delivered to my said factors; who have orders to bring all to me; and fearing the sloop may be uncapable of going to sea, I have sent a ship to bring away the cargoe and men."

The devout humility of honourable John, when in his teens, is well shown in the remaining paragraphs of this unique epistle.

"Several Englishmen, who, in former years, have been in your Majesty's kingdoms, and have obtained liberty of returning, doe declare the greatness of your Majesty's glory. If there be any now remaining under the misfortune of captivity, I humbly beg your Majesty will please to grant their liberty, that they may spread the fame of your Majesty's splendid greatness from the rising sun to the setting sun.

"Adrian Tilbury, a merchant of this place, was my servant for many years. He made a voyage from hence to Mortavan, and there dyed. His widow hath acquainted me that your Majesty's governours have, according to the usuall justice of your Majesty's laws, secured his estate, being a stranger. I humbly pray your Majesty will be pleased to order the same to be delivered to my factors, for the use of his widow and orphan.

"I humbly pray your Majesty to permit the speedy repair and return of the ship which I now send, and that my factors may be permitted to return, by the same ship, this monsoon. And if your Majesty will grant me leave to build a small ship, or two, I will send my people next year for that purpose.

"Your Majesty's most humble and
"Devoted servant,
"NAT. HIGGINSON."

"Dated in Fort St. George,
the 10th Sept., 1695."

If the golden-footed monarch can boast of a family library, it is possible that he sometimes recreates himself with the perusal of a document, which shows how, a century and a half ago, our fathers "ate dirt" in the presence of his ancestors. Nor was the crawling, pedlar-like style in which we went to work to get in the small end of the wedge, at all a matter of mere verbal degradation, in the presence of royalty. What would our modern commodores and high civilians say, if the present Governor of Madras sent them on an embassy to Burmah, with the following instructions: —

"If you receive any affront, or injury, from any native, you must not revenge it by any means; if it be of such a nature, as you think requires satisfaction, you must apply yourselves to the Government, who will do you right; and your prudence must direct you to avoid the offering any affront, or injury, to the natives, for they are excessive proud, and will not bear it; but will either seek an opportunity of revenge, or complain to the Government; one imprudent action of that nature may give you a great deal of trouble, and overthrow your whole business. At your first arrival at Syrian, inform yourselves in the custom of the country relating to strangers."

There appears to have been no need for uneasiness as to the possible effect of Mr. Fleetwood's high spirit. All his thoughts were directed towards accomplishing the object of his mission, and getting as much as possible in return for the governor's present. We have heard in what order Commodore Lambert presented his credentials, as plenipotentiary for the marquis, let us note how the like ceremony was performed for the merchant by his countrymen a hundred and sixty years since. Mr. Fleetwood is describing the manner of his reception.

"When we came to the garden gate, where the king was, we alighted, where we were met by one of the ovidores, who was there, ready to conduct me in, and to direct me in the manner of approaching the king; here I took the letter from Mr. King, and stayed almost a quarter of an hour before the gates were opened, when we fell down upon our knees, and made three bows, which done, we entered the garden, the present following; and having gone about half way from the gate to the place where the king was seated, we made three bows again as before; when we were gott within fifteen yards of the king, we made three bows again, as we had done before, and were ordered to sit down; after we were sat down, the king ordered the ovidore to receive the letter, and about half a quarter of an hour after, asked me the three usual qestions; viz. how long I had been in my passage from Madrass to his port of Syrian? how many days from Syrian to Ava? and, at my departure from Madras, if I had left my governour in good health? I told his majesty that I had been about thirty days in my passage from Madrass to Syrian; about forty-two days from Syrian to Ava; and that at my departure from Madrass (thanks to God) I had left my governour in good health, supplicating the Divine power for the continuation of his Majesty's health and happiness. After this I sat about half a quarter of an hour longer, and then was dismissed."

Counsellor Phillips wept for Courvoisier, and Serjeant Wilkins cried on behalf of Mr. Ramshay, but the tears of the lawyers were not half so affecting as the prayers of the governor. Now-a-days instead of "supplicating the Divine power" for the welfare of kings, we pray for their territories, and usually get what we piously ask for.

We may have, as a people, opposite opinions as to the propriety of modifying or abrogating certain forms of agreement between the Indian Government and the worn-out despots who continue to increase the sum of mortal evil; but nothing that can be said for or against such measures can possibly do more than retard their sure effect. Absorption will take place, whether we wish it or not: it is in the order of things; the handwriting is on the wall, in a language familiar to all, and which he who runs may read. It is fated that in time the remaining Mussulman and Hindoo dynasties shall be subverted at least for a season, and in those cases where the maintenance of a puppet sovereignty involves the perpetual misgovernment of millions we would fain aid the work of extinction.

It is true that treaties exist, by which we are covenanted to uphold the existing framework of power; but we deny, with the British Parliament and with the people of every European nation, that one generation has the power of binding all the future races of mankind. And there is this broad and never-to-be-forgotten distinction between the agreements made with native princes and those which are entered into by the potentates of the western world. In the one set of instances, they are personal only, whilst the other are national, or, at the worst, broadly political. An arrangement in the one case is made with the individual, in the other with the state. The people are not known in India. They are the payers of taxes, the veritable slaves of the soil or the loom; but there is no power in the masses, and neither right nor justice, except such as can be won by force. To think that the overthrow of any particular sovereignty to-morrow would offend the patriotic prejudices of the multitude, as folks are apt to imagine at home, is to fall into a grievous mistake. Provide for the ruler and his court as pensioners of the state, and the change would not cause a murmur of disaffection, but, on the contrary, be hailed as the greatest of blessings.

It has been held by writers of great influence, that we are responsible "before God and man" for the government of the whole of India, and that, in refraining to appropriate the whole of its revenues out of a foolish regard for the "letter of treaties," we make "a scandalous misuse of those opportunities which Providence has given us." This declaration of rights and duties is at least comprehensive enough, and if acted upon, would put an end to a great deal of bribing and petitioning on the part of native supplicants, for what is still considered in some quarters bare justice.

If Providence would sanction our seizure of the revenues of Hyderabad, where a monarch *de facto* still exercises an admitted right to do what he likes with his own, its approval may be certainly counted upon for the stoppage of the pensions now paid to deposed princes and dispossessed proprietors of estates. We take it that the Nizam has a better claim to his revenue than the Nabob of Moorshedabad has to his annual allowance; and if the one is a camel which we are prepared to swallow, the other is not a gnat to be strained at. Since the magnitude of the payment made constitutes the reason for repudiating the treaty by which it is secured, it must be frankly owned that an *honorarium* amounting to 160,000*l.* a year cannot be left out of the category of sins against Providence.

The least gifted amongst us may become acquainted with the events which Heaven permits, but the very wisest cannot distinguish all those which it looks upon with approbation. The only guide to our researches on this important point is a certain volume which in theory is supposed to lay down rules for the conduct of nations as well as individuals. A contract made by a community in one hemisphere with a people residing in another, through the rulers or representatives of both, is as binding as an agreement concluded between individuals. The English Government, in its relation to the people of India, stands precisely in the position of a strong man who had forcibly possessed himself of the management of an estate, giving bonds at the outset of his usurpation for the payment of perpetual annuities to the parties previously exercising the rights of ownership. Now, admitting that there was no redress for the wrongful entry upon the land, or that the persons ousted had renounced their claims, the obligations imposed upon the holder would be restricted to the duty of seeing that the soil was properly cultivated, the tenants amply cared for, and the rent charges duly paid. If the estate produced less than was sufficient to pay the expenses, it is clear that no surplus would be left for the annuitants, who would lose all the benefits recited in their various securities, without having more grounds of complaint against the manager than a merchant has against a shipowner, when the cargo which he counts upon is lost at sea. But if the administrator of the property had taken under the head of necessary expenses more than the reasonable costs of management; if he had ruined some farms by a system of rack rents, and suffered others to go out of cultivation by neglect of repairs, and inattention to the reasonable wants of the peasantry; whilst at the same time his own private expenditure was most lavish and uncalled for, a Court of Equity would doubtless afford relief to the bondowners, and if need be, appoint a receiver of rents for the general benefit. Upon the same principle, if the Indian Government is able to show that in spite of the utmost care and frugality, the income of the State is not sufficient to discharge the whole of its obligations, the treaties made from time to time with various parties must remain suspended. Putting out of sight the question as to the duty of making ourselves responsible for acts that we are unable to perform, it is clear that one class of obligations may have a weightier significance as compared with another. It is more binding on us to promote the prosperity of the toiling ryot than to feed the luxury of a deposed prince, who would most probably, but for our career of conquest, have been reduced by some one amongst his own countrymen, long ere this, to a state of destitution. But if we have agreed to do both things; to cherish the worker and maintain as well the useless drone, the force of our duty is only to be measured by the extent of our means. In either case performance must equally wait on promise. We are no more justified in refusing to continue the payment of subsidies, because they are applied to no good purpose and are inconvenient to be raised, than in declining, as private individuals, to discharge a debt justly due to a miser, or to furnish the means for reckless profligacy to the worthless scion of an ancient house. It was beyond all question a foolish policy which dictated the majority of our stipulations with the native princes of India, but hardly more unwise, than that which prompted the twenty years' war with France, and entailed upon Great Britain a debt of some six hundred millions sterling. Few venture to justify the conduct of our rulers during that period, which has bequeathed a burden that will be felt by our native posterity, but the man who talks of applying a sponge to the list of national creditors is looked upon as a public enemy. It was wrong to contract the debt, and it was very inconvenient to discharge it, but the obligation is clear, and until the means of fulfilment are wanting, we are bound in the sight of the universe to comply with its terms, both in the letter and the spirit.

The dogmas frequently uttered with regard to the uses of Oriental revolutions, and the extent of our rights as lords paramount of India, are miserably unsound and hardly specious. To contend that a nation is benefited by the frequent recurrence of civil wars and foreign invasions, terminating in a change of dynasty, is as reasonable as it would be to assert that a man's life was best preserved by the periodical accession of disorders which should bring him each time to the verge of the grave. As to our dormant claims, under the plea of being lords paramount of the entire country, it is hard to say what these may amount to, since the extent has never yet been defined by any competent authority; but we venture to assert that they stop short of a title to the whole of the revenues collected at present by the various independent and protected states. We have taken a great deal, and may possibly obtain more; but are very properly chary of putting forward the doctrine of abstract right. If we are entitled to claim the revenues of every district, we are bound as well to distribute universally the blessings of internal peace and good government. In India, as elsewhere, property has its duties as well as its rights; and if we do not fulfil the one, we have no title at all to the other. If our dignity as lords paramount is expected to bring us solid advantages, let us show that we are willing to make a proper return for them. In those parts of Hindostan and the Deccan where the worst occupation is that of honest industry, the most powerless office that of the minister of justice, and the greatest enemy of the public the absolute monarch, a very slender amount of coin will satisfy the just demands of the British Government on the score of tribute. The ultimate absorption of every native state is, perhaps, merely a question of time. They are always weak and prone to give opportunities for being despoiled: we are always strong, and usually found willing to take advantage of our good fortune. But these are reasons why the work of years should not be precipitated. With destiny on our side, we may be surely content to await the appointed hour. It is enough to acquire riches and glory whilst we are advancing the cause of civilisation and true religion, without acting so as to raise doubts with regard to the honesty of our motives and the reality of our mission.

CHAP. XVIII.

THE NOBLES AND JAGHIREDARS OF INDIA. — THEIR WRONGS AND MISERABLE CONDITION. — THE INQUISITION IN BOMBAY. — CASE OF THE NAWAB OF WOODIAGHERRY. — PROPOSED REMEDY.

But besides the inheritors of empty kingships, there is the numerous and daily increasing class of their families and those of their chief retainers, who are yoked to us by bonds which they have neither the energy nor the means to sever, nor we the honesty and wisdom to make pleasant or profitable. The family and adherents of the great Mogul, of the house of Tippoo Sahib, and of the late Nabob of the Carnatic, would alone make a goodly army, at least in point of numbers, and we know not how many thousands of able-bodied men are vitally interested in the overthrow of our dominion, by which alone they can hope to retain the means of existence. During the half century that we have had control over the destinies of the members of the three great families alluded to, whilst we have been steadily encroaching on the fund set apart originally for their maintenance, we have done nothing whatever in the way of training their children, or affording them the opportunities of employment. There is no opening for them in the army except as private soldiers; no room for them on the bench except they mingle with the mass of witnesses that haunt our courts, and are content to crawl upwards, all dirt and servility. Without land they cannot live by agriculture, and without capital they cannot embark in trade. Not a year passes over which does not make large additions to the stock of misery and discontent, in the shape of disinherited heirs who have licked the dust in vain for the chance of being allowed to retain the estate or the pension enjoyed by their fathers. In Bengal and Madras the work of retrenchment is well nigh over, and aristocratic pauperism is as wretchedly fed and clothed as need be; but in Bombay, at this moment, a commission is sitting, which has been in existence since 1843, charged to inquire into the validity of all titles to rent-free lands held in hereditary occupation. The total claims in the southern Mahratta country up to the date of a parliamentary return, issued on the 28th of August last, amounted to upwards of 108,000, and less than 7000 decisions had been given in the course of the fourteen years past. This leaves more than 100,000 claims standing over, which at the same rate will be settled A. D. 2,058. The gain in revenue from the resumptions is 15,846*l.* per annum, at present, and a further sum of 27,000*l.* after the lapse of one, two, or three lives. The cost of the survey was, perhaps, 100,000*l.* in cash, and how much in good will and loyalty?

The case of the jaghiredars of the Carnatic, most of whom are related to the family of the late nabob, may be taken as an example of the wrongs inflicted generally throughout India upon men of their class.

A thousand arguments might be adduced to show the impolicy and cruelty of the conduct pursued towards the Mahomedan nobility of Madras, but they can afford to rest their case upon the ground of admitted rights. Their dignities and estates were created in the most valid way by the Mussulman sovereigns of the Carnatic, and have been publicly and officially recognised by the English Government times out of mind. In the treaty which was made by the Marquis Cornwallis with Mahomed Ally, the possessions of the jaghiredars were declared exempt from interference, even in the worst extremity. The rights of the sovereign power, which extended over all the rest of the country, were barred with respect to their estates. In the third article of the treaty, it was stipulated "that in the event of war breaking out in the Carnatic and countries appertaining to either party, and dependent on the Carnatic, or contiguous thereto,"--for the better prosecution of it, and as long as it should last,—" the Company should " possess full authority over the Carnatic, except the jaghires belonging to the family of the said nabob, amounting to star pagodas 213,911, which on condition of the good behaviour of the jaghiredars of the said jaghires, and of their fidelity to the said nabob, and to the said Company, shall be continued to them, subject to the pleasure of the said nabob only.

No clearer proof can be required to show that the jaghires were perfect alienations from the property of the state, which could not be made subject to the provisions of a treaty between sovereign powers. Mahomed Ally himself renounced all legal claim, and he could not share or transfer that of which he was not in possession or expectancy. It is true the words " subject to the pleasure of the said nabob only," serve to indicate the possibility of his resumption of grants made in perpetuity; but the law of his country and religion would not justify him in so doing; and the European inheritors of his throne were not able to vindicate a wider range of lawless power. Oaths might be broken, and all the conditions of trust between monarch and subject openly violated, but the wrong would be palpable to earth and heaven. And there is this marked distinction to be drawn between the examples of native and British violence, where the Indian aristocracy are in question, that in the one case, the class rarely suffers by the loss of the individual. The aggregate wealth is not diminished; what is taken from the disgraced favourite, is given to his successor; and the caprice which ruins a man to-day, may restore him with added possessions to-morrow. But the water which the English ruler diverts from the stream is never restored to the fountain, or distilled in dew over the surrounding country. It is carried away to fertilise a foreign soil. Under Christian sway, the ryot and the noble are tending to the same result of lowest poverty, only the one has nearly reached the firm ground of ultimate wretchedness, whilst the other has still the rags and the recollection of better days clinging to his mind and person.

The jaghiredars of the Carnatic place great reliance upon the abstract validity of their titles, and the repeated proclamations in which the British Government pledged itself to respect them; but there is extant a paper, which shows what the very administration that subverted the dynasty of Mahomed Ally thought of their claims. It is a report from the Board of Revenue "On the Jaghires in the Carnatic," dated 26th March, 1802, only eight months after the annexation of the country. The writer, Mr. Falconer, after narrating the difficulties which stood in the way of getting at a thorough knowledge of the subject, gives the results of his investigation of the titles by which ninety-five persons held their estates. Most of the holders, he remarks, had a "plurality," and many of them a multitude of Sunüds. After proving that the united annual value amounted to nearly five and a half lakhs of pagodas, he says, "The jaghires may be arranged into three classes.

"The first class comprises the Altumgha tenures, of which the deed of gift expressly and emphatically describes them to be hereditary." The reporter enumerates the various individuals included in the first rank, and goes on to say:

"The second class comprises those which had originally been conferred by padshahi grants, or grants so termed: —and which, though not specified to be hereditary, have nevertheless been suffered to remain in the hands of the original grantee (the extent of the jaghire being sometimes curtailed), until the death of the late nabob. This class being generally killadars, were expected originally to perform military service as such, and the jaghires were bestowed to defray their personal expenses, and those of their garrisons. They latterly however became sinecures."

At the head of the list of jaghiredars of the second class, stands the name of Syed Abbas Khan, of Woodiagherry, who held under various Sunüds, the most ancient bearing the seal of the Soubahs of the Deccan. For five generations the estate had been in the possession of the same family. It yielded 10,000*l.* per annum; and they had independent jurisdiction within its limits. In 1839 the holder of the estate was an old bedridden man who had lost the use of his limbs for twenty years. Such a condition of physical impotence is unfavourable to the nurture of ambitious hopes; and it will be reasonably concluded that a petty Indian rajah, who had conceived the design of making himself master of the Carnatic, must possess many rare gifts both of body and mind. The poor jaghiredar in question had never been suspected of genius or insanity; but, at the time we speak of, the collector of Nellore took it into his head that he intended to carve out for himself an independent kingdom. The merit of the discovery, though ascribed to the collector, is claimed by a moonshee, who has since had his deserts, and upon the representation of the former to the government of the day, a commission, consisting of a single individual, was appointed to take evidence in the case; and the result of it lies before us. It is our earnest hope to have it laid some day on the table of a committee of the House of Commons, as a sample of the machinery by which men obnoxious on account of their wealth are ruined in India. It is the hearsay scandal of menials and policemen anxious to conciliate the minister of justice. It is so worthless that disgust at the open villany of the swearers is neutralised by the contempt for the intellect which could accept it as the revelations of honest men. There was not a single question put in the way of cross-examination. It was assumed from first to last that the witnesses knew all that they had to say, and had come prepared to say it.

The nawab begged for a hearing. He said it would be a boon for which he should feel ever grateful if they would allow him to confront his accusers. His request was denied: such a form was thought needless in the way of helping the collector and commissioner to a knowledge of the truth. People who are averse to toil look with natural reluctance upon the prospect of labours overthrown; and had the nawab been heard, according to the fashion that prevails in the civilised world, a new hypothesis of guilt would have been required to ensure his deposition. So they gave him, in answer, a message delivered by the officer of a sepoy guard, and sent him in custody to Chingleput, where a broken heart finished his career. His estate was confiscated, and a pension of a hundred rupees a month granted by the charitable clemency of the government to two of the surviving sons. The net profit on the transaction is 6760*l.* per annum. We have heard of the gain of godliness; but here are undeniable proofs of the gain of guilt.

For examples of broken faith, violated laws, and systematic oppression, the government of India is able to challenge the universe. In the main, things are done very quietly in that part of the world. We hear of the decay of a district only when a civil servant is suspended. A member of the Madras Board of Revenue is imprisoned in the common jail for perjury; and forthwith the public ear is filled with stories of how justice had been put up to sale for many years past, and the practice of corruption universally known, if not openly avowed. The people are timid and ignorant. They are afraid to clamour for redress, and know not where it is to be obtained for the asking. The press is deficient in a knowledge of facts, and the government officials, with but few exceptions, are a band of brothers.

Mr. Falconer closes his catalogue of grants of the above description with the remark, that, "these were conferred for services performed by the ancestors of the present claimants, who were all descended from families of some distinction."

"The third class," says Mr. Falconer, "comprises all other jaghires, which may be considered as life grants merely; or tenures depending on the good will of the donor." In the course of his inquiries, the reporter discovered that "a tract of territory, to the amount of 168,806 star pagodas," in addition to the recognised estates, "had been granted in jaghire tenure, but by the death of the occupants, or other circumstances, had reverted to the State." We draw attention to the reasons which Mr. Falconer assigns for this concealment.

"It is natural to suppose that these escheats would have been re-annexed to the khalisah or state lands. They however retained their denomination of jaghires, and were kept under a distinct management; the revenues being remitted to the exchequer's general treasury. The policy of this may be traced to the immunity provided for the jaghire lands of the family in the event of the Company assuming the country, and the advantage of reserving as large a proportion as possible of their resources, from the peril of eventual sequestration."

The poor jaghiredars had laid up for the rainy day which they dreaded was in store for them; but no man in that generation knew the full force of the storm, and that half a century would elapse before its worst ravages would be felt. Lord Clive and his councillors and revenue officers never intended that their policy should be interpreted as a series of covert and cruel confiscations, or they would not have left on record these damning proofs of their wilful dishonesty. The document from which we have quoted was not intended for the public, and is not only conclusive as to the rights of the jaghiredars, but it affords the most convincing evidence of their full recognition by the British Government.

It suited the policy of the Company, when they annexed the Carnatic, to take the jaghires into their possession with few exceptions, and grant pensions in lieu of them. The lands were freehold, and of course the allowance should have been hereditary; but, after the lapse of a few years, the Government found it inconvenient to continue such heavy and perpetual burdens on the resources of the State. So they began to talk of the annuity being only granted for the lives of the existing incumbents, whose children must look to the bounty of the ruling power. When the lapse occurred, half the rate of pension was paid, as being all to which the family were entitled "under the orders of Government." Unruly or ill-treated members applied occasionally to the agent for assistance or justice, and by degrees a practice grew up of dividing the allowance heretofore paid to the head of the family, into a certain number of shares, the amount of each being fixed by the agent, in conjunction perhaps with one or two Mussulman officials. As time wore on the recipients grew more numerous, and the rupees were diminished.

There were descendants of nobility living perhaps on forty shillings a month, and allowances were divided until some of those highborn people had but a couple of shillings weekly to subsist upon. And all this while, there were millions of acres of land lying waste in Madras, with no prospect of being brought into cultivation under the Company's rule. That which had not enriched us, had made them miserable.

Our remedy for this state of things is the universal recognition of all titles to land, for which even bare colourable testimony can be adduced; the return of jaghires instead of the payment of pensions, and the imposition of an income tax in all cases of rent-free lands. If posterity has no claim upon jaghiredars, it will be admitted that jaghiredars have no claim on posterity; and since they cannot do without government, we must make them pay at least a share of the cost of it. The measure of a government's requirements must be the measure of its income; and whatever expectations a man may have been led to form with regard to the smallness of the sums that he would have to pay in taxes, it is clear that the State can take no heed of them.

Of the right of Government to impose an income tax on state pensioners and holders of rent-free lands, there cannot be the smallest question; and if a legacy duty were added, the heirs of those persons would not be a whit worse off than the Englishman who is taxed from his cradle to his grave. If the Nabob of Moorshedabad were compelled to return some 10,000*l.* to the treasury of Calcutta, we, who uphold the necessity for paying his pension, whilst there are funds sufficient to furnish it, should not say that he was hardly dealt with. Three years ago the British landowner or merchant paid seven per cent. upon their several incomes in the shape of direct taxation, exclusive of imposts upon every article of consumption or needful appliance: and looking at the almost perfect exemption from fiscal charge which is enjoyed by the titular sovereigns and nobles of India, we assert that an income and property tax of ten per cent.

would not be an unreasonable compensation to the State, for the peculiar privileges that are bestowed upon them.

There are various opinions as to the proper mode of our future dealings with the princes of India, but there can only be one opinion as to the propriety of making a change in the state of our existing relations with them. We have indicated the course that in our judgment ought to be pursued, having a due regard to the mitigation of Indian burthens and the care of English honour. We would maintain unimpaired the substantial portions of every treaty, but abrogate without scruple those stipulations which acknowledge rights and titles, of which not a vestige actually remains. The heir of a deposed dynasty should rank in the first class of Eastern nobles, thus faring better than the Bourbons of our time, and they should be treated as an English Parliament would treat the English aristocracy. The period has arrived when we are bound to legislate on general principles for this numerous class of persons, and we trust that the nature of the enactments will not expose us to the reproach of mankind.

CHAP. XIX.

THE RESPONSIBILITY FOR CONQUEST. — REPUBLICAN NOTIONS OF THE RIGHTS OF MANKIND. — THE FIGHTING INSTINCT UNIVERSAL IN ALL CLASSES. — VALUE OF AMERICAN LESSONS. — THE RIGHTS OF CONQUEST AND THE CLAIMS OF THE CONQUERED.

We are half tempted to smile at the earnestness with which some of our countrymen in the East repudiate the charge of being favourable to the farther extension of the Anglo-Indian Empire. The blame of conquest must rest somewhere, but they prefer that it should be ascribed to some score or so of men, who from time to time have held the reins of government. It follows of course that these rulers did not represent the views or embody the passions of the British people. The latter were pacific and just, and would not have held a single acre of the soil in absolute possession, had they been consulted on the matter. They are the receivers of stolen property, but they did not authorise the theft. The robbers, from the days of Clive to those of Gough, have been fêted and rewarded at home on account of their spoils, but it was not the nation that honoured them. A few guilty aristocrats in Downing Street and grocers at Leadenhall Street are at the bottom of the whole matter.

It is hard to say what might have been the aspect of affairs at this moment, had every man in England, for the last century, been referred to for his vote on all public occasions; but we are afraid that our countrymen might have appeared less wise, and scarcely more honest. Two centuries ago a few of them emigrated to the far West, and laid the foundation of a mighty dominion in peace and justice. Their descendants invented a form of government for themselves; they abjured kingship, prelacy, and hereditary rank and title, and set up, as the sole rule and standard of authority, the sovereignty of the people. Well! do the republicans regard the rights of their neighbours? Are they better in this respect than the nominees of our aristocracy? The Red Indians will not reply in the affirmative, nor the millions of domestic slaves, nor the Mexicans, nor the Spaniards, nor the weak with whom they have come in contact in any part of the world. The nominal heads of the Government have sanctioned aggressive wars as readily as the "legitimate" powers of Europe; and when there are no state plans of hostility to be carried out, Jonathan gets up an invasion in shares, as you would a joint stock bank, and starts off to annex Central America as a private speculation. If conquest is as bad as robbery from the person, the Americans are worse than the Spartans of old, for they steal universally, with no pretence of a moral end in view.

Do we justify aggressive wars then? No! for they are clearly opposed to the genius and precepts of Christianity; but we look upon them as the natural fruits of civilisation — of the vices or the strength, whichever you please to term it, of the whole European race. As well say to the fire, do not burn the stubble, as to the Englishman, do not subject the Asiatic if you come in contact with him. Their intercourse is sure to end in the mastership of the former; but the result is not the consequence of a dogma—it is the effect of an instinct. The natives will not adopt our religion, because they are convinced that it is not so good as their own. They have no relish for our literature or music, but in the depths of their hearts they acknowledge the controlling force of the white man. The belief is mutual, for the meekest professor of the Gospel feels that he condescends when he treats the Asiatic as a "brother." We have only to bear in mind the additional fact that, even amongst missionaries, there is a per centage of worldly-mindedness, and the theoretical fairness, with which some folk contend we ought to treat the dusky tribes, is seen to be past praying for.

Were the nations to turn honest, there would be a very extensive exchange of valuables; and unless they make full restitution, the sense of abstract right will still be outraged. Who shall define the just claims of separate jurisdictions? Can England retain even the Channel Islands? We doubt it; for the sea is her natural boundary. She has no right to Ireland, and ought to poll the Welsh and the North Britons, to ascertain if they are willing to obey the Queen. As for the kingdoms of the Continent, we are at a loss to conceive upon what ground, except that of universal popular agreement, their just limits could be marked out. They have stolen from each other little or much, according to the strength of their opportunities. Not a gem in any diadem but has been obtained as questionably as the last bright ornament of the British Crown, for which Her Royal Majesty neglected to reward the captors.

We are aware that the members of the Peace Society are ready with a method of solving the difficulty which stands in our way. They wish England to turn over a new leaf, and give up entirely the military occupation of foreign parts.

We are to work, write, and pray for all the world, but to fight with nobody, white or black. The national faith should inculcate the sole duty of providing for the greatest happiness of the greatest number; the common creed should consist of a single article, that it is proper to buy in the cheapest and sell in the dearest market. In the latter sentence lurks the error of the theory. Justice between man and man requires that there should be no advantage taken of poverty or ignorance. The fair day's work should always be rewarded by the fair day's wages, and the buyer of an article should never be asked to pay more than its intrinsic worth. If capital be allowed on the one hand to take advantage of the necessities of labour, and the workmen, on the other, are permitted to combine whenever they see a chance of forcing a higher rate of payment, we can only recognise in such a state of things the alternate struggles and triumphs of contending enemies. Honesty and good feeling are out of the question. The law which rules is the right of the strongest, and the Society of Friends is not a whit less belligerent than the Board of Control.

All over the world there is a never-ceasing contest for mastery, and it will not begin to be ended in our time, unless we are near the latter days. In the century which has witnessed the triumph of Mormonism and other kindred impostures, we ought not to feel surprised at the efforts of the Peace Society. The doctrine that all men are mad upon some point or other would seem to derive confirmation from the speeches and writings of the leaders of the anti-fighting association. It may be very proper to form a league for the extirpation of a single political evil; but why should we combine with such labour and cost for the vindication of a single moral precept? Why not organise for the purpose of making all men veritable Christians, instead of the mere advocates of peace, which only forms a single clause in the Divine code? It has been well observed that the pursuit of riches is as strongly denounced in Scripture as the levying of war; but unless the principle of selfishness can be eradicated from the human heart, and the pure love of mankind implanted in its stead, what hope is there of hindering men from making war upon their fellows? Less than the universal practice of Christianity will not suffice to destroy the belligerent feeling; and if innumerable teachers have only succeeded, after the lapse of eighteen hundred years, with a small portion of the children of men, what prospect of usefulness is there in store for the Peace Society?

No doubt it is abhorrent to the best feelings of humanity, that soldiers should wish for an opportunity of slaughtering their fellow creatures, and of turning as much of this beautiful earth as their feet can traverse into a howling wilderness; but when a class of men profit by the misery of others, we must expect them to rejoice in the spread of evil. Ask the lawyer if the absence of litigation amongst a civilised people is not a cheering sign of progress, and he will reply in the affirmative; but for all that, if his bag be empty of briefs, he will curse his hard lot. A rich client and a long suit are the chief sources of his happiness. As a member of the human family he would rejoice at the cessation of strife, but as an advocate he must live by his profession, and is anxious to gain reputation. Just so with the physician, whose vocation it is to cure diseases. He will do his utmost to alleviate the ills which flesh is heir to, but it would task his philosophy to bear with patience a universal freedom from sickness. Is it not then unreasonable to expect that a soldier should obey a nobler class of impulses, and look upon his occupation as being designed for the benefit of the mass and not of the individual? We talk to him of the "God of battles," consecrate the flag under which he serves, and teach him to look to renown and the death of his seniors as the only roads to the enjoyment of a quiet competence in old age; and, in spite of those incentives, he is to uphold the dogmas of universal brotherhood whilst the rest of the world are fighting with brain and heart,—each man trying to wrest an advantage from his fellow and keep it for his own especial use. Competition is the soul of trade, almost the sole spring and source of human effort, yet what is it but a state of perpetual antagonism of interests? To say nothing of the indifference as to the welfare of others, which is the necessary consequence of such a state of things, the business of life is so carried on that the prosperity of one man must be built mainly upon the ill fortune of others. But little of the trade of a thriving shopkeeper is created out of nothing. If customers crowd in upon him it is at the expense of his fellow tradesmen; but who complains of him for doing his best to make money? Who says it is criminal in the merchant prince to absorb the small speculator? in the successful advocate to overshadow and keep in the background numbers as well educated as himself, and as keenly desirous of fame and profit?

These members of the Peace Society, dealers in merchandise and money! is there one of them who will part with his wares for less than the market value? or, in other words, for less than the highest price that opportunity enables him to demand? Surely not, and yet each great advance in the nominal worth of commodities is to many productive of mischief, to some of absolute ruin. We recollect when Cajeput oil was declared to be a specific for the cholera, at that time raging in England: there was but one holder of the drug in the kingdom, and he stood out till the price advanced from 9*d.* an ounce to 30*s.* Here was a profit of four thousand per cent. made upon an article which Christianity would have prompted him to vend at the rate at which it bestows the highest of all gifts — without money and without price. But the world had no blame for the transaction; it was a lucky hit — the reward of mercantile shrewdness and sagacity. It is not likely that the fortunate individual was a Quaker; but at any rate there was no reason why he should not have been an active member of the Peace Society, and set forth on platforms and in newspapers the blessings of universal brotherhood.

For one short year, if we could sum up the killed and wounded in the daily battles of our countrymen with each other, the sum of misery inflicted in the course of a campaign would appear very small in proportion. To slaughter a man, it is not absolutely needful to encounter him with wrathful brow and armed hands. Dry up by whatever means the source of his income, and he is as effectually disposed of as if he were laid face upwards on a field of slain. Shylock, when told that his existence would be spared but that all his estate was confiscated, spurns the partial clemency, and exclaims —

> "Nay, take my life and all, pardon not that:
> You take my house, when you do take the prop
> That doth sustain my house; you take my life,
> When you do take the means whereby I live."

We wish that the Anglo-Indian were colonist as well as conqueror. It is an evil thing for the people of India, that he leaves his household gods and his sympathies behind him in the land of his fathers. Had he chosen to take root in the Indian soil fifty years ago, we should by this time have had railways in some districts, and good roads everywhere. We should have supplied England with cotton, and been independent of the law commission in the matter of legislation. Stores of exhaustless wealth, which now lie unheeded, would have been opened up; duties, which are now only getting faintly recognised, would have been the practice of men in authority; and, in short, the India of the twentieth century would have been realised at this moment. A plentiful crop of heroisms may always be raised on the spot which a man inhabits, to console him for the fading memories of his distant birthplace. It is but ninety years since the inhabitants of America only shared in the glories of Britain; and now they have a roll of chivalry, on which are inscribed the names of deathless men, the product of the western world; they have a growing literature, and a dominion which is every hour enlarging its wide boundaries. Had the "pilgrim fathers" taught their children to look upon the land of their birth as a place of exile, in which they were to cherish above all things the memories of the past, it is more than likely that Washington would have died a retired officer in the royal army, and the affairs of New York and Pennsylvania been administered just now by Mr. Labouchere and the Colonial Office.

Ask the physiologist of nations what it is that prompts our schemes of foreign conquest; and he will answer, "a restless love of acquisition." We would pour the world's wealth into a goblet, and drink it off at a draught. We would anticipate the course of time, and enjoy, in our generation, the treasures of futurity; but in the instance of our Indian dominion, we seem to have gained without any desire to enjoy the usual fruits. Whenever we have encountered opposition, our track has been like that of the desolating lava; but, like that molten wave, we have congealed to stone when the strength of the fire-birth is expended. The wealth which we acquire is obtained by the exercise of the commonest appliances of labour; the exertions which we make are the result not of great thoughts or of noble emotions, but are prompted by the mere animal instinct of self-preservation. The land is teeming with wealth which we never use, and apparently never covet—for the simple reason, that we are ignorant of its existence. Two hundred millions of human souls wait, patiently, from father to son, for deliverance from mental and moral bondage; and we, who might almost be gods in our distribution of blessings, feel that we have performed our duty if we always rank a little above the fallen angels.

Every man is conscious of having at various times received new impressions, such as have totally altered his views and feelings upon particular subjects. The profound thinker can trace in his own mind the constant action of change, and follow in their proper sequence the influences which have moulded his opinions; and the mass of the people, though they do not consider these matters curiously, become aware at certain periods that a new light has dawned upon them. When feudalism was forced to acknowledge that the tiller of the ground was not a divinely-appointed slave — when priests were led to own that their mission was to convert heretics, and not to burn them — when the source of political power was declared to reside in the people — when the bonds of commerce were loosened and the entire freedom of international intercourse finally asserted, our English kindred saw they were about to open fresh chapters of history. They have taught themselves and the world some of the noblest lessons; but for the present it seems that they must put off the pedagogue, and go to school again. The Americans have set them a few exercises, which we hope will soon be learned and extended by the pupils.

We do not owe to our Transatlantic friends any improved ideas of religion, morals, or freedom. We are content with our monarchy, our church, and our share of liberty; but we have to thank them for the most decisive proofs of the omnipotence of common sense. They have shown us the monstrous absurdity of the rule of Red Tape, and the folly of allowing a government to regulate the social arrangements of a nation. Their progress is the most wonderful in the annals of the world, because they have hindered it from being interfered with. As soon as they have satisfied themselves that a thing ought to be done, they go and do it. The men who resolve are the men who execute. There is no waiting for sanction, or presentation of humble petitions to persons who are most likely known to be profoundly incompetent to give any opinion, much less an authoritative one, on the matter. The notion that a useful scheme could be set aside at the mere will of a State servant, is incomprehensible to them. They would as soon think of allowing the veto of the Emperor of China. The Yankee, who has so much in common with ourselves, looks at politico-social questions from a totally different point of view. He judges the acts of Government by the same criterion that he would judge the conduct of a body of traders. They ought to accomplish whatever lies in the compass of their ability, and in the cheapest and most satisfactory manner. The fool ought neither to be trusted nor rewarded; and the idler should be punished without mercy. Now, take an Englishman who happens to be both merchant and East India director, watch his conduct in both capacities, and you will note his application of two different rules to circumstances which are precisely alike. As a merchant he will only employ men to do the tasks they are fit for, and has proper notions of responsibility and power. He will not, as a member of a railway board, ask Mr. Stephenson to submit his plans to the approval and control of the secretary's department; but as a director of the East India Company, he insists that Colonel Cotton shall obey the Madras Revenue Board, the governor, and the authorities in Bengal. Tell him, as a merchant, that his workmen, whom he is bound to take care of, are many of them starving, but that, if he merely gives the word, abundant employment can be found for them, and his own income thereby largely increased, and see how readily his humanity and interest will dovetail in each other; but in his capacity of manager at Leadenhall Street, such considerations are mostly disregarded. Why questions of a purely social kind should be dealt with so differently is what brother Jonathan cannot comprehend. If we had the "'cutest" of all Yankees in Bombay or Madras at this moment, we should find it utterly impossible to make him understand why we keep up governors and councils under present circumstances,— why certain men in certain offices, who merely sign a few papers in the course of a week, are paid higher wages than English judges in Westminster Hall,—why the roads in the interior are impassable and the cities unsewered. He would ask us if we approved of such a state of things; and being answered in the negative, and furthermore assured that the power, wealth, and information at the disposal of the State were unbounded, he would emphatically tell us we were "the darndest fools in all creation." And it is difficult to say how the imputation could be got rid of.

If India had been only for the last ten years an appanage of the United States, all its capabilities would be known by this time, and most of them improved to the utmost. Whereever iron could be laid down or water made to flow with advantage, railways and canals would be made. In every town a Yankee trader would be found selling idols, and a Yankee missionary giving away Bibles. Spittoons and a senate would be introduced into Calcutta. A House of Representatives would be located somewhere on the Strand; and colonels at the head of commission houses would hold forth therein on the blessings of liberty and cheap rule. If resistless energy and never-failing shrewdness were the highest national gifts, it would be a glorious day for the East if it passed under the dominion of the younger branch of the Anglo-Saxons.

But something more than profound selfishness on the part of the governing class is requisite to promote the well-being of subject millions. The American admits no rivalry of interest and tolerates no admixture of races. No gifts of nature or position can, in his estimation, atone for a darker skin. He is the Western Brahmin, and looks upon all Asiatics as men of a lower order of being. We will content ourselves, then, with wishing that our countrymen may adopt American modes of performing public duties, but retain their own standard of social rights. We would ask Jonathan to show us how to deal with our courts of directors and legislative councils, but decline to take his advice as to the proper treatment of the dusky millions.

It cannot be denied that the natives lost rather than gained by the last change in the government of India. In theory, they stand upon the same footing with the Europeans; but who does not see that now and henceforth the latter will continue to engross for a time all the higher posts in the government of the country? The necessity of being educated in England, and of standing a competition with the whole body of the English educated youth, is fatal to the hopes of the Hindoo student, however naturally gifted, and though left entirely free to enter the lists as a candidate for the rich prizes of the civil service. It is true that hitherto the Company have always acted as though there had been no recognition of the equal right of all the Queen's subjects to aspire to high employment in the service of the state. We have no natives on the bench of the Zillah Courts, or dark-skinned engineers. Policy shuts them out from high command in the army; and interest has effectually prevented them from effecting an entrance into the ranks of the civil branch. But there was a change which appeared to effect all that could be desired. The monopoly of office was utterly overthrown; all distinctions of caste were abolished; rank and wealth were to be the sure rewards of the ablest. You cannot find a flaw in the scheme which is to ransack all the broad dominions of Britain in search of the most gifted intellects, and which gives to the service of the public the concentrated talent of the whole array of nations which own the sovereignty of Queen Victoria. And yet, the direct exclusion, by name, of the natives of India could not have hindered their advancement in the way of self-government more completely than this liberal measure. In the race which is thrown open to half the world, they will never be the victors. They might have extorted, under the old system, some concessions from the remorse and shame of the Indian Government; but, in future, they can hope nothing from the justice of the examiners at home. The latter are bound to select the best-instructed of the youth that offer to undergo the ordeal; and how can the poor Asiatic, weighed down with the prejudices of caste, and forced to unlearn, by way of a commencement, the foolishness of his previous lifetime, pass through the furnace with triumph? It is a pity that those to whom the guidance of affairs were intrusted, should not have had the courage to stand on the great truth which lies at the bottom of all this contradictory legislation for India. The Asiatic can never occupy the same platform with the European; and it is a cruel mockery to teach him to the contrary. So long as the value of his learning and capacity is tested by an Eastern standard, he may obtain, in reputation at least, the full measure of their worth; but when opposed to Western ability, he fails as much in the comparison of mental as of bodily power. The law that affected to put the two races on a level, would be at variance with the decrees of nature, which has ordained that there should be an eternal wall of separation between them. The time has again come round in which India must be legislated for; but we protest beforehand against any attempt to establish equality by Act of Parliament, in the teeth of the wiser legislation of Providence. There is a great debt owing to India, of which it is time to commence at least the payment of the first instalment; but those who would tender, for that purpose, a declaration of equal rights on the part of Hindoos and Englishmen, and practically enforce it, would create a balance on the other side, which would have to be adjusted again in an inconvenient way. The cry of "Justice to India," will receive various interpretations; but no honest politician can lend the slightest countenance to the notion which appears to be uppermost in the minds of leading Hindoos, that English institutions can be established in that part of the Queen's dominions, or that the country can be governed by and for the people. We may as well attempt to assimilate the natural productions of the two hemispheres, as strive to naturalise in the East the growth of Anglo-Saxon civilisation. Even where the soil is fitted for its reception, the tree of liberty will not flourish as a transplanted root. It must be raised from the seed, and not the graft. Instead of being inaugurated with pomp and ceremony, its silent up-springing must be watched and tended by anxious generations, ready at all times to water it with blood and tears. India created, thousands of years since, her own peculiar system of civilised existence. It is worn out, and now wants replacing; but the new law must grow out of the old,—you cannot change the national character. The Hindoo is always a "man;" but he will never be a "brother," in the sense which implies an identity of feelings and interests with the Englishman.

If the native reformers had the option to-morrow, they would reject the British constitution as a model. What they ask is, to be allowed to pick out a bit here and there; to have the means of being on an equal footing with Europeans, at the same time that they preserved their own class privileges to the fullest extent. They would like a house of lords composed of Brahmins, and a house of commons to which Sudras might be admitted; but if a barber's son claimed to lead the first, and the child of an apostate was appointed to rule the second, they would forego all the benefits of legislative authority rather than acknowledge them as superiors. The keystone of British freedom is the equality of all men beneath the law, whereas the fundamental principle of Hindooism is the irreversible subordination of classes. To the Englishman, the past and present teaches the grand lesson of the people's sovereignty. To the Brahmin, the voice of Deity ever inculcates the right of despotism on the one hand, and the duty of obedience on the other. Before the smallest fragment of a true representation is found in India, the existence of caste must be wholly annihilated.

And if it is vain to expect that the country can be governed by the native aristocracy, it is equally idle to imagine that it will be ruled by foreigners, for the population at large. As well may the servant expect to be allowed to labour for his own profit instead of his master's. The English exercise sway from purely selfish motives; and if heaven so ordains it that we are made the instruments of good, the merit is not to be ascribed to us. Every member of the alien race will try and extract as much individual profit as he can honestly obtain. To sow where they have not reaped, is the privilege of conquerors throughout all time. But, in addition to the good of which we are unconscious instruments, we are willing, as a body, to soften the inevitable evils of dominion over a strange land. We must have money — we will not part with power; but if the one can be raised with less of suffering to the people, and the other may be exerted to better results, there is abundant inclination on the part of the English people at home to make such changes as are requisite for both ends. It is usually admitted that inordinate taxation is injurious to the government as well as to the community, and that a defective administration of justice is a scandal to all those who have authority to effect its reformation.

The revision and abatement of taxation, the cheapening of law, which costs so much of the poor man's time, the legal education of judges, and the universal boon of English teaching, — these are the objects for which native associations might exert themselves with effect, and to which we should like to see them voluntarily restricted. Their neglect of the great social questions tells most unfavourably on the interests of their countrymen. If some of their complaints are voted unreasonable, it will be concluded that no grievance has been forgotten. When the patient appears unconscious of suffering, the state physicians will hardly act on the diagnosis of disease drawn up by one who will be set down as an over-zealous friend.

It frequently happens, however, that whole races, as well as individuals, are unmindful of their true interests, in which case it is the more imperative that they should be cared for by the rest of the world. It is the lot of society in the East to be moulded into new forms in spite of itself; to have freedom thrust upon it, and knowledge made a conquering power. Never in the history of mankind did a nation take such pains to subvert its own dominion, as the English have taken to destroy their empire over the goodly regions of Hindostan.

We can sum up at this moment all the results of attempts which may be made by the natives of India to extort political privileges; but it would be hard to say what might not be gained for the country, if they would Daguerreotype the face of the land, and present in colours its worn and melancholy features. We can at best only give a profile,—they could furnish a full portrait, and attest its fidelity.

The Baboos of Bengal, the Chetties and Moodeliars of Madras claim to be entitled to equal privileges with the Englishman; but they have to learn that, although freedom has no geographical limits, and the gift of liberty is a heirloom of all others the most precious, it must never be bestowed on those who would cut off the entail. To entitle themselves to be joined with the Englishman, and allowed to share in his privileges, they must adopt the covenant which binds him to look on the whole human race with sympathy. To the members of that undivided family, freedom is a property in common, and to claim the right of enjoying is to acknowledge the obligation to share it. But will the sticklers for caste accept the liberty they demand on those equitable terms? Will they allow the barber's son to preside over their legislative chamber, and see without murmur a pariah promoted to the highest offices? We are afraid that it is not in that spirit they would recognise the uses of power. They would exercise it not as trustees, bound to act for the common benefit, but as the members of a sect claiming the right of exclusive enjoyment and the opportunity of persecution for conscience' sake. They wish to get possession of freedom that they may assassinate her. In proportion as their licence is extended, the just privileges of others must be abridged. The consistent assertors of equal rights demand in the same breath that they may stand on a level with the English Christian, and be allowed to trample the Hindoo believer under their feet. We are to confer upon them the giant's strength, with the full knowledge that they intend to use it as tyrannously as a giant.

Under the heads of civilisation, literature, and commerce, our countrymen are not justly chargeable with having diminished the sum total of Hindoo blessings. If it is said that Suttee, Infanticide, and Thuggee, are amongst the comforts of civilisation, it will be allowable to charge us with Vandalism; but the Churruck Poojah is still left to console the devotees of the East. Every year they hang up, without molestation from the authorities, a dozen or so of civilised persons, who rejoice in the polished pastime of revolving round a huge pole by means of iron hooks passed through their quivering flesh. Not a temple has been thrown down by the English, not a single deity removed by proclamation from the calendar. They are at liberty to practise any of the arts for which their forefathers were famous, as well as those for which the European is renowned. In literature they have not lost Menu, but they have gained Milton. They can study their own shastras as well as our sciences, and read Shakspeare along with the Vedas and Puranas. As for commerce, our friends the Baboos, Moodeliars, and Chetties will hardly pretend that their fathers' sons have anything to complain of on that score. They are at liberty to trade with all the world, and when they have counted their gains, may rely on being permitted to keep them. They are fast making India an unprofitable place of residence for the British merchant, and might, if they chose, entirely monopolise the commerce of the country. The noble has become a pauper, the ryot barely contrives to keep body and soul together; but in every part of India the native trader thrives and fattens. It is he who gathers up the crumbs that fall from the Company's table, and gleans in the fields which have been ravaged by the collector and his locust brood. Our government and laws have been, and continue to be, full of evil; but they will certainly sustain a comparison with those of the native sovereigns to whose annals we can point with any degree of historic certainty. We know little about what was said and done in the remote periods of history; but the forefathers of the present generation can hardly be said to have experienced the qualified happiness which the Greek poet ascribed to his ancestors under the rule of Miltiades, when he sang —

"Our tyrants then
Were still at least our countrymen."

They lived and suffered under the changing rule of despotism. In one generation the Hindoo rajah killed pigs in the sacred places of the Mahomedans; and in the next, the descendants of the Arabian slaughtered cows on the hallowed floors of the pagoda. Life and property were the toys of authority, and liberty a blessing equally unknown to monarch and to slave.

Englishmen who have a proper sense of their responsibility to God and mankind, feel that they have not done justice to India; but the ruler who wishes to escape censure is only too glad to institute a comparison between the acts of his own government and those of his native predecessors. To come to modern times, there are men now living in the territory of Mysore who remember Tippoo Saib, and have paid obedience to the heir of the ancient Hindoo dynasty who was set up in his room: if their suffrages could be taken, they would not be inclined to vote in favour of native sovereigns, however orthodox in their practice of idolatry or sincere in their profession of respect for Allah and the Prophet.

For the people of India, the down-trodden masses,—for the beggared rajah whose patrimonial estate has been wrested from him,—for the Brahmin who sighs over the decay of a religion which, in his heart, he believes to be of divine origin—we can feel respect and sympathy; but we have not much regard for the majority of Hindoo politicians, who talk of wrongs which they have not suffered, and aspire to the enjoyment of privileges to which they have as yet no rightful claims. Let them first earn a title to freedom and understand the uses to which they would be bound to apply it. When they are of the same heart and mind with the Anglo-Saxon, they may be allowed to share in the fruits of his centuries of toil, and labour with him in the great field of human improvement. The terms of the partnership may be arranged with our descendants.

Though daily losing ground amongst their own people, the advocates of caste are still a power in India; but what share can they have in the triumphs of European civilisation?

They would retain the old forms of society, the ancient exclusiveness of rank. They would still punish heresy as a crime, and make belief a fixity. We on the contrary wrestle daily with the few remaining barriers that remain on the social highway. It is long since the peasant was shown how he might rise to be a noble; ages ago, the poverty-stricken scholar learned to tread the path which led to the highest seats in the tabernacle. We have made the expression of thought as free as the thought itself. We have introduced the horny-handed craftsman to the saloons of greatness, and everywhere proclaimed the universal brotherhood of mankind. How then can we sympathise with those who seek to perpetuate social and religious distinctions of the most intolerant class, who would press down the lowly, and set up again the broken images of pride and power? The Englishman who fights, in the same ranks with the champions of caste, the opponents of the *lex loci*, is a traitor to his name and birthplace, who will meet with no respect and obtain no support amongst his own countrymen. For every social hardship which presses on the people of India unfairly, for every act of administration which sets at nought their just rights, thousands of disinterested men at home will be found willing to provide a remedy, or set up a shout of execration; but the great dogmas of civil and religious liberty claim respect equally in Calcutta and London. We must uphold them in every clime under the sun where our influence has penetrated. They will flourish under every kind of temperature, and dispense enjoyment to every class of mortals. When we have taught the people of India as much as we know ourselves of the nature and extent of political rights, we shall have accomplished the most glorious part of our mission. As soon as they have learnt that lesson, we may feel less apprehensive as to the future of the East. The natives will know their own wants and the means of supplying them. The collector and the Brahmin may do their worst, in the face of an enlightened public.

CHAP. XX.

THE RELIGIOUS QUESTION.— NOBLE LORDS UPON CHRISTIAN RULERS. —THE DESPOTISM OF KNOWLEDGE. — THE WISE AND GOOD MAN ALWAYS A MISSIONARY. — FALSE IDEAS OF NATIVE HOSTILITY TO CHRISTIANITY.

In the House of Lords, on the 9th of June last, Lord Ellenborough spoke on the subject of the disaffection in the Bengal army. The former Governor-General of India said, in the course of his speech, "I can scarcely believe it now to be true, though I saw it distinctly stated in the papers, that the Governor-General himself, Lord Canning, subscribed largely to a Missionary Society, which has for its object the conversion of the natives. I deem that fact of these subscriptions of Lord Canning, the Governor-General of India, to societies having for their object the conversion of the natives, if it be true, to be one of the most dangerous things that could possibly have happened to the security of our government in India." The President of the Council, the Marquis of Lansdowne, followed Lord Ellenborough, and said that, "having the strongest public and private friendship for Lord Canning, he was yet prepared to state that if by any error or mistake in judgment, which he did not believe, and he would not believe without proof, Lord Canning had so acted as to give countenance to such belief as the noble earl inferred, he would no longer deserve to be continued in his office as Governor-General of India. (Hear, hear.)"

It is held in substance by his lordship and those who agree

with him, that a small body of men have no right to endeavour the subversion of an ancient faith which fills and satisfies the mind of a nation; but if this rule of action be correct, Sir James Brooke was not warranted in putting down head-hunting in Sarawak. The Dyaks had practised it from time immemorial. It was, at the same time, a religious duty and a custom of chivalry. They believed that it brought increase of riches as well as honour. The English civiliser murdered, then, the man who was put to death by a virtual ex post facto law for only abiding by the law of his priests, and the traditions of his fathers. And the like measure of disapproval must be awarded to every man who has suppressed foreign customs alien to his own preconceived notions, no matter whether cannibalism, human sacrifices, or self-immolation. It will only be necessary to prove, what no one will attempt to deny, that the said customs were agreeable to the habits and feelings of the people; and forthwith it is made a crime to disturb them. According to this doctrine, civilisation could only be advanced by supernatural means, and the idea of superior wisdom is absurd.

It is surely not necessary to employ argument, to show the folly of idol-worship, or the miserable vices of the Hindoo character in a national point of view. Those who sneer at Christianity will hardly vaunt, as a proof of their better appreciation of the ideas most worthy of man's homage, their own reverence for Hindoo symbols of divine power. The hatred of priestcraft, the recognition of the universal rights of mankind, and the acknowledgment of the just superiority of great powers — no matter in what station of life the possessor may be found — are altogether incompatible with the support of Brahmins and the advocacy of the division of castes; nor will any man uphold the superior advantages of Indian progress, unless he is prepared to deny the uses of knowledge and the benefits of science. Such a man must avow his desire to roll back the tide of time, and wholly erase the fairest pages of the world's history.

We repudiate then altogether the idea that the Hindoos are competent to offer valid opposition to the march of European ideas in religion or science, just as we would the resistance of a child to the projects of the matured intellect. The fact of an enlightened Englishman rationally espousing the cause of Hindoo hatred to innovation, is not capable of belief. Such a man can no more in his heart uphold the doctrines of native theology, or the follies of native pretensions to science, than he can prefer the bullock-tracks to the railway, or the tappal to the electric telegraph. We claim the right, by virtue of superior power, acquired from the incessant exercise of all the faculties of mind and body, to pronounce upon the value of mental efforts, and map out the course of the nation's travel upon the great highway of human improvement.

But then comes the question, how far are men, in their individual capacity, bound to spread abroad the superior knowledge which has been imparted to them? In physical affairs the question is easy of solution. The man who by chance discovers a remedy for a disease hitherto deemed incurable, and which annually swept off great numbers of the population, would be deemed a public enemy if he confined the secret to his own breast. The fate of almost every discoverer reflects but little honour upon his contemporaries. Opposition, contempt, and obscurity — neglect in the market-place and homage in the tomb make up the common lot of the world's greatest benefactors; but, could Jenner have foreseen with the clearness of prophetic vision that he should have been spurned as a quack, and treated as a cheat, alike by the men of his own profession and the untaught public, would that knowledge have justified him in the estimation of posterity in withholding his glorious discovery of vaccination? According to the magnitude of a gift, just so is the extent of our obligation to share its blessings with others. He who knows most, must work hardest. The knowledge which is not communicated loses nearly all its inherent value. And if such is the case with regard to mere temporal affairs, how much stronger is the obligation in spiritual matters! The man who would cure an aching finger, or as a matter of duty increase the enjoyments of the passing hour, would hardly deem himself justified in withholding the knowledge of immortality.

We hold that the government of India have no right whatever to interfere with the private missionary efforts of their highest officers, and that the natives have no cause to complain, so long as these efforts are not backed by the coercive power of the state. The employment of force defeats its own object, and is, besides, wholly unchristian; but what restrictions can the Court of Directors really place upon the efforts of their servants to disseminate the light of a purer faith? Granted, that they could prohibit a governor-general or a secretary from appearing upon a missionary platform, they could not prevent them from subscribing for the maintenance of a Schwartz or a Carey, they could not, without imminent danger to their own miserable and narrow interests, hinder them from founding Christian schools, or from exhibiting, in a thousand ways, the force of Christian example. And what on the other hand, should induce any man, holding in his heart the inevitable belief that truth will always prevail, to hinder the conflict of the opposing principles of reason and folly? We absolutely deny the right of the state to prohibit any man, however high or humble his station, from doing his utmost to obtain, with the weapons of mind, victory for his own peculiar opinions. We give toleration to all creeds, and equal external power to all forms of belief. It is as competent to the Hindoo as to the European to battle with pen and tongue in defence of his faith; and this claim of liberty, which is held to be undeniable in the case of the humblest, we cannot, surely, withhold from the highest in the state. A ground of complaint exists when the power which is held in trust for the common benefit of the community is exerted to forward the objects of a few. To say that the apparent bias of members of the ruling authority, exhibited only in speech or writing, is held to be equivalent to a demand of obedience, is to declare the absolute slavishness of the multitude,—an inference which would most probably be repudiated by those who uphold what are called the rights of the Hindoo.

Upon these broad grounds, then, that the opposition offered to the growth of European thought is not rational, and that the state has no right whatever to proscribe the moral influence of truth, or even of error, if we may be pardoned the seeming paradox, we hold that the Hindoos have no just ground of complaint when the peaceable subversion of their religion is contemplated, and that the officers of Government are entitled to exert themselves to promote missionary objects, on all occasions, in their private capacity. As servants of the state, they are bound to protect all; as heirs of immortality, they are bound to enlighten all.

There are questions upon which the laws and opinions of the Hindoos ought not to have any weight whatever. If an innovation sought to be made is in accordance with the true interests of civilisation (and of that the dominant race only are qualified to judge), we are authorised to carry it into effect. On what other grounds can we justify our forcible interference with so many cherished customs and religious duties? The Rajpoot thought it was for the benefit of his race, that female infants should be murdered. The Khond believed that the blessing of heaven would attend him if he offered up human sacrifices. The Hindoo widow anticipated a glorious hereafter, if she were permitted to burn with her dead husband. Well, our people converted all these meritorious acts into crimes. They debarred heaven from the widow. They exposed the Khond to famine and pestilence. They punished infanticide with the penalty of murder. Whence did they get authority to do this? Not from the Shasters or the lips of Brahmins. Not from Rajahs or the native commonalty. They walked by the light, and acted by the force of civilisation. They imposed humanity and liberty upon the ignorant and weak. There was no waiting for the national sanction. If darkness were not better than light, the natives would bless them by and by; and meantime they were prepared to encounter all the consequences of hatred and misunderstanding.

The priests and teachers of the Hindoos regard us with a feeling which is not to be conciliated by any act of apostasy on the part of our rulers. They care nothing about the subscriptions of the governor-general in aid of religious societies, or the preaching of the Gospel. It is our civilisation, and not our Christianity, that they dread; not the doctrine that the Saviour died for all men, but the teaching of the fact that the earth is round. Banish on the morrow all who take an interest in the spread of the glad tidings; pull down the pulpits and scatter the congregations, and so long as a school remained open, or a Hindoo child recollected the first lessons in geography, we should fail to satisfy them. Wherever our footsteps penetrate, the pundit finds that his income lessens and his influence withers. His defeats are not to be measured by our victories. The deist is a rebel to Hindooism, though he refuses to fight under the Christian banner. Young Bengal is not gained by the missionary; but he is lost to the Brahmin.

Let no man of our race harbour the foolish thought that the example of the Emperor Julian might well be imitated by our chief ruler in India, or that we can win the affection of the orthodox Hindoo by hindering the growth of Christianity. From the highest to the lowest, they will gladly tolerate us if we will only consent to tolerate them. They have not sought the life of the missionary or the holdings of the planter. They wish to retain their lands and religion, and believe in their hearts that we intend to deprive them of both by violence. Let us give them assurance to the contrary, and our Sovereign will have no firmer allies than the princes of Hindostan, no subjects more peaceful than the Brahmin and his followers.

CHAP. XXI.

TORTURE IN THE NORTH-WEST.—HOW STATES ARE "PROTECTED." —EXAMPLES OF INDIAN JUSTICE.

In dealing with the subjects of Indian law and police, one cannot help giving way to occasional bursts of uncontrollable laughter. You are obliged to indulge either in cursing or cacchination, and the latter is the more harmless, if the less satisfying mode of venting your feelings. The tyranny is so unrestrained, the illegality so outrageous, as to be really comic. Neither are matched by any species of rule under the sun. We are not going to quote examples from the report of the Madras Torture Commission, which is three years old, nor from Mr. Halliday's minute on the condition of the police in Bengal, but will begin with citing instances from a Parliamentary return ordered by the House of Commons, on the 22nd of June last, nine days after the Gagging Act was passed in Calcutta. The public must please not to murmur, if we ask them to turn back with us at the end of a few pages.

Amongst the chief allies of the British Government, is the Rajah of Puttialah. The territories of this prince, who is a Sikh, form a portion of what are called the "Protected States," and are situated on the south side of the Sutlej. When the rebellion broke out, Lord Canning called upon him for assistance; and he met the claim halfway, sending his troops amongst the very first reinforcements to Delhi, and affording, by word and deed, the greatest proof of zeal and friendship. It is reported, on good authority, that he has lent the Government of the Punjaub large sums; and it is more than likely that if, instead of aiding us, he had raised the standard of the Khalsa, and called on the Sikhs to make a second fight for their independence, he would have been joined by thousands of the men who are now fighting on our side, and whose numbers and bravery enabled us to capture Delhi. How needful it has always been to avoid giving this influential chief just ground for offence, is a point that need not be dwelt upon.

Amongst the list of civilians attached to the North-West Provinces, is Mr. Henry Brereton. This gentleman has been fourteen years in the service, and in April, 1854, and for some time previously, was deputy-commissioner, in charge of the Loodianah district. He is described by Sir John Lawrence as being a man of vigorous ability. In October, 1854, certain native petitions were addressed to the chief commissioner, complaining against some proceedings in the criminal department, and making various statements, which he ordered to be enquired into. The result was a report from Mr. Barnes, superintendent of the Cis-Sutlej States, the greater portion of which we must give in that gentleman's own words. After stating his arrival in Loodianah, in November, Mr. Barnes proceeds as follows: — "Before your communication, I had visited the gaol, in company with the deputy-commissioner. I had found all the wards crowded with prisoners, some of whom, for want of accommodation, were placed in tents. I was surrounded by men who complained loudly of the means by which they had been arrested and confined. I had also heard that Mr. Brereton maintained informers, some on a fixed salary, who were always with him, and some on special duty, who were only in occasional employ. I heard also numerous complaints against Moosahib Khan, and his brother Futteh Jung; and petitions from zemindars of Jugraon, belonging to castes who have not a good name, had been presented to me, complaining of the police measures adopted by the acting tehsildar, Moosahib Khan. Deedar Sing and Lukh Sing declare that their houses were searched last May, on suspicion of being concerned in the Koop robbery case, but that none of the stolen property was found therein. Nevertheless, all the valuable articles found in their houses were carried off to the cutchery, and still lie there. The property was paraded in the bazaar, and people were invited to inspect and claim it, if their own; but no man has appeared to identify the property. The search was instituted at the instance of a prisoner in the gaol, who had a cause of enmity with these sahookars, and with the Sirdar of Kuneitch, whose house was simultaneously searched. There appeared to me no sufficient grounds why they were subjected to this indignity, nor any reason why their lawful property has been so long withheld from them.

"On the same information, the house of Sirdar Chimmun Sing, of Kuneitch, a jageerdar of this district, was searched. On the 29th April last, Mr. Brereton commissioned Futteh Jung Khan Perwanah Navees, the brother of Moosahib Khan, to undertake this duty. The Sirdar came into Loodianah, and, at my request, has furnished a narrative under his own seal of all that occurred. He is a respectable native gentleman, and has always borne a good character. He has the testimony of Lieutenant Lake, then assistant agent at Loodianah, that he behaved with great loyalty in the campaign of 1845-6. One evening, late in April last, Futteh Jung Khan came with a posse of sowars and footmen to his residence. The Sirdar was treated with great violence; and shortly after, the deputy commissioner himself made his appearance, and began the search. The floors were all dug up, and according to the Sirdar, his houses at Raepoor were thrown down. All the property found was carried away; he mentions also that eight respectable zemindars of the village were seized at the same time. They were immediately placed in irons, and made over to Futteh Jung Khan. Three months they were kept in arrest, and subjected to treatment which he 'cannot describe.' These eight men were also sent for; they are Jâts, and I believe perfectly innocent of this crime; they were severally subjected to torture, and kept in confinement in Futteh Jung's own house, which is in a secluded part of the city. The hair of the head (they are Sikhs) was tied to their leg irons; wooden pegs were driven into the joints of their elbows and other sensitive parts. Others were merely bound tightly and beaten with fists, so that no marks might remain, I inspected two men, Ram Ditta and Dittoo; they bear large scars on their elbows, and on other parts of their arms. The cicatrix in each wound is recent; and they all solemnly state that these pegs were forcibly inserted, so as to lacerate the flesh. The man who operated in all these cases was a wretch called Allah Buksh, a servant belonging to Futteh Jung. Ram Ditta and Dittoo were so severely wounded with these pegs, that they were sent to the gaol hospital, and were cured there.

"Eventually, although there was nothing whatever against them, except the malicious statement of a convict, all these men were required to furnish heavy securities of 200 rupees each, and they were not released till these securities were produced.

"After I had taken these depositions, I went to the Hawalut, where I found fifty-seven men under confinement. In one case of robbery of 8,700 rupees, at Raepoor, six men and women were under arrest. Some of these were arrested in August last, and some in September last; yet in two instances only had the defence been taken. The other four did not know on what grounds they had been seized. They had not been called upon for their defence, and had been in Hawalut for many weeks. The arrests were made by Futteh Jung, on the information of a single 'Goindah.' Dewa Sing, one of the prisoners, declares he was tortured by Futteh Jung into a partial confession. On his testimony, Hurnam Singh, a Jât of the Puttialah territory, near Thaneysm, was seized, and also Roopa, his mother. Hurnam declares that he was confined at Futteh Jung's quarters in the city. A tent-peg was driven into his anus, and eventually he was sent to hospital; he was never confronted with his accuser, nor was his defence even taken. I found him in the gaol hospital; and he appears a young Jât, with a countenance that does not indicate crime. There is no proof against him. His mother, Roopa, states that Futteh Jung and Alla Buksh, and a third man, seized her at her home in Puttialah, and wanted to strip her. They placed her under an August sun, and gave her nothing to drink. Futteh Jung tied a bag of filth over her mouth and nose, and endeavoured to get her to confess. Roopa also declares that her house at Puttialah was dug down in the search for stolen property, none of which was discovered. Money found concealed there, belonging to herself, was appropriated by Futteh Jung.

"Boodh Sing, Jât, made a partial confession in this case. He declares it was extorted from him by false representations and torture. His statement is that Kheema, an informer, and Sheik Chund, a burkundaz in disguise, came to his house. He entertained them. A month after, Futteh Jung came to his village, placed a guard round his house, dug up the floors and walls, and destroyed it. He himself was absent, but was seized shortly afterwards. Red pepper was stuffed in his nose, and a peg driven into his anus. In his agony he was induced to make a false confession. He has been under confinement since 27th July; but no order has been passed in his case. He lent out money to his neighbours, and the list of his debtors was seized by Futteh Jung, who realised and appropriated the money. The two men who confessed partially have had their statements taken down. The other four were cast into prison; they have never seen their accusers, nor have their defences been written. They do not all state that they were tortured. Hurnam Sing and Roopa state that torture was employed against them in vain; the other two simply state that they were arrested, the reasons thereof they know not. I found two men under arrest on a charge of highway robbery, value 48 rupees; there is no proof whatever against them. The extra assistant recommended their release on the 29th October last, but they are still in custody. There were two persons seized by Ahmed Yar Khan, of the same party as Futteh Jung; their offence is alleged bad livelihood. Ahmed

Yar is not a police-officer; he holds an unauthorised appointment as "provider of supplies" to troops marching; he seized these two men on 12th October last, a month ago; they are in strict arrest; no proof has appeared against them, and their defence has not been taken. I found also four men arrested since 7th August last, at the instance of an informer called Mootsuddie, on the charge of false coining; there is no proof whatever against them, and no defences have been recorded, although these men have been under arrest three months. There are other instances of injudicious arrests and illegal treatment among the persons in the Hawalut, but I have noticed only those cases in which mention was made of Futteh Jung and Ahmed Yar Khan, or in which the circumstances were more flagrant than in others.

"There were six men in the hawalut at the city Kotwallee. Some of these had been there several weeks, none less than twenty days, and their defence had not been recorded. While I was visiting the gaol four men complained to me of Futteh Jung and Ahmed Yar Khan, and I took their depositions; they are imprisoned for no specific crime, but for alleged bad livelihood. Two of these men are subjects of foreign states arrested by Futteh Jung; and a third is a resident of Dhurm Kote, Zillah Ferozepore. Their arrest and confinement in the Loodianah gaol on such charges is unjustifiable. Futteh Jung and Ahmed Yar appear to have had a commission to rove in foreign territory. They were at Maleir Kotta, Puttialah, and Nabha, at different periods from last January till the present time. Futteh Jung is perwanah navees in the Fouzdarry office. Ahmed Yar was specially employed in the Koop robbery case on your recommendation, suggesting that a special party should be deputed to investigate the particulars of this crime. No clue whatever has been obtained and the establishment sanctioned was discharged on the 30th September last; subsequent arrests made by Ahmed Yar were entirely illegal, as he had no police powers whatever."

These are the particulars of the cases represented to the

Chief Commissioner in which these men have been employed. Allowing for some exaggeration, I feel convinced that Futteh Jung Khan has held almost unlimited power, which he has grossly and most cruelly abused. Holding a subordinate appointment in the Fouzdarry office, he has been commissioned by Mr. Brereton to investigate crimes, with permission almost to do what he liked, to go where he pleased, and to arrest any one upon whom his suspicions might fall; he has also been allowed to hold a separate court as it were, prisoners having been kept for weeks at his quarters, and, as he was directly interested in eliciting confessions, I most firmly believe that he exercised great oppression for this object, particularly in the instance of the zemindars of Kuneitch; I am convinced that the wounds their bodies show were caused by the torture he applied. During his long sojourns in foreign territory it is reasonable to suppose, as alleged by the victims, that such a man, armed with such power, committed many atrocities and levied much money. The chiefs themselves did not complain; it is not etiquette to mention such matters, and oppression might proceed to almost any length before the commissioner would hear of it from the chiefs themselves. Futteh Jung Khan entered the district with Mr. Brereton; he had accompanied him for some years; he is own brother to Moosahib Khan, and is a villain of the deepest die. Ahmed Yar Khan is one of the same clique, but he is no relation to the other two; there are complaints against him, but he appears to be milder and more humane than Futteh Jung. I have no doubt he has extorted much money in his long forays into foreign territory; but he was not so active nor so cruel in torture as Futteh Jung; he should simply be dismissed from employ, a light punishment for the numerous crimes he has doubtless committed. There have been many complaints preferred against Moosahib Khan for the surveillance he has imposed upon certain villages in his jurisdiction, supposed to have a bad name. The means employed to prevent the occurrence of crime are very harsh and the remedy appears far worse than the evil. A burkundaz is stationed in every suspected village; he is ordered to assemble every man, woman, and child residing therein three times a day. A fourth "parade," as the people call it, is taken about eleven at night; any person found absent from these roll-calls is fined two rupees, ten annas, and on a repetition of the offence he is fined twenty-five rupees.

Moosahib Khan admits the truth of this account, and gives as his authority the verbal orders of the Deputy Commissioner. He states that on the second offence, not a fine, but a recognizance of twenty-five rupees is taken. If so, the first fault is punished more severely than the second, which seems unlikely. These villages are inhabited by a race called Harnees, and one or two by communities of men called Rajpoots. They are the proprietors of mouzahs, paying revenue to Government, and, as far as I know, bear a terrible character. Many of them are in the service of the Raja of Kupoorthulla, and hold high rank on his establishment. Admitting, however, that the race generally is predatory, I think so indiscriminate and severe a system as that enforced by Mr. Brereton and Moosahib Khan is quite indefensible; a people might be driven into rebellion by measures like these. Harnees, like other men, have legitimate calls upon their time which oblige them to leave their homes: to interdict them, and to deprive them entirely of their liberty, is a measure far exceeding the exigencies of the case. Besides, to place a single burkundaz in that position, with leave to compel the attendance of every soul four times within twenty-four hours, is to give him a license to bully, extort, and plunder at his discretion. Mr. Brereton is actuated by undoubted zeal; he pursues a system which he thinks will suppress crime, and be formidable only to the worst of mankind. But his judgment is entirely defective. In order to punish and prevent crime, he creates a hundred evils, which in my opinion cause more mischief than the offences he would put down. In his pursuits after the ducoits of the Koop robbery he has seized numerous persons quite innocent of the crime. He has allowed men like Futteh Jung to roam over the protected states without control; he has alarmed the respectable section of the people by the injudicious and causeless searches he has instituted for stolen property; and, lastly, he has been entirely deceived in the character of his agents, who have robbed, and tortured, and bullied guiltless men in his name.

Another phase in Mr. Brereton's system is, his dependance upon spies. To hear Mr. Brereton himself speak on the subject one is impressed with a belief that he is fully aware of the abuses and evils to which a reliance on such sources will lead. Yet he has three informers constantly about him. I may say they are domesticated in his house; they live in his compound, and act occasionally as private servants. Their names are Mootsuddie, Shurfoo, and Jowahir. Mootsuddie has seized several persons, and many unjustly; he has received rewards, and all three draw fixed salaries from Government. They are soucars, and, I believe, coiners of false coin; they should be remanded to the Thuggee department, and removed from this district without loss of time. I have heard numerous complaints against these men, and especially against Mootsuddie.

I forgot to mention in the body of the letter, that no less than eighty men have been apprehended since the commencement of the year on the charge of "budmashee." Of these, thirty have given in their sureties, and have been allowed to return to their houses; but fifty men still remain in gaol on this charge. I am engaged in looking over the records of their cases. In many instances, I have found that the accused have been thrown into gaol on the bare report of the thaunahdar. There is no proof whatever against them, and yet they have been imprisoned in default of heavy security, far beyond their means, for one year. They are all in irons, although the law as construed by the Sudr Nizamut expressly forbids this aggravation of their punishment. In the neighbouring zillah of Ferozpoor, with the same aggregate of prisoners, and within the same time, viz., 1st January to 31st October, with much the same population and the same amount of crime, the district officer has arrested only five men; and yet in Loodianah eighty men have been seized. This fact alone indicates the indiscriminate severity with which Mr. Brereton employs the means at his disposal for the criminal administration of his district.

We have reproduced the exact words the report in this instance, because it would have been impossible to obtain credence for any other form of statement in which such facts might be embodied. The knock at the portals of the English ear must be an official one, or the truth will not be allowed an entrance. Let us try to realise in a more familiar way the state of things which prevailed in Loodianah three years since. The emperor Napoleon is not the chief of a "protected state," and is bound to take care of himself, but he is a neighbour and ally. He has helped us in our wars like the rajah of Puttialah, and gives shelter to a portion of our rascaldom. The magistrate of Dover had a character for vigorous ability, and deserved it. Spies served him at table, and informers followed his footsteps wherever he moved. The head of the latter was the magistrate's copying clerk, "a villain of the deepest dye," coiner by profession, and thief by the accident of his position. A respectable inhabitant of Dover complained that the people living in the same street with him, "could not sleep at night for the cries of his victims." At times he would have the latter operated upon under his own immediate inspection, and in one instance, he arrested eight respectable tenant farmers, took them to his own house, and tortured them for a period of three months, the men being totally guiltless of crime and accused only by a convict. Bankers, retired officers, and landed proprietors, whoever had money, were liable to be seized without a warrant, thrown into jail, and their assets collected for the benefit of the clerk aforesaid. In all the villages near Folkstone, he ordered his brother, who was a police inspector, to station a policeman, who assembled the whole population, man, woman, and child, three times a day during daylight, and again at ten o'clock at night, the fine for absence being five shillings and threepence, the sum of three weeks' wages. Whenever he required change of air, or wanted to make up the price of some little property that he had set his mind on, he was accustomed to run over to Paris and invigorate himself in health and pocket. An elderly French lady deposed, that he knocked her house down, and stole the money that she had concealed on the premises. He placed her in the sun with the thermometer at 125°, kept her without water, and tied a bag of filth over her mouth. Her son was taken to the clerk's house in Paris, and tortured so horribly, that they were obliged to send him to the hospital. A third brother, having no official appointment whatever, roved about Calais, and ran across into Belgium or Germany "without control." Owing to the disregard of "rules regarding returns and reports, supervision on the part of superior authority became impossible; as the detectives worked only on verbal orders, or no orders at all, they eluded all the usual checks; no one knows the number of arrests they made and did not report, and the amount of property they seized, and did not account for." Neither the emperor, the magistrates of Antwerp, or the burgomasters of Brussels ever complained. The Dover official and his robber retinue might have gone to any length before our Government would hear of it from those gentlemen. "It is not etiquette to mention such matters."

India is still the land of romance, but men who have resided there for years and are familiar with its social life, feel, on reading the story of Mr. Brereton, much as a boy who lays down the book of "The Arabian Nights," to take up a report of the performances of Mr. Anderson. Sir John Lawrence, who knew that the detailed iniquities might only be a tithe of what had been perpetrated under Mr. Brereton's authority, was "sorry to declare his opinion, that a mere warning cannot be depended upon to prevent any future recurrence of these evils under Mr. Brereton's administration. He seems possessed with a species of infatuation in regard to the use of espionage, the employment of personal attachés, and the application of indiscriminate severity; from this vicious system experience does not seem to deter him, nor advice dissuade. It will be observed from the papers, that some of the very employés now arraigned, had attracted some kind of notice in connexion with Mr. Brereton at various periods and places. The late Board had reason to fear that latterly these abuses had even crept into the Thuggee department; of these suspicions Mr. Brereton was made fully aware; indeed, a circular was afterwards issued on the subject. These circumstances, however, seem to have left but a transient impression on Mr. Brereton's mind, and the same men who, as he himself says, have followed him for years, are now figuring in the present report. The chief commissioner considers that some mark of the severe displeasure of Government is necessary, which may operate as a stern lesson to Mr. Brereton, and may serve to keep his judgment straight in these matters for the future. Moreover, the chief commissioner would submit, that when great faults are clearly brought home to an officer, some example is called for to vindicate the administration before the people, and to preserve it pure from the like scandal hereafter. The chief commissioner would further be disposed to suggest, that after what has occurred Mr. Brereton is not suited for employment in the Punjaub. That officer needs more supervision than can well be given by any of our commissioners, whose duties are so numerous. In the older provinces there are judges to supervise and restrain as well as commissioners. It has been suggested that Mr. Brereton should be appointed to some station which forms the head quarters of a commissionership. But there are many practical difficulties in this course. Such stations usually require the best officers; and there are usually reasons why those districts should continue to be held by their present incumbents. Indeed, with this very view of securing supervision, the chief commissioner had contemplated transferring Mr. Brereton from Loodianah to Lahore; but waived this intention in consequence of the judicial commissioner urging that this officer's peculiar system would be particularly mischievous at the capital, as calculated to irritate and distress a large city population. If Mr. Brereton should remain in the Punjaub, it will be undesirable, after all that has happened, that he should reassume charge of Loodianah."

Sir John Lawrence felt towards Mr. Brereton as an English overseer feels towards a troublesome pauper. He was anxious to get him carted into the adjoining parish, and cared nothing about the trouble he might give the next board of guardians that had to deal with him. But Lord Dalhousie, to whom the papers in the affair were transmitted in due course, objected to this method of getting rid of the difficulty of "how to punish a civilian." "The Commissioner," said the Governor-General, "has suggested no specific measure; but he casually hints that he wishes that Mr. Brereton should no longer be employed in the Punjaub. I cannot accede to this wish. The faults and irregularities of Mr. Brereton have no particular heinousness in the Punjaub. They would be open to the same degree of objection if committed anywhere else in the Indian territories. If Mr. Brereton is unfit to be employed in the Punjaub, he is equally unfit to be employed in the north-west provinces. I should object to his being sent back to those provinces. I do not consider it fit that the rest of the Presidency of Bengal should be used as a preserve, whence very many of the best men have been drafted to the Punjaub, and that it should be made use of also as a penal district, to which every offending officer in the Punjaub should be immediately transferred." Lord Dalhousie pronounced upon the case as follows: "I am of opinion that the Government of India, consistently with a due regard to its own character, and to the protection which it owes to those who are placed under its charge, cannot consent to leave in Mr. Brereton's hands the power which he has so grievously abused. I am of opinion that Mr. Brereton cannot, for the present, be fitly entrusted with the authority of a deputy commissioner; that he ought to be removed from that grade to the grade of a first-class assistant; and that he ought not to be restored to the grade of a deputy commissioner, or to any corresponding authority, until his conduct shall have satisfied his superiors that he better appreciates the responsibilities of a British officer in this country, and can better use the civil powers with which he has heretofore been entrusted."

The case had still to go before the Court of Directors, and the consummate tact with which they managed it was worthy of their reputation in the East. In an unwise moment, Sir James Hogg, standing counsel for the Company in the

House of Commons, had allowed his sympathies to get the better of his judgment, and knowing that torture had never been sanctioned by the Government, he went to the length of asserting that it was wholly unknown in India. The *lapsus* was most unfortunate; the enemies of the company persuaded Lord Harris, the Governor of Madras, to appoint a commission of inquiry, and the subject was busily agitated at the very time that Mr. Barnes made his report. The Torture Commission did not send in its report till the 15th of April 1855, and it would have been madness to let it be known in the previous January, that in the territory recently acquired from the Sikhs, torture was so common, that its application by men having no authority to make arrests, disturbed the nightly sleep of quiet inhabitants; whilst hope of redress was so idle, that the people never complained to Mr. Brereton on the subject. What would parliament say if they heard of the atrocious outrages perpetrated on the subjects of foreign states by servants of the Government that annexed Oude? If this state of things prevailed in the country of the warlike Sikhs, what might be reasonably assumed with regard to the treatment of the cowardly Bengallee, and the down-trodden peasantry of Madras? "Hush! gentlemen of the Chairs and Committees; let the sleeping dog lie: tide over the perilous time, and remember that you have to be 'astonished and pained' when the Torture Commission makes its statement."

Eighteen months after the date of Mr. Barnes's report, the Court of Directors addressed the Governor-General in Council on the subject. They approved of the decision by which Mr. Brereton had been removed from the grade of deputy-commissioner to that of assistant, "not to be promoted until his superiors are satisfied of his being fit to be entrusted with higher authority." Their delay in pronouncing on the matter was, it may be inferred, the result of their having "hesitated whether official misconduct so glaring, and the cause of so much injury and suffering, ought to be visited with a punishment less severe than dismissal from the public service." The Directors go on to say, "Mr.

Brereton's superiors acquit him of any knowledge of the cruelties which were inflicted by the worthless agents whom he employed. We observe his assurance, 'So utterly was I in ignorance of the truth, that even to the last, I could not realise the fact that any atrocities had been committed. When the veil was once lifted from my eyes, I perceived at once the whole occurrence, and need hardly observe the distress of mind and horror which I have suffered at the bare thought of being, however unconsciously, the cause of misery to others;' and are of opinion that, however much, therefore, Mr. Brereton is condemned for acts in excess, and in abuse of legal authority, both on his own part, and on that of the unprincipled agents in whom he placed a blind and unlimited confidence, we are nevertheless persuaded that he fully participates in the abhorrence with which acts of wilful cruelty and oppression are regarded by the European officers of Government in India! Under this impression, we are induced to refrain from carrying the punishment of Mr. Brereton's misconduct further than you have done. We desire, however, that you will inform Mr. Brereton that any similar misconduct will result in his immediate dismissal from the public service." To show that they were in earnest, the Directors pointed out that the doctor of the Loodianah gaol had two of Mr. Brereton's victims under his care for two months in a private room, their injuries arising from torture. The doctor must have seen the wounds and ascertained how they were inflicted. Why did he not report the facts? They desired that his conduct, and that of every body in the gaol at all concerned, should be made the subject of general inquiry.

Mr. Brereton took his furlough and went home, receiving of course the usual allowance paid to a civilian in England. At the end of three years from the date of "leaving the pilot," he will come back, and find no difficulty in satisfying his superiors that he is fit to be entrusted again with power; so that the entire measure of his punishment, will be the amount of salary that he lost whilst under suspension. Futteh Jung was sentenced to eight years' imprisonment, and his brother was dismissed from Government employment, and their victims were compensated out of the public treasury for their sufferings by torture. The Loodianah jailer, who received the prisoners with only a verbal order, and the doctor who attended them, were "warned," and at the end of two and a half years the whole matter was rounded off. The Puttialah Jâts will perhaps exhibit their scars to match those which their countrymen may show who fought for us before Delhi, and the rest of the late prisoners will of course pray for the continuance of the Company's Raj.

There are now thirty thousand Sikhs in the service of the East India Company. We believe they will be true to their salt; but when the disciples of Nanuk meet in the sacred city of Umriosur, there will not be wanting, amongst the stories of English greatness and Sikh courage, narratives of the cruel mode in which we have occasionally dealt with the rich noble and the humble retainer. We have seen how Sikhs have been treated in the Punjaub: let us now tell of the way in which law has been administered to them in the north-west.

Some forty-eight years ago, a Brahmin from Saharunpoor made his appearance at the Court of Runjeet Singh. He was of handsome person and winning address, and accomplished as most Brahmins are in the arts of pleasing. His religion stood in the way of his advancement, but not for long. Khoushal Singh became a Sikh, and in time rose to be Jemadar of the Deoree, or Lord of the Entry, the virtual prime minister of the Punjaub. His two brothers hastened to share his fortunes, and rose to offices of distinction. One of them had a son named Tej Singh, the traitor who sold his country to the British in the first Sikh campaign; the other is represented by a boy of whom more will be said in season.

The influence of Khoushal Singh lasted for many years, during which time he amassed enormous wealth; but a youth, named Goolab Singh, was one day accepted as a recruit in his regiment of horse, who soon caught the eye of the Maharajah, and rapidly mounted the ladder of advancement. He, too, called his relatives about him, and the Rajpoot faction in time gained paramount sway. Khoushal Singh sank quietly into a subordinate position; but it was not until the life of his master was drawing visibly to an end, that he began to put in practice a long-meditated resolution of transporting his family and riches into the British territory. He fixed one portion of his household at Hurdwar, and commenced building a magnificent palace at Ekree, near Sirdhana, in the Meerut district. The house was built under the superintendence of an Italian architect, Signor Reghelini, who had designed the Cathedral, and the Begum Sumroo's palace at Sirdhana; and when finished, it was inhabited by the favourite wife of Khoushal Singh, and the two wives of his eldest son, Kishen Singh, for whom the chief part of his wealth was intended. Treasure to the amount of 300,000*l.* was said to be deposited in the vaults at Ekree, in gold mohurs, ingots, and jewels. The money for building the Ekree palace was entirely disbursed by Motee Ram, a Hindu of the writer caste, who, during the lifetime of Khoushal Singh, managed his domestic affairs. At that place he paid the pensions and salaries of all the servants, and was even entrusted with the superintendence of the household; the females of the family being authorised to enter the zenana, and see that matters were properly conducted in the absence of the lord. Dewan Kour, the wife of Khoushal Singh, with her daughters-in-law, received their allowances at his hand, and, in every respect, Motee Ram acted as the representative of the head of the family.

Khoushal Singh died in 1844, and his son Kishen Singh, then at Lahore, performed the funeral ceremonies of his parent, and claimed the property. But the troubles in the Punjaub hindered him from coming to take possession. On the application of Motee Ram, who was confirmed in his position of steward, he sent down a reinforcement to the Sikh guard at Ekree, from the retainers of the family at Lahore, with orders that they were to obey his cousin, a boy of twelve or thirteen, and Motee Ram. The force now amounted to nineteen men, under the command of Jemadar Kyroddeen, a Mahomedan of good family, and a zealous adherent of the house of Khoushal Singh.

In the latter end of 1844, the magistrate and collector of Meerut was informed that there were two parties contending for the right of possession at Ekree — the one representing the interests of Kishen Singh, and the other being a Brahmin of Deobund, named Bhugwan Singh, who married a daughter of Khoushal Singh's, by Dewan Kour. Motee Ram gave in a petition, and claimed protection, which was opposed by a counter-petition from the widow, who affirmed that she wished to be placed under the guardianship of her son-in-law. The magistrate ordered the Kotwal of Sirdhana to inquire into the facts of the case. He did so, and reported that the family of Motee Ram were living in the house, as they had done for years past, and that there had been no breach of the peace.

Here was a case for the sole intervention of the civil tribunal, but the nature of rights and the claims of jurisdiction are sometimes confounded in courts which claim to be ruled by equity and conscience, rather than by statutes and precedents. The matter was again brought before the magistrate, who bound both parties, under heavy recognisances, not to go near the house; but on reference to the judge, Mr. Begbie, that functionary decided that the order should be relaxed in favour of Bhugwan Singh, who it was considered had a right, in consequence of his near relationship, to visit the widow and offer her advice and consolation. As for Motee Ram, he was debarred from all access, and induced to beg that he might be formally released from his responsibility. "Since it is the pleasure of the Sirkar"— such was the purport of his petition,—"that I should not be allowed to look after my master's property, let Bhugwan Singh, or the servants of the Great Company, come and take an inventory of everything, and give me a receipt for it. How else shall I look my master in the face, when his wealth, which he left in my care, is carried away and ruined?"

Does not the reader already divine how affairs will terminate? Some thirty lakhs are in dispute, the rival claimants are a Brahmin residing close at hand, the other, an unknown Sikh at Lahore, who is represented by a writer and a boy, and who will soon be a national enemy of the British! The contest is carried on in an obscure corner of the East, where journalism has no influence, and public opinion is unknown. We feel that the defeat of Motee Ram is certain, but no one can guess the fate which is in store for him.

A word or two of necessary digression at this point of the narrative. Fourteen years since, the collectorate of Meerut had a very bad reputation, as any one may find out who will take the trouble to read the reports upon the civil and criminal administration of justice in the North-west at the period in question. It was declared that more fraudulent suits were instituted in that district than in any other. Great numbers of persons were arrested, and subsequently dismissed without apparent cause, and the highest authorities debated upon the most effectual means of enforcing the execution of the decrees of the civil courts, which in the Meerut district were little better than waste paper in most instances. A man might get his verdict, but to realise the fruits of it was altogether another matter. If the law had favoured the plaintiff, the fact was a good reason why the native officials should favour the defendant, except, indeed, the former could show better reasons than he dared to produce in court for being allowed to get execution. Hence the course of justice was impeded, and a host of evils encouraged; the growing prosperity of the Omlah being the only signs that any class of men in a zillah, containing a population of nearly a million of souls, were reaping benefit from the mode in which it was governed.

The native officers in the district were remarkably unanimous, and strictly co-operative in carrying on their business. There were thirty-four who belonged to a single family, the head of which, a Rajpoot, some few generations back, embraced the Mahommedan faith, to which his descendants have since adhered. A Hindu proverb has immortalised a striking trait of the family character; the treachery of a Kumbo is set down as a fact which the Asiatic world may take for granted. At the time we speak of, they held every post of importance at Meerut.

The magistrate and collector was very fond of society, and society in turn was very fond of him. In the hot seasons, he was an invaluable acquisition to the sporting circles at Simla and Mussouri, inasmuch as he played for large sums, which he always lost and always paid. No one ever suspected him of unfair play, since the longer he sat at table, and the higher the stakes were raised, the more money he had to pay at settling time. Folks pitied his ill-fortune, but since somebody must lose, it was agreed on all sides that the lot could not fall upon one who was likely to bear it with more good temper, and repair it with greater facility.

We must now pick our way over a very difficult bit of ground, which requires to be trodden with much care and circumspection. In May 1851, a small band of prisoners might have been seen on the road from Agra to Meerut. Their guards were strictly enjoined to prevent them holding communication with any person whatever, and, to that end, they closed up round them at meal times, and diligently watched them as they slept. One of the criminals was a Hindoo of mature age, with a broken and dejected air, who seemed to have abandoned all hope of change. The other was a fine-looking, courtier-like man, whom chains and a felon's garb had not robbed of a natural grace and dignity. They were Motee Ram, and Kyroddeen, who had been sent for from the Agra jail to give evidence in the inquiry then pending, and the object of the jealous precautions observed during the journey was to satisfy the mind of the commissioner, that they had not been instructed or informed in any way as to how they should act, or what was expected from them.

The testimony on which the collector and magistrate's conduct was sifted, must be taken just for what it is worth. It charged two of the Kumbos with corruption, and we had better not say what else it pretended to show.

Motee Ram was declared to have given one of these men 10,000 rupees, and a promissory note for 40,000 rupees, on condition of being allowed to hold Ekree, which, coming to the ears of Bhugwan Singh, that shrewd individual, who knew the influence of ready cash, offered half a lakh down, which was accepted. Most likely there is not a word of truth in either case. What follows is beyond the reach of doubt and cavil.

Some days after the judge had decided that Bhugwan Singh had leave to visit the house at Ekree, word was brought to Motee Ram that the treasure was in the course of removal to Deobund, and would soon be entirely carried away. As stated beforehand, his request to be furnished with a receipt for the delivery of the property to the magistrate or Bhugwan Singh, had not been complied with, and in an unlucky moment, he addressed himself to Kyroddeen and the Sikh guard, and asked if they intended to prove unfaithful to their salt, by allowing their master's property to be made away with? The Sepoys replied that of course they would obey the orders of himself and Dabee Sehaee; on which the whole party marched over to Ekree, and finding the entrance defended by the servants of Bhugwan Singh, forced their way in, one man being wounded in the scuffle. The ejected faction hastened to give the alarm that a band of dacoits had stormed and held possession of the house; but first they took the precaution to lock the outer doors on the declared ruffians, a proceeding which evinced a great deal of reliance on the mildness of their demeanour to the inmates of the zenana, and equally anxious wish to take care of their persons till the arrival of assistance from without.

The entrance into Ekree was effected about 9 P. M., and soon after daylight the following morning a portion of the police battalion, under Captain Chiene, and a large body of men, headed by the magistrate, reached the spot, which is twelve miles from Meerut. Captain Chiene, who marched with an advanced guard, and all due military precaution, was surprised, on coming up, to see Motee Ram at one of the verandahs. "What are you doing there?" said the Captain. "I am taking care of the house," replied Motee Ram; "but Bhugwan Singh's people have locked us in." There is reason to believe that the Captain was puzzled what to make of the matter; but he summoned the party inside to surrender, and the doors being unfastened, twenty men, each armed with a musket and sword, came out, and fell in as prisoners, in regular rank and file. Motee Ram, and the child, Dabee Sehaee, were also seized, and the captives being marched some distance out of the village, were seated on the ground and searched. In the sand near them, were found some articles of jewellery, said to have been taken from Ekree. The Sepoys denied all knowledge of them; but of course they were not believed. They proved that, on entering the house, they had placed guards over the apartments of the females and the treasury, and found that the latter contained only 25,000 rupees. Perhaps they urged that robbers, after having had the opportunity of ransacking houses, were always anxious to make their escape, whilst, if they found that hopeless, and knew that a force was coming to capture them, they would take care that none of the plunder should be found on them. What their line of argument really was, we cannot say; but in due time they were committed to the sessions, and sentenced by Mr. Begbie as dacoits, to periods of imprisonment varying from fourteen to ten years, in the Agra jail. Here is the definition of the offence with which they were charged. "Dacoity: robbery by open violence;—any person or persons who in the day or night, go forth with any offensive weapons, or in a gang, with or without an offensive weapon, with the criminal intent of committing robbery."

Thus those poor foreigners, the Sikh Sepoys, for their fidelity to their master, were punished as burglars. Their sole duty in this life was to render obedience to the man who fed them. What did they know of decrees of ejection, and bonds of recognisance? Their chiefs said to them, "Go," and they had gone. They did the work which they had covenanted to perform, and their English judge estimated and rewarded it.

It was an effective way of terminating a lawsuit and creating a title. To charge Motee Ram, the original "man in possession," with the offence of dacoity; with stealing that which, in the eye of the law, was his own property! Mr. Begbie scorned the aid of John Doe and Richard Roe. His law was as swift as that of Judge Lynch, and almost as much to be venerated.

Years rolled away, many of the Sepoys died, and the rest might have been seen grinding otta daily, with fetters on each limb. Dabee Sehaee, who was released on account of his tender age, lives at Hurdwar. His uncle Kishen Singh, died in 1850, and in the attempt to have the case re-opened, Dabee Sehaee brought forward the evidence that we have detailed. Tej Singh, the present head of the family, enjoyed the reward of having given Lord Hardinge a victory, and a step in the peerage, and was not likely to trouble himself with the fate of the poor retainers of his house. But at last, Motee Ram and Kyroddeen were released. The collector died a judge; Bhugwan Singh bought a zemindary, and no one was greatly discontented, except it might be the people who are too low, or Providence which is too high, to interfere in such matters.

Our next illustration is drawn from the Madras Presidency. It contains a greater variety of incident, and shows how powerless even the Privy Council and the Queen are to enforce the doing of justice in India.

The northern districts of Ma as bear a marked resemblance to the Highlands of Scotland, both in physical conformation and the social condition of the people, as both existed a hundred years since. The head men were feudal chiefs owning large tracts of land partially reclaimed, and paying but a nominal tax to the sovereign power. When the English found their way to this remote part of the country, they thought it advisable to deal liberally with the petty rulers of the Northern Circars, both from the difficulty of coercing them, and the unprofitable results of severe measures. They settled the land tax, therefore, at sixty per cent. of the net income realised, and allowed the landholders to levy certain petty dues and customs. The latter were afterwards abolished, but the revenue demand was unaltered, sunnuds having been given to the zemindars at the outset of our connection with them, in confirmation of those granted by the previous rulers of the country.

Amongst the most distinguished of those great landed proprietors was Vencatreddy Naidoo, the Rajah of Vasareddy. His estates stretched for more than a hundred miles along the fertile banks of the Kistnah, and consisted of many hundred villages swarming with inhabitants, and rich in every kind of tropical cultivation. His father and himself had helped the English in their attempt to get a footing in the country, and of all their tenants, none paid so well and regularly. There were frightful famines in Guntoor and other northern districts in 1791 and 1802, arising in a great measure from the total neglect by Government of the tanks and watercourses built by former possessors of the land; a great fall in prices occurred in 1796-7, and in 1816 the Pindarries swept like a combined whirlwind and pestilence over the whole face of the land, but the Rajah paid up in all cases the full revenue claim of 68,000*l.* per annum, and this in spite of the most lavish personal outlay during his whole lifetime. He had built palaces and pagodas without number, and spared no cost in the way of buying power in this life, and a title to heaven in the next. The Nizam gave him the title of Munnay Sultan in exchange for an offering of 35,000*l.* Bajee Rao, the ex-Peishwa of the Mahrattas, took his money and gave compliments in return. He weighed himself once against gold, and twice against silver, and each time emptied the scales into the yawning pockets of the Brahmins. He maintained the largest following, purchased the most devout prayers and the most beautiful wives, and at his death, died the possessor of wide spread fame, and of half a million in hard cash. It was needful to dwell upon this example of Eastern wealth and extravagance, that the reader might realise the full significance of what is about to follow.

The Rajah Vencatreddy died in 1815, and his son, who succeeded to the estates, lived ten years, during which time the greater portion of the half million in money disappeared. Rajah Jugganatha left two wives and two adopted sons. The one, Lutchmeputty Naidoo, who was first chosen, was a child of only six years, the other Ramanadha Baboo, had reached the age when, according to Hindoo law, he might enter into the possession of property. The wives, who had procured the respective adoptions, took, of course, separate sides: a law suit was commenced in 1829, and pending its settlement the government officers took possession of the land. In other words, the estates were put into chancery, only that, in Madras, it is the Board of Revenue that appoint the receiver. In this case, the property passed under the control of the authorities, not only unincumbered, but with a surplus of nearly 50,000*l.* in the public treasury.

If vultures have any sense of gratitude for fat carcases vouchsafed to them, we may infer that the revenue officers thanked the gods for this glorious opportunity of plunder. The tenures of subordinate posts in the districts where the estates lay became materially shortened. The hungry Brahmins came from all quarters, fed, grew fat, and dropped off, to make room for friends and relations, all keen of appetite, and skilled in tearing up the corpus, from which law and industry, the life and soul, had departed. No more was heard of surplus revenue, and the estates soon ceased to yield even the amount of the government tax. The reserved fund was attacked, and vanished almost in an instant. It was a race against litigation, which might possibly be terminated at any moment, when the lands would revert to the management of the proprietor. To guard against the consequences of such a calamity was the ceaseless occupation of the collectors' establishment.

The result of the suit in the Company's Court, was favourable to the pretensions of Ramanadha Baboo, who was declared the lawful heir to the zemindary, and petitioned to be put in possession. But the guardians of Lutchmeputty had appealed to the king in council, and a law, passed by the imperial legislature, specially provided for such cases. Either the appellant or respondent might have the management of the estates, on giving full security for the satisfaction of the final decree. It was but fair that Ramanadha should have the control of the property, but since the decision of the highest tribunal might be against him, when he would be liable for every shilling of profit that he had received, he must place in the hands of the Court the most complete security for the amount of surplus rent. In answer to an application, the Sudder Court fixed the security at the sum of 25,000*l.* per annum.

The finding of such an amount at the end of every twelvemonth, suited neither the means nor the inclinations of Ramanadha, but a shrewd man in the East is seldom at a loss how to get over such a difficulty, when in such a position. The Court's decree had given him possession of the personal property of Jugganatha, and he could raise money without trouble. At this crisis of his fortunes, he sent a sum of 17,000*l.* to the Presidency, and soon after it reached the capital instructed his vakeel to renew his application for possession without giving security. In the teeth of the clear letter and spirit of the law, and of the Court's previous decision, it seemed little else than an impertinence to the judges and a waste of money to the client; but, strange to say, the Sudder reversed their previous conclusion, and in spite of king's and Company's law they now decided that Ramanadha should have the estates. Nothing, it must be understood, is ever considered to be finally settled in the Company's highest Court. The judges, some of whom, perhaps, have never sat on a bench of justice until the day when they were placed at the head of the civil and criminal jurisdiction over the teeming millions of Hindostan, are enlightened enough not to care for precedents. It was no matter for wonderment, therefore, in Madras or Bengal, that a "final order" should be reconsidered and reversed; but in this instance it was thought to be rather stretching a point, to set aside an Act of Parliament which was in accordance with the simplest principles of equity. However, that was a mere matter of opinion, nothing more!

The interests of Lutchmeputty were considerably damaged by this last decision. Hitherto, Ramanadha had a common cause with himself in guarding against the spoliation of the estates; but henceforth, the latter would only seek to make a purse for himself, so as to be independent of the final disposition of the property. The Sudder Court, in assigning reasons for allowing him to get possession, said no security was required, because the zemindar's profits had disappeared, whilst, as to the government revenue, the public officers would of course take care to realise that as it fell due. The reckless dishonesty of this statement was patent to themselves, and to all who were acquainted with the revenue system of Madras. The regulations gave, to be sure, the most ample powers for the recovery of the state dues, either by the immediate seizure and confinement of the defaulter, the sale of personal property, or the attachment of the land; but, owing to the frightful pressure of the government demand, it was found expedient, in the case of all settled estates, to take what could be had from the zemindar, and allow the arrears to accumulate at twelve per cent. interest. Ramanadha, it was known, would exact all that he could get from the ryots, and hand over as little as the collector's people would consent to take. The goose had merely changed hands; the mode of obtaining the golden eggs was the same under the rule of either party.

The assigned reasons of the Sudder Court for its last order, gave Lutchmeputty, of course, a right to come forward at any time, if he could show that they were not consistent with the state of the facts. This privilege he availed himself of, by frequent remonstrances, until at last the judges were worried into addressing a letter to the Revenue Board, in which they asked whether it was true, as the appellant repeatedly asserted, that Ramanadha was wasting the property for his own gain? The public departments in question are located four miles apart, but it took seventeen months to get an answer to this communication. At the end of that period, the Revenue Board replied, that all which had been alleged on the subject was quite true. The estates were now heavily indebted on account of arrears, and they had just given an order to attach the zemindary.

It is but a small leap from the frying-pan into the fire. The collector's men were again in possession, and there was still some good pickings on the bones. The government authorities had first swallowed up the 50,000*l.* a year that used to find its way into the pockets of the zemindar, next they got rid of the balance in the treasury, and thirdly they accumulated a debt of 140,000*l.* for arrears. Ramanadha's addition to the latter reached 76,000*l.*, so that at the time of the second attachment, the entire arrears standing against the estate amounted to 216,000*l.* The stone had now got to the middle of the descent and was sure to reach the bottom.

In 1842, the Court of Directors were induced to make one of those benevolent interpositions in favour of their Indian subjects, which read to such advantage in Blue Books and speeches in parliament. They wished to save from utter ruin those fine old families whose estates were now hopelessly involved, mainly, of course, through their own dissipated course of life and want of business habits, but owing, perhaps, in a small degree, to hard times and a very little of undue pressure on the part of the local government. The Madras authorities were directed to call on the zemindars to surrender their title deeds, so as to enable Government to deal with the estates as effectually as if they had been acquired at public auction. The collectors were then to set on foot a detailed survey of each property, to execute works of irrigation and general improvement, and finally, to make liberal agreements with the cultivators before giving back possession to the owners. Attributing in some degree, the depressed condition of the estates to the frequent changes of management, arising from the constant transfer of collectors from one district to another, they proposed that these gentlemen should be tempted, by the offer of higher salaries, to remain in their appointment. The zemindars were to have a suitable allowance, and the discharge of their private debts should be left to the discretion of the authorities.

The government of Madras handed the above instructions to the Board of Revenue, and the latter passed them on to the collector, directing that "Mr. Stokes should, in the first instance, ascertain from the zemindars whether they are willing to surrender their estates on the terms proposed by the Honourable Court, which he should take especial care to have explained to them, and," said the Board, with a touch of grim humour, "considering the alternative, the application is not likely to be refused." Ramanadha Baboo did, however, hold out for a time, but on being threatened with a sale, he gave up his title deeds, received a pension of 1200*l.* a year, and waited, with the rest of the Guntoor landholders, for the good times which the Honourable Company had in store for them.

The collector received the instructions of the Board, and acted thereupon as the Company's servants have been in the habit of proceeding since the days of Warren Hastings with regard to similar documents. He filed them, and took no further notice. Whenever he drew the increased allowance suggested as the proper compensation for the increased labour imposed upon him; when the zemindars sent in their quarterly petitions; when he saw the cattle of the peasantry dying in the beds of the dry water-courses; or passed in his palanquin through the roofless and deserted villages, he might possibly think of his duty of promoting works of irrigation,—of giving comfort to the ryot, and restoring wealth to the ruined noble; but such reflections would only have a temporary effect. The district must send forward its usual quota of revenue, and those who left him without a surplus were answerable for the neglect of public works and the breach of private obligations. And hence it was, that the zemindaries progressed from bad to worse for four years longer. No single step had been taken in the path chalked out in 1842, and at last, the Marquis of Tweeddale, a pious, conscientious governor, gave his consent to the absolute sale of the estates. There was no one near him who had cared to say that Government had already obtained possession of the lands as absolutely as if they had acquired them by purchase; that improvements could be made neither cheaper nor better by a change of title, and that, above all the estates had been surrendered on the express condition that they should be given back. Such considerations concerned no one in office, and so the Vasareddy zemindary in Guntoor, the debt upon it increased by the sum of 38,000*l.* since the title deeds and responsibility had been transferred to the state, was put up to auction in 1846, and bought by the Government for 500*l.* Now they had got rid of the rival rajahs and their claims, and could see their way in the matter of making paying improvements.

All this time, the appeal to the King in Council was pending. The papers had gone home in 1832, and fourteen years had elapsed without the slightest notice being taken of the matter. There were no witnesses to be examined, and the lower courts had taken care to exact the deposit of what was considered a sufficient sum to cover costs. But the East India Company were not concerned in the settlement of such causes, and what could women and children in India know of the way to proceed? What would a Leicestershire squire of the old school be likely to make of a suit which must be carried on in a strange tongue, in courts sitting fifteen thousand miles off? Perhaps the Vasareddy appeal might have been unheard at this moment, had not Lord Brougham, with that practical sagacity which has made him so truly famous, discerned a mode of redressing one of the evils of Indian administration of justice. A bill was passed compelling the Company to prosecute all such appeals as were then on hand, and making provision for the proper disposal of such cases in future. Under the provisions of this Act, the Vasareddy suit was brought to a hearing before the judicial committee of the Privy Council in 1848. The decision of the Sudder Court was reversed, and Lutchmeputty Naidoo declared sole heir to the entire zemindary.

There was much feasting in the halls of Lutchmeputty Naidoo, now a man of twenty-three, when the Queen's decree was made known. Old ryots thought of the days of Vencatreddy, and believed that they might come round again, and his friends lauded the justice of the Queen's courts, where a man's rights could only rest in abeyance for a season. In due course, Lutchmeputty presented a petition to the Sudder Court, and, filing the decree of the Privy Council, prayed to be put in possession. The judges took the matter into consideration, and, reciting in their proceedings, the absolute title now vesting in the petitioner to the property left by Jugganatha, they decided to collect the costs of the appeal in the first instance. The Company's bill for bringing the case to hearing, amounted to 32,000*l.*, which they required to be paid as a preliminary measure. The securities deposited in the first instance, might realise perhaps, with interest, 10,000*l.*, and he had now to find the balance. The rajah, though rich in parchments, had no cash, and the judge of the district where he resided was instructed to seize his horses, elephants, and whatever personal property could be laid hold of. Lutchmeputty remonstrated against a proceeding which seemed to imply that he was rather worse off than before, and had made a heavy loss by being declared the heir to 50,000*l.* a year. The judge consented to stay the sale of his household gear for a short time, but asked what he wanted with elephants and their trappings? They were only for rich men, and he was not of that class.

The lapse of another month enlightened the landless rajah to the true worth of the decree for which 32,000*l.* had been charged. When the Company's Courts had sold him up entirely, he was told that there was nothing to be handed over to him. The Government had bought his Guntoor estates two years back, and as for the Masulipatam villages, he might have them upon payment of the arrears, amounting to 280,000*l.* Neither oyster nor shell came into his possession. The Revenue Board cared nothing for the decree of the Privy Council, of which he should have speedy proof. It declared him the sole owner of the estates, and nothing could divest him of that title short of new legal proceedings, or of his own act of alienation. The decree was filed in the

Sudder Court, in October 1848, and in April 1849, the Board put up to auction the Masulipatam property, as the estates of Ramanadha Baboo, and bought it as such on behalf of Government. There! let him tell that to the Queen and the Judicial Committee.

It was told to the Queen and the Judicial Committee, and in July 1854, the members of that august body, after hearing the Rajah's petition, which, perhaps, startled them somewhat, recommended her Majesty to make another order for putting Lutchmeputty in possession. The second mandate was issued, and it was now thought justice would be done at last. Two hundred pounds more were spent in getting the matter argued in the Sudder Court, which finally dismissed the petition for execution of the Queen's decree, and told the rajah, that if he wanted the estates, he must begin by filing suits against the Company in the Zillah Courts. There must be a suit for each estate, and a third for the sum originally deposited in the treasury. The first sheet of paper used in each cause, would cost 100*l.*, and each separate page of the proceedings would cost four shillings. In time, the cases would come to the Sudder in appeal, when the same expense would be incurred over again, and, at last, it would be appealed to the Privy Council, when the rajah must deposit in hard cash, security for the full amount of the estimated costs. Lutchmeputty, who is a fine specimen of the Hindoo gentleman, still occasionally visits Madras, vaguely fancying that changes of ministry in England might help him; but he has given up that hope, since the last appointment of a secretary to the Board of Control. In reply one day to a remark of condolence, he said, "You think it is a hard case? I can assure you that there are a hundred stories much worse than mine."

We have spoken of suits and suitors; let us now speak of judges. The highest judicial tribunal under the Company's government, is called the Sudder Adawlut, on the civil, and Sudder Nizamut on the criminal, side. It consists of three judges, who sit regularly, and a member of council, who is ex officio, and only takes his seat on very rare occasions.

Every civil cause except the very lowest, may come in appeal before the Court, and every criminal sentence passed by a judge or magistrate, is reviewed as a matter of course. It has the privilege of enhancing as well as mitigating punishment, and can order a man to be hanged whom the judge below only considered deserving of transportation, or it may release him unconditionally. A single judge sitting on either side of the court has the same power as if the whole were present. If the entire authority of the courts of assize throughout England were vested in the Court of Queen's Bench, the judges would have no wider jurisdiction than is exercised by the Sudder Courts in India.

Exactly ten years since, the Marquis of Tweeddale, then Governor of Madras, suspended the three judges of the Sudder Court in that Presidency, and the Court of Directors on being appealed to, made the removal permanent. Of course the circumstance excited much local comment, and gave rise to a lengthened correspondence between the Government and the judges; but when the latter had spoken their minds with regard to the conduct of Lord Tweeddale, they proceeded to give their opinions of each other. The first judge speaking of the third, asked the Court of Directors as follows: "Why should the responsibility of such an appointment, which placed the disposal of landed and other property, and of sums of money unlimited in value and amount, together with the powers of life and death, in the hands of an incompetent person, or to speak more correctly, why should the results of such an appointment, and which, as evinced by the memorial, followed as a matter of course, attach in any way, direct or indirect, by inference or otherwise, to your memorialist?" Of the second judge, the same weighty authority wrote, that "he was in a state which had prostrated his judgment to a degree subversive of official usefulness;" and the third judge wrote of the first, that he was "a canting hypocrite, a pitiful scoundrel,—held in the lowest repute, and incapable of adhering to the truth in any statement, verbal or written." We have tried to fancy what the public would say in England, if Sir Samuel Coleridge drew such a pen-and-ink portrait of Lord Campbell; but the imagination refuses to compass it. In Madras, the statement scarcely provoked notice; it seemed to be in accordance with the system of things; a little too violent, perhaps; but then allowance must be made for excited feelings. Any astonishment that a stranger might have felt on the subject would have been mitigated a few months afterwards, when a member of the Board of Revenue, who had repeatedly officiated for months as a Sudder judge, was sentenced by the Queen's Court to six months' imprisonment for the crime of perjury.

The fool, the firebrand, and the judge denounced by his colleague as something worse, had sat on the highest seats of justice for years; and, if what they said of each other were true, what an amount of mischief and misery they must have wrought amongst twenty-three millions of people! Yet neither in their cases, nor in that of the official who was so terribly punished, did the Government ever think of interfering to check the scandal, of the existence of which they could not possibly be ignorant. The judges were removed because they had quarrelled with the local authorities, and not on the score of their proved unfitness for office. They were degraded as civilians, but not as judiciaries; for being insubordinate, and not for being destitute alike of wisdom and self-respect. Too bad at last for Lord Tweeddale, they had always been good enough for the people.

A similar result was exhibited in Bombay, where, in 1853, Lord Falkland removed two of the Sudder judges on account of comments made upon their private characters in a Bombay newspaper. Had the welfare of the public or the purity of the judicial bench been objects of the smallest regard, the Government would have saved themselves much pain and the service much discredit. Men asked why it was that a measure, which ought to have originated with the highest authority, was allowed to become the work of a journalist? It was honestly enough avowed that the articles in the newspaper formed the grounds upon which the judges had been deposed from their high places; but the editor neither created the public scandal nor intensified it, so far as Bombay was concerned. He merely related to persons at a distance facts which everybody in the western presidency were long acquainted with. It was impossible not to see that the judges were in reality punished, not for indebtedness, immorality, or for exposing the Sudder Court to the chances of contempt and suspicion, but for having been written about in a public journal. Whatever of actual mischief resulted from their conduct existed independently of newspaper comments. All the circumstances which had been treated as a bar to their continued employment as dispensers of justice, must have been currently talked of in English drawing-rooms and native bazaars long before the "Gazette" dared to allude to them. It was an error, in fact, to assert that the scandal grew out of the leading articles, as it was a blundering policy to let people see that the press took better care of the public interests than the Government. If the judges were innocent of offences which deserved so severe a punishment, no difficulty in the way of convicting their slanderers could justify the Government in disgracing them; and if they were guilty, it should not have been left to a private individual to ordain and ensure their downfall.

The Court of Directors approved in each instance of the removal of the judges; but the latter had to be provided for in future, and it is in the mode of caring for them that we detect the true character of Indian rule. Of the Madras officials, two had served their time, and accepted retiring pensions; but the third judge had no desire to leave the service, and, by prescription, the Government were bound to give him a salary equal to that which he had last enjoyed. There were no posts, except in the Revenue Board, to which such a rate of income was attached, and, under any kind of administration, it was thought indispensable to have none but clever men in that department. It was needful, then, to secure the main object in view, that he should go into the judicial line again, and so they gave him a sessions judgeship, and, in due time, his decisions came up to the Sudder Court to be reviewed by the men whom he had reviewed five or six years beforehand. One of these decisions concerned the right of certain parties to a piece of ground. Witnesses for the plaintiffs deposed that to their knowledge the ground sued for had been in the possession of the claimants' ancestors, on which the moonsiff gave it in their favour. The defendants appealed to the judge. They said these witnesses are all men of middle age, and it is proved beyond doubt that we have held possession against one part of the family claiming for sixty, and against the other for forty years — how can they speak, except from hearsay? The judge saw no force in such a statement, and affirmed the judgment, observing, that "the decision of the district moonsiff had been based on the evidence adduced, and that the Court cannot discover any substantial reason advanced against it in the appeal to question its correctness." It was nothing that what the witnesses swore to happened before they were born, nor did he stop to consider a plea based on the adverse possession for at least forty years by the defendants, though but a month before the Government defeated a suit against themselves by pleading the Statute of Limitations!

On a second occasion, the Sudder judge then extant, said, of his predecessor's verdict, that "he was wrong on every point of law save one, and that was immaterial."

We might multiply to utter weariness examples of the thorough degradation of law and justice in India, and the chances would still be, that every man who has resided for a few years in the country, could, from his own experience, tell of some instance more strange and grotesque. There are differences of opinion with regard to every topic of Eastern reform, except upon the subject of the Company's judicial system. It provokes no discussion, since it has no defenders. It is incapable of improvement, and therefore no one suggests plans of amelioration. Young men, when they are placed on the Bench, have had no opportunities of acquiring a knowledge of the principles of jurisprudence, and persons of mature age find common sense a guide sufficiently reliable to serve in lieu of law, statute or common. It was one of the oldest judges in Madras who fined a man 5,500*l.* for bringing a civil suit, which the Sudder Court afterwards decided in his favour, and it was the civilian who is called the ablest man on the Bench who gave validity to a Papal bull, and decided that His Holiness had dominion in India.

The reforms needed are, the appointment of trained lawyers to sit as judges, and the use of English as the language of the courts. If the choice to be made lay between retaining as judges the men who at least knew the language of the country, in preference to replacing them by men who only knew the law, we should still advocate the change, because it is infinitely better that the judge should be able to give a sound decision, than that the suitor should understand the words in which he pronounced it. But it is not true that in the majority of cases the judges know the language of the district over which they preside. In Bengal and the north-west the greater number may be able to converse with their Sheristadars, but of the dialects familiar to the people, they know next to nothing, whilst in Bombay and Madras, no heed is taken of such a test of fitness. The civilian who speaks Mahratta is perhaps promoted to a judicial post in the Guzerattee country. The apt scholar in Tamil is appointed to a court where people only speak Telogoo. We happen to know an instance, where the utter ignorance on the part of the judge of even the rudiments of the native tongue, was apologised for by the plea that "the defect was of no consequence, since he was as deaf as a post." He was thought no worse of by the rest of his judicial contemporaries, and for the best of reasons.

Of course it would be better that a judge should know the native languages, but there is not the slightest ground for supposing that the barrister whose whole life is devoted to the legal profession will be less anxious to fit himself in every respect for the discharge of his duties than the civilian, who may be taken any day from the Bench to the Revenue Board, sent over the country with a roving commission, or comfortably lodged in the secretariat. The one man shines or fails as a judge, and is always exposed to the severe criticism of the legal profession: the other scarcely knows the meaning of the term "responsibility;" is sure of pay, and careless of censure. He accepts the office which binds him to dispose of human life and liberty, as a labourer would undertake a new job, trusting that in time he may learn to handle his tools well, and get accustomed to the work placed before him.

If provision be made for the settlement of small disputes by native punchayets, and the right of appeal is abridged to the limits which regulate it in England, we shall be quite content to know that the suitor in the superior courts is obliged to have the judge's English translated to him in future, as he is now compelled to get translations of his Hindostani or Tamil. There are few of us in England who care to comprehend the meaning of what is said on our behalf in a court of justice. We take law as we take physic, a nauseous draught, about the composition of which we had better not be too curious.

CHAP. XXII.

STATE EDUCATION IN INDIA ALMOST WHOLLY CONFINED TO THE UPPER CLASSES.—MISTAKEN NOTIONS AS TO ITS RESULTS.—PURELY SECULAR CHARACTER OF THE INSTRUCTION.—THE FIELD FOR CHRISTIAN EFFORT.

THE Court of Directors, in a letter to the Madras Government of the year 1833, observe:—"The improvements in education which effectually contribute to elevate the moral and intellectual condition of a people are those which concern the education of the higher classes, of those persons possessing leisure and influence over the minds of their countrymen. You are moreover acquainted with our anxious desire to have at our disposal a body of natives, qualified by their habits and acquirements to take a larger share and occupy higher stations in the civil administration, than has hitherto been the practice under the Indian Governments. The measures for education which have been adopted or planned at your Presidency have no tendency to produce such persons." They subsequently add:—"We consider this as the scope to which all your endeavours with respect to the education of the natives should refer." In another letter of the Court, quoted by Lord Auckland in his minute of 24th November, 1839, they observe:—"That, with a view to the moral and intellectual improvement of the people, the great primary object is the extension, among those who have leisure or advanced study, of the most complete education in our power. By raising the standard of instruction among these classes, we should eventually produce a much greater and more beneficial change in the ideas and feelings of the community than we can hope to produce by acting more directly on the more numerous masses."

We entirely concur in the objects sought to be obtained by the Court of Directors, but utterly deny the wisdom of the mode by which they seek to achieve them. Upon what grounds is it asserted that the best way to advance the moral and intellectual welfare of the people is to raise the standard of instruction amongst the higher classes? The history of the past affords no warranty for it. The universities of England are nearly five hundred years old; in every age they produced distinguished men: but did the enjoyment of these facilities for learning elevate the morals and intellects of the people? Why, it seems but yesterday when women were burned for witchcraft; and at this moment there are millions of people in England and Wales wholly unable to read the letters of the alphabet. So strange a doctrine we have not heard for many years; and yet it has survived through the journey from Leadenhall Street to India, and has still some signs of life remaining in it! There is not a writer, whose vocation is to deal with the existing questions of morals and politics, who does not believe that, so far from its being necessary to retrace our steps, we must march forward on the great highway to change with accelerated speed. And what is it that has so entirely altered the aspect of the thinking and acting world? Is it the greater spread of knowledge amongst the higher classes, or the greater intensity of moral feeling amongst them? Are there more well-educated persons in their ranks, than at any former period; so that, observing the close connection which has always existed between the increase of their knowledge and the progressive amelioration of the people, we can say that the latter are better off, because the former are more wisely instructed? A glorious argument this for aristocracy, were it only tenable. To show the growth of the national happiness, it would only be necessary to refer to the number of pupils at the colleges, and the lists of academic degrees. Each wrangler would be accounted a national benefactor; and the existence of deans and proctors would be associated, like the game laws and the ten-pound franchise, with the best interests of the Constitution.

Many ages have elapsed since peculiar resources were afforded to the Brahmins; but the most considerate cosmopolite would hesitate to enroll them amongst the benefactors of the world. They boast of vast stores of ancient learning They have amassed great riches, and been invested with unbounded power; but to what good end? They have cherished the most degrading superstitions and practised the most shameless impostures. They have arrogated to themselves the possession and enjoyment of the rarest gifts of fortune, and perpetuated the most revolting system known to the world. It is only from a diminution of their abused power, that we can hope to accomplish the great work of national regeneration. Amongst the various arguments by which the Government have from time to time advocated their favourite plan, they have never once appealed to examples furnished in the history either of the past or the present.

They have bought scholars who, it is thought, would in time vend learning "without money and without price." "If we can only inspire the love of knowledge in the minds of the superior classes, the results will be, it is contended, a higher standard of morals in the cases of the individuals, a larger amount of affection for the British Government, and an unconquerable desire to spread amongst their own countrymen the intellectual blessings which they have received." We have never heard of philosophy more benevolent—and more Utopian. It is proposed by men who witness the wondrous changes brought about in the Western World purely by the agency of popular knowledge, to redress the defects of the two hundred millions of India by giving superior education to the superior classes, and to them only. It is admitted that the attempt to implant religious feelings would be wholly abortive; and yet it is thought, that by making the few more powerful, the welfare of the many will be cared for! We expect that the result of our system of intercourse and Government will be to pull down, in a great measure, the religious superiority of the higher class; but we propose to make atonement by setting up fresh claims on their behalf, which shall at all times be backed by our authority! We will give them strength of intellect, without the soft humanities of religion! When they have renounced the gods of their fathers, whilst disbelieving the faith of the stranger, — when they are armed with exclusive privileges and own no tie binding them to their humble fellow men, — we expect that they will surpass ourselves in moderation, and form an aristocracy of worth such as the world in every age has vainly sighed for.

Power instinctively knows its rights, and always reconciles the assertion of them with abstract notions of justice; but it never originates the knowledge of its duties. Whilst learning was confined to the upper classes at home, they governed for their own sakes. When the folios of literature gave way to the octavos, and the author was patronised by the bookseller instead of the nobleman, opinion questioned the theory that Heaven had intended one law for the rich and another for the poor; but when the last change had been effected, and the flying sheets, which uttered the noblest thoughts of great men, were read by the labourer at his fireside, then it was that the revolution of power was accomplished, and the solemn truth proclaimed that all men were equal in the sight of the law, and that all authority should be exercised only for the benefit of the multitude. The learning of the few has enlarged the bounds of human speculation and refined the manners of its votaries; but the crude knowledge of the masses — rude and imperfect as it is — has added to the empire of truth and brightened the prospects of the future.

We ask the friends of Indian universities to favour us with a single example of the truth of their theory from the instances which have already fallen within the scope of their experience. They have educated many children of wealthy men, and have been the means of advancing very materially the worldly prospects of some of their pupils; but what contribution have these made to the great work of regenerating their fellow men? How have they begun to act upon the masses? Have any of them formed classes at their own homes, or elsewhere, for the instruction of their less fortunate or less wise countrymen? Or have they kept their knowledge to themselves, as a personal gift not to be soiled by contact with the ignorant vulgar? Have they, in any way, shown themselves anxious to advance the general interests and repay philanthropy with patriotism? Have the few intelligent heads of Hindoo families, as they grew more and more acquainted with the nature of the disinterested exertions made in their behalf, given any help to the good cause? Has any party amongst the natives, rich or poor, urged on the scheme? That they are not indifferent to the necessity of offering opposition to the success of missionary effort in the cause of education, we admit. But five years since the middle classes of the great district of Bellary forwarded a petition to the Madras Government, which discloses fully their notions of what a national education should be, and what is the nature of their expectations from the state. The petitioners say:—"We deem it proper here to notice that our schools at Bellary, being founded by the respectable portion of our community, are adapted for the higher classes; and, consequently, admission is given therein, not only to Hindoo youths, but also to the children of respectable families of the Mahomedan population. Having schools of our own, we scarcely have any connection with the school recently established by the mission at Bellary, in which the lowest classes form the majority of the pupils; and neither do we wish to have any concern whatever therewith."

This, it must be known, is an extract from a letter requiring the assistance of the Government. The "respectable portion of the community" at Bellary have maintained their own schools for eight years; but hearing that at Madras 10,000*l*. is annually expended in the great cause of teaching the higher classes, they naturally desire to be placed on an equal footing. Education of itself is good, but education for nothing is better. They are proud of the fact, and allege it as a recommendation, that they have no connection with the lower classes, but they are not above begging. They will part with their independence, but not with their rupees. They are the lowliest servants of the Government, but they will not tolerate the acquisition of knowledge by their own countrymen. Let the state, which is upheld by all, found schools and support them out of the common funds, but in the reception of scholars only consider the "respectable portion of the community," and adopt free teaching to the higher classes! We have asked for an illustration on the other side of the question, but will manage to make shift with the present for want of a better.

It is not well that the existing system should be upheld. An age may, perhaps, elapse before the light of a better faith sheds its equal rays over the land; for after the demolition of a creed there is a time during which the ruins must cumber the soil, and, until those are cleared away, the task of the restorer cannot be commenced; but the action of political and social wrongs is never for a moment intermitted. The unjust rule and the frequent privation are felt equally by the Christian and the idolater, and though we may fail to teach the natives the truths of our theology, we may easily acquaint them with the nature of our legislation. Our object should be to protect them against the better knowledge of their own countrymen, who charge upon British authority their own acts of monstrous oppression. We want to see the Hindoo armed by his knowledge against the assaults of power, and made as impervious to an illegal act as the European or East Indian. We cannot teach him Socrates and Shakspeare; but we can make him acquainted with the powers of native officials, and instruct him in the method of procuring redress for injustice. We may fail, for some generations to come, in making him a moralist, patriot, or Christian; but we may convert him into a contented subject: we can train his selfishness in the right direction, and enable him to curb the exercise of inimical power by showing him the secret of his own.

CHAP. XXIII.

TENDENCY OF THE NATIVE MIND TO IMITATION.—VALUE TO ENGLAND AND INDIA OF AN EXTENDED SYSTEM OF EDUCATION.

AMONGST great multitudes of people the elements of strength are invariably found more or less abundantly, and it only requires skilful management to evolve them. Granted that the natives of India are averse to change, and therefore indifferent to the acquisition of foreign knowledge, they are also imbued with the most intense love of wealth, and their avarice will always overcome their apathy. Show them by palpable evidence that they can get more power and profit by adopting European modes of action,— make it plain to them that change will produce the most beneficial results,—and they will not hesitate to follow the example of the Western World. Their faculty of imitation is proverbial for its excellence; and wherever the means of advantage have been fairly exhibited to them, they show no lack of inclination to avail themselves of opportunity. It is a mistake to suppose that their conservatism is the result of inaptitude or indifference. They follow the ways of their fathers because they believe in their sufficient excellence. They are incapable of originating new ideas; and hitherto it has not been thought worth the while of those having means and authority to teach them the absurdity of existing modes of thought and action. In ten years a judicious scheme of national education would effect an almost entire revolution in the habits and condition of the people. Instead of adapting instruction to the use of the higher classes, we would address it to the capacities and selfishness of the multitude. A board of competent persons should be formed in each Presidency, to whom ought to be confided the tasks of rendering into the vernacular languages the simplest forms of European knowledge. To the agriculturists should be distributed tracts showing the best methods of increasing the riches of the soil. To the workers in metals and manufactures the most approved processes of labour ought to be explained. Each trade and branch of industry should be furnished with the information best calculated to increase the worth of the various products of industry; and when it was once thoroughly understood that the land could be rendered more fertile, the sources of employment more abundant, and the general value of all articles greatly increased, we might easily depend upon the strength of the selfish impulse in urging forward the great work of improvement. Within the reach of all persons, and clothed in the very simplest garb, should be placed the knowledge which it most concerned them to obtain; and to each and all we would afford the means of arriving at a correct understanding of the relative powers and duties of the various officers entrusted with the work of administering the government of the country. It would be absurd to attach as much value to the influence of publicity in India as is properly awarded to it in England, and we do not expect that Asiatics would be as prompt as our own countrymen to resist the arbitrary exercise of authority; but by degrees a feeling of opposition to injustice — at all times existing in a latent state — would be brought into action, and, at the very worst, the sins of actual commission only would be charged upon the British Government. We have no belief whatever in the patriotism of the Hindoos, and therefore think it unwise to place any reliance upon the supposed good intentions of the superior classes; but perhaps the surest guarantee of good government in any country whatever is the consciousness, on the part of the rulers, that the people are acquainted with the nature and extent of their own privileges. As it is the interest of the many to be well governed, it naturally follows that the best way to keep rulers honest is to array the instincts of the masses in opposition to the corrupt impulses of the few. When oppression becomes dangerous to the chief actors in the work, a great advance in the march of liberty is gained; but if it is made almost impossible, it is astonishing what service is rendered to the cause of public virtue.

A great incidental advantage would also accrue from the performance of this work of national education. Whilst teaching the lessons of European civilisation, we might ourselves acquire a knowledge of Indian resources. Perhaps no race of conquerors ever occupied, for so long a time, a vast territory with so little advantage, in the way of adding to their own stock of information. The English character, in this respect, offers the strangest contradictions. In all other parts of the globe we rake the depths of the sea and shore in quest of the riches which in India we refuse to scrape off the surface with our nails.

At home the art of the chemist is employed to conquer, by the most refined combinations of capital and skill, the difficulties of nature. In India, where the most costly products might be created at the expense of a little time and knowledge, the outlay is often considered too great. We are the most skilful artisans in the world, but our tool chests are invariably left at home. We complete our education in the land of the setting sun, and think life too short to make any additions to our stock of knowledge when we have quitted its shores for the East.

The world has never yet seen an example of a well-governed people becoming vicious and insubordinate, and we have no fear that the Hindoos would prove an exception to the rule. There are opportunities given to the humblest classes in Britain which the people of India have never been permitted to hope for, but to the use of which they could never be insensible, whilst wealth, and fame, and power have charms which are worth struggling for. It should be our policy to assimilate, in this respect, the condition of all British subjects, — to give ambition the hopes of advancement, enterprise the means of employment, and talent of every kind the opportunity of growth, in whatever part of the soil its roots are found implanted.

A future in which these objects should be realised is not shut out from the Indian vision; but to render it possible it is requisite that the education we propose to impart should not be confined to the superior classes.

It is not supposed by the present heads of the universities that the study of knowledge for its own sake, however great the opportunities afforded for its acquisition, can prove an incentive strong enough in the minds of the native youth to induce them to enroll themselves as scholars. This circumstance, considered by itself, provokes some mortifying reflections, but it also gives rise to some serious inconveniences, which in a great measure detract from the utility of educational projects. It is all very well to hold out as an incessant bribe the prospect of Government pay, as a reward for the inhalation of the weakest portion of Locke, Bacon, Pinnock, and other kindred spirits; but there is such a thing as over-cramming public offices, as well as scholars;—added to which, the aspiring alumni, who have scraped away some portion of the shell of knowledge, and written essays almost as good as new, are prone to institute comparisons between their salaries of thirty and forty rupees as writers, and the huge sums melted by men, their superiors, as they are willing to admit, in all things except intellectual culture. They have been taught that the tree of knowledge always bears fruit of a kind sufficient to satisfy the most craving appetite; and they find that, like the famous apples of the Dead Sea, though pleasant to the sight, it turns to ashes in the mouth. Men are ever prone to consider themselves undervalued and underpaid; and it seems strange to imagine that a system of culture which sets up material benefit as the chief, nay, almost the sole, reward of exertion, whilst the means of satisfying the hope are so notoriously small, should be thought likely to increase the amount of affection entertained for the present rulers of the country. We believe that, so far from having brought about this desirable result, it has prompted those who have been trained under its influence to reason in the spirit of the worst philosophy upon the curses of refinement and the evils of intellectual superiority.

We are not weak enough to separate the wish for learning from the desire of ultimate benefit, nor to seek to hinder the educated portion of the Hindoo community from reaping the just reward of superior ability; but, instead of drafting them in crowds to the public offices, there to waste existence in fruitless repinings and objectless efforts, they should be taught to combine the love of gain with feelings of a higher and worthier cast. We would have the colleges changed into great normal schools, and the students trained for the work of teaching their countrymen throughout the length and breadth of the land. The first step in the great work of general education must evidently be the training of a body of competent teachers; but it is altogether out of the question to suppose that European agency can be employed, except upon the most limited scale. A great plan which, beginning with the establishment of village schools, after a competent body of teachers had been formed, would afford the opportunity of filtrating the native intellect till the rarest products were found in a university, would command the cordial support of all classes. It is a question by no means decided, whether the instruction now afforded in the highest schools is really the best calculated to advance the mental or moral condition of the pupils; but, putting this aside, as a needless subject of discussion, it is clear that the results obtained are not worth the cost, either in the estimation of Europeans or Hindoos. In no country in the world do class interests and class prejudices obtain so much as in India; and it is the plain duty of a Government which is paid by all, and which exists nominally for the benefit of all, to bring to bear in their fullest force all the levelling principles of education. It should be the especial duty of our people to afford equal facilities to all ranks. They ought, above all other things, to proclaim the republicanism of knowledge, and that Nature makes no distinction of castes in bestowing her gifts of intellect and beauty. So far is such an idea from obtaining acceptation, that we believe it has never been enunciated by the supporters of the existing state of things. The scholars of the universities are at this moment almost exclusively composed of the superior classes, and above one half of them are remunerated in hard coin for their attendance. The one fact telling somewhat against the catholicity of the system, and the other militating as strongly against the feeble belief in its popularity.

The establishment of boards of English and native professors, who should be instructed to prepare, for universal distribution, elementary tracts, conveying the wisdom of Europe in the language of the East, would be the first step in the right direction. Unless we anticipate that the impoverished Hindoo, to whom the progress of the world is all a mystery, should make greater advances in mental study than the nations amongst whom knowledge has grown up from infancy to maturity, we cannot expect that our language and literature will become extensively familiar to him. What the dead languages are to our own countrymen, our own tongue is to the Indian; and how few of the former are familiar with them! To the few who enjoy great opportunities or are prompted by strong inclination, the obstacles in the way of gaining even an ordinary acquaintance with the higher branches of study may not prove insuperable; but we shall have done much if, in the course of the next fifty years, we can succeed in imparting even the rudest outlines of knowledge to the dusky masses. To make any sensible progress, however, it will be necessary to begin in another direction, and look upon a university, not as a starting point, but as a final halting-place—the goal of the best and wisest amongst two hundred millions of human beings.

We have not lost sight of the fact that the point at issue is not what should be the character of a truly national scheme, but what is the best use to which the limited resources at the command of the Government shall be applied. We do not oppose colleges, but we more strongly advocate village schools. The best interests of a community require that each of its members should be educated to the top of his bent; but if we are to choose between the system which turns out annually, at an enormous cost, a half dozen "practically" uneducated "proficients," whose intellects add nothing to the general stock of knowledge, and whose cultivated moral sense has scarcely, in each presidency, produced a Christian in theory or a patriot in practice, and the system which should teach the masses the great simple truths which lie at the very foundation of all human learning!—why, we have no hesitation in coming to a conclusion on the subject. So far as eleemosynary aid extends, we would rather bestow it in teaching twelve ryots the truths which our English boys become acquainted with in the nursery, than in the vain endeavour to impart European wisdom or modes of thought to members of the upper class. We are not dealing with a question upon which freedom of choice is permitted; we have only a poor alternative — a little for the many of that which is surely useful, or much for the few of that which often neither benefits nor adorns.

Had we proposed that the State Education now given should be abolished in favour of a plan which gave instruction in mechanical vocations, we should have been prepared to defend the suggestion. We contend that hitherto the Government have not succeeded in making even a fraction of the population, morally or intellectually, wiser, and we see no encouragement to hope for a different conclusion in times to come. Amongst the alumni of the universities, past and present, are to be found the greatest sticklers for caste, the bitterest haters of Christianity, the most prejudiced and exclusive, in short, of the Hindoo population. Are we then to care for the upholding of such a system of "national education as this?" Would it not be a thousand times better to advance the national welfare of the masses, in the rear of which ever advances the incalculable blessings of an improved morality and general enlightenment?

We are weary of reference to the regenerating influence of Socrates, Milton, and mathematics. What we seek is to cultivate amongst this people the existence and knowledge of Power. Instead of aiding the Brahmin and the upper classes generally, we want to raise a counterpoise to their baneful influence,—to defend the Hindoo against the assaults of the native aristocracy. If we saw any signs, however remote, of the growth of patriotic feeling amongst the higher ranks, we might be content to witness, for a few years longer, the further trial of the present experiment; but so far from inducing a better feeling towards their destitute and low-caste countrymen, the instruction which they imbibe seems only to sharpen the natural appetite for the power to exert oppression. It is universally admitted, by those who have studied the statistics of crime, that education has the happiest effect in diminishing the amount of evil; but it is not necessary to impart the higher branches of study to realise the moral benefits of training. The ability to translate Euripides, or master the hardships of the differential calculus, affords no superior guarantee for the moral worth of its possessor. The harvest of piety to be reaped at the university is not more abundant than that which the despised grammar-schools afford; and hence, until it is universally held that the State is equally bound to maintain policemen and schoolmasters, no case can be established, either in favour of universities or Protestant colleges. We know that the immortal part of one man is as precious as that of another in the sight of Heaven; and the good behaviour of the many ought to be infinitely more valuable to the State than the mere intellectual superiority of the few. The moral value of education lies in the first few lessons, and not in the recondite truths of learning. Teach a whole people to read, and cheapen all access to knowledge, and the consequences will be visible in the decay of gaols and the increase of churches; but found colleges and sneer at grammar-schools and village tuition, and you will have the pedant at the top of your pyramid of society, and a broad basis of crime at the bottom.

It must not be supposed that we are hostile, or even indifferent to, the existence of the highest seminaries of learning; but we have to deal practically with a question of comparisons. Here is a little money to be laid out upon national education, in the way most conducive to the public benefit; and how can the end be best achieved? Our opponents contend that, by training a few youths in the knowledge of the highest branches of human wisdom, we are creating a force which, in time, will penetrate to the remotest parts of the body politic. We, on the contrary, argue, not that their wish is improper or their machinery intrinsically useless, but that they are pursuing the wrong path and embracing the smaller instead of the greater good. It is certain that the principle of evil is active in all minds, and requires repression; hence the necessity of universal education: but it is not true, either that moral beauty resides in the mysterious depths of nature, or, that to induce a youth to exert for the public good some rare faculty with which he may be gifted, it is necessary to found universities at the public expense. Whatever genius resides in him may be developed in a grammar-school;—if the innate power is there, it will be seen to defy obstruction, rather than require forcing. If all men could receive such a measure of education as is afforded at grammar-schools, the question as to the existence of "mute inglorious Miltons" would be set at rest for ever. A cursory examination would show that few authors of prize poems and gainers of mathematical prizes have made for themselves places in the world's estimation, in comparison with the host of men who obtain their knowledge from the parish pedagogue and earn their living by the sweat of their daily toils.

It is no more just to call upon the State to found universities than to demand that it should support workshops, rice depôts, and fever hospitals in every locality. Labour is good, and rice not to be despised, but the task of providing either of them is not the duty of a government; and we should not incur the odium of being thought indifferent to human welfare, were we to resist the proposal of looking to the State for due supplies. The very restricted task which we would impose upon the guardians of the community is perhaps open to challenge on the part of those who contend that, of all aids to happiness, self-help is the most efficacious;

but we are disposed to make an exception in this instance to an otherwise valuable rule. The masses do not understand the value of education; and where the knowledge of its uses and the will to improve it exist the means are often wanting; it becomes therefore a duty on the part of the Government to provide that, so far as their power extends, the task appointed to every human soul, of working out, with Heaven's help, its own regeneration, shall not be left undone for want of the necessary tools. But it is not in the universities that the manufacture of implements can be carried on successfully; and we are not therefore concerned, so far as Government grants are required, to prolong the existence of the one or help the other into being. As the brick-and-mortar results of extended education, we should rejoice in their prosperity; but as a portion of the means whereby knowledge may be universally spread abroad, our judgment honestly refuses to acquiesce in their propriety.

On the great subject of religious teaching, we must do justice to the Indian Government. It hinders no man from teaching and preaching Christianity. It does not seek to plant its foot within the circle of missionary influence. It merely adds to the list of State obligations a duty hitherto imperfectly recognised; and as Hindoos, Mussulmans, Jews, and Christians, have always been declared equally entitled to the benefits of civilised government, it has resolved to give all classes the advantage of that training which is deemed requisite to fit them to discharge their several duties to society. It holds that worldly knowledge is good, though religion is better, and that an educated heathen is better than an ignorant one, just as an educated Christian is better than one who knows nothing but theology, and perhaps but little of that. It cannot, if it would, coerce men's consciences, but it can inform their intellects and refine their manners. It looks upon the Khoud as being lower in the scale of humanity than the Brahmin, and the latter again as inferior to the schoolboy who understands astronomy and the use of the globes. It recognises God's handwriting on every leaf and wave; in the caverns of the earth and the motions of the stars, as well as in the inspired volume; and leaving to the ministers of religion their appointed tasks, claims to work only a portion of the machinery by which the Almighty deigns to reveal His wisdom and goodness to mankind. The founders of our faith, whose example we ought to follow, preached everywhere, and to all people, the sublime truths of religion; but they never levied taxes for the support of their mission, and had no doubts as to the right solution of much that is classed by ourselves amongst the mysteries which pass human understanding.

The precepts and the doctrines of Christianity have remained unchanged for nearly two thousand years, but the interpretation of them is different in every age. At this moment the wisest and best of men are to be found professing opposite creeds, and drawing from the plainest texts irreconcileable inferences. Some of the highest dignitaries of our church are warm friends of secular education, whilst others believe, that when you teach the Bible you teach everything; that learning and intellect, strength and prosperity, are the results of Bible training; that to know all which can be known, and enjoy all that can be gained in the temporal world, it is only necessary to read and obey; to meditate in silence and reap all the fruits of industry.

A union between the State and the missionary is not possible; antagonism, real or apparent, is not wise; but what should prevent the friends of Christian knowledge from taking over the whole of the existing Government machinery of education, and making the Bible a class book in every school? Government might retain the colleges for the study of medicine and civil engineering, and fulfil all the functions performed for the British Isles by the Royal Society of Arts. It might enhance in many ways the social welfare of the people, and direct the aims of the trained intellect, whilst abandoning to the care of the missionary the interests of literature and religion. It would thus give in native estimation full value for taxation, and by tolerating all religions, secure in time the supremacy of a solitary creed, the triumph of the highest and holiest interests of mankind.

The entire net sum paid by Government in India for the maintenance of colleges and schools is in round numbers about 120,000*l.* per annum, but under missionary supervision perhaps half that sum would suffice. The latest returns give a total of 14,319 scholars receiving instruction in the State schools of Bengal, at a cost, after deducting school fees and the sums received for the sale of books, of more than 50,000*l.*, or 4*l.* 10*s.* each. We do not think the average cost of tuition, is less than that sum in the other Presidencies, and it is for the missionary societies to say whether they will undertake the contract at a lower rate, with Bible instruction included. The English public need have no fears on the score of slack attendance at missionary schools, or of the growth of a feeling hostile to missionary effort. In 1853 there were two thousand pupils receiving daily instruction in three missionary schools at Madras. Not fifty of the number were of low caste origin. Many of the boys came in carriages, and each and all had to read a portion of the Scriptures daily. Is it worth adding, say, another 100,000*l.* to the income of missionary societies to secure the like results in the case of rich or poor, Brahmin or Mussulman, in every quarter of the East? That is the question for the consideration of the Christian people of England.

CHAP. XXIV.

THE LAND REVENUES OF INDIA.—EXPLANATIONS OF THE VARIOUS MODES OF LEVYING TAXES ON THE SOIL.—THE ZEMINDARS AND THE POLICE OF BENGAL.—FAILURE OF THE VILLAGE COMMUNITIES IN THE NORTH-WEST.

AND now we have to consider the gravest portion of this subject. Can we make India pay? It has been shown that the East India Company would be unable to conduct the future Government of the country, were it only on the score of financial difficulties, and we should fare no better under the Imperial rule, if the system of taxation were not wholly revolutionised. Nothing more can be had from land, nothing from salt, nothing from opium. And we see no prospect of reducing expenditure whilst the present need for the supremacy of force continues to exist. Under the present system, we cannot do without the bayonets of Europeans, the honesty of the civilians, or the numbers of the revenue officers, and hence we must continue to maintain an enormous army, pay high salaries, and support a countless multitude of native subordinates. Our income is derived, not from surplus profits, but from capital; not from luxuries, but from the poorest necessaries. It is the product of sin and tears.

The Chairman of the Court of Directors told the House of Commons, on the anniversary of the battle of Plassey, that "there was a cuckoo cry about the miserable condition of the people. It was said that the people were so miserably poor that they could not develope their resources; but how did that assertion agree with the fact that the balance was always against us, and that we were always under the necessity of exporting silver for what we received? (Hear.) The truth was, the manufacturers of Manchester were altogether careless about Indian tastes and fancies, but if they would not give themselves any concern about the wishes of the people, they must not expect them to become customers. (Hear, hear.)"

We must not be angry with Mr. Mangles, or with the members of Parliament who cheered him. The one spoke and the others applauded according to their convictions, and it is a positive gain to the cause of good government, when men in high places give vent to their real views and feelings. But light is not more opposed to darkness than the statements of the Chairman of the Court of Directors to honest truth. We hope that he is only ignorant; blindness from whatever cause is bad enough in the case of a man so placed, but we will not assume that it is wilful, an example of social malingering.

Of the entire revenues of India, amounting in round numbers to 29,000,000*l.* per annum, 16,000,000*l.* is derived from the rent of land, Government being at the same time sovereign and landowner. The land rent is collected under three different fiscal systems: — The Perpetual Settlement, which prevails only in Bengal; the Village Partnerships, which obtain in the Punjaub, Scinde, and a part of Bombay; and the Ryotwarry, under which nearly the whole of the Madras and a portion of the Bombay tax is collected. The perpetual settlement had its origin in 1793, when the Marquis Cornwallis fixed in perpetuity the annual rent payable by the presumed owners of the soil. The village partnerships sprang out of the desire of the authorities in the North-West Provinces to keep up what was considered the old framework of village society. Tracts of land were surveyed and leased to certain castes, or persons having what was thought the right of occupation. The rent was fixed latterly for a term of thirty years, and each member of the partnership was bound to pay his share of a defaulting member's proper contribution. The ryotwarry, as its name implies, was a form of holding direct from Government. The cultivator paid at the close of the official year for the land he had in possession, and renewed, relinquished, or altered his holding at pleasure. The tenure was a yearly tenancy, to be undisturbed so long as the peasant paid the rate agreed upon.

In spite of what our Government has chosen to assume, it is an undeniable fact that, in every part of India, land under cultivation was in the private ownership of some one or other previous to the English conquest. Where violence and general insecurity prevailed, there would of course be frequent mutations of property. The estates of the nobles would experience the consequences of their changing fortunes; and the village communities, made up of what we should call peasant-yeomen, were occasionally scattered abroad, but always to reappear and unite when the wave of ruin had subsided. The land furnished nearly the whole of the State's revenue; and the tax was raised or lowered, paid or evaded, according to the character of the ruling power and the dexterity of the agricultural interest. To simplify the collection of the Government dues, a class of agents was created all over the country, called Zemindars,—literally, landmen, not landlords,—who received all the tax, and paid it into the public treasury, less their commission, which was usually fixed at about 40 per cent. It is the tendency of all official employment in India to perpetuate itself, and, in the course of time, the zemindar claimed and was allowed a vested right, as permanent as that of the owner of the soil. It was to these men that Lord Cornwallis, in 1793, made over the whole territory of Bengal, rent-free estates excepted, which they were to hold for ever on payment of the tax then existing. The outcry against this act has never been intermitted; but the civilian condemns it because it excludes the Government from any share in the growing value of the soil, the just cause of complaint being that the rights of the proprietors were entirely sacrificed by the law. If the ownership had still remained with the cultivator, it would have been of no moment to him that Government had agreed to give the zemindar 40 per cent. of the amount which the former was obliged to pay; but what happened was this, — the zemindars complained to the Government that they could not gather in the rents unless they were vested with summary powers of imprisonment and distraint, which were granted; and from that hour to the present the ryot has remained in a state of hopeless slavery. The law took no note of under tenures or leasehold rights. If the rent due by the zemindar was not paid at sundown on the appointed day, the estate was sold, and the buyer received it clear of all claims. The default of the proprietor was ruinous to all beneath him, and that law is unaltered at this moment. Of course every estate was purged at once of village proprietors; and though there is hardly a holding which is not let and sublet many times over, the speculation involves risks which none but a Bengalee would undertake. English planters strive of course in all cases to obtain an independent footing on the soil; but the task is a hard one, and neither money nor cudgels, which are the influences next in potency throughout Bengal, will at times suffice to uphold them.

Take the case of a public common, or a public orchard, if the latter could exist in England, and either would bear an exact resemblance to the condition of the Bengal ryot. Cattle would nip the herbage almost before the blades reached the surface of the soil; children would gather the apples before they were ripe. The fear lest others should appropriate exclusively what each man feels he has a right to share in effectually hinders growth and maturity in the case of the grass and the fruit, and just so with the miserable Bengalee under the common ownership of the zemindars and policemen. The one does his best to prevent the growth of property, the other is always on the watch to detect the signs of it. The peasantry are born and die in debt; somebody owns them from the cradle to the grave; and what matter for the colour of the master's skin or the nature of his profession? With the rich soil at their feet, and the burning sun over head, possessing nimble fingers and willing hearts, the ryots have all the elements of a prosperous strength; but faculty lies within them, like the vigour of a man who is worn down to the last stage of weakness by famine. The nourishing food and the refreshing drink are spread out only a short mile from the spot where he lies, and yet he must die of hunger, from sheer inability to crawl the distance. No one has an interest in the ryot, except for his performance of tasks for their benefit. The missionary would clothe him in righteousness for the next world, but is obliged to leave him in rags during his stay in the visible portion of the universe. In this state of existence he has literally no friends, and is so drained of manhood as to have few or no enmities. Since the harrow and the roller must pass over him, why should he care who guides and drives them?

To award the ryot the very smallest share of the wealth derived from the soil, is the never-ceasing object of the zemindar; and when he has reaped all that he can in that field, the police come in and pick up the scattered ears. They are ready at any moment to convert a murder into a case of cholera, or a death by disease into an atrocious homicide. They will tie up and torture, without hesitation, a whole village, for the sake of a few rupees. It is a matter of mere chance whether they make the subject to be operated upon a culprit or a witness, and there is scarcely any difference in the consequences. Crime cannot be detected, if the criminal is willing to pay; innocence cannot escape, if it is poor and believed to have the means of bribing. Upon such a subject, declamation is so facile, and therefore so suspicious, that it is necessary to quote authority for the character of two important classes of Hindoos. Here is what the present Lieutenant-Governor of Bengal, Mr. Halliday, says of the police and the magistrates appointed to watch over and dispense justice to forty millions of people. "For a long series of years, complaints have been handed down from administration to administration, regarding the badness of the Mofussil Police under the Government of Bengal, and as yet very little has been done to improve it;" that, "throughout the length and breadth of the country, the strong prey almost universally upon the weak, and power is but too commonly valued only as it can be turned into money;" that "it is a lamentable but unquestionable fact, that the rural police, its position, character, and stability as a public institution, have, in the Lower Provinces, deteriorated during the last twenty years;" that "the criminal judicatories certainly do not command the confidence of the people;" that, "whether right or wrong, the general native opinion is certainly that the administration of criminal justice is little better than a lottery,—in which, however, the best chances are with the criminal,—and this is also very much the opinion of the European Mofussil community;" that "a very small portion of heinous offenders are ever brought to trial;" that "it now appears that half of those brought to trial are sure to be acquitted;" and that "peculiar and accidental circumstances, partly temporary and partly arising out of the constitution of the Civil Service, have, at this moment, made the inexperienced condition of the magistracy more observable than it has ever been before; while it seems certain that the evil during several successive years is likely very seriously to increase."

The missionaries, speaking of the Bengal zemindars, in their petition to the House of Commons presented last session, say, "It is manifest that the tenants suffer from a lax administration of laws passed for their protection; that they are oppressed by the execution of other laws, which arm the zemindars with excessive power; that they do not share with the zemindars in the advantages derived from the development of the resources of the country; that the profits thus monopolised by the zemindars are already incalculably valuable; and that, year after year, the condition of the tenants appears more and more pitiable and hopeless. Other evils increase the wretchedness of the condition to which a tenant is thus reduced. The village chowkeydars are the servants of his landlord; the government police are corrupt, and he cannot vie with his landlord in purchasing their favour; the courts of justice are dilatory and expensive, and are often far distant from his abode, so that he has no hope of redress for the most cruel wrongs; and he is frequently implicated in affrays respecting disputed boundaries in which he has not the slightest personal interest.

Ignorant of his rights, uneducated, subdued by oppression, accustomed to penury, and sometimes reduced to destitution, the cultivator of the soil, in many parts of this Presidency, derives little benefit from the British rule beyond protection from Mahratta invasions.

The area of Bengal is 149,000 square miles, or 97,000,000 of acres, and on the productive surface of 64,000,000 of acres the taxation amounts but to a fraction more than 1*s.* per acre, the total paid to Government being 3,333,150*l.* The value of the exports for 1856–7 was not less than 18,000,000*l.* sterling; and, as very little of skilled labour enters into the price of Bengal produce, it may be estimated that at least 16,000,000*l.* is represented by raw material. Calcutta, however, is the principal outlet for the sea-board exports of the north-west, and perhaps it will only be fair to add to the Government demand on account of the total shipments, 25 per cent. of the land-tax paid by the latter territories. This will bring up the revenue of the whole of Bengal and a fourth of Upper India to 4,500,000*l.*, which is about 28 per cent. of the worth of raw produce exported. The rent of land leased by the zemindars varies from 8*s.* to 14*s.* per acre, averaging perhaps 10*s.* Wages, over the whole country, average, for an able-bodied ryot, not more than 1*s.* a week; and we have been assured by the head of a firm in Calcutta, having extensive dealings with the interior, that in some portions of Tirhoot, where the great indigo factories are situated, twenty-seven men had been contented to work the entire day for 2*s.*

In the North-West Provinces, which cover an area of 72,000 square miles, without including the non-regulation districts, the Bengal system was everywhere adopted on the country first coming into our possession; but subsequently the talookdar, or government agent, was compelled to show his title, and where that was found to be defective, he was set aside, and the village proprietors treated with alone. A broad distinction was, however, always preserved between the mode of dealing with the cultivators in Northern and Southern India. The sum to be paid as rent being defined, Government, under the ryotwarry system, took the whole of it, as a private individual would have done, but in the north-west no less than 38 per cent. was set apart, 20 per cent. of which was returned to the proprietors and 18 per cent. to the talookdar. But it sometimes occurred that the latter was proprietor as well as Government agent, in which case he received 30 per cent. of the net rental; and in cases where the Government collected the rents which he had a right to realise they paid him a commission of 22½ per cent. free of all risks and charges. In broad terms, it may be stated that the Government returned, all over the country, one-third of the net rental to those in whom the right of cultivation and the right of collecting the tax were vested.

Of course, under such a system, land grew very valuable; and though it was never so difficult to purchase estates in the north-west as in Bengal, owing to various social causes, the soil never lacked eager buyers. But whilst the village settlement favoured the views of capitalists and traders, who availed themselves of every opportunity of buying out or ejecting by force of law the village proprietors, it was not calculated to secure the great aim of its founders. The scheme was unsound in its essence, as every attempt must be to regulate by law arrangements which depend for success on the exercise of free-will and the indulgence or restraint of passions.

If an English parliament were to attempt to restore the ancient guilds and corporations, on the ground that in old times they were the nurseries of trade and the strongholds of liberty, it would not commit a greater mistake than that which the Government of India fell into in this respect. No doubt, in the turbulent centuries, when the tillers of the soil suffered almost equally from the ravages of the foreigner and the protection of their lawful chiefs,—when the distinctions of caste were rigidly observed, and the village boundaries were the peasant's horizon,—it was good to establish and maintain brotherhoods of labour; there was a common interest to support and a common danger to repel: but when peace is the natural inheritance of the ryot, and the bonds of prejudice are falling from every limb, why should we yoke him in these new fetters? why seek to restrain the course of free effort, and map out by authority the tasks that he shall perform and the way that he must go? We may be sure that the instincts of selfishness are wiser in these matters than the dictates of authority. Long before the outbreak of the rebellion it was visible that the scheme was crumbling to ruin. In the north-west the suits to obtain possession of lands were continually on the increase, and every decision against the right of a shareholder was scarcely less hurtful to his copartners than a judgment against the property of a merchant would be to the firm of which he might chance to be a member. The author of "Modern India" is so impressed with the gravity of this result that he deprecates the application of the law of sale to landed property in the Punjaub. The system will not stand the wear and tear of litigation; the mutation of proprietors is everywhere fatal to it. If the cultivator indulges in the natural desire for selling, mortgaging, or devising, except amongst the limited circle of his coproprietors, the law must refuse to give validity to his acts, or the fabric of society, which has been built up at so much cost, will avowedly tumble to pieces!

As affecting the existence of village communities, the North-West System entirely failed; but, as regards the general public, the objections to it were, the perpetual interference of the Government officers, its cost to the Government and to the people, and the inefficiency of the tenure, as a means of developing the resources of the country. If a man took new land, which could be very seldom obtained of late, he had only a term of thirty years to count upon; but in general the lease of property available for a new comer would not have more than fifteen years to run: and who would undertake extensive works, build factories, or make great embankments, with the knowledge that at the end of his lease Government would assess the rent for the next term upon the current value of the property? The interest of the tenant, during the last years of his term, tended in the way of depreciation and not of improvement. The system was for a time much better for the interests of the cultivator than either the perpetual settlement or the ryotwarry, because it gave him a share of the rent;

but in the long run he found it impossible to remain suspended between the condition of a capitalist and that of a mere labourer. Extravagance and bad seasons worked his sure ruin: and when this happens, and he is ousted by the decree of a court, "his enmity," according to Mr. Thomason, late Lieutenant-Governor of the North-West, "is transferred from the individual to the State. He feels that there is no hope for him but in the downfall of the system. He becomes as much a disaffected man as though he had been ruined by some direct act of the Government." Without any idea of showing the unsoundness of the system, Mr. Thomason, in the next paragraph of the paper from which the above quotation is taken, tells us that "it is not many years ago that an insurrection was occasioned in Ramghur and the Cole country from the unrestrained operations of the courts of justice. The Government perceived the evil, and at once, by excluding the regulations, put a check on the obnoxious proceedings." The Coles evidently knew how to deal with the Honourable Company: but a system which requires the occasional suspension of laws and the shutting up of courts of justice could hardly advance the welfare of any people, whether civilised or barbarous.

The poverty of the Bengal ryot is not to be attributed to the direct action of the East India Government, who are responsible only for so much of the misery that prevails amongst the forty millions inhabiting the great Gangetic valley as may be traced to the appointment of those whom the Deputy-Governor of Bengal terms "boy magistrates," to the nomination of inefficient judges, and the support of the police. To ascertain the true character of the Company's government, we must turn to that portion of their dominions where their influence, both social and political, has been absolute for a hundred years past, where there is no middleman to intercept the profits of the cultivator, where peace has been uninterrupted and obedience has never failed. The condition of Madras is the true touchstone of the value of that Government which, according to Mr. Mangles, needs no teaching to understand its duties and no additional incentive to perform them.

CHAP. XXV.

THE RYOTWARRY SYSTEM IN MADRAS.—MELANCHOLY RESULTS OF A CENTURY OF RULE.—THE HOPELESS POVERTY OF ALL CLASSES.

In a Parliamentary paper, dated May, 1857, there is printed a copy of a dispatch from Lord Harris, the Governor of Madras, upon the proposed general survey and assessment of that Presidency. "Much has been published of late," says His Lordship, "respecting the unsatisfactory state of this Presidency, of the poverty of the inhabitants, of the hopeless position in which they are placed, and of the exorbitant taxation; and all this misery has been stated to be the result of British misgovernment. I have serious doubts of the correctness of these assertions. That the majority of the cultivators of the soil are poor, is certainly true; but that is almost certain to be the case where the soil is divided into innumerable small holdings, each insufficient to provide for the most ordinary wants of a family of the lowest class.

"That the position of the ryots is not very hopeful, may be attributed to many circumstances; but I am inclined to think that their depressed condition is as much the result of moral as of economic causes.

"That the taxation which they have to pay is excessive may, in some instances, be the case; but I cannot allow that the amount of public funds contributed by the Presidency is exorbitant. Neither am I prepared to admit that the state of the country, generally, is deteriorating. I believe, on the contrary, from all I can learn, that there is a marked improvement in many districts, though probably not to the extent which might have been attained had circumstances permitted more active measures for improvements on an extensive scale to have been undertaken by the Government.

"That the general state of the country has not become less prosperous, is sufficiently shown by this one fact,—that, though remission of taxation has been made to some extent within the last few years, the general income has not diminished."

The views enunciated by His Lordship in the above passages were shared by his colleagues in the Government; they have been approved of by the Court of Directors; and we propose to examine and test their real value.

In dealing with the great social questions of India, the inquirer is materially aided by the simple and permanent character of Eastern life. The tides of nature and of human existence flow in the channels which were worn for them in remote ages. Whatever was true of a thousand years past, is almost literally true of the present day. A change of masters, a little more wealth or poverty, and you have all that mark, for the teeming millions of Hindostan, the progress of time. Now, as heretofore, the records of the tax-gatherer furnish an index to the state of the nation: when we know what is paid to the Government, it is easy to find out what has been earned by the people.

This absence of complexity in the business of life, which is characteristic of every part of the country, is especially so in Madras, where government, trade, and tillage are all carried on upon a scheme of first principles as naked as need be. In that highly favoured Presidency there are neither nobles nor landlords; the priests are maintained on the voluntary system; and for every acre of cultivable land under the ryot, there are five or six lying fallow. In other words, it is an Eden of the mind, with many thousands of good angels keeping watch inside the boundaries.

Such an innumerable multitude of persons—many of them able, and most of them honest—have written in praise of the Revenue system of Madras, that were it not for the reflection that the Corn and Navigation Laws have been repealed scarce ten years since, we should be tempted to doubt the accuracy of returns and the evidence of the senses. Still it could hardly escape observation, that whether the Government of the day was painstaking or otherwise, whether the "Board" had ruled in favour of zemindars or direct holdings, the upshot to all concerned was the same. The ill wind blew nobody good. The superstructure of society gave way and was overturned, without in the least relieving the foundations. Where the zemindars were absorbed, the district yielded no more profit to Government, frequently less; whilst the wages of labour and the prospects of employment were decreased as well. The class disappeared, and with them vanished not only pomp and extravagance of living, but the means whereby their state had been upheld. The hut and the starved bullock took the places of the palace and the elephant. The rich man became a beggar, and the ryot remained a slave. The working of the machinery is rather different now, since there are no more wealthy proprietors to be amalgamated. The fire must needs go out when the fuel is exhausted. Poverty must be allowed to live because it is required to toil; but, truly speaking, no other reason can be assigned as the cause which has hindered the depopulation of the Southern Presidency.

In the last report of the Madras Government, the inhabitants are set down as amounting to nearly twenty-three millions, three-fourths of whom are engaged in agricultural pursuits. At the usual rate of five persons to a family, this gives, say, three and a quarter millions of able-bodied ryots; and since the peasant's wife works as hard as her husband, and the children are put to labour as soon as they can crawl, we shall be far within the mark when we assume that the work of two labourers is done by each family of five persons. We have then six and a half millions of workers diligently toiling on the land, and more than ten millions depending for food upon their exertions. Now what do they earn from January to December? Never was problem more easily solved, and never did the result of a few simple figures so put to shame the working of a Christian Government. The official estimate of Land Revenue for 1856-7 gave a total under three and a half millions sterling; and we have to find out what proportion of the gross produce of the land is represented in that sum. Colonel Baird Smith says, that in Tanjore, the most favoured district in the Presidency, the Government share is two-fifths of the gross produce.

We doubt if in any part of Madras the amount actually taken by the servants of the state is less than one half, and know, from personal investigation, that over the greater portion of the country the tax swallows up two-thirds. But let us take Tanjore as the standard by which the impost is assessed, and the entire value of the cultivation is shown to be eight and three quarters millions. If no portion of the above sum were taken by Government,—if the crops grew spontaneously, and the reaping were done by fairies,—the sum to be divided amongst the people would not amount, for each household, to five shillings monthly. But, inasmuch as the Government in their mildest mood take two-fifths, and the cost of cultivation, excluding labour, cannot be set down at less than one-fifth, we have for distribution amongst the people as many pounds sterling as there are heads of families, or about half that sum as the annual wages of each labourer. Did the bitterest denunciation of the Company's rule ever reach the accusing height of these simple facts? Think of it, conquering countrymen of ours! Fivepence a week for the joint labour of man, wife, and children, or two shillings and a penny in the currency of London and Liverpool, where money is said to be worth only a fifth of what it will buy in India; in the shape, however, of food and shelter only! What interest can Manchester have in the living or dying of any conceivable number of fathers of families, whose incomes are but twenty shillings yearly? They do their best to encourage British trade, for they consume of yarn, cotton, wool, and piece goods, imported from all quarters, as much as amounts to twopence per head per annum. Our friends at home can judge for themselves how far that sum will go in the purchase of their wares, and may form a lively idea of what the seventeen millions have to spare for food, education, and pastime when they can afford to lay out on their wardrobes just twopence a year.

There are upwards of ninety millions of acres in Madras, and, including rent-free lands, not above twenty per cent. of the whole area is cultivated. Indigo, sugar, cotton, oil-seeds, and coffee grow to perfection; but they are only produced by fits and starts, as the agents of exporters come forward with advances, and select the crop to be sown. Excellent raw sugar can be laid down at the sea-board for 8*s.* 6*d.* per cwt.; cotton gives a capital return when the grower obtains 2*d.* per pound. It is said that 70,000 maunds of indigo will be shipped this year; and to the production of oils there is literally no limit. And for every ounce of produce there are eager buyers; and if the field were increased twenty times over, no portion of it would be left on hand. Yet this is the land of which the richest tracts lie waste; which furnishes the Honourable John Peter Grant with the following illustration when combating the arguments of the Calcutta missionaries: — "There are no such contentions and affrays about land in Madras, as are justly complained of by the memorialists here. But this is not due to a good police and judicial administration, a survey and registration, or the absence of a zemindary system in the greater part of that Presidency; it is due to the fact, that in most Madras districts land is valueless, by reason of the revenue system there in force; the contentions there being, when a ryot is forced not to give up, but to take land." Mr. Grant might have stated his instance even more forcibly. Thousands of men labour on the public works, and prefer leaving the acres untouched, for which they are obliged to pay rent, experience having taught them to select the least of two evils. And under present circumstances, there is not the most remote chance of the waste lands being taken up, for emigration absorbs more than the annual increase of the population. The labour that might find such profitable returns at home is drafted off to a dozen ready markets. The man who should raise sugar on his own plot of ground, is only too glad to hire himself out to the planter in Mauritius. Wealth lies at his feet, yet he is obliged to expatriate himself to procure the means of existence.

And if ancient zemindar and modern ryot have been equally ruined by the operation of the Madras system, it has not proved in the least favourable to European enterprise. No great amount of capital has, perhaps, been sunk in agricultural or manufacturing operations; but whatever has been ventured has either been lost entirely, or is so unproductive that the parties concerned would gladly retreat were it possible to do so without sacrificing all. We are not aware of a single instance where a European has gone home with a competence achieved by planting or manufacturing operations. The attractions of more than a thousand miles of sea-board, and of a climate suited to the growth of every kind of tropical vegetation, would inevitably draw capitalists to settle in Madras, were it not that the long catalogue of disastrous results warns them off a coast which is fatal alike to all the producing classes.

Even if an energetic man can overcome the natural jealousy of the authorities, who look upon him as an enemy to the ryots and the Government in virtue of his position,—if he can contrive to do without roads, and has no necessity for law,—his ultimate defeat is certain. The weight of bad seasons falls upon him, though he may not rent a single acre. It is his money in that case that pays the tax; for though remissions are sanctioned by Government, they are granted not on account of the ryot's loss, but in view of his inability to pay. Like the Borderer of old, the collector says to the planter, "Thou shalt want, ere I want;" and unhappily for the latter, the raid is always resistless. What death is to life, the Government demand is to capital; it swallows up all, sooner or later.

As a consequence of this state of things, the preparation of raw produce for the European market is, with the most trifling exceptions, left wholly to the natives, whose will and poverty combine to make them prefer an inferior and adulterated, to a good and therefore costly article. They are able to make indigo as good as the finest Bengal sorts; but the great bulk of the Madras production is wretched stuff, much of it mere clay veneered with the real drug. The greater part of their sugar comes to market in such a state that the pumps of the vessels in which it is shipped are often choked with the drainings of the cargo, the loss from deliquescence being usually ten per cent. Cotton is wetted, and mixed with rubbish and stones. Oils are mixed without scruple, often to the serious detriment of the buyer, though the adulteration increases the seller's profit perhaps by the poorest trifle. These facts will explain the cause of the standing inferiority of Madras products in the markets of Europe, and help to show how it was that the mere increase last year in the exports of Bengal amounted to forty-two per cent. of the whole trade of the former Presidency.

We contemplate, in the case of Madras, a population whose growth has been everywhere obstructed, which is always miserable, always decrepid, neither wiser, nor stronger, nor wealthier than it was a century since, but, on the contrary, more weak, more ignorant, more poverty-stricken;—a population which declines in everything; which is losing its hold of an ancient religion, without adopting a new creed in the place of it, since the pagodas are destroyed faster than new chapels are built. The Hindoo schoolmaster is usually extinguished, not supplanted. The traditions of national prosperity are dying out; the consciousness of power which was always sufficient to avenge tyranny in the past, if it could not render it impossible in the future, is no longer entertained. Where else on the face of the globe shall we find peaceful millions so cruelly dealt with?

Growth is the necessity of nations. In numbers, in knowledge, in material prosperity, a people must inevitably increase in every generation. Not more surely do the houses of the dead outnumber those of the living, than the evidences of past labour overshadow those of the present. But in Madras, the only surplus is that of the Government revenue. Nature and industry in all else are but barely equal to the requirements of present existence. The country teems with mineral wealth, but there is not a mine sunk in it; the mechanical dexterity of the natives is not to be surpassed, but there is not a single factory the property of native capitalists. The sugar is crushed by wooden mills, and drained in earthen pots. The rice is ground by hand, the cotton cleaned by the rudest of all machines, the indigo prepared by the cheapest instead of by the best process. The increase of population, instead of augmenting the general wealth, is felt to be an evil; and thousands of the hardiest and ablest men annually expatriate themselves to countries where, inferior natural advantages being turned to better account, their labour enriches their masters, and secures a competency for themselves. The ryot, who would gladly stay at home to cultivate his ancestral fields, leaves the rich sugar soil untilled, and wends his way to the coast, where a discriminating Government has kindly provided machinery for putting his industry in motion. In the course of time, he finds himself in a distant island, engaged by a master, who has had to compete for his services, at three times the rate of wages he would have been content to receive at home. He still makes sugar, only now by the aid of the most costly appliances. He learns that God's rain and sunshine, and man's careful toil, are all valuable, if rightly understood and dealt with.

We have all need of Heaven's help; but if any class of mortals more than another require their eyes to be couched, their ears to be opened, and their hearts to be softened, it is surely those who administer the affairs of the Indian Government.

CHAP. XXVI.

SOCIALIST DOCTRINES OF LORD HARRIS AND THE EAST INDIA COMPANY.—GRADUAL DECAY OF EVERY FORM OF NATIONAL OR CLASS PROSPERITY.—THE FUTURE ARISTOCRACY OF THE EAST.

Lord Harris has a doubt as to whether the burdens of the peasantry have been fairly distributed; but without discussing at this moment the relative incidence of taxation in various districts, we assert without hesitation that, in all the ryotwarry talooks, it is imposed solely with reference to the amount that can be obtained from the people. In every other part of the world the cultivator benefits by the natural or social advantages of his position. Land which is well watered by running streams, or which is in the vicinity of great markets, brings a larger profit to the farmer as well as to the proprietor; but in Madras all the profit goes to the Government, the risk only falls to the lot of the ryot. Whether he cultivates largely or otherwise,—whether he grows sugar, indigo, or dry grains,—the result is precisely the same. The State leaves him but the barest subsistence. If he digs in North Arcot, he pays forty shillings an acre, because produce fetches a high price as compared with the inaccessible villages of the interior. If the land yields a double crop, he is taxed twice over; if it is poor in quality, his own gain is not the less in reality. If bad harvests occur, remissions are made, not on account of his loss, but in consideration of his inability to pay. When a country is ravaged by invaders, the poor rejoice in their immunity from mischief; when famine rages in Madras, the ryot thanks his gods that ruin has long since done its worst by him.

In no other country can the condition of the people be described in a few generalising sentences. Everywhere else there are diverse orders of society, with opposite interests and varying fortunes; sources of wealth which are hidden from curiosity; armouries of strength that only require to be properly handled, to save or regenerate the life of nations. But in Madras, the story of the merits of the Government and the misery of the population fills less than a dozen lines of narrative. The native aristocracy have been extinguished, and their revenues lost equally to the rulers and the multitude. The native manufacturers are ruined, and no corresponding increase has taken place in the consumption of foreign goods. Not a fourth of the cultivable land is taken up for tillage, and yet 20,000 men annually leave these shores to seek employment on a foreign soil. The taxation of all kinds, and the landlord's rent, amounts but to five shillings per head; and yet the surplus production of twenty-three millions is but two shillings and sevenpence, and the imports but one shilling and sixpence each person. The exports of the slave state of Brazil amounted, in 1852, to upwards of eight millions sterling. Madras, with a population three times as great, never produces a third of the amount.

Railways, roads, and canals will not cure the evil, and we should be sorry to see it made more bearable. What we require is an abstinence on the part of Government from interference with the operations of agriculture, as absolute as that which they are compelled to observe with regard to the workings of trade. A man should be as free to buy and sell land, as to deal with any ordinary chattel. The belief that it is to the advantage both of the state and the public that the soil should be declared the property of the former, is one of the most fatal errors that ever prevailed. Does any one believe that if the British rulers had been compelled, from the outset of their career of conquest, to levy taxation by the ordinary methods, Madras would be now in its present miserable state of poverty and degradation? Is it credible that from the industry of twenty-three millions of souls, living under a tropical sun, and raising, almost without effort, the costliest products of the world, a sum of five and a half millions sterling — but one-tenth of the taxation of Great Britain—could not be raised without difficulty? The statistics of crown colonies and of slave states furnish the best answer to such a query!

The Governor of Madras is a member of the British Peerage, an estated noble who has a "place" and a rent roll which we suppose he would not wish to have diminished. Yet we find him, in the forty-fifth year of his age and the fourth year of his Governorship of Madras, addressing the grave bankers and landlords who sit in Leadenhall Street as follows: —

"I consider that the land of a country belongs to the Government *de facto,* and should be held by it, and should be distributed by it amongst the population in such a manner as is likely to cause it to be most beneficially cultivated, both as regards the interests of the cultivators and of the whole community. There may be, and we know there are, many hindrances to this principle being even openly allowed, much more to its being fully carried out in all countries; but in those cases wherein the opportunity is afforded of starting from first principles, it should not be neglected. I think this opportunity exists in the ryotwarry districts of this country."

It will not do to identify the Anglo-Indian Conservative, Lord Harris, with a member of the upper or middle classes of England who wishes to maintain the aristocracy as an institution, nor with a Birmingham Radical who would destroy the House of Peers and abolish hereditary titles. The principles which he advocates are neither more nor less than socialism: his apostle and teacher is M. Proudhon, who advanced in Europe the theory that Lord Harris enunciated, and which his honourable masters have reduced to practice in Southern India for a period beyond the memory of the oldest man living.

A hundred years since we found an aristocracy existing in every part of the East. They were not more enlightened, perhaps, than the nobility of England in the days of the Plantagenets; not more moral than the courtiers of Charles II., or those of Louis XV.; not more thrifty than certain model peers; in fact, not more lovable or useful, in the main, than the highest classes of Europe have shown themselves to be in ancient or modern history. But the Indian aristocracy oppressed and governed, attained wealth and lavished it, fought and intrigued as passion prompted or ability served, and so satisfied what the majority of people, even in these enlightened days, are prone to term "a real social and political want." As a governing class, the remorseless English heel has long since trampled them out of existence. So far from realising the European ideal of a ruling minority, which makes laws by prescriptive authority, fills the highest posts in Church and State, and influences the public weal without regard to considerations of fitness or respectability, they have been reduced to a state of abject dependence. The parish constabie would feel himself degraded were he made to change stations with the rajah. Every private soldier in the Queen's service has the prospect of a higher destiny before him than the head of the noblest Asiatic family. The title which adorns the beggar, and the phrases of respect that greet the ears of the slave, are all that remain to the descendants of the masters of the East.

We recognise and sanction the penalties of weakness. There are no political rights for the nation which has suffered itself to be vanquished, except those allowed by the grace of the victors. But the question with which we have to deal is one apart from politics — it is the right of the State to confiscate the wealth of the upper classes upon no pretext of crime or proof of public utility.

We know of no right which a Government has to prevent the growth of large estates, which does not as readily apply to the creation of small ones. We can think of no reason that can be urged against allowing a man to become the owner of half a county, which may not just as forcibly be applied to his acquisition of a score of acres. Our Indian socialists, with the same objects in view as their co-thinkers in Europe, have not had the sagacity to perceive, or the boldness to carry out, their principles to the full extent. The latter recognised and acted upon the dogma, that property, to be interfered with, must be declared altogether illegal and opposed to the best interests of the community. They saw that the rule must be made universal, that accumulations in every form, and to whatever extent, must be made subject to the same law of interference. Men must be allowed to keep all or nothing. If individual action were allowed, no limits could be set to it.

For the last thirty years the British Government in India have been steadily uprooting the landed gentry of the country, on the sole ground of their inutility. They are no worse than the common run of aristocracy; on the contrary, are much better; but it is said society can do without them. They neither grow the rice nor milk the cows. The young children are taught, if taught at all, without their assistance; and old men go down to their graves with a sound persuasion that it is God's blessing, and not the zemindar's, to which they were always indebted for food and health. No one can question the justice of premises that have grown axiomatic in Europe, but the difficulty to be reconciled is the opposite character of the conclusions which are drawn from them. Human nature in the East has its shades of variance, but hardly affords such contradictions as are implied in the policy of the Honourable Company.

Why should the supreme authority, having most at heart the greatest possible welfare of the greatest possible number, care to maintain a class whose members are sometimes dissolute, sometimes tyrannical, sometimes idiotic, and in almost every case mere burdens on the industry of the people?

Why should so large a portion of the stream of wealth be diverted to flow over those barren sands which yield neither herbage nor flowers? No one is able to give satisfactory answers to such queries—on paper; and so the socialists in these parts have it all their own way. They have set up a standard of bare utility, and would compel all men to pass under it. He that refuses to work shall not be suffered to eat. The only poor which a Government can recognise, is the present generation of princes and nobles, who may be allowed to receive out-door relief for a season.

The first member of the Madras Council was for three years at the head of a revolutionary tribunal in the Northern Circars, and in that capacity he destroyed more ancient families and confiscated more estates than any member of the National Convention could boast of having ruined in his day of republican triumph. Now, if M. Proudhon were to claim him as a zealous practical disciple, would Mr. Elliot give him the kiss of fraternity? He could hardly help doing so, for the Frenchman would assail him with remonstrances something like what follow: —

"Fellow worshipper of the great mystery of the right of nations! you acknowledge with myself the claim of the producers of wealth to its full enjoyment, less the cost of cheap and good government. The study of the past has led us both to the only rational conclusion. Your rajahs are the exact counterparts of our grand seigneurs; your zemindars are our farmers-general; the Indian ryot is the very image of Jacques Bonhomme. Our common object is the abolition of all middlemen. We would have but one class of rights — those which spring from the exercise of industry; and but one kind of power — that which is necessary for the public safety. You have no peers, no chamber of deputies, no aristocracy; but only the ryot at one end, and an executive of retired tradesmen at the other. Go on and prosper, in the name of the friends of a regenerated world!"

We should not agree with M. Proudhon in the above tribute of praise, but confess that we do not see how the zealous champions of the Company can avoid being identified with the advocates of democratic equality. If you pull down all above, it does not follow that you must elevate all who are below; and there is not, to our mind, a single reason for the overthrow of the landed gentry in India which would not apply with tenfold force in the case of England. Is it that they are a heavy drain upon the productive resources of the country? Why, the rental of real property at home is more than all the annual profits of trades and professions.

There are three noblemen whose united incomes amount to more than a million sterling a year, and hundreds may be counted who receive at least a tenth of that sum. But the Indian aristocrat is useless; his proper place is occupied by another; the community are able to do without him, and should therefore cease to pay a double rate for the services of which it stands in need. Well, what does the Marquis of Westminster or his "order" do for our countrymen, that the latter need care to support "Corinthian pillars" that require so much gilding? The weaving and ploughing would go on just as well if they were all banished to dig in Australia. Their castles are no longer places of shelter for helpless serfs and burghers. They are no longer relied upon for security against foreign invasion and domestic plunder. It is not they who invent steam ploughs and reaping machines, and make pathways for the spirit of man over and around the globe. Manchester asks no assistance from lords or ladies to fulfil its mission of making cloth for all mankind. Birmingham is wholly plebeian; Liverpool essentially low. Every great interest is cared for by busy brains and willing hands, who work from necessity and not from choice; and of the amateur labourers, the most distinguished are men of humble note. The agriculturist relies much on Mechi, the owner of the "toy shop," and parson Huxtable, and half suspects that his landlord is a worse enemy than Cobden. Why maintain, then, a set of drones at such a frightful cost? If the landlords' rent throughout England were confiscated, it would pay all the taxes, and leave a large surplus to defray the expense of national education. In India rent is devoted entirely to public objects. If you abolish your landed gentry here, where wealth is scarce, learning confined to a few, and dignified employment almost wholly engrossed by a race of foreigners, how much more readily ought you to vote for the destruction of aristocracy at home, where property, knowledge, and industry are all independent of its aid! To our thinking, the civil servant who would hand over all the soil of India to Government and the peasants, ought to take his place, when in England, amongst the Cuffeys and O'Connors. He should have no thought of the danger of dislocating society, after having uprooted "houses" to whose antiquity the Norman baron is a creature of yesterday. For the reckless extravagance of the zemindar he can find parallel examples in the condition of half the peerage. The gaming table and the opera do the work of ruin as effectually as the overgrown suwarry and the dancing girls of the East. For the tyrannical interference with ryots, of which so much is said, he will find kindred illustrations in the conduct of men who avow that they will "do what they like with their own;" and when the race of folly is at an end the collector steps in to manage the zemindary, and the solicitor to nurse His Lordship's estate. The rajah goes on a pilgrimage, and the peer travels on the continent. In the next generation the evil will reappear; the vice is in the blood. Your only remedy is to compel the spendthrift to live on sixpence a day,— and earn it.

But in proportion as our Government are destroying the landed proprietors they are calling into existence the class of rich native traders, who will be the future aristocracy of the East. So would democracy at home foster the progress of the bourgeoisie. If the House of Lords were voted useless and dangerous, and all the property of the peerage confiscated to-morrow, the cotton spinners and growers would undergo, perhaps in still greater numbers, the process of transmutation into gentlemen entitled to sit at home at ease. And there is this striking difference between the class of new men in the two countries,— that whereas the native shopkeeper merely changes from young Hunks to old Hunks, and will cheat for pice after he has accumulated a fortune, the Englishman marches abreast of his destiny, and outwardly, at least, becomes the livery of greatness.

The father of the first Sir Robert Peel wore a patched coat and wooden shoes, — his grandson was a member of the Privy Council before he reached the age of thirty, and at his death his family had intermarried with the noblest of the land. We sneer at the aristocracy of wealth in enlightened Britain, and have many a bitter word for cotton lords and rich parvenus, but what could be said for the bunneahs and soucars of India as samples of the "best and bravest" of the country? Will they command the respect of the people? Can they create that sentiment of veneration which an aristocracy ought to inspire, and wanting which they are fated to suffer speedy extinction? We fear the answers must be in the negative.

We look with dismay on a system of rule which is wholly destructive, and which, if successful, will leave two hundred millions of human beings without a religion, without an aristocracy, and with but the scantiest portion of wealth. We are undermining at the same moment every part of the social edifice. The priest, the noble, and the rich man of whatever denomination, are threatened with the same fate. The great ends of civilised teaching are the filling of the pockets, the heart, and the head; but the masters of India neglect two-thirds of their duty, and perform the rest in a very unsatisfactory manner.

For the effects of Godless colleges a cure will be found at last in the strong necessity of belief. When Hindooism has been thoroughly wrecked, and the ruins are cleared away, a nobler creed will spring up in its room; but with the Brahmin degraded from his high place, and the zemindar lost in the ranks of the peasantry, where will the nation find the materials to build up an aristocracy? It will not always consent, as now, to find its masters and guides in the youth of the Civil Service. It will yearn for the excellence of home growth, and the lordship that is not a sign of servitude; and Heaven forgive us for having done our best to render the craving a hopeless one.

Men who have studied natural phenomena tell us, that if all the earth were levelled and made smooth as a lawn, the uniformity would be purchased at the price of perpetual barrenness hereafter. It is the mountains and forests that bring down the fertilising rains; and so they counsel that the tall trees should be suffered to remain for the sake of the indirect good to be derived from them. In like manner we would urge that the axe should be withdrawn from the roots of the few remaining specimens of native aristocracy. If they do not yield the best of fruits, they serve to invite the refreshing showers. Let the levelling process cease for awhile, till we note the tendency of our wayward experiment.

CHAP. XXVII.

THE LEVELLING CHARACTER OF THE COMPANY'S RULE. — THEIR INFLUENCE PURELY DESTRUCTIVE. — THE RAJAH AND THE YEOMAN EQUALLY RUINED, WITHOUT PROFIT TO THE GOVERNMENT.

We acquit the opponents of property in India of any design to uproot the foundations of society. It is their misfortune to apprehend but rarely the consequences of their policy. Civilians who have been all their lifetime engaged in annihilating every interest interposed betwixt the state and the cultivators of the soil, would deem it an insult to be classed with the lowest order of democrats in Europe. They will each go home in due season, and if fortunate, either inherit or purchase estates, which they will bequeath to their children in the full assurance that the legislature will permit their lands to pass unchallenged to the latest posterity. The fate which they have decreed to Hindu and Mussulman will not descend on the heads of their own children, — the public welfare in Great Britain not being so well cared for.

But let us ignore principles, and deal merely with the question of profit. The Socialist only advocates the destruction of private rights, in order to increase the sum total of the general happiness; and we will not suppose that he would willingly destroy the native zemindar, to whom wealth and the importance that it brings are naturally very dear, unless he felt assured that his ruin would be a blessing to the community. We are content to narrow the discussion to this single point, and to give up the case of the ancient land-holders, if it can be shown that their loss has been a gain to others.

With the facts patent to the world that in Cuddapah, Bellary, and Guntoor, three of the naturally richest districts in the Madras Presidency, land is wholly unsaleable, whilst in Chingleput it is only worth six months' purchase; we shall take it for granted that the ryot is not richer now than he was fifty years since. Proof to that effect has already been furnished, and we shall content ourselves with disclosing the results of the overthrow of the zemindary system, so far as Government, the universal landlord, is concerned.

The permanent settlement was made in 1802, and founded on the basis that thirty and in some cases forty per cent. of the rental should be allowed to the zemindars. If we may believe Mr. Walter Elliot, whose authority in such cases must be entitled to great weight, the landowners took care to exact even a more liberal allowance for themselves, by means of false measurements, and the use of corrupt artifices. We have not been able to get the revenue returns for the twelve years immediately following the settlement of the proprietary estates; but, from 1814 to 1818, the average yearly revenue in pounds sterling was 3,339,666*l.*, the last year of the series being that in which the ryotwarry system was first introduced. The subsequent collections are as follows:—

1819 to 1824	£3,285,592
1825 to 1829	3,291,832
1830 to 1834	2,996,999
1835 to 1839	3,124,530
1840 to 1844	3,259,948
1845 to 1849	3,528,022
1850 to 1853	3,579,231

We should of course be fully justified in taking the average of the thirty-five years, during which the ryotwarry system has been in operation, and comparing them with the five years ending in 1818; but we elect the mode of comparison that gives the largest share of advantage to our opponents, and test the results of the latest by those of the earliest period.

From 1814 to 1818 the annual revenue was	£3,339,666
From 1850 to 1853 . .	3,579,231
Increase . . .	£239,565

Let us now see how this increase has been obtained, and whether any portion of it is owing to the absorption of the zemindars.

Since 1814, the revenue of the single district of Tanjore has been raised by upwards of 150,000*l.* Kurnool, annexed in 1844, yields a surplus of 85,000*l.* Various works of irrigation executed since 1836, give an annual revenue of 40,000*l.*; so that whilst the income of 1853 only exceeds that of 1814 by

	£239,565
The sums due to the above sources amount to .	270,000
Showing an annual loss of . .	£30,435

If we take the increase of population as equivalent to that of Ireland,—$12\frac{1}{2}$ per cent. in ten years,—we have an addition of forty in the hundred to the number of workers and consumers, a loss of from 30 to 40 per cent. to the zemindars, and a decline in the four most prosperous years, in the sum realised by Government! We challenge the world to match the mournful picture!

The company has always estimated its successful collectors above jurists and men of science, and yet in this department its failure is notorious, simply because it has always ignored the lessons of civilisation.

Neither of the great modes of settlement, the zemindary, village, or ryotwarry, has succeeded, nor can possibly do so, for in no case are the natural laws which affect the distribution of property allowed to have free action. The zemindar is over taxed and always hampered by the interference of the Government officers. The village cultivator is a member of a compulsory partnership, which is not founded upon stable grounds; and the Madras ryot is a beggar and a slave, who can never be a capitalist or an honest man. And the various systems react upon the rulers. They damage public as well as private morals. If the people have no sense of obligations, the Government has no regard for rights. The one cheats like a bondsman, and the other oppresses like a despot who owns no law but his own will; and if we may trust public despatches and speeches in Parliament, the onus of the admitted failure of the zemindary system, rests entirely with the rajahs and the bad seasons. It is shared between Providence and the proprietors, sometimes in equal proportion, but the responsibility generally varying according to the nature of the object to be served, and the position of the writers or speakers. Some useful information on the subject is to be found in a return made by the India House to an order of the House of Lords in May 1852, which states the case on behalf of the Government.

In 1802 settlements were made on the zemindary tenure to the amount of 1,079,250*l.* Of these estates, five belonged to ancient families, who shared between them the district of Guntoor, and paid 122,548*l.* The amounts thus specified formed two thirds of the net rental, which must therefore have reached 1,539,675*l.* on the total zemindary settlement, and 184,822*l.* in the case of Guntoor. There is no reason to believe that the tax then imposed was based upon a wrong calculation of the gross produce of the estates, for in 1813–14–15 the possessions of the Vasareddy family, amounting to 383 villages in that district, yielded an average revenue of 83,230*l.*, from which deducting the Government tax of 54,730, the remainder, or landlord's profit, is shown to be 28,500*l.*

The Guntoor estates have all, without exception, passed into the hands of the Company; and whereas we are assured on the authority of the first member of the Board of Revenue that they once produced magnificent incomes to their proprietors, the Parliamentary return shows that the present revenue is only seventy per cent. of the amount fixed by the permanent assessment in 1802.

In other words, the Government, standing in the place of

the landholders, receives no more than the share of profit taken by the latter after the tax was paid, so that the zemindaries yield less by upwards of a million sterling than they did fifty years ago. The barbaric pomp that disgusted the collector so much has passed away, and the heirs of the ancient chieftains of the northern Circars may be seen occasionally hanging round the doors of the Revenue Board Office, waiting with anxious looks for permission to present begging petitions. And who has benefited by their destruction? Not the Government, as we have seen; not new men who have come forward to occupy their places, for their lands do not bring by a third the amount of tax fixed upon them, and have therefore no value in the market; not the ryots, for they are amongst the most wretched in the Company's dominions. The wealth thus coveted, and which nature so liberally rendered up to despised natives, is lost as absolutely as if it had never been realised. The test of the superior excellence of the Company's rule will ill bear such a commentary.

But we have yet to see the cause of this vast deterioration in the resources of a district. A paternal Government which knows its duty, and has ample means to fulfil it, waits for more than fifty-eight years before it undertakes a work of proved necessity — till it kills off, in one famine out of many, five times the number of British that perished at Waterloo, and curses the land with barrenness: this Government, at the end of a few after years, when the bones of the dead have been gathered into heaps, and the sites of ruined villages are overgrown, sternly taunts the proprietors of Guntoor with neglect of the duties that belonged to their position! Poor wretches! they have paid the penalty of their improvidence. Their debt has been liquidated; but justice has still to enforce, either in this world or the next, its heavier claim on the East India Company.

Upon their plea of exemption, that of their superior management of the zemindaries as compared with the results of Government rule, we have but to cite a single instance, which is commented upon at length in another portion of this volume. For twenty-five years the revenue authorities held possession of those estates which Vencatreddy Naidoo, the Rajah of Vassareddy, bequeathed to his descendants. They came into the hands of the collector without a rupee of liability, and at the end of that time they were saddled with arrears due to the Government, and created by its own acts, to the extent of no less than 460,000*l.*, exclusive of interest. From 1790 to 1815, the period of his death, Vencatreddy held possession: the records of Government tell how he feasted and revelled, and what store of wealth he gave away. The wise and strong English Government took this property into its care, in trust for the lawful owner. It erected neither temples nor palaces; it made no pilgrimages, and gave away no hundredweights of gold and silver; and when called on to surrender its charge, instead of having half a million sterling to hand over to the heir, it handed him its own little bill for a trifle more than that amount, or 588,666*l.*

As compared with the balance sheet of Vencatreddy Naidoo, the accounts of Government management showed a loss of more than 108 lacs, or 1,080,000*l.* sterling, in the case of a single zemindary, to say nothing of the ruin inflicted on the ryots and the country.

Of course if rajahs will keep elephants, maintain large followings, make presents to nautch girls, and take no heed of their affairs, they must expect that Government will sell them up and utterly extinguish their pretensions to lordships and honours. If the folks in authority at home had had the honesty to do their duty like the East India Company, there would have been no House of Lords, nor great landed gentry in England by this time. Where the heir came into possession at a ripe age and succeeded to an encumbered estate, a few years of heavy taxation and loose living would bring the property to the hammer. Where he was an infant, out of debt, and the title was litigated, they could take the estates into their own management by way of nursing and protecting them, as in the case of the Vassareddy estates. It would come to the same thing in the end. So, if you please, we will say nothing against the policy which the Company has pursued, and the Queen's Government ought to have imitated, save this, that had the landlord's profit been abolished at home, somebody would have been the better for it. The Company have pursued the right course, and as is often the case in this strange world, their virtue has been an unprofitable one.

But it is not alone the great families that have been steadily rooted out of their ancient places. The class of mootahdars or "gentlemen farmers," as men of a corresponding rank would be called in England, have shared the fate of poligars and rajahs. In 1803, twenty-six small estates in Rajahmundry were put up for sale, and bought from Government for 33,494*l*. Forty years afterwards not a single acre remained in the possession of the original holders or their descendants. "They had not been more fortunate," says the Parliamentary Report from which the facts are taken, "than the thirteen ancient zemindars" of Rajahmundry, of whose possessions only one sixth remained in 1843. Purchase money, working capital, the produce of mortgages, all had been swallowed up by the inexorable landlord, and still the demand was not satisfied. As the last efforts of despair, the resources of nature were anticipated. The soil, tasked beyond its strength, refused to yield its treasures to the cultivator, and in fifty-one estates, repurchased by Government up to the close of 1843, in Rajahmundry, the resources of the villages had decreased upwards of 40 per cent. per annum. Government it will be seen never exceeded its just demands, but these unfortunately happened to be 40*l*. in the hundred more than the land could pay. Nobody could say that they confiscated the estates; they only asked for their own; but to get that, it was necessary that the mootahdars should be sacrificed, as their betters before them had been — that the pucka house and the bullock coach should follow the palace and the elephants, and nothing but the mud hut of the ryot be left to cumber the ground.

There is a story told of a man who sold his dog whenever

he required money, the sagacious animal always finding its way back to his old master, a little lean perhaps and tired on some occasions, but only wanting rest and food to get into flesh and look as well as ever. It is likely the dog's master had been in the service of the Company, and had studied the operation of the zemindary settlement.

The marvellous increase that has taken place in the value of Eastern exports during the last three years has revolutionised to some extent the commerce of Madras, and of every other part of the world with which we have dealings. There is now a small balance in favour of the Presidency, that is to say, more money and goods are brought in than are sent out of the country. The value of the imports for the year ending 30th of April last, was 3,645,057*l.* 4*s.*, including treasure, against 3,358,965*l.* 10*s.*, the value of the merchandise and treasure exported. But to see how the revenue system of Madras has operated on the wellbeing of the country, we must look to the records of past years, and watch the gradual drain of capital into the coffers of the state.

During the eighteen years from 1834 to 1852, both inclusive, the exports from Madras amounted to 25,506,197*l.* 12*s.* in round numbers about 1,400,000*l.* per annum. The imports in the same period reached only 14,439,449*l.* 6*s.*, or 800,000*l.* per annum. We naturally look for the balance under the head of treasure imported, but strange to say more money was sent out of the country than was brought into it, and in the list of exports we have not included the precious metals. Still dealing with the same period of time, we find that 3,338,810*l.* 10*s.* was shipped from Madras in the shape of treasure, and but 3,190,767*l.* 10*s.* brought back again. The total of money and merchandise put on board, or sent across the frontier by land, was 28,445,008*l.* 2*s.*, and the total imports 17,630,217*l.* 4*s.* A sum then of 11,214,798*l.* 18*s.* is wholly unaccounted for, and if we allow the merchant a profit of 10 per cent. on exports, we shall find that for every two shillings' worth sent out of the country, whether in the shape of produce, manufactures, or the precious metals, but thirteen pence half-penny came back again. But the value sent forward and the traders' profit must return to Madras through some channel or other. The London banker would remit to his correspondents the amount which the latter had advanced on bills of lading, either by paying their drafts upon him in cash, making advances on goods shipped to them in return, or remitting bullion. Every merchant or agent who received money's worth, had to pay for it in some shape or other; but there was one firm that neither paid money nor sent out a shilling's worth of goods, who yet demanded and received every year the seven annas in the rupee that we have found missing. In the four years ending 1851, the East India Company carried off from the Southern Presidency nearly 2,470,000*l.* of coined money, exclusive of the sums raised by advances on goods and the sale of bills. In 1851-2 they shipped from Madras 651,200*l.*, and obtained money on bills to the extent of 303,000*l.* If this sum be added to the imports of that year, the whole will amount to 2,854,965*l.* 10*s.*, against a total export of 2,670,444*l.* 8*s.* merchandise and treasure in 1850-1, and gives Madras back the worth of its ventures and a profit of more than 7 per cent.

No one will quarrel with us for saying that the above statistics are strange and melancholy beyond all conception. Here is an English Government, which takes all the state tax and all the landlord's profit upon 140,000 square miles; which exists in perfect peace; and yet is obliged, in order to defray its expenses, to seize and carry off half the surplus profits of twenty-three millions of souls! The Madras ryot, growing the most valuable products of agriculture; the native manufacturer, with his curious examples of patient industry; and the European capitalist, sugar refiner, indigo maker, and cotton grower — each and all surrounded with illimitable space for expansion and improvement — pay 5*s.* a head in taxes; create, as the combined product of their daily lives, a surplus of 3*s.* yearly, and consume of imported goods as much as amounts to 1*s.* 9*d.* each person! The negroes of Africa are wealthier by far than the Madras

Hindoo; the beggars of Europe are better customers to the rest of mankind.

There is hardly a fact more thoroughly recognised than that of the successful competition of English mill-owners with the cotton manufacturers of the East. The most prosaic of statists is apt to warm into enthusiasm, when dilating on the wondrous results of that union of energy, skill, and capital which has enabled the costly workman of Lancashire to supplant the exquisite fabrics of Dacca, and undersell the labour which considers 2*d.* a fair day's wages for a fair day's work. We are constantly reminded that the art of weaving had its rise in India, and that the term "calico" is derived from Calicut, a town in Madras.

It is not our present business to discuss the question, whether Madras derives as much comparative benefit from imported cottons as England is said to do from foreign corn; but that the substitution of Manchester goods for those of native make is an advantage to the bulk of the community cannot be denied. With all the willingness of the labouring class to encounter any amount of risk and fatigue in the hope of procuring profitable employment, there is no increase in the number of weavers. The very lowest rate of wages is still too high for the man who has to compete with the work of the iron fingers that never tire, and can be multiplied to any extent. The use of English thread or cloth is only limited by the means of the consumers.

We stipulate beforehand against any expressions of incredulity with regard to the fact we are about to disclose. Disbelief would be natural, but not proper. This is a land of wonders; and the story of the Indian Government, and of the real condition of the people, is of all others the most difficult of comprehension. But it is nevertheless true, that the whole extent of cotton-twist and manufactured goods, printed and plain, imported into the Madras territories, by sea and land, amounts but to 2*d.* per head.

We have searched for a proper standard of comparison, but without success. The crown colonies within the tropics, which are said to be wretchedly governed as contrasted with the countries under the sway of the East India Company, are so small in comparison with Madras, that the disproportion is ludicrous. Ceylon and Mauritius receive about a third more than the total imports of Madras, and pay about one eighth of its revenue. We prefer, therefore, to quote the South American States, where the Negro works for a bare maintenance, where the rulers have never been trained for the duties of government, and the hunter wears a dress of deer-skin, and seldom requires the aid of the dhobie. Our authority is the Parliamentary return of "British cotton manufactured goods exported in the year 1851," from which it appears that Brazil and nine South American Republics, having in the whole a population of less than twenty-two millions, took more than four millions worth of manufactures, or a trifle less than four shillings per head. One can account for slight discrepancies in the working of human institutions, but how the slaves and mestijos of South America should be able to purchase of one single class of English manufactures, twenty-four times as much as the free, enlightened, and happily-guided Hindus, is a problem which we ask the public at large to assist us in solving. It is not compatible with any notion of honesty and wisdom on the part of the governors, or of any comfort on the side of the people.

CHAP. XXVIII.

THE CONDITION OF THE MADRAS RYOT DESCRIBED BY AUTHORITY.—FOLLY OF ATTEMPTING TO INVEST CAPITAL IN THAT PRESIDENCY.

It requires thirty-seven thousand men to collect the revenue of Madras, or more than three-fourths of the whole force of the fifty-two regiments composing the native infantry of the southern army. The cost of maintaining them is close upon half a million sterling, a sum which, if rateably distributed, gives about fourteen shillings a month to each individual employed. It is of course hard to say how much is contributed by the country in addition. Folks who pretend to have accurate information on these points assert that the rupee obtained from the ryot is always divided into two equal parts, one going into the general treasury, and the other remaining in the pouch of the subordinate tax gatherer; but the estimate is most likely exaggerated. Where the knavery is greatest, and where poverty is most utter and desolate, the native tax gatherer will reap the greatest harvest; he will be bribed heavily for allowing the rich man to cheat and the poor man to live.

The state of things disclosed in the foregoing pages might still be thought reconcilable with the existence of a race of peasant farmers elevated above the sphere of labouring wretchedness; but such is not the case. The present Secretary for Government in the Revenue Department, Mr. Bourdillon, published a pamphlet in 1852, in which he showed, from the official list of holdings for the revenue year 1848–49, that out of 1,071,588, the total number of leases, excluding joint holdings in the fourteen principal ryotwarry districts, no fewer than 589,932, being considerably more than half, were under 20*s.* per annum each, averaging in fact only a small fraction above 8*s.* each: 201,065 were for amounts ranging from 20*s.* to 40*s.*, averaging less than 28*s.* 6*d.*; 97,891 ranged between 40*s.* and 60*s.*, averaging 49*s.* 6*d.* In other words, nearly 900,000 leases out of a total of less than 1,100,000 were for amounts under 60*s.*, and averaging less than 19*s.* 6*d.* per annum.

Upon the general condition of the people, Mr. Bourdillon remarks as follows: —

"Now it may certainly be said of almost the whole of the ryots, paying even the highest of these sums, and even of many holding to a much larger amount, that they are always in poverty, and generally in debt. Perhaps one of this class obtains a small sum out of the Government advances for cultivation; but even if he does, the trouble that he has to take, and the time he loses in getting it, as well as the deduction to which he is liable, render this a questionable gain. For the rest of his wants he is dependent on the bazarman. To him his crops are generally hypothecated before they are reaped; and it is he who redeems them from the possession of the village watcher, by pledging himself for the payment of the kist. These transactions pass without any written engagements or memoranda between the parties, and the only evidence is the chetty's own accounts. In general there is an adjustment of the accounts once a year, but sometimes not for several years. In all these accounts interest is charged on the advances made to the ryot on the balance against him. The rate of interest varies with the circumstances of the case and the necessities of the borrower; it is probably seldom or never less than twelve per cent. per annum, and not often above twenty-four per cent. Of course the poorest and most necessitous ryots have to pay the highest.

A ryot of this class of course lives from hand to mouth; he rarely sees money, except that obtained from the chetty to pay his kist; the exchanges in the out villages are very few, and they are usually conducted by barter. His ploughing cattle are wretched animals not worth more than from three and a half to six rupees each (seven to twelve shillings), and those, perhaps, not his own, because not paid for. His rude and feeble plough costs, when new, no more than two or three shillings; and all the rest of his few agricultural implements are equally primitive and inefficient. His dwelling is a hut of mud walls and thatched roof, far ruder, smaller, and more dilapidated than those of the better classes of ryots above spoken of, and still more destitute, if possible, of anything that can be called furniture. His food, and that of his family, is partly thin porridge made of the meal of grain boiled in water, and partly boiled rice with a little condiment; and generally the only vessels for cooking and eating from are of the coarsest earthenware, much inferior in grain to a good tile or brick in England, and unglazed. Brass vessels, though not wholly unknown among this class, are rare. As to anything like education or mental culture, they are wholly destitute of it. Even among the more wealthy ryots, and indeed among all ranks throughout the country, with the few and rare exceptions where there is a missionary school, the whole education consists in learning to read and write, with a little arithmetic. The only books read are foolish and trifling, not to add immoral, legends. There is no true knowledge communicated even on matters of physical science, or any useful training of the mind."

When we look on the Indian ryot, we see one upon whom man's curse presses harder than the Deity's; when we contemplate the Madras Government, which, if it has not helped to make him what he is, takes care to keep him in the wretchedness which he inherits from his forefathers, we are led to wonder at the combination of circumstances which confers authority, and prompts obedience. Why the man who works and creates good should pine in misery, whilst the useless member of society, the drag on the wheels of time, receives wealth and honour, is a strange and humbling mystery.

At present, with the aid of a little concealed cultivation,

a few prayers and entreaties, occasional sore bones, much lying and chronic abjectness of soul, the ryot manages to live; but the way of it is unknown to himself, and unhappily as well to the good people of England.

Wide as is the range of the English dominion in the East, various and exceptional as are the modes of raising revenue, costly and desirable as are the products raised within its borders, it is beyond all doubt that, under the present system of taxation, the public revenue can obtain no increase. A vast addition everywhere to the breadth of land cultivated, would add both to rent and customs; but the soil of Bengal has been sold in fee simple. Bombay, settled mainly on the ryotwarry basis, must, in the nature of things, pass from bad to worse. In Madras, the annual emigration more than balances the natural increase of the population. In the north-west, the village system is tumbling to pieces, and the land revenue has for years been stationary. Only one fourth of the Punjaub is cultivated; the country requires outlets for trade, and recent events have drawn away a large portion of the male population for military service.

There are many millions of acres of the finest land in the world lying fallow in Pegu since the days, perhaps, when first upheaved above the waters; but the country lacks population, having only a million of souls throughout its whole extent of 30,000 square miles. Not one fifth of the cultivable area of British India is turned to account; and yet the limits of cultivation appear to have been reached. God has made the land fertile; but man has reversed his decree, and consigned it to hopeless sterility.

Where is the remedy? Under the Company, or the Company's Government, there is none to be hoped for. The most cursory examination might have satisfied the Court of Directors, any time within the last quarter of a century, that the sole cause of the vast and permanent prosperity of Bengal is the perpetual settlement which they never cease to denounce and lament. The commerce of India has increased from two and a half millions, in 1813, to sixty-five millions in 1856-7, and there is no limit to its further expansion. Crowds of the native landholders and merchants accumulate princely fortunes; and many a fair estate in England and Scotland has grown up from the savings of the few years' labour at the desk or by the side of the indigo vats. There is no lack of the enterprise which would achieve results as favourable elsewhere. Calcutta is not the best outlet for trade, nor Bengal the only rich soil: the land is everywhere in India, the men and the capital are waiting at home; and why are they not brought together?

The answer is, simply because, beyond the limits of the Bengal Presidency, there is no permanency of tenure. In the north-west provinces and Bombay, the settlement is made for a short term; in Madras and Pegu the tenancy is only yearly. In the Cis and Trans-Sutlej states, leases are given for twenty or thirty years; in the Punjaub proper, the term is ten years, with a promise that it may be further prolonged. The tenant is in the situation of a leaseholder whose property does not absolutely pass away from him at the end of his term, but which may be assessed at a rate which amounts to virtual confiscation. He may then be called upon to pay, not merely an enhanced rate for the soil, but an assessment upon the full value of his improvements. The capital that he has sunk becomes a part of the fixed property of the landlord; and he must either abandon it, or pay what is demanded of him. Such a state of things is never contemplated in the theory of the Court of Directors. They profess to see nothing which can possibly prevent the employment of British capital in any part of India, though we have shown that four-fifths of the cultivable area of Madras lies waste, and is not likely to experience change. The fact of its fertility, the extent of its mineral resources, the general excellence of the climate, the almost perfect security of property from violence, are generally known; yet moneyed men forbear to build mills or dig mines, or become great landholders.

The opportunities seem tempting, the facilities are perfect; why do not people avail themselves of the chance of getting rich without much trouble? Simply because the Company's system is a perpetual lion in the path of the settler. What is his energy, however great, in the midst of universal wretchedness and apathy? What can his example effect, when there are none to imitate it? What marvels can his wealth exhibit, when all around are poor to destitution? To take land in his own person and improve it, would be to court certain defeat. If he quarrelled with a collector, his rent would probably be raised, and his plans of amelioration thwarted in every possible way. If he offended the great man's subordinates, he might count upon being harassed by scores of false suits, and exposed to a thousand losses and humiliations. On the other hand, if he merely sat down, and gave out that he was willing to purchase produce, his task would be easy enough for the first twelve months, after which difficulties would occur. He could not obtain a measure of rice or a cake of indigo without previously making advances; or, in other words, taking a mortgage upon Providence, with only one signature to the bond. If the next season turned out favourable, he would get back a portion of his money, and perhaps make a fair profit upon it, but a goodly balance would remain to be accounted for; next year, if bad harvests occurred, he must make up his mind to get a new set of books, and begin with fresh accounts and altered expectations. If he perseveres for some years, he finds it profitable to maintain a native lawyer, at a fixed salary, and keep a staff of permanent witnesses. The occupation is neither pious nor profitable; and the most enduring and reckless speedily become tired of it.

CHAP. XXIX.

THE REMEDY.—IMPOSSIBILITY OF RAISING MORE REVENUE UNDER THE PRESENT SYSTEM OF GOVERNMENT.—DIFFICULTY OF OBTAINING CORRECT INFORMATION.—COST OF CULTIVATION AND PROFITABLE CULTURE.—OVERTHROW OF THE SLAVE-HOLDING INTEREST.—THE BALANCE OF TRADE.

THE task that we have to perform is the changing of a rebellious into a contented people, of a deficient into a surplus revenue, to abolish the slave trade and slavery, and enable England to be the mistress of her own destiny. The work seems heavy enough; but harder labour has been undertaken by Englishmen before now—for less wages than can be paid in this case—and with the certainty of no eventual profits.

Let us thoroughly comprehend our present position. India must be held by the English, that is a point about which no discussion can be tolerated; but by no State device can we equalise, under the present system of taxation, its income and expenditure. If we could restore to-morrow the land, the loyalty, and the fixed capital that has been destroyed, still with the necessity for keeping up an additional force of twenty-five thousand Europeans, the annual deficit would amount to some millions, with no prospect whatever of a change for the better.

The only fiscal resource as yet untried is a property and income tax; but it would utterly fail, owing to the insuperable difficulties in the way of getting at the knowledge of what your supposed rich man possesses. On inquiry, his land would be found nominally in the hands of a score of holders, his Company's paper all mortgaged for advances. He would bury his coin, and hide his securities; and all that we should gain by the attempt to make income contribute to the State, would be measureless ill will from the only class that now wish for the continuance of our rule. The Hindoo and Mussulman method of accusing a man of riches, and torturing him into confession, is the sole mode of raising direct taxation in the East; and our civilisation objects to it.

We must increase our deficit if we would vastly augment our surplus. We must lay out English capital if we would have English profits. We must look upon India as a great joint-stock property, of which all the Queen's subjects are entitled to have a share. We have but to yoke sun, soil, and human efforts together, and in hopefulness of heart and brain wait the outturn.

We have done nothing whatever for Bengal, except to bestow the land in perpetuity at a fixed rate of taxation. We have steadily opposed the settlement of Europeans, and upheld the worst judicial and police system in the known world; and yet the sole fact that the zemindar holds his property in fee simple, at a mere nominal rent, has made the soil so valuable, that estates are scarcely ever to be obtained by our countrymen on any terms, whilst the export tonnage has increased twelvefold within the last sixty years. The land-rent on the cultivated area only amounts to a shilling per acre; and the zemindar at least obtains six times that amount. The ryot on the average gets a shilling a week; and the native traders make enormous gains. Bengal wants an Encumbered Estates Act, and a law of Tenant Right; and then, with English judges and a reasonably honest police, we discern no limit to the growth of trade and prosperity. As matters stand, the soil of Bengal is far too valuable. The zemindar lords it in reality over all the trading interests of India, and has the English merchant and the native peasant equally underfoot. We want a counterpoise in the shape of an increase in the labourers' earnings, and of a value given to land elsewhere. We are equally concerned in cheapening the cost of produce, and raising the rate of wages.

We have seen that, after paying the Government land tax and the cost of cultivation, the five and a half millions of Madras families engaged in agricultural employment, have only one shilling and eight pence per month each to subsist upon. We want to raise that sum to ten shillings, a range of income beyond their wildest dreams, which would give them seven millions sterling to lay out in the purchase of our manufactures, and still leave a considerable surplus for extravagance or hoarding. Four shillings monthly suffice to maintain a household in riotous profusion, so far as food is concerned; and after laying out forty shillings in imports, the ryot would have a yearly balance of one third more than his present total income.

We propose to effect this change by reducing the land tax, over the whole of India, to two shillings per acre, and selling the fee simple of it for twenty shillings. We should then be better off in the matter of revenue than the colonies of the Crown, where the land is disposed of outright for a pound an acre. There should be no distinction of soils recognised, the object being to induce a rush for investment, and so draw out the hoards of the capitalist. Land held in proprietary right would of course only pay the annual assessment, the owners, if their title was clear, standing in the same category with the new purchasers. Works of irrigation should be kept up under the supervision of trusts, as in England we maintain the turnpike roads and other corporate conveniences, the Government selling or leasing such as they have hitherto maintained. Roads and canals should be made and repaired at the cost of the country, rates being levied for that purpose, and the inhabitants encouraged to look to the proper application of the funds.

The cultivator should in every case have, during twelve months, the right of pre-emption in the purchase of the land actually held by him under tillage, on paying the five per cent. which Government would gain by closing at once with the offer to buy. At the end of that period no further impediment should be offered to the entrance of the capitalist, whose co-operation in the work is a matter of the utmost importance. The ryot would find plenty of favourable localities in which to labour whilst earning the small sum requisite to make him a landed proprietor.

The cost of the reduction would be, in the case of Madras, taking the assessed area at fourteen millions of acres, just two millions sterling. In Bombay it is difficult to say what the exact sum would reach; but a million and a half would cover it. The North-Western deficiency would be nil as yet; Nagpore, Oude, the Punjab, and Pegu only pay in the aggregate 1,655,000*l.*, and are scarcely assessed at three shillings per acre. An allowance of a million is ample in the instances of the countries alluded to, which brings up the total reduction to four and a half millions.

With regard to the North-West there is the certainty that in the new arrangements for taking land, necessary in consequence of the numerous confiscations that must ensue from the rebellion, and the destruction of title-deeds and records, most men would prefer to receive the fee simple of their holdings, and pay a reduced scale of taxation, instead of re-entering under the old system of a terminable lease, subject to an enhanced rental at each renewal. Whenever this occurred, Government would only be selling one-third of their annual rent at twenty years' purchase; but if the tenant elected to remain on the old footing, of course the terms of the agreement must be carried out. It is not likely that extensive purchases would be made, for a time, by the ryots in Oude or Pegu; but in the old presidencies and the Punjab, we calculate that every rupee would be drawn from the earth for the purpose of being laid out in the purchase of land. It is almost the only mode in which men of capital can turn their savings to account; and once assured, as they soon will be, of the permanence of our rule, we shall see land as scarce and valuable in all parts of India as it is now in Bengal, and as it was but lately in the North-West provinces. There will be an end to emigration after the first six months of the new system of land tenures.

Less than 40,000,000 of acres additional brought into cultivation, would make up the whole deficiency of revenue; for at least 1,000,000*l.* sterling would be saved in the reduction of revenue establishments. Madras, in proportion to its population, should have 30,000,000 of acres under tillage; and many thousands of disbanded Sepoys and Government servants of all kinds will be available for field labour in 1858. Crowds of ryots would flock in from all the Native States, anxious to share in the blessings of the new rule; and every man would have a real interest in the preservation of law and order. We hardly expect to create a Paradise on the site of what is now Pandemonium; but at any rate we should succeed in making happiness a possibility, and put future revolt utterly out of the question.

And now to come to the question in which the two hemispheres are vitally interested,—the prospect of getting cheap and abundant supplies of cotton, sugar, and other tropical produce. It is beyond all doubt that India can grow any kind as well as any quantity of cotton. Every variety of climate, every degree of moisture is to be found within her ample borders. Sugar, silk, tea, seeds, rice, and wheat can be raised to the full level of the demand for them, if that reached to the exclusion of Southern America and the Slave Islands from the markets of Europe. Let us weigh a few agricultural and financial facts, and then make the fitting comparisons.

A man and his family can do the work of two labourers, and they will be rich if in the receipt of 6*l.* per annum. They can cultivate with ease five acres of land, growing, say, one acre of sugar cane, one of cotton, and three of rice or oil seeds. To avoid the chance of error, we will take each acre separately, both for cost, product, and outturn of cultivation.

We must premise by saying that the difficulty of obtaining reliable information for general use upon questions of Indian social economy is as great as that which stands in the way of acquiring political knowledge. An Anglo-Indian, who fancies that he thoroughly understands the state of affairs in the East, stumbles perhaps upon a body of evidence upon Indian topics which utterly confounds him. He vows honestly, on being questioned, that the secretary to Government is not such a person as is represented by the witnesses, that he is incapable of doing anything so foolish or tyrannical as the act ascribed to him. The army, instead of being discontented, and in a state of disorganisation, is well satisfied, and in the highest state of efficiency. The land tax is by no means oppressive; the collectors have nothing to say to the standing crops. The Sudder Court has a couple of able judges in it; and the English functionaries in the lower tribunals are not all ignorant of law, as would seem to be inferred. The indignant critic goes on, perhaps, till out of breath and scant of charity, and then discovers that the testimony impugned relates to Bombay or Madras, whilst his own experience is wholly confined to Bengal. The machinery of government is nearly alike in construction, and the parts are called by the same names—a ryot in Bengal is identified with the class of ryots all over the surface of the English dominions; but in other respects, the Company's servants and subjects in one presidency know as little of each other as Spaniards know of Frenchmen, and transact the business of their lives in entirely different ways. The diversity tells heavily against the interests of the people when questions have to be decided at home which demand, for their wise settlement, the attention of more than a single individual. There is, at this moment, but one man in the East India direction who can pretend to the slightest knowledge of Madras affairs; and he is a general who retired from the country some years since. Men who have achieved reputation as able administrators in one part of the East will honestly admit their ignorance of the state of things which prevails elsewhere; and how should it be otherwise, if their plea of a special aptitude for the performance of their own proper tasks is a valid one? The languages spoken, the methods of raising taxation, the habits and manners of the natives, are all peculiar to each great section of the Queen's Eastern possessions, and require, on the part of the Englishman, facilities for learning, and an interest in rightly understanding them. Take from the Court of Last Appeal the elements which are either hurtful or innocuous in the way of arriving at a just decision, and, when your body of Directors is dwindled down to a solitary person, add the influence of the fact that he has been several years away from India, and only knew it as an official; and the conclusion must be, that great things as well as small ones are left to the rule of thumb. The persons charged to decide upon matters of vital concernment to India may have the will to do justice in most cases; but it is beyond their power to administer it, if knowledge of the subject is requisite for that purpose.

In assigning credence to official statements, equal care must be taken to ascertain the character of the facts upon which they are based. The mode in which averages are struck is one of the most fruitful sources of erroneous impressions. In preparing statements on the incidence of taxation, the Indian authorities adopt a principle which gives results that are as correct as those of a process which, adding the wages of half a dozen farm-labourers to the rental of the Duke of Bedford, would make out that each had an income of 30,000*l.* per annum. The Madras statists put down the area of cultivation in that presidency at twenty millions of acres, and show that the tax only amounts to 3*s.* 6*d.* per acre, whilst, according to the statements of the Revenue Board, sugar in Madras is not cultivated, "in general," on lands assessed below 21*s.* or above 48*s.* per acre, the plain English of which is, that the collector takes care that sugar land shall not pay less than the smaller amount; and the range of prices in the English market forbids attempts on the part of the ryot to raise it under the higher scale of taxation. It is a positive fact, that in 1832 the tax imposed upon sugar lands varied in Tinnivelly from 13*s.* to 8*l.* 3*s.* 6*d.* The Government have, within the last twelvemonth, reduced the assessment in Bellary with regard to five classes of land, fixing the highest at 18*s.*, and the lowest at 15*s.* per acre. Facts tending to the same result crop out with reference to the North-Western Provinces. The average of taxation, which, according to Thornton's Gazetteer, is 3*s.* 3*d.* on the total assessed area, gives no clue to the real extent of the Government demand, which, as in all other parts of India not permanently settled, was merely regulated by the ability of the cultivator to pay. Take from the North-West system its distinguishing characteristics, of a return of one third of the gross produce to the holders of the proprietary right and the granting of thirty years' leases, and it would be found scarcely to differ in essentials from the ryotwarry, which the advocates of the former condemn and repudiate.

An acre of land will grow, with careful irrigation, 200 lbs. of clean cotton and a ton of oil seeds. The cost of cultivation will be as follows: —

	£	s.	d.
Rent and interest of purchase money . .	0	4	0
Seed, hire of bullocks, and cost of water .	0	14	0
Proportion of annual income . . .	1	4	0
	2	2	0

And the outturn will be —

	£	s.	d.
200 lbs. of clean cotton @ 2*d*. per lb. . .	1	13	4
One ton of oil seeds @ 4*s*. per cwt. . .	4	0	0
	5	13	4
Profit on the cultivation of one acre . . .	£3	11	4

Sugar cultivation will yield the following result: —

	£	s.	d.
Rent and interest	0	4	0
Cost of cultivation and water . . .	1	0	0
Proportion of annual income . . .	1	4	0
	2	8	0

The product in this case, single crop, will be: —

	£	s.	d.
1500 lbs. of ordinary Madras sugar @ 8*s*. per cwt.	5	4	0
Profit upon one acre	£2	16	0

Rice and oil seeds mixed, a double crop, will show the following: —

	£	s.	d.
Rent and interest	0	4	0
Cultivation	0	10	0
Proportion of annual income . . .	1	4	0
	1	18	0

And the outturn will be —

	£	s.	d.
Clean rice, 10 cwt. @ 3*s*. 6*d*. per cwt. . .	1	15	0
Oil seeds, 1 ton @ 4*s*.	4	0	0
	5	15	0
The profit in this instance being	£3	17	0

Implicit reliance may be placed on the above figures, which show, in round numbers, a profit of more than 3*l.* per acre upon the four articles of produce cultivated, after the ryots' income has been deducted. Cotton grown in the North-Western Provinces, has yielded as much as 380 lbs. to the acre; sugar raised in Madras has given considerably over two tons. The experience of a Chinaman would put these statistics to shame, as affording proof of what might be made from such an area of soil; and in due time we shall have India as well irrigated, and almost as densely peopled, as the Celestial Empire. The difference between barrenness and the most glorious fertility is merely a question of water; and between wretchedness and prosperity, a matter of low rent and permanent tenure.

Let us now see what would be the cost of the above commodities to the people of Europe, allowing for all charges incurred, and profits expected. If we assume that the produce is raised at an average distance of 200 miles from the port of shipment, and the cost of carriage is 2*d.* per ton per mile, we shall surely cover all the expenses of transit. The cotton and the grain of Pegu will not cost a tenth part of that amount; and along the 1600 miles of seaboard belonging to the Madras Presidency, there is land enough to supply all the requirements of England far within the limits now assigned. But we are content to let the figures stand; they show as follows:—

Cotton.

	d.
Cost of raw material per lb.	2
Carriage to the coast	0¼
Baling and screwing	0¼
Shipping charges	0¼
Freight @ 20*s.* per bale of 500 lbs.	0½
Insurance and other charges	0¼
Cost in Liverpool on shipper's account per lb.	3½

We assert, without hesitation, that at the above rate, and under the conditions laid down, any quantity of excellent cotton can be produced in India and Pegu, yielding the profit stated to the growers.

Sugar.

	s.	d.
Cost of raw material per cwt.	8	0
" gunny bag	0	3
Carriage to coast per cwt.	1	8
Charges, @ 10 per cent.	1	0
Freight @ 80*s.* per ton, and insurance	4	6
London charges	1	6
Cost to sell without profit or loss	16	11

Rice.

	s.	d.
Cost of clean rice per cwt.	3	6
Gunny bag and shipping	1	0
Freight @ 80*s.* per ton.	4	0
Insurance and London charges, average	1	3
Cost to the shipper	9	9

Oil Seeds.

	£	s.	d.
Cost of mustard or gingelly per quarter	0	19	0
Gunny bag, insurance, and shipping charges	0	4	6
Freight @ 90*s.* per ton	1	2	6
London charges	0	4	0
Cost to the shipper	2	10	0

On the 7th of November last, under great depression of prices, Madras native sugar averaged in bond, 23*s.* 6*d.*; in July the same quality was worth 37*s.* The lowest rate would give the merchant a profit of more than 6*l.* per ton; and at what may be called, under the present state of things, the natural value, he would realise at least double that amount, or more than a hundred and seventy per cent. on his outlay of capital. Adopt at once our proposed scale of taxation in Madras; and despite the want of roads and machinery for crushing the cane, sugar could be made at a profit to the grower when the native merchant only obtained from the shipper 5*s.* 6*d.* per cwt., which would reduce the cost of the article, laid down in London, to 14*s.* 5*d.*

Madras cotton was quoted at Liverpool on the 7th of November at 4¾*d.* The advance of a farthing in the price of cotton adds a million sterling to the outlay of the manufacturers; but what would be the gain when we could not only import cotton of the present quality at an aggregate reduction of 5,000,000*l.*, but suit at the same rate all the requirements of the spinner? It needs but a glance at the samples on view at the India House, to convince the public that water and tendance only are requisite to raise from the indigenous seed nearly all the varieties of cotton now in use. Three years of English culture would set the question of Indian sufficiency in this respect at rest for ever.

How cheaply rice can be grown, and how pleasant annexation may be made to a people who as yet scarcely know us except as traders, may be ascertained from a glance at the present condition of the inhabitants of the eastern coast of the Bay of Bengal, as compared with what it was under the rule of the Burmese. The taxation fixed by the Court of Ava consisted of an impost of about ten shillings sterling levied on each homestead, and an equal amount charged upon each yoke of buffaloes, in lieu of land rent. Our government has retained the capitation tax, but has substituted, for the charge on cattle, a land tax of two, three, and four shillings an acre, according to the quality of soil. The aggregate sum now levied is hardly greater than the regular taxation fixed by the Burmese; but, whereas the hundred baskets of table rice, weighing 7400 lbs., formerly sold at Rangoon for 18*s.* on the average, the same quantity now realises 5*l.*

It would pay us well as a nation, to dispense entirely with taxes in the case of a people who would consent to give us rice at threepence per cwt. We compensated the Mughs of Arracan and the Karens of Pegu for the loss of their independence, if they ever had, or cared to preserve such a gift, and might safely go to a popular election in that part of the world on the question of the maintenance of British sovereignty.

The objects that we have kept steadily in view, apart from the improvement of the condition of the ryot, are the incentives to the employment of capital in the cultivation of land, and a vast increase of production. As matters now stand, every mill that is built tends to make cotton dearer; for, toil as it may, production cannot overtake consumption. The buyers increase faster than the sellers; and so long as that is the case, it is hopeless to expect a diminution in the price of the raw material. The manufacturer is obliged to pay far more than the worth of the inferior article, because he cannot get enough of the better sort. Every advance in the price of American cotton, which the grower improves to the best of his ability, is a bounty to the Asiatic agriculturist, who will make no change in his modes of culture or dressing if he can help it. The Englishman is obliged to take the adulterated stuff, whether he likes it or not, simply because that, bad as it is, it is better than nothing. The effect of high prices in the home market for East India produce tends more to change the nature of the cultivation, than to increase the breadth or improve the quality. Cotton lands are made to grow sugar, or vice versâ. Advances are made by the native traders to the ryots during the time that high rates rule in Europe; and the article is delivered perhaps at a period of great depression, when value has been forced down below its natural level. All trading under such circumstances partakes more or less of a gambling character; and the European merchant is mainly the loser. If demand is active, buyers compete with each other, and prices go up enormously; and if it flags, the native middleman has made so much profit by his previous transactions, and lives at such a trifling cost, that he can afford to hold on, and wait till the necessity for fulfilling charters, or of finding freights for vessels consigned on commission, compels the English house to buy on the native's terms, as an alternative preferable to that of sending ships away in ballast. In Calcutta, where the supply is enormous, and the native merchants are more acquainted with the true principles of commerce, the latter state of things can scarcely prevail; but it is quite common at Akyab or Rangoon for merchants to be forced to pay a great deal more than the real market value of grain, because the first holders, being few in number, and very wealthy, are enabled to keep back supplies till the ships' laying days have run out, when the merchant is either obliged to surrender at discretion, or lose the full amount of freight. That mischievous power is, of course, at an end, when the proper balance between supply and demand is obtained, and commerce can be carried on to the mutual benefit of all parties engaged.

The result of imparting a high value to cultivation will be, of course, to improve the quality as well as to increase the quantity of all Eastern products. Englishmen will grow cotton, sugar, and rice as they now grow indigo, and with the same good effects. Care and continual irrigation will entirely change the character of the great staples; and capitalists will be encouraged to make advances when they are sure of obtaining what they have bargained for. The grower would never want a market; the shipowner would never lack a freight; and the merchant might count upon always realising a profit.

The profit of more than three pounds per acre, allowed everywhere to the proprietors of the soil, will doubtless be objected to in some quarters; but we hold that, if the production of raw material can be doubled or quadrupled, no amount of gain should be grudged to the men who accomplish it. We can never cheapen produce, so long as the demand is greater than the supply. The cup must be filled in the first instance; and what runs over goes to the share of the public. When the existing vacuum is entirely filled up, the next ounce tells in favour of the buyer. From getting the same rate of prices as the owners of slave labour, the Indian grower would be gradually brought into competition with the former. After awhile a struggle would commence as to which interest, that of free or servile labour, should supply the world's markets; and the contest must of necessity terminate on the side of civilisation. No efforts of slavery could avail against the countless millions of willing labourers, happy in the enjoyment of family earnings amounting to fourpence halfpenny a day, Sundays excluded. What they now want in the way of useful knowledge, will be imparted to them. No men are more industrious or more desirous to earn money. We have only to show them how a competency is to be realised, and they are sure to achieve it.

Until the world can stumble on another India, or we are false to ourselves and our forefathers, we shall be able, under the new social system, to occupy the foremost place amongst the nations, in reality as well as in appearance. At this moment our condition resembles that of the Hindoo universe, which is supported on a snake, which rests on a tortoise, which latter rests upon nothing. Our prosperity has no solid foundation. It could scarcely exist, and perhaps we should scarcely care to uphold it, if national independence were wrenched from it; and so long as we are dependent on a single foreign nation for the means whereby alone millions of our best citizens are enabled to exist, we cannot be said to be actually masters of our own fate. There is a choice left to us. In a period of hostility, which may one day overtake us, we must cast our lot either with the beggar or the slave; but the alternative is not a pleasant one.

Members of Parliament and directors in Leadenhall street ask what becomes of the immense supplies of bullion that go forward by every mail to India; and the question is easily answered. The average value of Indian exports is doubled; but the ryot gets little or none of the increase, and rain and sunshine cost no more to the grower than of old. Such portion of the middleman's profit as he can employ with advantage in extending production, is directed to that end; and after he has clothed himself according to the custom of his tribe, and decked his wife with jewels, the rest returns to the soil from whence it originally came. He has no opera to subscribe to, no turf to patronise, no wine merchant's or milliner's bills to pay. His sons' education may cost him perhaps twenty pounds a year, if his family is numerous. His daughters' accomplishments are taught, from first to last, in what we should term the nursery. He makes and spends money, lives, and is buried, after the fashion of his fathers.

Level the houses of our Manchester operatives, and let each family reside in a mud hut, with a grass mat for bed and bedding, a couple of three-legged stools for furniture, and for cooking utensils an earthen pot. For clothing, let the worker have a cotton rag round his waist, for food a handful of the cheapest grain — let himself, his wife and family, exist from infancy to old age without comfort, knowledge, or religion, — without a sense of decency or a hope of amelioration more than is possessed by the beasts that perish; and then if the work of his hands brought the same price as now in the world's markets, and the mill owners spent each but a hundred a year, we should have no trouble in finding out why gold and silver were more largely imported, and where the greater portion went to. Do we wish to restore what a certain section of political economists call "the balance of trade" in favour of England? We have only to give the Indian ryot an equal interest with the Manchester spinners in the fruit of his labour. To contend that the former has no desire to be well fed and clothed, that his wife has no love of finery, and his children no capacity for instruction, is to mock common sense, and despise the responsibilities of civilisation.

CHAP. XXX.

POLITICAL CHANGES REQUIRED.—NECESSITY FOR THROWING INDIA OPEN TO ALL THE QUEEN'S SUBJECTS. — ORGANISATION OF A STAFF CORPS. — MONOPOLY OF THE CIVIL SERVICE AT AN END.

LET us have the right to buy lands anywhere in India, and with lawyers for judges, and Englishmen for zemindars, we should take little heed as to the composition of the governing power. That portion of the Anglo-Indian population, which has the largest amount of interest in the well-being of the country, only cares to interfere in public affairs for self-defence; but, from the nature of things, Government in the East has so much to do with social questions, and has done its work so badly, that men who would as soon think of meddling with state matters in Calcutta, as of neglecting their business for parish politics at home, have been obliged to come forward and agitate for a total change in the system of rule. Their aims are solely directed to the advancement of the English in India; but inasmuch as they cannot benefit their own important class, without at the same time serving the interests of the people, they deserve the support of the home public.

In dealing with this great matter, we put classes and cliques equally aside. We have no respect for the Indian Government, because its members belong to the middle ranks, and no abstract dislike to the wider influence of the imperial authority, on the score that it is usually exercised by titled persons. It is said with justice that appointments made by the ministry of the day, are rarely bestowed with reference to the capacity of the individual promoted; but there is no reason to suppose, that in the selection of candidates for the highest offices, the Court of Directors are a whit more considerate; and it is not always that lucky indiscretions protect the public from the consequences of unwise partiality. Fools and firebrands have sat in the highest seats before now, and will do so again, whether the choice of selection rest with the Crown or the Company. One day your ablest man is a soldier, and the grey-headed civilian a type of imbecility. The next you are called upon to admire a Dalhousie or a Thomason, the choice of each and all being equally the result of accident. It is the merest chance whether the Commander-in-Chief is a Napier or a Godwin; fate and the exigencies of party dominate over all.

Even if we could obtain a guarantee, that the ablest member of the services should always be at the head of the Government, it would by no means follow, that we should witness the adoption of a liberal and enlightened policy. Long residence in India narrows the understanding and strengthens the prejudices of a man, however gifted he may be by nature. Obliged to enact the despot for the better part of his lifetime, he becomes incapable at last of identifying himself with the broad principles of popular progress. He has never been accustomed to deal with the rights of the people; the good and the evil that he has done, have proceeded from his own volition, or the mandate of his superiors. Remonstrance displeases and opposition provokes him. He abhors publicity, and chafes at the strictures of the press. We know members of the service to whom none of these objections apply, who sympathise with every plan of improvement, and would make Government instead of being, as it is, the mystery of quacks, a thing to be understood and reverenced. But they are sadly few in number, and labour under the disability of not being admired in high places.

No one can deny the soundness of the axiom, that it is for the general good that the ablest man should always be appointed to office, without reference to the class he belonged to, and all we contend for is, that no body of men, however well selected, shall be allowed to monopolise the government of an empire.

At forty years of age, a man of good character may enter the church, the law, or the army. Bishops, chief-justices, and generals of approved ability, have commenced, even later in life, the career in which they were destined to be famous; and why should not similar facilities for the exercise of genius, learning, and enterprise be afforded in the Civil Service of India? No one expects that the outsider should be planted at once in the front ranks. It is only governors that are made out of the purely raw material; but just as you allow a Wilde to exchange his profession of attorney for that of advocate, which chance shall, in due time, enable him to become Lord Chancellor — just as a Graham, sorrowing for the loss of his wife, is permitted to become an ensign at fifty, and afterwards Lord Lynedoch, the victor of Barossa — should a capable man be suffered to make his way to an Indian judgeship.—Providence, which has not made ability the sole product of a single country, or the attribute of a particular class, punishes, in the prevalence of foolish counsels, the attempt to support such a monopoly as that of the East India Company. Of course, there will be many to point out the dangers of such a policy, but only a few years since it was as vigorously contended that the interests of India and England were intimately bound up with the Company's trading system. If tea was bought by any other than covenanted servants, and carried home by any other than Company's vessels, you might enrich a few grasping speculators, but it would be at the expense of British supremacy in the East.

Since that change was effected, which the ablest servants of the East India Company, including Sir Thomas Munro and Sir Charles Metcalfe, so much deprecated, the Indian trade has increased from two and a half millions annually to sixty millions, and there is reason to suppose that, by opening up the service to the competition of the whole empire, men as well as youths, the profit in politics will be as great as the benefits in commerce. In India, at this moment, there are scores of first-rate men available for the public service, of all classes and colours; and why should the state be denied the benefit of their labours? We have no objection to the maintenance of the present system of recruiting the ranks of the Civil Service; but it does not exhaust the stock of ability, and in many instances fails to disclose the presence of it. The dunce at school often turns out a successful administrator, and the winner of the prize at the examinations a poor bookworm. There is work to be done in India, such as mere scholarship can hardly forward. The tasks are various, and let us, if such are to be found, everywhere intrust them to fitting hands.

It is rank cowardice on the part of the public to give way to the fear of making the minister of the day too powerful. Such an objection to the overthrow of the India House was valid enough when Parliament was a close assembly, ruled by class influences, and the newspaper was made up of advertisements and gossip. If the nation is true to itself, why should it dread a lord? If men are too idle to qualify themselves to pronounce a just verdict on the conduct of those placed above them, or too timid or dishonest to say what they know ought to be said, no scheme that the wit of mortals can devise will obtain for them the blessings of good government. Under any system of rule, the fool will creep into the post of honour, and the knave will get to be trusted, unless a never-ceasing watch is maintained by the people. Let us cast our lines everywhere, on the surface, and in the depths of society, and take for public use the best of the haul. The capable man will need to be looked after as well as his opposite; but the one in that case is sure to achieve good, the other can only be kept from doing harm.

The late change, by which entrance into the Civil Service was made the prize for competition amongst the pupils of the great seminaries of learning, was a great step in advance of that system, which maintained a dozen families for the sole purpose of raising the future governors of the East, and left the general public dependent on female sterility. But another great reform is needed. We require, as well, that appointments in the army should be thrown open to all the adventurous and able. Let Government take a fourth of the whole number of nominations, to be dealt with as human infirmity may suggest, and let us bestow the rest upon the most deserving applicant for military distinction.

The employment of more European agents in India will be a necessity under the new system of rule. There will be less work for the politician, but more for the magistrate and overseer. When the civilian has nothing to do with law, and the collector merely sits in his Cutcherry to regulate the receipt of revenue, the labour of governing will be materially simplified, and officials will be sufficiently paid at half their present rates of income. We shall find in the army a large reserve of practical ability; and can, at any time, lay our hands upon men who have been acclimatised, and obtained a certain knowledge of the country. Their constant sense of the impossibility of achieving civil distinction without much study, would call forth whatever of faculty they had within them. The boatman who would contend in the race takes care that his oar shall never be long out of the water.

A list should be opened in London, wherein every young man amongst the Queen's subjects, who had passed a preliminary examination, should be permitted to inscribe his name. At stated seasons a number of candidates should be drawn by ballot, and examined as to their proficiency in the course of study laid down, the most competent being selected to receive commissions. On arriving in India they should be posted to regiments, and made to do duty for not less than two years, at the end of which time they would be eligible for staff employment, on passing in the language of the district in which they were to labour. We would do away with the present evil of taking an officer from his regiment, to spend the prime of his days in staff duties, and sending him back to command the corps, when both intellect and activity were either gone altogether or greatly deteriorated. At the end of three years, the absentee should elect to remain on the staff, or go back to his regiment. If he chose the former, his place should be filled up by the junior next in succession, and henceforth his military rank would be purely nominal. He should be styled Captain or Major when he would have attained those grades in the corps; but if obliged to leave the staff, either from sickness or incapacity, he should never be allowed to return to the army. Whatever interest he could make should only be available to get him returned to civil employment. If he was unfit, either morally or intellectually, for the one set of tasks, he should not be declared good enough for the performance of the other. Under such a system men, who had interest enough to get appointed, would hesitate as to their use of it, and take more heed of their conduct when they had abandoned the worse paid but surer position of a subaltern in the army. Officers who had no friends to push them forward, or who had a love for the military profession, would rejoice in the appointment of a senior to the staff. Every such case would be as profitable to their interests as a death vacancy, and far more pleasant, we would hope, to their feelings. They would rejoice at what is now considered usually a hardship, and often an insult to them. Those who did the work of soldiering would get its rewards; and we should have no more instances of men, after spending a lifetime in civil employment, and in the receipt of high pay, coming back to command their corps over the heads of majors who had never left their regiments, or received more than mere army allowances. Both classes would be greatly benefited by being restricted to the choice of a profession, and secured in the enjoyment of the privileges which properly belong to it.

But whilst we hold out this immense boon to the middle classes, who find it so difficult to get employment for their younger branches, — whilst we provide for a large accession to the stock of available administrative ability, and do away with the heart-burnings which now prevail in the army, — we must not ignore the existence of indigenous capacity in the East. There are crowds of men — European, East Indian, and native — who seek employment and can exhibit proofs of fitness for it; and we must remember, too, that whilst the home-bred candidate for office has all the world before him wherein to pick out a sphere for exertion, those men are restricted to the opportunities afforded in the place of their birth. A great many of them actually perform the tasks for which civilians draw high salaries, and some possess an aptitude for work which defies rivalry. We would allow them in all cases to come in and prove their claims to share in whatever was held out as the reward of proved fitness in India, and abolish altogether the prevailing distinction between covenanted and uncovenanted employment. The men appointed at home should always have work and pay; but we would do away at once, and for ever, with the system which makes certain offices the sole heritage of those who hold civil or military commissions. It is not difficult to detect the interest which such persons have in the continuance of the present monopoly; but what compensates the public for its existence? If the official at the head of financial affairs is totally ignorant of all that he should know, it is surely no set-off against a deranged money-market and a damaged state of public credit, to show that he is a member of the Civil Service, and not a mere adventurer, East Indian, or native, selected only because he possessed knowledge and ability. In Ceylon, seven years since, the Queen's Advocate, and member of the Legislative Council by virtue of his position, was a gentleman of the darkest shade of colour, yet no one grumbled at an appointment which in this case was filled by the ablest man in the island. If East Indians can collect customs in Rangoon and elsewhere, why should they not do so in Bengal and Madras? If adventurers are good enough to be deputy-commissioners on rare occasions in Pegu and the Punjaub, why should they be kept in general upon a lower scale of pay, and taught that the rich prizes of the service are exclusively for those who have received their appointments at home? If one man is set to do certain tasks, and steadily and ably gets through them, upon no principle of fairness to the individual or advantage to the public can we withhold from him the rate of remuneration which is given to others employed in like manner.

The system of promotion in the navy bears some resemblance to the state of things which prevails in the East; but though a lieutenant is often allowed to grow grey in the Queen's service, he is never made to believe that a positive class inferiority is the cause of his being passed over for promotion. He accounts himself as good a gentleman as the post-captain, and never regards his own elevation as a sheer impossibility. Were it otherwise, the nation might raise an outcry, and the efficiency of the fleet would be in danger; but the injustice which would not be tolerated for a moment in the one hemisphere is universally inflicted in the other. The civil and military servants of the East India Company form literally two castes, who, by virtue of their covenants or commissions, engross, to the absolute exclusion of all other Englishmen, all the dignified and lucrative offices in the East. The wife of the high civilian may look down upon the family of the military man as being "trash from the fort;" but both unite in the feeling of unmeasured contempt for all without the pale of privilege. And they have a right to be proud of their position as matters are managed and worth estimated in that part of the world; for, let the emergency be ever so great, or the stock of capacity ever so small, no "uncovenanted" person has a chance of holding high rank even for an hour. If he is thrust in, like a handful of tow, to stop a leak which would otherwise speedily send the ship to the bottom, every one knows that he is but a temporary plug, to be thrown aside at the first convenient moment.

This state of things will of course be abolished under the Queen's Government; it could only exist under a corporation like the East India Company, and makes the cost and the result of ruling exhibit very different results from what ought to be produced. Some men find it hard enough to bear with the existence of an aristocracy; but merit in every quarter of the globe can find an entrance into the ranks of the nobility. It was reserved for a knot of merchants to establish a system of exclusiveness such as the world never saw before, and is not likely to witness again.

APPENDIX.

THE GAGGING ACT.

From the CALCUTTA GAZETTE.

Legislative Council, 13th June, 1857.

THE following Act, passed by the Legislative Council of India, received the assent of the Right Honourable the Governor-General this day, and is hereby promulgated for general information.

ACT No. XV. OF 1857.

"An Act to regulate the establishment of Printing Presses, and to restrain in certain cases the circulation of printed books and papers."

Whereas it is expedient to prohibit the keeping or using of printing-presses, types, or other materials for printing, in any part of the territories in the possession and under the government of the East India Company, except with the previous sanction and license of Government, and under suitable provisions to guard against abuse; and whereas it may be deemed proper to prohibit the circulation, within the said territories, of newspapers, books, or other printed papers of a particular description: It is enacted as follows:— Preamble.

I. No person shall keep any printing-press or types, or other materials or articles for printing, without having obtained the previous sanction and license for that purpose of the Governor-General of India in Council, or of the Executive Government of the Presidency in which such printing-press, types, or other materials or articles for printing are intended to be kept or used, or of such other person or persons as the Governor-General of India in Council may authorise to grant such sanction or license; and any person who shall keep or use any printing-press, or types, or other materials or articles for printing, without having obtained such licenses, shall be liable, on conviction before a magistrate, to a fine not exceeding five thousand rupees*, or to imprisonment not exceeding two years, or to both. No printing-press to be kept or used without the license of Government.

* £500.

Power to search for and seize unlicensed printing-presses, &c.

II. If any person shall keep or use any printing-press, or types, or other materials or articles for printing, without such sanction or licenses aforesaid, any magistrate, within whose jurisdiction the same may be found, may seize the same, or cause them to be seized, together with any books or printed papers found on the premises; and shall dispose of the same as the Governor-General of India in Council, or the Executive Government of any Presidency, or such other person as the Governor-General in Council shall authorise in that behalf, may direct; and it shall be lawful for any magistrate to issue a search warrant for the entry and search of any house, building, or other place, in which he may have reason to believe that any such unlicensed printing-press, types, or other materials or articles for printing are kept or used.

Application for license to keep printing-press.

III. Whenever any person or persons shall be desirous of keeping or using any printing-press, or types, or other materials or articles for printing, he or they shall apply by writing to the magistrate within whose jurisdiction he proposes to keep or use such press or other such materials or articles as aforesaid, or to such other persons as the Governor-General in Council, or the Executive Government of the Presidency, or such other person as the Governor-General in Council shall authorise in that behalf, may appoint for that purpose. The application shall specify the name, profession, and place of abode of the proprietor or proprietors of such printing-press, types, or other materials or articles for printing, and of the person or persons who is or are intended to use the same, and the place where such printing-press, types, or other materials or articles for printing are intended to be used; and such application shall be verified by the oath, affirmation, or solemn declaration of the proprietors and persons intending to keep or use such printing-press, types, or other materials or articles for printing, or such of them as the magistrate or other person to whom the application shall be made shall direct: and any person wilfully making a false oath, affirmation, or declaration, shall be deemed guilty of perjury.

Government may grant license subject to conditions, and may revoke the same.

IV. The magistrate shall forward a copy of such application to the Governor-General in Council, or to the Executive Government of the Presidency, or to such other person as may be authorised to grant the license; and the said Governor-General in Council, or such Executive Government, or other person as aforesaid, may at his or their discretion grant such license subject to such conditions (if any) as he or they may think fit, and may also at any time revoke the same.

Penalty for using press contrary to conditions, or after revocation of license.

V. If any person or persons shall keep or use, or cause or allow to be kept or used, any such printing-press, types, or other materials or articles for printing, contrary to the conditions upon which the license may have been granted, or after notice of the revocation of such license shall have been given to, or left for, him or them at the place at which the printing-press shall have been established, he or they shall be subject to the same penalties as if no such license had been granted; and such printing-press, types, and other materials or articles for printing may be seized and disposed of in the manner prescribed in Section II. of this Act.

VI. All books and other papers, printed at a press licensed under this Act, shall have printed legibly thereon the name of the printer and of the publisher, and the place of the printing and publication thereof; and a copy of every such book or printed paper shall be immediately forwarded to the magistrate or to such other person as the Government or other persons granting the license may direct; and every person who shall print or publish any book or paper otherwise than in conformity with this provision, or who shall neglect to forward a copy of such book or paper in manner hereinbefore directed, unless specially exempted therefrom by the Governor-General in Council, or other person granting the license, shall be liable, on conviction before a magistrate, to a fine not exceeding one thousand rupees, and in default of payment to imprisonment for a term not exceeding six calendar months.

Books, &c., to have the printer's and publisher's name printed on them, and copies to be forwarded to the magistrate.

VII. The Governor-General of India in Council, or the Executive Government of any Presidency, may, by order to be published in the Government Gazette, prohibit the publication or circulation, within the said territories, or the territories subject to the said Government, or within any particular part of the said territories, of any particular newspaper, book, or other printed paper, or any newspaper of any particular description, whether printed within the said territories or not; and whoever, after such prohibition, shall knowingly import, publish or circulate, or cause to be imported, published, or circulated any such book or paper, shall be liable for every such offence, on conviction before a magistrate, to a fine not exceeding five thousand rupees, or to imprisonment not exceeding two years, or to both; and every such book or paper shall be seized and forfeited.

Government may prohibit circulation of particular books or newspapers.

VIII. The word "printing" shall include lithographing. The word "magistrate" shall include a person exercising the powers of a magistrate, and also a justice of the peace; and every person hereby made punishable by a Justice of the peace may be punishable upon summary conviction.

Interpretation.

IX. Nothing in this Act shall exempt any person from complying with the provisions of Act XI. of 1845.

Act not to exempt compliance with Act XI. of 1835.

X. No person shall be prosecuted for any offence against the provisions of this Act, within fourteen days after the passing of the Act, without an order of the Governor-General in Council or the Executive Government of the Presidency in which the offence shall be committed, or the person authorised under the provisions of this Act to grant licenses.

Prosecutions.

XI. This Act shall continue in force for one year.

Duration of Act.

W. MORGAN,
Clerk of the Council.

From the CALCUTTA GAZETTE *Extraordinary, Saturday,* 20*th June*, 1857.

NOTIFICATION.

Fort William, Home Department, 18th June, 1857.

With reference to the provisions of Act No. XV. of 1857, it is hereby notified that applications for licenses to keep or use any printing-press, or types, or other materials or articles for printing within the town of Calcutta, are to be made to the commissioner of police.

The Lieutenant-Governor of Bengal is authorised to grant licenses under the said Act, and to appoint any person or persons to receive applications for such licenses in any part of the lower provinces of the presidency of Bengal except the town of Calcutta.

The Lieutenant-Governor of the north-western provinces is authorised to grant licenses under the said Act, and to appoint any person or persons to receive such applications in any part of the north-western provinces of the presidency of Bengal.

The Governor of the straits settlements, the chief commissioners of the Punjub and Oude, and the commissioners of Mysore, Coorg, Nagpore, Pegu, and the Tenasserim and Martaban provinces, are authorised severally to appoint any person or persons to receive such applications within the provinces, districts, and settlements, under their control.

The conditions upon which licenses to keep or use any printing-press, or types, or other materials or articles for printing will ordinarily be granted, are as follows:—

1. That no book, newspaper, pamphlet, or other work printed at such press, or with such materials or articles, shall contain any observations or statements impugning the motives or designs of the British Government, either in England or India, or in any way tending to bring the said Government into hatred or contempt, to excite disaffection or unlawful resistance to its orders, or to weaken its lawful authority, or the lawful authority of its civil or military servants.

2. That no such book, pamphlet, newspaper, or other work, shall contain observations or statements having a tendency to create alarm or suspicion among the native population of any intended interference by Government with their religious opinions and observances.

3. That no such book, pamphlet, newspaper, or other work, shall contain observations having a tendency to weaken the friendship towards the British Government of native princes, chiefs, or states, in dependence upon or alliance with it.

The above conditions apply equally to original matter, and to matter copied from other publications.

A copy of every book, pamphlet, newspaper, or other work published in the town of Calcutta, is to be immediately forwarded to the commissioner of police.

By order of the Right Hon. the Governor-General in Council.

CECIL BEADON.
Secretary to the Government of India.

THE FIRST FRUITS OF THE ACT.

No. 298.

From the SECRETARY TO THE GOVERNMENT OF BENGAL, *to* J. C. MURRAY, Esq., *Printer and Publisher of the "Friend of India."*

Dated Fort William, 29th June, 1857.

Sir,—I am directed to forward for your information the accompanying copy of a letter No. 1202, dated 29th June, 1857, from the Secretary to the Government of India in the Home Department relative to an article which appeared in your paper of the 25th instant. General.

I have the honour to be, Sir,
Your most obedient Servant,
A. R. YOUNG.
Secretary to the Government of Bengal.

No. 1202.

From CECIL BEADON, Esq., *Secretary to the Government of India, to* A. R. YOUNG, Esq., *Secretary to the Government of Bengal.*

Dated the 29th June, 1857.

Sir,—The attention of the Governor-General in Council has been given to the first leading article headed, "The Centenary of Plassey," which appeared in the *Friend of India* of the 25th inst., and especially to the two last paragraphs, which in the judgment of His Lordship in Council are fraught with mischief and calculated at the present time to spread disaffection towards the British Government, both among its native subjects and among dependent and allied states. Home department.

The article in question infringes every one of the three conditions upon which licenses to keep a printing-press are now to be granted. It tends to excite disaffection towards the British Government amongst great masses of the people; it tends to create alarm and suspicion among the Hindoo and Mahomedan population of intended interference by Government with their religion; and it tends to weaken the friendship towards the Government of native princes, chiefs, and states, in dependence upon and alliance with it.

Whatever the intentions of the writer may have been, the tendency of the article is as above described, and the publication of such remarks, even if innocent and admissible in ordinary times, is now, under the critical circumstances which rendered the passing of Act No. 15 of 1857 necessary, most dangerous not only to the Government, but to the lives of all Europeans in the Provinces not living under the close protection of British bayonets.

I am directed, therefore, to request that with the permission of the Lieutenant-Governor the views of the Government of India may be communicated to the Publisher of the *Friend of India*, and that he may be warned that the repetition of remarks of this dangerous nature will be followed by the withdrawal of his license.

The Governor-General in Council has no intention of interfering with the fair discussion of public measures, but he cannot now permit the circulation in India of writings so framed as to excite popular disaffection.

I have, &c.,

(Signed) C. BEADON,

Secretary to the Government of India.

Council Chamber, 29th June, 1857.

(True Copy.)

A. R. YOUNG.

Secretary to the Government of Bengal.

From the FRIEND OF INDIA, *June 25th.*

THE CENTENARY OF PLASSEY.

WE have glided into the second centenary of English rule in India, and Hindus and Mussulmans who study the mysteries of fate are well nigh in despair. The stars and scriptures told them that on Monday last we had completed our allotted term of mastership, when the strength which had hitherto been resistless, the courage that never faltered, would pass away, and we should become in turn the easy prey of our vassals. The favour of the gods is not a perpetual gift, and though sire and son have witnessed so often what must to them appear supernatural results, it was but reasonable to suppose that our store of miracles would be exhausted at last. We share with them the belief in hidden influences, only what they look upon as being natural and common place, is to us the domain of the marvellous. It is easy to understand how we gained power, and wealth, and glory, at the commencement of the cycle, but hard beyond measure to find out how we have lost all three at its close. When you can succeed in realising to the imagination the most foolish thing, the most improbable thing, and the most timid thing; and have blended all these together and multiplied them, and worked them into what is called a policy, you may perhaps get some clue to the solution of the problem, but all other modes of induction will hopelessly fail.

The qualities of mind which enable a man to accumulate wealth are often those which hinder him from making a proper use of it. It was necessary for the conquest of Hindustan that the East India Company should exist, for it is only the intense greediness of traders that could have won for us the sovereignty of the country. The enemies of the Company's rule assert that they made and broke treaties, planned and fought battles, for the mere love of gain. Whatever degree of interference with private or public rights was needful for the purpose of collecting revenue, received instant and eager sanction; whatever concerned merely the welfare of Asiatic souls, or the social interests of the great body of

Englishmen and Hindus, was either coldly ignored or bitterly assailed. They imported for their own use the might of civilisation, but never cared to exhibit to the nations its beneficent features. Wealth embodied all the attributes of their good deity, to whom was rendered with cheerful devotion the homage of heart and brain. The evil principle was symbolised by power, and where they failed to vanquish they fell down and worshipped. Without a spark of patriotic feeling they set on the brow of England a gem of priceless value; without care for Christianity they paved the way for the overthrow of idolatry. Be it so, but the evil which they wrought has well nigh passed away; the good of which they have been the not unconscious instruments will go on multiplying for ever.

A hundred years is but a small point in the lifetime of a nation. It may be a period of sowing or of reaping the harvest, of giant labours such as shall influence the destiny of remote generations, or of utter folding of the hands to sleep. We found India destitute of invention and enterprise; ignorant of liberty, and of the blessings of peace. We have placed her face to face with the forces of our civilisation, and have yet to see if there are no subtle invigorating influences that can be transmitted through her aged frame. We have given her liberty such as she has not enjoyed for centuries, and never save by brief and long interrupted snatches. The Hindu stands upon the same platform with the Englishman, shares equal privileges with him, and challenges for himself as great a measure of the protection and immunities accorded by the state. He has no political enemies, and his grievances are all social. There is much to be remedied within, but without all is quiet and secure. If he has a new part to play in the world's history, the stage is clear for him, and there is an audience ready to sympathise and applaud. Whatever he has in him of creative ability may find easy vent and ready acceptance. We have swept away the obstacles which stood in the path of intellect and courage, it rests only with Nature and himself, whether he achieves success or otherwise. A second Sevajee is happily impossible, but another Luther would find an easier task than that which was imposed upon the monk of Wittenberg. The inventor, the author, the man of science will meet ready welcome and sure reward. We spread out before the dormant Asiatic soul, all the mental treasures of the West, and feel only too happy in being allowed to distribute them.

It is a great crime in some instances to trample out a nationality; to strangle in infancy what might have grown up to be one of the fairest births of Time, but except in the case of the Sikhs, there is no example of the kind to be alleged against our countrymen. The Mussulman power was effete long before the battle of Plassey, and such as Clive found the Mahomedans in the days of Surajah Dowlah, we encounter them in the time of the deposed king of Oude. Cruel, sensual, and intolerant, they are unfit to rule and unwilling to serve. Claiming to exercise sway as of Divine Right, and yet destitute of every gift with which Nature has endowed the races meant by destiny to dominate over the world, they fell by necessity under the power of a nation replete with energy and resolution, and loathe with all the bitterness of hate the infidels who have subdued them. They will never tolerate our gifts or forgive our supremacy. We may load them with blessings, but the reward will be curses. We stand between them and a fancied earthly paradise, and are not classed in their list of good angels.

The Mahrattas have none of the elements of greatness in their character, and speaking in the interests of the dusky millions, we do not regret Assye, Deeg, and Maharajpore; but it is otherwise with regard to the Sikhs, who had they flourished as we have seen them, two centuries back, or never come in contact with the might of England, would perhaps have uprooted the tenets of Hindu and Mussulman, and breathed a new spirit into the followers of Mohamed and Brahma. Humanity, however, will be content with their overthrow. The Bible is a better book than the Grunth, and Christianity is superior to the Khalsa. Regenerated Hinduism might have obtained a new lease of existence, but it would have gained nothing in morals, and effected but little for human happiness. Its sole gain would have been power, and the example of universal destruction.

It may also be alleged against us that we have deposed the Kings, and ruined the nobles of India, but why should the world sigh over that result? Monarchs who always took the wages, but seldom performed the work, of Government, and aristocrats who looked upon authority as a personal right, and have never been able to comprehend what is meant by the sovereignty of the people, are surely better out of the way. No Englishman in these days deplores the wars of the Roses, and would like to see the Cliffords and Warwicks restored again to life. France bears with calmness the loss of her old nobility; Europe at large makes steady contributions to the list of kings out of employment. Had princes and rajahs in Hindustan been worth conserving they would have retained their titles and power. The class speedily die out in the natural course of mortality, and it is not for the benefit of society that it should be renewed.

Array the evil against the acknowledged good; weigh the broken pledges, the ruined families, the impoverished ryots, the imperfect justice, against the missionary and the schoolmaster, the railway and the steam-engine, the abolition of Suttee, and the destruction of the Thugs, and declare in which scale the balance lies! For every anna that we have taken from the noble we have returned a rupee to the trader. We have saved more lives in peace than we have sacrificed in war. We have committed many blunders and crimes; wrought evil by premeditation and good by instinct, but when all is summed up, the award must be in our favour. And with the passing away of the present cloud, there will dawn a brighter day both for England and India. We shall strengthen at the same time our hold upon the soil and upon the hearts of the people;

tighten the bonds of conquest and of mutual interest. The land must be thrown open to the capital and enterprise of Europe; the ryot lifted by degrees out of his misery, and made to feel that he is a man if not a brother, and everywhere Heaven's gifts of climate and circumstance made the most of. The first centenary of Plassey was ushered in by the revolt of the native army, the second may be celebrated in Bengal by a respected Government, and a Christian population.

The *Madras Athenæum* was "warned" and the *Bangalore Herald suppressed*, for reprinting the above article before the Government notification appeared. The latter journal was afterwards allowed to reappear on condition of the editor being dismissed.

No. 329.

From the SECRETARY TO THE GOVERNMENT OF BENGAL *to* J. C. MURRAY, ESQ., *printer and publisher of the "Friend of India," Serampore.*

Sir,—I am directed by the Lieutenant-Governor of Bengal to forward for your information the accompanying copy of a letter from the Secretary to the Government of India, in the Home Department, No. 54, dated the 3rd inst., relative to the article which appeared in your paper of the 2nd idem, headed "The First Warning." General.

I have the honour to be, Sir,
Your most obedient Servant,
A. R. YOUNG,
Secretary to the Government of India.

Dated Fort William, 3rd July, 1857.

No. 54.

From C. BEADON, ESQ., *Secretary to the Government of India, to* A. R. YOUNG, ESQ., *Secretary to the Government of Bengal.*

Sir,—In consequence of the article which appeared in the *Friend of India* of the 2nd inst., headed "The First Warning," the Governor in Council would have felt it necessary to direct the revocation of the license which had been granted to the publisher of that paper. His lordship in Council only abstains from adopting this course in consequence of an assurance he has received on the part of the representatives of the absent proprietor, that the newspaper shall, during his absence, be carried on so as to avoid all cause of complaint, and within the terms of the license. Home department.

The Governor-General in Council desires me to request that this may be conveyed to the publisher.

I have the honour to be, Sir,
Your most obedient Servant,
CECIL BEADON,
Secretary to the Government of India.

Council Chamber, the 3rd of July, 1857.

From the Friend of India, *July 2nd.*

THE FIRST WARNING.

Lord Canning has done us the honour to select the *Friend of India* as the subject of his first experiment under the Gagging Act. We are, it appears, an *imperium in imperio*, studied by the native masses, watched with anxiety by Moollah and Brahmin, stronger than the East India Company. We have only to insert a couple of paragraphs, and the rebellion broadens and deepens. The chief priests amongst Hindoos and Mussulmans tremble for the safety of their creeds, and allied and dependent princes, looking upon their treaties as so much waste paper, turn a deaf ear to Governor-General and Resident, and prepare to array their fighting men against the Sirkar Bahadoor. Say that our power is complimented at the expense of our patriotism, yet what journalist could resist the temptations that beset us? What would even the *Times* give to possess such vast means of doing mischief? Who else is there of all the tribe of editors, that has authority over a hundred and fifty millions of souls, that stirs equally the ryot in his hut, the devotee in his temple, and the ruler on his throne? A few words and we can subvert the allegiance of the people. The servants of the sacred shrines, dear to all races of Asiatics, seek their destiny in these columns; wherever the English soldier is absent, we hold the lives of Europeans in the hollow of our hand. So says Lord Canning, and we may not question the truth of his statement. Here is the Governor-General's opinion of an article in our last which we dare only refer to, except for home purposes.

* * * * * *

If we were on our defence in a trial for libel, we should be allowed to reprint the obnoxious paragraphs, but it will be sufficient to say that they occurred in the course of a rapid sketch of the results of a century of British occupation, and formed the best apology that we were able to make for the East India Company. We had to speak of a policy which has swept away monarchies and aristocracies in all parts of the land, as if they cumbered the earth; a policy which bore its first fruits in 1757, and its latest just a century afterwards. We advocated it as has been the habit of this journal for a score of years, and however prepared for hostilities on the part of the present administration, we certainly never expected that the grounds of indictment would be found in the first leading article of our last issue. We have no objection to recant one of the obnoxious paragraphs, but must stand by the hope expressed in the other. We will say, if required, that from Suraj ool Dowlah to the King of Oude, the princes of India have been vilely dealt with, but we cannot forego the pleasing vision that in 1957, a Christian people may live happily under a respected Government.

But what is the use of beating about the bush, and assailing us under false pretences? Our fault is no question of orthodoxy, or want of sympathy with mockery Kings. It is, that whilst doing our utmost to keep eyes and ears closed to much that we were bound to receive, we were forced to denounce the vacillation of purpose, the utter want of organisation, and the wretched crop of results, which have given such a melancholy character to the proceedings of Government since the commencement of the mutinies. We had to choose between the utterance of unpleasant censures or a dishonest silence. Between saying what in the interest of England it were traitorous to suppress, and what it was for the reputation of a few high officials should never have been written. The time had come when it was needful to take a side, and without hesitation we fell into the imperial ranks. As it turns out, we had not counted the cost, but such as our course seemed to entail we were willing to defray. On the score of public support we have no martyrdom to boast of, having gained a hundred and eleven subscribers since the 1st May, after allowing for all the deaths and withdrawals.

We venture to say that there is not a man in Calcutta, or elsewhere, who will put upon the excepted paragraphs the construction which Lord Canning has chosen to fix on them, or who will adopt any other conclusion than the palpable one, that it is thought more desirable to gag the *Friend of India* at once, than to waste time in finding a sufficient reason for the act. But we submit to his Lordship the following matter for consideration. The people of all classes, who are said to read and study this journal, know as a matter of course that it has always been the advocate of annexation and of Christianity. But all of a sudden it is silent upon those important topics. The shrewd Asiatic need not ask the reason, for he can see for himself that the Government has interfered to prevent their discussion, but he will carry the inquiry a step further, and ask what it is that has prompted the interference. If they intend to reverse the policy of their predecessors, why let them reinstate Kings, restore Jagheers, and deport Missionaries. But if they are not repentant, but merely timid; if they do not abjure the acts, but only shrink from enduring the consequences, why what a dullard he must be, to be duped into inaction by such shallow artifices! Either we advocate what is always injurious to the body politic, or it is the poorest cowardice to coerce us into silence. No man, Mussulman or Hindu, if he has half the brains that the Governor-General allots to him, can fail to recognise in this open tabooing of subjects hitherto left free for comment, the newest and most damning proof of the mistrust which the Government entertains of the allies and native subjects of the Crown of England, and the Honourable Company.

Three weeks since Lord Canning had the sympathy and support of every man of European birth or parentage. To-day there are not half a dozen who would lift up their hands in his favour. But why should he do for himself, what he has failed to do for England? Why care to retain personal when public reputation is irrecoverably gone? When the goodly ship goes down with all her rich freight on board, it is better that the captain should exhibit no anxiety to save his cabin furniture.

And now a word as to the policy of this journal—say for the next three months. We have no intention of testing the ability of Government to put down a rebellion at Serampore. To-day is the last of our independence, and we will not write under compulsion, or invite, for interests which have been created by industry and intellect exerted for a quarter of a century, the ruin which it will now cost Lord Canning nothing to decree. We accept the situation that is made for us, and take leave of political discussion—till the times mend.

THE DACCA NEWS "WARNED."

No. 393.

To A. Forbes, Esq.

Dacca.

Sir,—I have the honour to forward herewith a copy of a letter No. 456, dated the 7th instant, from the Secretary to the Government of Bengal referring to an article published in the *Dacca News* of the 1st instant, and headed "The Tenure of Land by Europeans in India."

I have the honour to be, Sir,
Your most obedient Servant,
C. F. Carnac,
Officiating Magistrate.

Foujdary Adawlut, Zillah of Dacca.
The 10th August, 1857

No. 456.

From the Secretary to the Government of Bengal *to the* Magistrate of Dacca.

Dated Fort William, the 7th August, 1857.

Sir,—The attention of the Lieutenant-Governor of Bengal has been given to an article in the *Dacca News* of the 1st instant, headed "The Tenure of Land by Europeans in India," which, in his Honour's judgment, manifestly infringes the conditions on which the license to the publisher of that paper was granted. I am directed, therefore, to request that you will warn the publisher that a second infringement of these conditions on his part will compel the Lieutenant-Governor to withdraw his license.

I have, &c.
(Signed) A. R. Young,
Secretary to the Government of Bengal.

(Copy.)
C. F. Carnac,
Officiating Magistrate.

From the Dacca News, *August 1st.*

THE TENURE OF LAND BY EUROPEANS IN INDIA.

Mr. Ewart has moved in the House of Commons for a return showing on what tenure land is allowed to be held by Europeans in India, whether in fee simple, for life or lives, or for years; and if so for what terms of years, and whether renewable on payment of fines or otherwise. — As we may expect that the Court of Directors, which first denied that it had received a copy of Mr. Halliday's police minute, and then furnished, as the police minute, a minute which was not the police minute — as we may expect that Court to give a false return to Mr. Ewart's motion, we shall give a return of our own, as to the terms on which Europeans hold land in the perpetually settled districts. But before doing so we would remind our readers, that the Perpetual Settlement is a bargain entered into between Lord Cornwallis, on the part of the British Government, and for which he staked the good faith of England — not of the Court of Directors, or the "Company Bahadoor," for that is nil — and the land-holders, that as long as they paid a certain rent to the Government, they were to enjoy in perpetuity the possession of the lands contained within certain boundaries specified in the books compiled at the time of the settlement by the various Collectors, and which had been sanctioned with regard to each particular district by the Government. This is the theory of the Perpetual Settlement. The practice has been very different, especially with regard to Europeans, who about twenty years ago were allowed to hold land on the same terms as natives. The practice is as follows: —

A European is allowed to hold lands as long as these lands do not excite the concupiscence of the Government of the East India Company, administered by a Civil Service, whose salaries depend upon the amount of revenue that can be realised, *per fas aut nefas*, from the country. — Example: Mr. George Lamb, a gentleman well known for many years in the Dacca district, purchased an estate called Chur Doopooriah, paying, under the aforesaid Perpetual Settlement, a rent to Government of two hundred and ninety odd rupees. By the encroachment of a large and rapid river, the whole of this estate was carried away. Mr. Lamb, aware, from long observation of the oscillations of the rivers in Bengal, that the land would re-form, continued to fulfil his part of the bargain entered into with the Government — that is, to pay the revenue during eight or ten years, while the estate in question formed a part of the bed of the river, which is from four to five miles broad. He of course expected that, when the river retired, he would be allowed to take possession of the lands re-formed. There is a law, however, in connection with the Settlement, which states, that if an island is thrown up in the channel of a navigable river, it becomes the property of the Government; and this law is perfectly just, for it presupposes the drying up of the river — a circumstance of frequent occurrence in Bengal — and the formation of land on a spot which had not been included in the Perpetual Settlement, as there was no land existing there at that time. There is also another law very useful in preventing disputes, which is to the effect, that lands which are formed by the retiring of rivers from one bank and their encroachment on the other, are to belong to the proprietor on to whose lands they form. In the case before us, when the river was retiring, the Government in the first place took possession of the dry land which first appeared, as an island; and then of all the lands successively emerging from the river, as formations on to the island the property of Government. Mr. Lamb, up to the present date, hoping against hope that justice may be done to him, pays the Perpetual Settlement Revenue for Churr Doopooriah, though he is not in possession, nor has had for the last twelve or fourteen years a single bigah of land belonging to this estate. The Collector receives the rents without a murmur, though we believe the Commissioner of Revenue has ordered him to strike the very name of the estate off the books. The case, moreover, was five times decided in Mr. Lamb's favour by the Judges of the Company itself; and only gained by them when they had succeeded, after a number of years, in packing a bench. We would refer the curious with regard to this case to our supplement of the 19th of July, 1857.

A European is allowed to hold lands as long as these lands do not excite the concupiscence of any native; for, if any native should desire to possess them, they will certainly be decreed to him by the Judges of the East India Company, who find none so impracticable as European owners of land. Example: Mr. G. Lamb purchased at a sale for arrears of Revenue, from the East India Company, an Estate said to comprise within its boundaries certain specified villages. A native about the same time purchased an adjoining estate. Mr. Lamb, from information gathered from the Collector's books, brought a suit for certain villages in the possession of the native, as belonging to his estate. The native brought a cross suit claiming villages of the value of Rs. 1,500 a year against Mr. Lamb. Mr. Lamb lost his suit. The suit of the native was decreed in his favour, giving him villages producing Rs. 6,000 a year, instead of Rs. 1,500, which he had sued for. The document on which the Sudder decreed against Mr. Lamb was a forgery. It purported to be one of the original papers of the Decenial Settlement (on which the Perpetual Settlement was founded) of Zillah Tipperah. Mr. Lamb proved that the whole of that settlement was made in Arcot Rupees, while this paper was summed up in Sicca Rupees. The Sudder Dewany Adalut, The Supreme Civil Court of Bengal, decided that the word "Sicca" meant "current," and might apply to any rupee. They themselves were, at the time of this decision, receiving their salaries in Sicca Rupees of more than 6½ per cent. greater value than the Company's rupee, and would have repudiated with scorn the proposition of being paid in the Company's rupees.

A European is to be prevented from becoming the possessor of land at any cost whatever.—Example: While the last mentioned case was passing through the courts, Mr. Lamb's opponent got deeply into debt, and his creditors put up his estate for sale. Mr. Lamb was willing to purchase peace at any price, and therefore bid a large sum for this estate, which comprised the disputed lands. Mr. Lamb purchased the estate in his wife's name, in order to avoid, as he thought, all disputes. Mrs. Lamb, on becoming purchaser, sued for possession of the estate, but was nonsuited in the Superior Court, the Sudder, on the ground that she, as an English or Scotch woman, could not sue in her own name, but must be joined by her husband. We have got the best authority for saying that this is not good English law; but supposing it were, there was nothing on the record to show that Mrs. Lamb was either an English or a Scotch woman. She might have been of any other race, among many of whom—the Armenians, Mussulmanees and Hindoos, for instance—married women may possess property apart from their husbands. The objection was not taken in any of the pleadings, and we submit that the appellate court had no power to take it up—but there was an Englishman or Scotchman, well known in their private capacities to the judges on the bench to be such, to be prevented from possessing lands. The case was therefore nonsuited. On this decision being given Mr. Lamb brought a fresh suit, joining himself with his wife. The same objection would not serve now; but Mr. Lamb lost his case in the appellate court on account of an alleged irregularity in the sale, an irregularity for which no one was responsible but the court which sold, and therefore Mr. Lamb was punished—be it observed, that Mr. Lamb gained every one of these cases in the courts of first instance. It was only when they were appealed to the Sudder, when they were taken down to Calcutta, where Civil Servicisim is rampant, where the necessity of keeping the interloper from gaining a footing in the land is fully appreciated—it was only in Calcutta that he lost them. We could adduce many a case where the same gentleman, who, unfortunately for himself, had a desire to become a landed proprietor, and to improve his lands by introducing the culture of various crops unknown in this part of India, had decree after decree given against him in the Civil Courts; many of them so absurd, that they gave rise to fresh lawsuits in the vain endeavour to have them executed. We could bring instances of parallel cases, where natives only were concerned, where decrees were given in their favour, which would have made Mr. Lamb's fortune had the same law—we shall not desecrate the name of justice by applying it to any of the dicta of the Sudder—been dealt out to him. But the interloper was there. He was to be put down. If he had not been put down, he might have had the presumption to grow cotton; and by supplying Liverpool with that material, to have made the English people take as great an interest in, and become as well acquainted with, the affairs of India as they are with those of America.

However long a European may have been in possession of land, every means to the endangering of the salvation of the judges themselves is to be used to oust him from possession, and to give it to a native, with which class the Civil Service believed, till lately perhaps, they could do anything. This is an error on the part of the Court Service. Since Reg. II. of 1819, and the Public Works Loan, the native believes that there are no depths so low to which the Company Bahadoor cannot descend, so long as they have power on their side. The Englishman confesses that the Government is "awful dodgy," but cannot believe that the men whom he knows well, and knows to be tolerably honest in their private transactions, could be guilty of the rascalities which have been committed under the aforesaid regulation. But we are running away from our subject, which is that, however long a European may have possessed land he must be ousted somehow or another.—Example: Messrs. Lamb and Wise, two gentlemen settled in the Dacca district, learned from their attorneys that an estate was to be sold by the Collector, at the instance of the owner's creditors. They agreed to bid for the estate, and to purchase it together. The estate was put up for sale, and they bought it. Though many objections were raised to the manner in which the sale was made, &c. by the late proprietors, at the time of and immediately after the sale, they were all overruled by the courts. Messrs. Lamb and Wise were put in possession, and continued in possession for eleven years eleven months and odd days. If the twelve years had passed, their title would have been secured by prescription. But before the twelve years had expired, a suit was brought to upset the sale, on the ground that the law prescribed that notice of sale should be affixed in ten places. It had been so in nine, but there was a doubt with regard to the tenth, whether the place where it was affixed was situated on certain lands or not. The case came on in the local courts and was decided in favour of Messrs. Lamb and Wise. It was appealed to the Sudder, where it was, as a matter of course, decided against the interlopers by two judges out of three—decided, we have almost the highest legal authority in India for saying, against the common-sense interpretation of the law. But what can be expected from judges who have absolutely no legal training, and who consider the interloper as a being who has no right to be in India!

Such are a few—we solemnly affirm a very few—of the instances we can give to Mr. Ewart of the tenures on which lands are allowed to be held by Europeans in India. Were we to unfold a half—one third, of what we know, we should be scorned as unjust traducers of the Civil Service of the Honourable the East India Company.. Fortunately we can prove every word we have said from the decisions of the Sudder Dewany Adalut—Lord Canning must have wondered why his proclamations were so little believed. It is long—as the evidence of every independent man will prove—since the assertions of the Government of this country have been believed by its subjects.

THE BENGAL HURKARU SUPPRESSED.

The *Hurkaru*, the oldest journal in India, was suppressed on the 18th of September, on account of the appearance, in different issues of the paper, of the following three articles:—

From the BENGAL HURKARU.

"The steamer which arrived on the 10th instant brought us the *Times* of 6th August, which contains a leader beginning 'There are some acts of atrocity so abominable that they will not even bear narration,' and ending, 'Let it be known that England will support the officers who may be charged with the duty of suppressing this mutiny, and of inflicting condign punishment upon the bloodthirsty mutineers, however terrible may be the measures which they may see fit to adopt.'

"The article in the *Times* from which the above quotations are made should be republished by Government, circulated to all civil and military authorities in substitution of Cecil Beadon's proclamation, dated 31st July, published in your paper of 2nd instant; and the article from the *Times* should be read also to every regiment in India, instead of Sir James Outram's order about the 10th regiment. Little did the *Times* know of Indian officials when he wrote 'Nothing more injudicious than Mr. Colvin's proclamation can be conceived.'

"What will the Thunderer say when he sees Cecil Beadon's proclamation, and Sir James Outram's order from Dinapore? and that the latter has since that order been reappointed commissioner in Oude, besides commanding the Dinapore and Cawnpore divisions, thus superseding Havelock and Neill? The latter is unquestionably the man who ought to have been appointed chief commissioner in Oude, for the energy he has displayed from the time he confined the railway people here, to the time he hanged the Brahmins at Cawnpore.

"The imbeciles are not all out of England yet, however; the board of control has Vernon Smith and the war department has Lord Panmure. Witness the answer of the latter, through his organ in the Commons, to Colonel North's question on the 5th August, 'Why it was that the Government were only sending 140 men to reinforce the artillery in India, when the number required to bring that force up to its war complement was 223?' Answer by Sir John Ramsden, 'vide *Times* of 6th August':—

"'Sir J. Ramsden said that the artillery force was put under orders for India, the same as the other troops, in compliance with a requisition of the East India Company; and the total force of artillery which they had asked for would be made up by the particular number which had been sent' (hear! hear!).

"That is, the artillery force was rendered inefficient before its departure for India, by reducing it even under the war complement required in Europe, that certain figures sent in by the East India Company might correspond with other figures in the estimates prepared at the war department!

"With such a specimen of the way things are conducted in that department, can any one be surprised that we meet with disasters, from the ruinous effects of which to the nation nothing saves us but the devoted courage of our soldiers and sailors?—yet these are the men whose feelings are being trifled with by old women in India.

"The cavalry horses in the Crimea were starved because Sir Charles Trevelyan, at his desk in London, thought he could there form a more correct estimate of the forage required than the commissary-general on the spot could do—and now we are to have the artillery sent out in an inefficient state because Vernon Smith and *the chair* think that the war complement, which experienced artillery officers have laid down as necessary in Europe, is too large for a fine climate like India, where they no doubt suppose ready-made artillery men grow in the Rose Gardens!"

From the BENGAL HURKARU.

THE FRIEND OF HINDOSTAN AND THE STATE-GRINDER.

AFTER GEORGE CANNING.

(The F. of H. represented by the Chairman of the Court of Directors, and the S. G. by a noble lord.)

F. OF H.

Needy State-grinder, whither are you going?
You're quite gone astray, your wheel is out of order.
There s a row blowing up—your actions are all rotten,
So are your speeches!

Weary State-grinder, little do those rascals
Who with their howlings hunt down all their rulers
Think what hard work 'tis, crying all day, "Red tape,
Red tape for ever!"

Tell me, State-grinder, how came you in this plight?
Did the supreme court lay its hands upon you?
Was it the chief, or editor of journal,
Or some low planter?

Was it some judge, for acting without Queen's law?
Rancorous chief, for keeping down his service?
Editor vicious, crying up the people,
Brought you in this fix?

(Have you not read the minute of Sir Thomas?)
Sparks of resentment smoulder in my headpiece,
Ready to blow up as soon as you have told your
Most wretched story.

S. G.

Story! God bless you! I have none to tell, sir,
Only one day, I, talking in the council,
Gagged the free press, and then made that J. P. Grant
Gen'ral Obstructor!

Campbell was sent out, for to take me into
His command; they took me before the Commons;
Public opinion then put me in the
Pound as a donkey!

I should be glad to drink your honour's health in
A small pension, if you will kindly give it;
But for my part I never more will meddle
With Hindostan, sir:

F. OF H.

I give thee pension! I will see thee d—d first—
Man whom we trusted, like so many asses;—
Taunted and jeered at, made no end of fun of—
Impotent failure!

(Kicks the State-grinder, overturns his wheel, and exit in a transport of official agony and lost hopes.)

From the BENGAL HURKARU.

All India is eagerly watching the progress of public opinion at home, the eventual declaration of which will decide the future policy of the Government. Our rulers are being put upon their trial, while a jury composed of many millions are weighing the evidence, preparatory to laying their heads together for the consideration of the verdict.

There are many good, honest, simple people in Calcutta, who are both surprised and disappointed that popular indignation has not boiled up to a higher pitch. They are astounded at finding that Lord Canning has not been already ordered home in irons, and that Mr. Beadon has not been sentenced to be tarred and feathered and ridden upon a rail, previously to being placed in some extremely uncovenanted appointment, under a native superior. We are very far from saying that these proceedings would not be appropriate in the cases in question, but we would say to our enthusiastic friends:—My dear sirs, you are too impatient. All in good time. Public opinion is not a mere dramatic performance, got up to make the overland papers exciting, for your pleasure. It is a real earnest process, which takes time for its development, which must be expected to "drag"—in dramatic language,—now and then; which will not always produce startling effects at the most desirable moment; which keeps one waiting a long time between the acts, with nothing but "apples and oranges and a bill of the play" to fall back upon;—but for all that there can be no rational doubt that the conclusion will find virtue triumphant, and that the villains of the piece will meet with their just doom. But,—we would add to our enthusiastic friends,—what more can you expect? What more would you have at the present moment? Have you not heard through private letters that the windows of the directors' town houses are by no means safe, and that any one of the honourable court showing himself at Bath or Cheltenham, or elsewhere where Anglo-Indianism most abides, would meet with a reception from the mob compared to which that of Marshal Haynau by the brewers was courteous and flattering? Do you not know that the Duke of Cambridge was heard to say that he should soon have the Indian army under his command? Are you not aware that the mode of communication adopted by the government of the crown towards the government of the court, at home, has already become savage and dictatorial to an extent that six months ago would have aroused Leadenskull-street to a fury of resistance? Do you not see that the comparative satisfaction which has been manifested at the mode of meeting the mutinies has been founded upon want of knowledge of the real facts of the case? Is it not obvious to the stupidest fellow among you, that where our rulers have been praised, they have been praised for doing what they have left undone, or for not doing that which they have done most thoroughly and completely? If her Majesty's Government approve eventually of the conduct of these gentlemen they will have to do so, not merely at the cost of their consisency—which they will care no more about than any other government—but at the cost of their offices, which they will not be disposed to part with for such an incidental consideration as Mr. Halliday, or such a matter of detail as Mr. Beadon—to say nothing of one or two others of the same stamp, and a higher functionary whom they have dragged into the same boat.

We ask the sanguine persons to whom we have addressed the above, what more they would have for the present? To us it seems that Parliament and the public at home have made immense progress towards a proper view of the question. In the House of Lords, the Earl of Ellenborough and the Marquis of Clanricarde have addressed themselves to it with profound knowledge and sagacity. In the Commons, Mr. Disraeli has made one of the most masterly and statesmanlike speeches that he has ever made in his life; and the question has been met by all who took part in its discussion with a high appreciation of its importance. The press has done its work well, and has been steadily drifting in the right direction, to a position which the *Times* has taken up with a decision and energy which sufficiently show that the voice of the country is on the same side. Throughout the discussion, both in parliament and the press, it is to the honour of all engaged in it, that no party feeling has been shown, however much may have been felt in some quarters. The utmost consideration has been manifested for the local government under the difficult circumstances in which they were placed, and no signs of any personal prejudice have been made apparent. Even the *Press* and the *Examiner*, the two most systematic opponents of the company's government, have handled Lord Canning as tenderly as if he was a baby, and have let Messrs. Beadon and Halliday alone with a magnanimity which is almost beyond belief, and suggests the suspicion that those usually well-informed journals have not yet acquainted themselves with the fact that there are such persons in existence.

In the meantime, the accused are awaiting the verdict which is to decide their official fate, in a highly characteristic manner, such as we see described in the London police reports as "treating the charge with the utmost levity," or "evincing a hardened indifference to the situation in which they were placed, that was painful to behold." But among these it is only just to remark that the most elevated personage stands out in honourable relief. His grand calmness under the ordeal is comparable to nothing but the demeanour of Miss Madeleine Smith, in similarly trying circumstances, which elicited the wonder and admiration of the rapt people of Glasgow. Let us hope that the omen is a good one, and, for the sake of an illustrious name, and as good intentions as have ever paved India or any other place, that the charges which have been brought against the individual in question will be "not proven."

THE ACT IMPROVED UPON IN PEGU.

To the PROPRIETOR OF THE RANGOON CHRONICLE AND PEGU GAZETTE PRESS.

Rangoon.

Sir,—I am permitted by the Commissioner of Pegu and Governor-General's agent to inform you, that in the event of your wishing to publish any articles concerning the affairs connected with the rebellion in Bengal, in your journal, you are, before doing so, to submit them to me for approval. Without such previous submission, you are not to publish such accounts or articles, whether original or extracted: this will be an especial condition of the *ad interim* protection being continued to you.

I have the honour to be, Sir,
Your most obedient Servant,
GEO. DANGERFIELD,
Officiating Magistrate of Rangoon.

Rangoon Magistrate's Office, the 5th August, 1857.

The proprietor appealed to the Commissioner, and received the following reply:—

To R. GODFREE, ESQ., *Proprietor of the* RANGOON CHRONICLE PRESS.

Rangoon.

Sir,—I have the honour to acknowledge the receipt of your letter to the address of the Commissioner and Governor-General's agent for Pegu, forwarding a letter from the magistrate of Rangoon, herewith returned.

In granting an *ad interim* for protection in publishing the *Rangoon Chronicle*, pending the receipt of orders from the Supreme Government on your application for a license, the Commissioner and Governor-General's agent has assumed a power not strictly vested in him by the law, and has in a measure, and for a time, made himself responsible for what is published in that paper; but he refuses to accept the responsibility unless upon such conditions as will, he trusts, justify him in having incurred it with the Government he has the honour to serve.

I have the honour to be, Sir,
HORACE A. BROWNE,
Extra-Assistant to the Commissioner of Pegu.

Rangoon Commissioner's Office, 7th August, 1857.

THE FIRST ATTACK ON THE LONDON JOURNALS.

The following letter has been addressed by the Magistrate of Poona to the Government of Bombay:—

Judicial Department, Bombay Castle, 23rd of September, 1857.

Sir,—In the *Times* newspaper of last Thursday, the Editor stated that a detachment of the 2nd Bombay Light Cavalry had mutinied at Deesa, and had been destroyed by Her Majesty's 83rd Regiment at that station;

and in last Monday's paper there is an article extracted from the English paper, the *Press*, the publication of which is calculated to have a very pernicious effect at the present time.

I am, therefore, desired by the Right Honourable the Governor in Council to request that you will be good enough to warn the editors of English and Native newspapers within your jurisdiction against republishing the articles in question.

I have, &c.,

(Signed) H. L. ANDERSON,
Secretary to Government.

To the Magistrate of Poona.

MADRAS A STEP IN ADVANCE.

No. 1106.

Extract from the MINUTES OF CONSULTATION.

Public Department, dated 10th August, 1857.

The attention of the Right Honourable the Governor-General in Council has been drawn to an article in the *Examiner* newspaper of the 6th inst., copying a false statement from the *Hurkaru*, regarding a supposed intention to remove the Government agent at Chepauk, and reflecting on that officer's official conduct.

Government resolve to notify to the proprietors of that newspaper, that this is a violation of the terms on which they hold their license, and that their license will be withdrawn on the appearance of any similar article.

(True Copy.)

E. MALTBY,
Acting Chief Secretary.

From the MADRAS EXAMINER, *quoted from the* HURKARU.

The Madras Government, we understand, has recommended to the Supreme Government the immediate removal of Dr. Balfour from the Government agency at Chepauk, for alleged acts of oppression.

THE END.